New Inside Out

Sue Kay, Vaughan Jones, Helena Gomm, Peter Maggs & Chris Dawson

Upper intermediate

Teacher's Book

Macmillan Education
Between Towns Road, Oxford OX4 3PP
A division of Macmillan Publishers Limited
Companies and representatives throughout the world

ISBN 978-0-230-00924-0

Text © Sue Kay and Vaughan Jones 2009
Text by Helena Gomm
Photocopiable resource materials and language and cultural notes by Pete Maggs
with Miguel Ángel Almarza, Vincent A Desmond, Ruth Sánchez García, Jon Hird,
Nicholas Sheard, Russell Stannard.
Design and illustration © Macmillan Publishers Limited 2009

First published 2009

Designed by 320 Design Limited
Page layout by Carolyn Gibson
Illustrated by Kathy Baxendale, Beach, Dave Burroughs, Peter Campbell, Ivan Gillet,
Peter Harper, Ben Hasler, Ed McLachlan and Bill Piggins
Cover design by Andrew Oliver

The authors and publishers would like to thank the following for permission to reproduce
their material: Quotation from *Language and Problems of Knowledge* by Noam Chomsky
copywrite © Noam Chomsky 1988 Massachusetts Institute of Technology, reprinted by
permission of The MIT Press, Cambridge, Massachusetts. Quotation from *Understanding
Second Language Acquisition* by Rod Ellis copyright © Rod Ellis 1985, reproduced by
permission of Oxford University Press.

The author and publishers are grateful for permission to reprint the following copyright
material: *Big Yellow Taxi* – Words and Music by Joni Mitchell, copyright © 1970 (Renewed)
CRAZY CROW MUSIC. All Rights Administered by SONY/ATV MUSIC PUBLISHING,
8 Music Square West, Nashville, TN 37203. All Rights Reserved. Used by permission
from ALFRED PUBLISHING CO. INC.; *Mozambique* – by Bob Dylan and Jacques Levy
copyright © 1975 Ram's Horn Music. All Rights Reserved. International Copyright
Secured. Reprinted by permission of the publisher; *When A Man Loves A Woman* – Words
and Music by Andrew James Wright and Calvin Houston Lewis, copyright © 1966
(Renewed) Pronto Music (BMI), Mijac Music (BMI) and Quinvy Music Publishing Co.
(BMI). All Rights Administered by Warner-Tamerlane Publishing Corp.; *Suddenly I See*
– Words by KT Tunstall, copyright © Sony/ATV Music Publishing (UK) Limited 2006,
reprinted by permission of the publisher. All Rights Reserved.

These materials may contain links for third party websites. We have no control over, and
are not responsible for, the contents of such third party websites. Please use care when
accessing them.

The author and publishers would like to thank the following for permission to reproduce
their material: **Alamy**/Pictorial Press Ltd pp160,170,180, Alamy/Jim Wileman p179(br);
Pete Maggs p179(bl); **Rex Features**/Everett collection p190(b), Rex Features/ Guitarist/
Future publishing p190(t), Rex Features/Alisdair Macdonald p179(tr), Rex Features/
Dave Penman p179(tl).
All other images taken for New Inside Upper-Intermediate student book. Please refer to
this publication for full credit details.

Although we have tried to trace and contact copyright holders before publication, in some
cases this has not been possible. If contacted, we will be pleased to rectify any errors or
omissions at the earliest opportunity.

Printed in Thailand

2013   2012   2011   2010
10 9 8 7 6 5 4 3 2

Contents

TEACHER'S NOTES

RESOURCE MATERIALS

Student's Book contents map

ⓌⒷ = **Workbook**. Each unit of the Workbook contains a one-page section which develops practical writing skills.

Introduction

Welcome to *New Inside Out!*

New Inside Out is the fruit of many years' teaching, writing and developing material. Everything we write is informed by the reactions we get from our students. Our aim is simply to produce a set of materials that will help you create optimum conditions in your classroom for learning to take place.

Sue Kay   *Vaughan Jones*

Engaging content

The American linguist and philosopher Noam Chomsky once said:

'The truth of the matter is that about 99% of teaching is making the students feel interested in the material. Then the other 1% has to do with your methods'.

While we might want to quibble with the percentages, we would nevertheless agree whole-heartedly with the central message in Professor Chomsky's assertion: namely, students learn best when they're interested in the material. It's as simple as that. A text might contain six beautifully-crafted examples of the past simple, a good spread of high frequency lexical items and exemplify some useful functional language, but if it doesn't engage the students, if they can't relate to it, if it feels alien to them, then the most important ingredient for successful learning is missing. In *New Inside Out*, we've drawn on our own classroom experience, and that of our colleagues around the world, to select topics, texts and tasks that engage students both emotionally and intellectually. Students are our richest resource. They come to class with their own knowledge of the world, their own tastes, feelings and opinions. It's up to us to exploit this rich resource by organising learning around topics that they can relate to – topics that are part of their life experience.

Structured support

We all know that learning a language is a messy, non-linear business. We're dismayed when there seems to be little correlation between what is taught and what is learned! However, there is plenty of evidence to suggest that 'instructed' learners (those who attend classes or follow a course of study) learn faster, and ultimately attain a higher level of proficiency than 'non-instructed' learners.

In *New Inside Out*, new language input is carefully controlled: we aim to maximise exposure to high frequency language appropriate to this level. Students are encouraged to notice new grammar and new vocabulary in contexts where the meaning is clear. They are then given opportunities to manipulate the new language and try it out in different situations. They discover why using one particular form rather than another one actually matters: not just because it's right or wrong, but because it does or doesn't communicate a meaning successfully. The emphasis is always on what students can do with the language rather than what they know about the language. The new language is systematically reviewed and recycled until finally the students feel confident enough to use it to make their own meanings. It becomes part of their available repertoire. It has been 'learned'.

Real world tasks

We're strong believers in the old adage: 'practice makes perfect'. *New Inside Out* emphasises output, particularly speaking, and there are a huge number of tasks that are designed to develop fluency. Students practise functional language in sections entitled *Useful phrases*. But for the most part, the speaking tasks simply encourage the students to talk about things that actually matter to them, rather than playing roles or exchanging invented information. One of our main objectives is to ensure that the language our students spend time rehearsing in the classroom is transferable to the real world. By orchestrating tasks that require the students to use grammar and vocabulary to make meaningful utterances, this objective becomes obtainable. As the linguist and academic Rod Ellis reminds us:

'It is the need to get meanings across and the pleasure experienced when this is achieved that motivates second language acquisition.'

www.insideout.net
'the art of communication'

Components of the course

Student's materials

- Student's Book *see page viii–x*
- CD-ROM *see page xi*
- Workbook and Audio CD *see page xi*

Teacher's materials

- Teacher's Book *see page xii*
- Test CD *see page xii*
- Class Audio CDs *see page xii*
- DVD *see page xiii*
- DVD Teacher's Book *see page xiii*
- Website *see page xiii*

Student's materials A typical Student's Book unit (Unit 4)

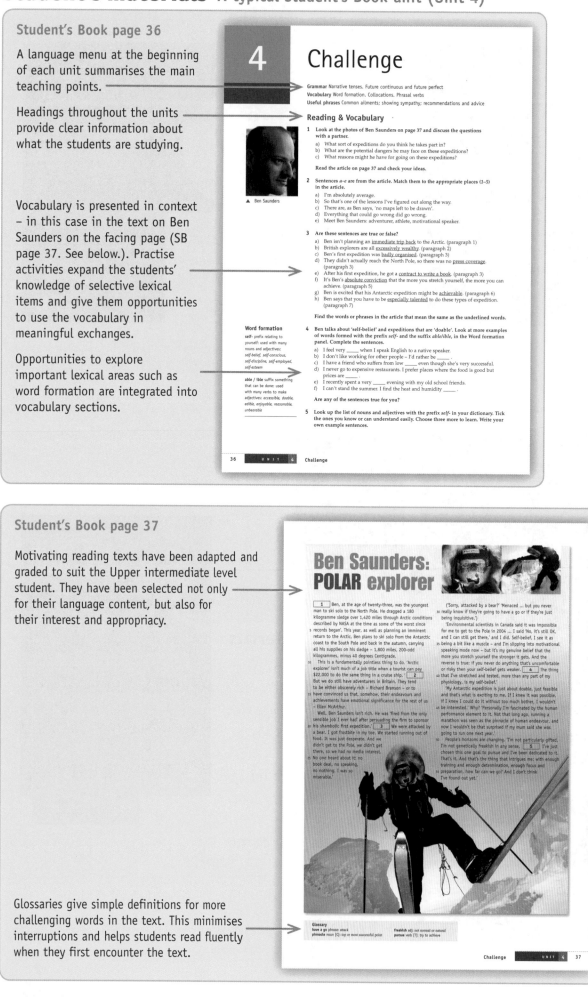

Student's Book page 36

A language menu at the beginning of each unit summarises the main teaching points.

Headings throughout the units provide clear information about what the students are studying.

Vocabulary is presented in context – in this case in the text on Ben Saunders on the facing page (SB page 37. See below.). Practise activities expand the students' knowledge of selective lexical items and give them opportunities to use the vocabulary in meaningful exchanges.

Opportunities to explore important lexical areas such as word formation are integrated into vocabulary sections.

Student's Book page 37

Motivating reading texts have been adapted and graded to suit the Upper intermediate level student. They have been selected not only for their language content, but also for their interest and appropriacy.

Glossaries give simple definitions for more challenging words in the text. This minimises interruptions and helps students read fluently when they first encounter the text.

Student's Book page 40

New Inside Out Upper intermediate is full of engaging material taken from modern authentic sources. As a first step, students are always encouraged to read or listen for meaning and enjoyment.

Comprehension work is often combined with a focus on a particular lexical area – in this case collocation.

Students are encouraged to relate the topics to their own lives, views and feelings.

Student's Book page 41

New Inside Out Upper intermediate includes an average of two grammar sections in every unit. Typically, these follow a three-stage approach.

1 Students 'notice' new grammatical structures that have been contextualized in the previous section. They focus on the way new language works.

   A brief summary of the grammar point is provided in the margin.

2 Language practice is designed to be realistic and meaningful.

3 Students use target language for controlled, personalised practice.

In addition, students are referred to the Grammar *Extra* pages at the back of the Student's Book for extended explanations and further practice.

The listenings include several authentic recordings, as well as text specially written for language learning.

Student's Book page 44

Useful phrases gives students a portable toolkit of functional language. These sections are designed to be fun and engaging and the phrases are recorded on the Audio CD.

Pronunciation work on particular areas of sound, stress and intonation is integrated into every unit.

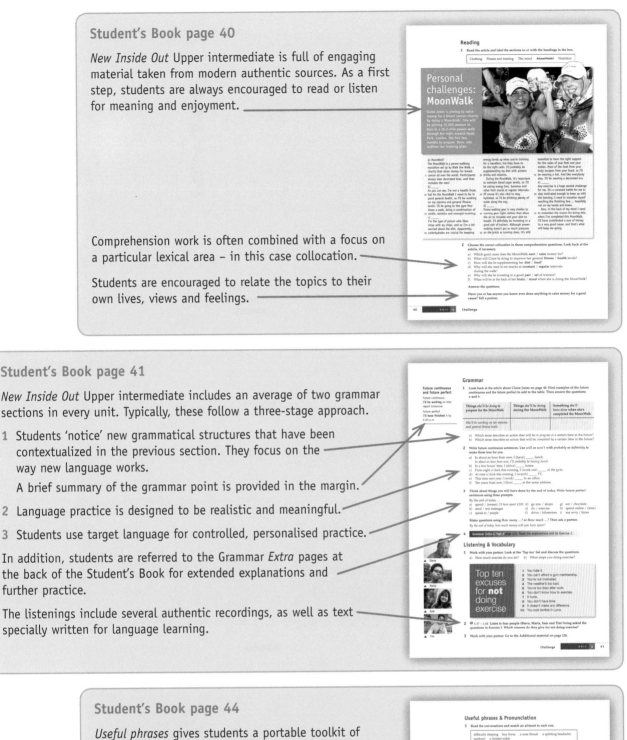

Student's Book page 45

The *Vocabulary Extra* pages at the end of units 2, 4, 6, 8, 10 and 12 explore key lexical areas such as collocation, metaphor and in this case phrasal verbs. They provide students with detailed practice activities and help promote useful dictionary skills.

Student's Book page 55

The *Writing Extra* pages at the end of units 1, 3, 5, 7, 9 and 11 develop important writing skills in a variety of genres. They compliment the complete self-contained writing course in the Workbook.

Student's Book page 66

There are four Review units in *New Inside Out* Upper intermediate Student's Book. Each Review unit revises the new structures taught in the previous three teaching units.

Student's Book pages 134 and 135

The *Grammar Extra* pages at the back of the Student's Book provide a summary of the new grammatical structures as well as extra practice.

CD-ROM

The CD-ROM in the back of every Student's Book provides a wealth of interactive practice activities along with integrated listening material and video clips contextualising the *Useful phrases*.

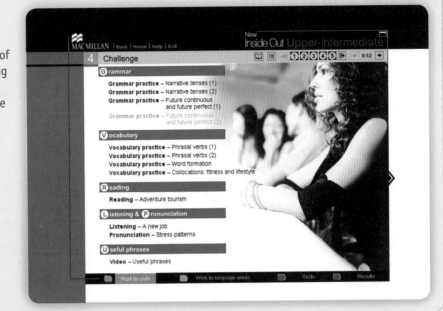

Workbook pages 22 and 23

The Workbook provides revision of all the main points in the Student's Book, plus extra listening practice, pronunciation work and a complete self-contained writing course. There are *with* and *without key* versions, and an extract from the *Magnetism* and *Three Hours Between Planes* (Macmillan Graded Reader) is included in the back of the Workbook.

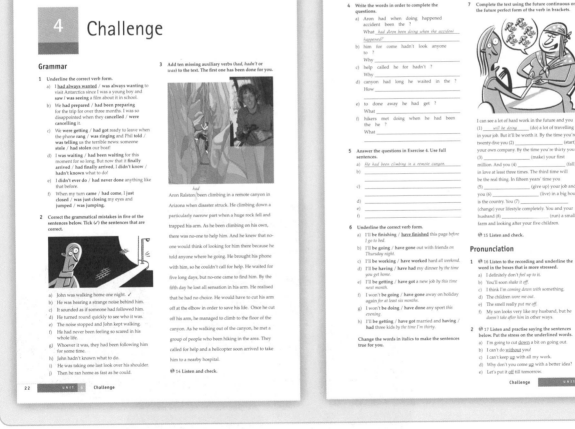

Teacher's materials

Teacher's Book

The 6-in-1 Teacher's Book contains:

- an Introduction
- Practical methodology
- Council of Europe (CEF) checklists
- complete teaching notes with answer keys
- a bank of extra photocopiable grammar, vocabulary and communicative activities
- a Test CD with word files that you can edit and the recordings of the listening test activities

Class CD set

The Class CDs contain:

- the dialogues and listening activities from the Student's Book
- recordings of the songs

DVD and DVD Teacher's Book

The DVD contains programmes which complement the topics in the Student's Book. There is a wide variety of formats including interviews, profiles, documentaries and video diaries. The DVD Teacher's Book contains related teaching notes and photocopiable worksheets.

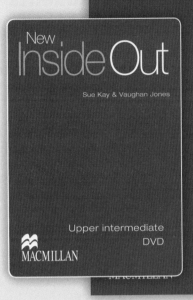

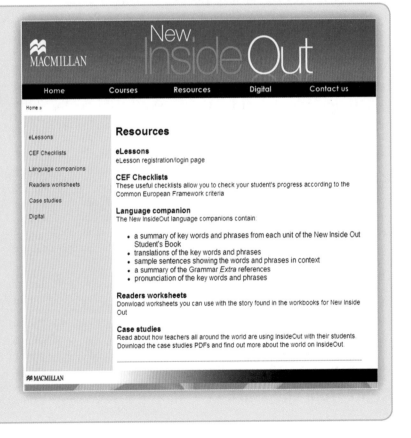

Website

www.insideout.net

Visit www.insideout.net to find out more details about the course and its authors. The new magazine-style website provides downloadable resources and more information about *New Inside Out*.

Practical methodology

Teaching upper intermediate students

A student who has reached the upper intermediate level is to be congratulated. Having managed to move off the so-called 'intermediate plateau', he or she is well on their way to becoming a competent communicator at an advanced level. The CEF descriptor for B2 is a useful summary of what a student at this level is aiming for:

Can understand the main ideas of complex text both on concrete and abstract topics, including technical discussions in his/her field of specialization. Can interact with a degree of fluency and spontaneity that makes regular interaction with native speakers quite possible without strain for either party. Can produce clear detailed text on a wide range of subjects and explain a viewpoint on a topical issue giving the advantages and disadvantages of various options. *

Progress towards this highly desirable goal is not necessarily automatic. Because upper intermediate students can get by in nearly every situation, and because they're more interested in expanding the quantity rather than the quality of their language knowledge – more 'new' words rather than more about 'old' words – there's a danger that 'half-learned' language will 'fossilize': i.e. that their language deficiencies will become permanent features of their competence.

In *New Inside Out* Upper intermediate we've tried to balance the natural inclination to race ahead and learn more and more 'brand new' language with an analytical approach, which encourages students to notice more complex aspects of language they already 'know'. We believe that time spent learning more about 'half-known' words – things such as collocation, range, connotation and register – can help iron out any residual problems students may have without compromising a sense of progress and forward momentum.

In common with all the teaching materials in the *New Inside Out* series, there's a relentless focus on meaning. In particular, the aim to help students make their own meanings in ever more communicatively competent and socially acceptable ways. This is built into every stage of the learning process. It's the core feature of *Inside Out* which helps students maintain their enthusiasm and motivation.

Right from the start

Every teacher has their own way of setting up their classroom, interacting with their students and conducting their lessons. Here are a few things that we've found useful to bear in mind.

The right environment

It's important to do everything you can to create a supportive learning environment. Start by memorising every student's name and learn as much information as you can about them. Make sure students learn each other's names too and that they all get to know things about each other early on.

Make sure you find time to 'chat' to individual students or small informal groups of students before or after class. More formally, it's a good idea to devote at least one lesson per term to counsel your students individually and discuss their progress.

Your classroom might be the only exposure to English that students get. Make that exposure as rich as you can by decorating the walls with maps and posters. Have several monolingual dictionaries available to refer to – a class set if possible. Also, try to have a selection of English books, newspapers and magazines lying around that students can pick up and browse before and after lessons. Here are some further ideas:

- Institute the 'Class Scribe' idea. One student in the class is given the role of recording any new language that comes up during the lesson that isn't necessarily the target language of that lesson. This unique record is then kept in a folder in the class and provides the teacher with valuable data for revision activities. The role of class scribe is rotated so that each student gets a turn at being responsible for recording the lesson. This shared responsibility can help promote positive group dynamics.

- Promote graded readers. There's a huge selection of readers available at the upper intermediate/advanced level: both simplified classics and original stories. Ask the students to always bring their reader to the lesson and occasionally set aside a ten-minute slot for them to talk about what they're reading. Alternatively, just devote ten minutes to silent reading. Most upper intermediate students will be best suited to readers where the basic vocabulary is in the range 2,200–3,000 words. Some may feel that

* Council of Europe, 2001. Common European Framework of Reference for Languages: Learning, Teaching Assessment p 24.

they want to tackle unsimplified, original versions. This is fine, but make sure the students understand that it's much better to read and enjoy ten easy books than struggle through one difficult one. Get your students hooked on books!

The right learning skills

Students will always benefit from help with learning strategies. Here are some thoughts:

- Encourage students to ask questions about language. If you have created the right atmosphere in your classroom, then students will be more likely to take an active approach in their own learning and this is important. Students should never feel intimidated about asking questions.

- Spend time encouraging students to experiment with how they record words and phrases from the lesson. Make sure they note the part of speech – verb, noun, adjective, etc. Tell them to find a way of noting the pronunciation of the word, either using phonemic script or by developing their own system. Ask them to write complete personalised sentences putting the new word or phrase in a real context and thereby making it more memorable.

- A dictionary is a very important language learning tool and most students will have one. Usually students prefer a bilingual dictionary but at the upper intermediate level they need to think seriously about investing in a good advanced monolingual dictionary. The Vocabulary *Extra* pages at the end of units 2, 4, 6, 8, 10 and 12 in *New Inside Out* Upper Intermediate have been designed to give students valuable dictionary practice and make them aware of all the useful 'extra' information that is available in a good monolingual dictionary.

The right amount of practice

In our experience, the most successful lessons consist of a manageable amount of new input, and then a lot of meaningful practice. For this reason, we've tried to provide maximum practice activities in *New Inside Out*, both in the Student's Book and in the other supporting components. But there is never enough time in the lessons alone. Always set homework, even if it's just reading a chapter from a reader, and make homework feedback or correction an integral part of the lesson.

First Certificate Practice Activities

Many students at the upper intermediate level will be considering the idea of taking a language exam such as the Cambridge First Certificate. In *New Inside Out* Upper intermediate we have included some examples of exam-type activities in the second half of the student book. It's a useful way of sensitizing students to the sort of exercises that are typically included in language exams. Look out for the following flash:

FCE Exam Practice

The top 10 activities for upper intermediate students

These tried and trusted activities can be used as lead-ins, warmers, fillers, pair-forming activities, or for revision and recycling. Most of them require very little or no preparation and can be adapted to cover a wide variety of different language points. The emphasis is on vocabulary revision as we all know that it's only through repeated, systematic exposure to new words and expressions that students are likely to transform 'input' into 'intake'. You may be familiar with some of the ideas and others may be new. In any event, we hope they provide a useful extension to your teaching repertoire. They certainly get used and re-used in our own classrooms!

It's always useful to have a stock of small white cards and access to a collection of pictures. Magazine pictures are ideal, and can be filed in alphabetical order according to topics.

1 Board bingo

Aim

This activity is good for revising any type of vocabulary.

Preparation

Write down twelve to fifteen words you want to revise on the board. They could be words from the last lesson, words from the unit you've just finished or a random selection of words covering the whole term.

Procedure

- Ask the students to choose five of the words and write them down. When they've done that, tell the students that you're going to read out dictionary definitions of the words in random order and that they should cross out their words if they think they hear the definition. When they've crossed out all five words, they shout *Bingo!* Make sure you keep a record of the word definitions you call out so that you can check the students' answers.

- If you teach a monolingual class, you could read out a translation of each word rather than an English definition. Alternatively, you could turn it into a pronunciation exercise by working on the recognition of phonemic script. Hold up cards with phonemic transcriptions of the words in random order. Students cross out their words if they think they've seen the corresponding phonetic transcription.

2 My criteria

Aim

This activity can be used to review almost any vocabulary.

Preparation

Choose up to ten words that you want to revise. You might want to start with recognisable lexical sets and then move onto groups of random words.

Procedure

- Write the words on the board in no particular order. Put the students in pairs or small groups. The activity consists of writing out the words in a specific order according to a particular criteria of the students' choosing. Each pair or group keeps their criteria secret. They then give their list to another pair or group who have to work out what they think the criteria is.

  For example, let's say you want to revise words for items you find in a house from Unit 12. You write eight items on the board: e.g. *coat hooks, a doormat, a rug, shutters, a knocker, a dustpan, an ironing board, blinds.* The students then rearrange the list according to a criteria that they've thought of. The criteria can be anything from 'alphabetical order': i.e. 1) *blinds,* 2) *coat hooks,* 3) *a doormat,* etc. to 'useful': i.e. 1) *coat hooks,* 2) *a dustpan,* 3) *an ironing board,* etc.

- Sometimes the criterion clearly suggests only one possible order (i.e. 'alphabetical order'). If the criterion is 'useful', then the order of items might be open to debate. This is fine and can lead to some interesting discussion. To get the students used to this activity, in the first instance, you might want to give them different criteria to choose from. Here are some more possible criteria for household items: *expensive, big/small, easy to find in shops, things I use or have.* Alternatively, you might want to give them just one criterion – one where the order is not obvious – and see if each group comes up with the same order.

- Here are some more ideas for lexical sets and criteria:

  1 Phrasal verbs (Unit 4 page 45)
  Possible criteria: frequent, useful, largest number of meanings, most idiomatic.

  2 Facial features (Unit 8 page 78)
  Possible criteria: attractive, distinctive, feminine/ masculine, likely to age.

  3 Professions (Unit 9 page 95)
  Possible criteria: creative, well-paid, useful to society, easy, fun.

3 Category dictation

Aim

This activity can be adapted to review almost any vocabulary. It can also be used to review certain pronunciation and grammar points.

Preparation

Choose the language you want to review and devise a way of categorising it into two or more categories.

Procedure

- Write the category headings on the board and ask the students to copy them onto a piece of paper. Two simple categories is usually best. More than four can get complicated. Then dictate the words (10–12 maximum) slowly and clearly, and ask the students to write them down in the correct category.

  For example, you might want to revise verb-noun collocations from Vocabulary Exercise 2 on page 25. So, write the following on the board and ask the students to copy it down.

have	make	take

- Then dictate some noun collocates, e.g. *a loss, a think, action, sense, a laugh,* etc. The students write down the words in the correct category. When you've dictated 10 or 12 words, ask students to compare their lists. When they've done this, ask them to call out their answers and write them on the board in the correct category, so that they can check the spelling. Alternatively, you could ask the students to take it in turns to write the answers on the board. This simple activity can be used to revise more or less any verb-noun collocation involving 'de-lexical' verbs such as *do, put, give, get,* etc.

- Here are some more ideas for categories:

  1 Revise verb patterns. (Unit 2 page 17)
  Suggested categories: *verb + gerund* or *verb + to-infinitive; verb + object* or *verb + no object.*

  2 Revise word formation. How to make adjectives negative (Unit 7 page 73)
  Suggested categories: *'dis'* or *'in'* or *'un'.* Read out the positive forms of the adjective, i.e. *loyal, appropriate, willing,* etc.

  3 Revise ways of saying 'hello' and 'goodbye'. (Unit 12 page 124)
  Suggested categories: *hello* or *goodbye.* Read out different useful phrases, i.e. *Safe journey, Long time no see, Keep in touch,* etc.

4 Whose dialogue?

Aim

To imagine what people in pictures are saying to one another and to write a short dialogue.

Preparation

You will need a selection of eight to ten magazine pictures. Each picture should show two people who could be talking to one another. Try to get pictures of as widely varying contexts as possible.

Procedure

- Divide the students into pairs or small groups. Display the pictures on the board, on the wall or on the floor where everybody can see them. Ask each pair or group to secretly choose a picture, but without pointing or touching it. The students then write a short dialogue between the people in the picture they've chosen. When they've finished, ask them to act out their dialogue to the other members of the class without indicating which picture it's based on. The other students guess which picture the dialogue goes with.

- This activity is particularly suited to revising some of the functional language from the Useful phrases sections in the Student's book. You could write six or more useful phrases on the board and tell the students that their dialogues must include at least one (or two, or three) of them. The Useful phrases could be part of a recognisable set (i.e. Unit 4 page 44: *Oh dear, you poor thing*; *Oh yes, I know what you mean*; *Oh well, it serves you right then, doesn't it?*, etc.) Alternatively, they could just be random (i.e. *It can't be her*; *Make yourself at home*; *I'm not made of money*, etc.)

- Alternatively, you could choose any ten to twelve words you want to revise and put them on the board. Then tell the students that they must include at least three (or four, or five) of the words in their dialogues.

5 Random letters

Aim

This activity is good for revising any type of vocabulary.

Preparation

None

Procedure

- Ask the students to call out any seven letters from the alphabet. (It doesn't have to be seven letters: anything between seven and twelve is fine.) Write the letters scattered on the board.

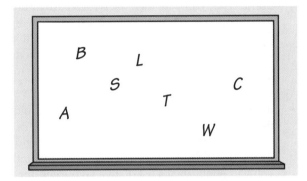

- Then ask the students in pairs to think of a word beginning with each letter on the board. The most obvious criteria is to revise words from a specific lexical set that you have taught recently. Alternatively, you could simply ask them for words they've noted down in lessons over the past two weeks.

- Another possibility would be to find the most interesting words they can from the Student's Book unit that you've just finished. If the lexical set you want them to revise is particularly rich, you could ask the students to think of as many words for each letter as they can in say three minutes: make it into a contest to find the most words.

- There are lots of possible variations using different criteria for words from the letters on the board. Here are a few:

  1 Use the same criteria as above, but ask the students to think of words ending with the letter on the board.

  2 Ask the students to write only nouns, or adjectives or irregular verbs or some other part of speech.

  3 Ask the students to write only words with three syllables or words with the same vowel sounds.

  4 Ask students to write only words that start with the same letter in their own language or only words that start with a different letter.

6 Five favourites

Aim

This activity is good for revising any words learned recently.

Preparation

None

Procedure

- Students look back through their lesson notes for the last two weeks and select from the words they've recorded five words that they think are particularly useful. They compare their list with a partner and together they produce a common list of five words from the combined list of ten. To do this they'll have to argue for and against words on the combined list until they are both satisfied that they have the most useful five.

- If you wanted to continue the activity, you could then have each pair join up with another pair as a group of four and repeat the procedure. Depending on the size of your class you might continue until you had established a list of 'five favourites' for the whole class.

- The value of this activity lies in the students looking back through their notes, choosing the words and then arguing for them to be part of the combined list. The whole procedure gives them valuable repeat exposure to words recently learned.

- A possible extension activity after each pair has formed their common list of five words is to collect the lists and redistribute them so that each pair has a different list. The pairs then write a dialogue or short story incorporating the five words they have on the list they've just received. You could then ask them to read out their dialogues or stories and the other students guess what the five listed words were.

7 Crosswords

Aim

This activity is good for revising lexical sets and can help with spelling.

Preparation

Choose a lexical set you want to revise. For example: *nouns that collocate with 'make'* (or *'take'* or *'have'*) (Unit 3); *words on the topic of weddings (Unit 5)*; *food (Unit 6)*; *positive adjectives to describe personality (Unit 8)*, etc.

Procedure

- Students work in pairs. They'll need a piece of paper, preferably graph paper with squares on.

- Choose a topic, for example, *food*.

- Student A writes 'Across' words, and Student B writes 'Down' words.

- It's a good idea to provide the first word across, and make sure that it's a long one (e.g. *vegetables*). Student B then adds another food word down the paper from top to bottom. This word must intersect with the food word written across the page.

- Student A then writes another food word across that intersects with the word Student B has written down. Students continue taking it in turns to write in their words.

- Students build up a crossword until they can't think of any more food words. (You could make it into a game by saying that the last person to write a food word is a winner.) Note that students must leave one square between each word – this is why it's better and clearer to use squared paper.

- At this level, with a topic as big as 'food', it might be advisable to narrow the category: i.e. *fruit and vegetables* or *meat and fish* or *food you put in the fridge* or …

8 Odd one out

Aim

This activity can be used to revise almost any language.

Preparation

Think of the vocabulary, pronunciation or grammar point you want to revise.

Procedure

- Write five words on the board and ask students which one is the odd one out. The students then explain why. This is usually relates to the meaning of the word.

  | milk | cheese | cream | butter | sugar |

- Here *sugar* is the odd one out because the other words are all dairy products.

- Note that it doesn't matter if the students can't explain in perfect English why *sugar* is the odd one out. The important thing is that they're looking at and thinking about the words you want them to revise.

- You can use this format to practise and revise all sorts of things. Here are some examples:

  1 For meaning:
  sister / nephew / daughter / wife / mother
  nephew is the odd one out because he's a man. The other words describe women.

  2 For spelling:
  pen / book / bag / phone / diary
  diary is the odd one out because you spell the plural *ies*. The other words you just add *s*.

  3 For pronunciation: sounds
  A / I / H / J / K
  I is the odd one out because the vowel sound is different.

  4 For pronunciation: stress
  hospital / banana / potato / Italian / computer
  hospital is the odd one out because the stress is on the first syllable. The other words have the stress on the second syllable.

  5 For collocation: *do* or *make*
  your homework / the washing / a training course / an appointment / the shopping
  an appointment is the odd one out because you use *make*. For the others you use *do*.

  6 For grammar:
  agree / promise / want / can't stand / offer
  can't stand is the odd one out because it is followed by a gerund – the other words are followed by the *to*-infinitive.

- You should tell the students what the criteria is, for example 'think about meaning' or 'think about the sounds'. To make the activity a little more challenging, instead of writing the words on the board, you can dictate them. As a follow-up, ask the students to write their own odd ones out.

9 Making sentences

Aim

This activity is good for revising any type of vocabulary. It works best if the words are a fairly random selection and not part of a tight lexical set.

Preparation

Choose 12 words you want to revise and write them in a circle (like a clockface) on the board

Procedure

- Students work in pairs. They choose two or more of the words and try to make a sentence with them.

  Example sentences:

  My brother is doing | yoga | *in the* | park | .

  The | snowboarder | *eats* | organic vegetables | *on* | Friday | .

  I | saw | *an* | ambitious | | puppy | *in the* | canal | *with a* | blue | | neck | .

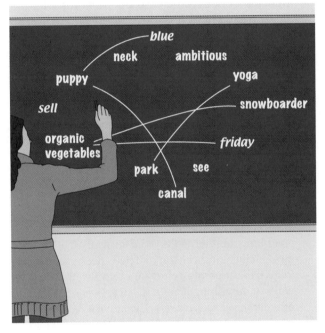

- The students then read out their sentences and you connect the words they have used on the board. You can correct the grammar as necessary or you can make it more difficult for the students by only accepting grammatically correct sentences. (You could make it into a game by saying that the pair who form the sentence including the highest number of words on the board is the winner.) It doesn't matter how bizarre the sentences are, the important thing is that students spend time looking at and remembering the vocabulary.

10 Spell check

Aim

To revise any vocabulary and focus particularly on spelling.

Preparation

Choose the words you want to review. They can be lexical sets or words at random. Eight to ten words is best.

Procedure

There are various different ways you can approach this, but the following four ways seem to work best:

1   The missing letter
    Student work in pairs. Write up the words with a letter missing from each one, e.g. *samon, courgete, rasberry*, etc. The students have to decide which is the missing letter in each case and rewrite the word correctly. Then give a definition.

2   The extra letter
    Students work in pairs. Write up the words with an extra letter in each one, e.g. *unfaithfull, sosciable, tollerant*, etc. The students have to decide which is the extra letter in each case and rewrite the word correctly. Then give a definition.

3   The wrong letter
    Students work in pairs. Write up the words with a wrong letter in each one, e.g. *nefhew, cousen, neece*, etc. The students have to decide which is the wrong letter in each case and rewrite the word correctly. Then give a definition.

4   Anagrams
    Students work in pairs. Write up the words as anagrams. The students have to unscramble the anagram and rewrite the word correctly. This is the most challenging version of 'Spell check', so it's best to give the students a clue, for example: 'these are all ways of describing hair', e.g. *lurcy, ssemy, cidenger*, etc. (*curly, messy, receding*): Then give a definition.

Anecdote tasks

New Inside Out Upper Intermediate includes a number of extended speaking tasks, where students tackle a longer piece of discourse. We've called these 'Anecdotes'. They are based on personal issues, for instance, memories, stories, people you know. When you learn a musical instrument, you can't spend all your time playing scales and exercises: you also need to learn whole pieces in order to see how music is organised. Anecdotes give students a chance to get to grips with how discourse is organised. We have found the following strategies helpful in getting our students to tell their Anecdotes.

1   Choose global topics that everybody can relate to

One of the main objectives of an Anecdote is to encourage students to experiment with and hopefully grow more competent at using language at the more demanding end of their range. It therefore seems only fair to ask them to talk about subjects they know something about. With familiar subject matter students can concentrate on how they're speaking as well as what they're speaking about. The eight Anecdote topics in *New Inside Out* Upper Intermediate have been carefully selected to appeal to the widest range of students, whilst at the same time, fitting in to the context of the unit.

Unit 1	A person who made a big impression on you.
Unit 2	Somebody's home you have stayed in.
Unit 3	Your most treasured possession.
Unit 4	A challenge you have faced.
Unit 5	A wedding you've been to.
Unit 6	Your favourite restaurant.
Unit 7	A childhood family holiday.
Unit 8	The most positive (or negative) person you know.
Unit 9	Your favourite historic place.
Unit 10	A blockbuster movie you have seen.
Unit 11	Your favourite (or least favourite) teacher at school.
Unit 12	Your favourite room.

As soon as you have got to know your students well enough, you'll be able to choose other Anecdote topics suited to their particular interests and experiences.

2   Allow sufficient preparation time

Students need time to assemble their thoughts and think about the language they'll need. The Anecdotes are set up through evocative questions. Students read or listen to a planned series of questions and choose what specifically they'll talk about; shyer students can avoid matters they feel are too personal. This student preparation is a key stage and should not be rushed. Research, by Peter Skehan and Pauline Foster among others, has shown that learners who plan for tasks attempt more ambitious and complex language, hesitate less and make fewer basic errors.

The simplest way to prepare students for an Anecdote is to ask them to read the list of questions in the book and decide which they want to talk about. This could be done during class time or as homework preparation for the following lesson. Ask them to think about the language they'll need. Encourage them to use dictionaries and make notes – but not to write out what they'll actually say. Finally, put them into pairs to exchange Anecdotes.

A variation is to ask the students to read the questions in the book while, at the same time, listening to you read them aloud. Then ask them to prepare in detail for the task, as above.

Alternatively, ask the students to close their books – and then to close their eyes. Ask them to listen to the questions as you read them aloud and think about what they evoke. Some classes will find this a more involving process. It also allows you to adapt the questions to your class: adding new ones or missing out ones you think inappropriate. After the reading, give them enough time to finalise their preparation before starting the speaking task.

3   Monitor students and give feedback

It's important for students to feel that their efforts are being monitored by the teacher. Realistically, it's probably only possible for a teacher to monitor and give feedback to one or two pairs of students during each Anecdote activity. It's therefore vital that the teacher adopts a strict rota system, and makes sure that everyone in the class is monitored over the course of a term. Constructive feedback helps students improve their delivery.

4   Provide a 'model anecdote'

It's always useful for the students to hear a model Anecdote at some stage during the Anecdote task cycle. The most obvious model is you, the teacher. Students will enjoy hearing real stories from your own life experience. Alternatively, you might ask a teaching colleague or friend to talk to the students, or record one of them telling an Anecdote and play it back in class.

5   Repeat the same anecdote with a new partner at regular intervals

Consider going back to Anecdotes and repeating them in later classes. Let the students know that you're going to do this. This will reassure them that you're doing it on purpose, but more importantly, it will mean that they'll be more motivated to dedicate some time and thought to preparation. When you repeat the task, mix the class so that each student works with a new partner, i.e. one who has not previously heard the Anecdote.

In our experience, most students are happy to listen to their partner's Anecdotes. If, however, any of your students are reluctant listeners, you might think about giving them some sort of 'listening task'. Here are three examples:

- Ask the listener to tick the prompt questions that the 'Anecdote teller' answers while telling the Anecdote.

- Ask the listener to time the 'Anecdote teller'. In *Teaching Collocations* (page 91) Michael Lewis suggests reducing the time allowed to deliver the Anecdote each time it's repeated: for example, in the first instance the student has five minutes; for the second telling they have four minutes; and the third three minutes.

- Ask the listener to take brief notes about the Anecdote and write them up as a summary for homework. Then give the summary to the 'Anecdote teller' to check.

The pedagogic value of getting students to re-tell Anecdotes – repeat a 'big chunk' of spoken discourse – cannot be over-stated. Repeating complex tasks reflects real interactions. We all have our set pieces: jokes, stories. And we tend to refine and improve them as we retell them. Many students will appreciate the opportunity to do the same thing in their second language. Research by Martin Bygate among others has shown that given this opportunity students become more adventurous and at the same time more precise in the language they use.

You can also use the Anecdotes to test oral proficiency and thereby add a speaking component to accompany the tests in the Teacher's Book.

Key concepts in *New Inside Out*

The following excerpts are from *An A–Z of ELT* by Scott Thornbury (Macmillan Books for Teachers, 2006). They give clear authoritive definitions and explanations of some of the most important concepts in *New Inside Out*.

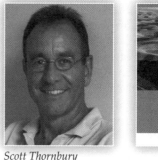

Scott Thornbury

Contents

Note: SLA = Second Language Acquisition

classroom interaction METHODOLOGY

Classroom interaction is the general term for what goes on between the people in the classroom, particularly when it involves language. In traditional classrooms, most interaction is initiated by the teacher, and learners either respond individually, or in unison. Teacher-centred interaction of this kind is associated with *transmissive* teaching, such as a lecture or presentation, where the teacher *transmits* the content of the lesson to the learners. In order to increase the amount of student involvement and interaction, teacher–learner interaction is often combined with **pairwork** and **groupwork**, where learners interact among themselves in pairs or small groups. Other kinds of interaction include *mingling* or *milling*. Pairwork and groupwork are associated with a more **learner-centred** approach. Rather than passively receiving the lesson content, the learners are actively engaged in using language and discovering things for themselves. The value of pairwork and groupwork has been reinforced by the belief that **interaction** facilitates language learning. Some would go as far as to say that it is *all* that is required.

The potential for classroom interaction is obviously constrained by such factors as the number of students, the size of the room, the furniture, and the purpose or type of activity. Not all activities lend themselves to pairwork or groupwork. Some activities, such as reading, are best done as *individual work*. On the other hand, listening activities (such as listening to an audio recording, or to the teacher) favour a *whole class* format, as do grammar presentations. The whole class is also an appropriate form of organization when reviewing the results of an activity, as, for example, when spokespersons from each group are reporting on the results of a discussion or survey.

The success of any classroom interaction will also depend on the extent to which the learners know what they are meant to be doing and why, which in turn depends on how clearly and efficiently the interaction has been set up. Pair- and groupwork can be a complete waste of time if learners are neither properly prepared for it, nor sure of its purpose or outcome.

Finally, the success of pair- and groupwork will depend on the kind of group **dynamics** that have been established. Do the students know one another? Are they happy working together? Do they mind working without constant teacher supervision? Establishing a productive classroom dynamic may involve making decisions as to who works with whom. It may also mean deliberately staging the introduction of different kinds of interactions, starting off with the more controlled, teacher-led interactions before, over time, allowing learners to work in pairs and finally in groups.

collocation VOCABULARY

If two words *collocate*, they frequently occur together. The relation between the words may be grammatical, as when certain verbs collocate with particular prepositions, such as *depend on, account for, abstain from*, or when a verb, like *make, take*, or *do*, collocates with a noun, as in *make an arrangement, take advantage, do the shopping*. The collocation may also be lexical, as when two **content words** regularly co-occur, as in *a broad hint, a narrow escape* (but not *a wide hint* or *a tight escape*). The strength of the collocation can vary: *a broad street* or *a narrow path* are weak collocations, since both elements can co-occur with lots of other words: *a broad river, a busy street*, etc. *Broad hint* and *narrow escape* are stronger. Stronger still are combinations where one element rarely occurs without the other, as in *moot point, slim pickings* and *scot free*. Strongest of all are those where both elements never or rarely occur without the other, such as *dire straits* and *spick and span*. These have acquired the frozen status of *fixed expressions*.

Unsurprisingly, learners lack intuitions as to which words go with which, and this accounts for many errors, such as *You can <u>completely</u> enjoy it* (instead of *thoroughly*), *On Saturday we <u>made</u> shopping* (instead of *went*), and *We went the <u>incorrect</u> way* (for *wrong*). Using texts to highlight particular collocations, and teaching new words in association with their most frequent collocations are two ways of approaching the problem. Nowadays learners' dictionaries also include useful collocational information, such as this entry from the *Macmillan English Dictionary for Advanced Learners*:

communicative activity METHODOLOGY

A communicative activity is one in which real communication occurs. Communicative activities belong to that generation of classroom **activities** that emerged in response to the need for a more **communicative approach** in the teaching of second languages. (In their more evolved form as **tasks**, communicative activities are central to **task-based learning**). They attempt to import into a practice activity the key features of 'real-life' communication. These are

- *purposefulness*: speakers are motivated by a communicative goal (such as getting information, making a request, giving instructions) and not simply by the need to display the correct use of language for its own sake
- *reciprocity*: to achieve a purpose, speakers need to interact, and there is as much need to listen as to speak

- *negotiation*: following from the above, they may need to check and **repair** the communication in order to be understood by each other
- *unpredictability*: neither the process, nor the outcome, nor the language used in the exchange, is entirely predictable
- *heterogeneity*: participants can use any communicative means at their disposal; in other words, they are not restricted to the use of a pre-specified grammar item.

And, in the case of spoken language in particular:

- *synchronicity*: the exchange takes place in real time

The best known communicative activity is the *information gap* activity. Here, the information necessary to complete the task is either in the possession of just one of the participants, or distributed among them. In order to achieve the goal of the task, therefore, the learners have to share the information that they have. For example, in a *describe-and-draw* activity, one student has a picture which is hidden from his or her partner. The task is for that student to describe the picture so that the partner can accurately draw it. In a *spot-the-difference* task, both students of a pair have pictures (or texts) that are the same apart from some minor details. The goal is to identify these differences. In a *jigsaw activity*, each member of a group has different information. One might have a bus timetable, another a map, and another a list of hotels. They have to share this information in order to plan a weekend break together.

Information gap activities have been criticized on the grounds that they lack **authenticity**. Nor are information gap activities always as productive as might be wished: unsupervised, learners may resort to **communication strategies** in order to simplify the task. A more exploitable information gap, arguably, is the one that exists between the learners themselves, ie, what they don't know – but might like to know – about one another (→ **personalization**).

context LINGUISTICS

The context of a language item is its adjacent language items. In the absence of context, it is often impossible to assign exact meaning to an item. A sentence like *Ben takes the bus to work*, for example, could have past, present, or future reference, depending on the context:

> I know this chap called Ben. One day *Ben takes the bus to work*, and just as …
> Most days *Ben takes the bus to work*, but sometimes he rides his bike …
> If *Ben takes the bus to work* tomorrow, he'll be late, because there's a strike …

Likewise, a sentence like *You use it like this* is meaningless in the absence of a context. By the same token, a word or sentence in one context can have a very different meaning in another. The sign *NO BICYCLES* in a public park means something different to *NO BICYCLES* outside a bicycle rental shop. It is sometimes necessary to distinguish between different kinds of context. On the one hand, there is the context of the accompanying **text**, sometimes called the *co-text*. The co-text of this sentence, for example, includes the sentences that precede and follow it, as well as the paragraph of which it forms a part. It is the co-text that offers clues as to the meaning of unfamiliar vocabulary in a text. The *situational* context (also *context of situation, context of use*), on the other hand, is the physical and temporal setting in which an instance of language use occurs. The typical context for the spoken question *Are you being served?* is in a shop, for example. Both co-text and context influence the production and interpretation of language. **Discourse analysis** studies the relationship between language and co-text, including the way that sentences or utterances are connected. **Pragmatics** studies the relationship between language and its contexts of use, including the way meaning can be inferred by reference to context factors.

Various theories have been proposed in order to account for the ways that language choices are determined by contextual factors. One of the best known of these is Michael Halliday's **systemic functional linguistics**. Halliday distinguishes three variables in any context that systematically impact on language choices and which, together, determine a text's **register**:

- the *field*: what the language is being used to talk about, and for what purposes
- the *tenor*: the participants in the language event, and their relationship
- the *mode*: how language is being used in the exchange, eg is it written or spoken?

For example, this short text shows the influence of all three factors:

> Do u fancy film either 2nite or 2moro? Call me.

The field is 'making arrangements about leisure activities', hence the use of words like *film, 2nite* (*tonight*), *2moro* (*tomorrow*). The tenor is one of familiarity and equality (accounting for the informal *fancy* and the imperative: *call me*); and the mode is that of a written text message, which explains its brevity, its use of abbreviated forms (*u, 2nite*) and the absence of salutations. A change in any of these contextual factors is likely to have a significant effect on the text.

Language learners, it is argued, need to know how these contextual factors correlate with language choices in order to produce language that is appropriate to the context. One way of doing this is to ask them to make changes to a text (such as the text message above) that take into account adjustments to the field, tenor, or mode.

dynamics: group, classroom METHODOLOGY

Dynamics are the actions and interactions, both conscious and unconscious, that take place between members of a group, whether the whole class or sub-groups. Group dynamics are instrumental in forging a productive and motivating classroom environment. They are determined by such factors as: the composition of the group (including the age, sex, and relative status of the members, as well as their different attitudes, beliefs, learning styles and abilities); the patterns of relationships between members of the group, including how well they know each other, and the roles they each assume, such as group leader, spokesperson, etc; physical factors such as the size of the group and the way it is seated; and the tasks that the group are set, eg: Does the task require everyone to contribute? Does it encourage co-operation or competition? Are the goals of the task clear to the group members?

Ways that the teacher can promote a positive group (and class) dynamic include:

- ensuring all class or group members can see and hear one another, and that they know (and use) each other's names
- keeping groups from getting too big – three to six members is optimal
- setting – or negotiating – clear rules for groupwork, such as using only the target language, giving everyone a turn to speak, allowing individuals to 'pass' if they don't want to say anything too personal
- using 'ice-breaking' activities to encourage interaction, laughter, and relaxation
- ensuring that group tasks are purposeful, interactive, and collaborative
- personalizing tasks, ie, setting tasks that involve the sharing of personal experiences and opinions
- defining the roles and responsibilities within the group, and varying these regularly, eg by appointing a different spokesperson each time
- monitoring groupwork in progress, and being alert to any possible conflicts or tensions between members, and reconstituting groups, if necessary
- discussing the importance of groupwork with learners, and getting feedback on group processes

fluency SLA

If someone is said to be fluent in a language, or to speak a language fluently, it is generally understood that they are able to speak the language idiomatically and accurately, without undue pausing, without an intrusive accent, and in a manner appropriate to the context. In fact, research into listeners' perceptions of fluency suggests that fluency is primarily the ability to produce and maintain speech in *real time*. To do this, fluent speakers are capable of:

- appropriate pausing, ie:
  - their pauses may be long but are not frequent
  - their pauses are usually filled, eg with **pause fillers** like *erm, you know, sort of*
  - their pauses occur at meaningful transition points, eg at the intersections of clauses or phrases, rather than midway in a phrase
- long runs, ie, there are many syllables and words between pauses

All of the above factors depend on the speaker having

a well-developed grammar, an extensive vocabulary, and, crucially, a store of memorized *chunks*. Being able to draw on this store of chunks means not having to depend on grammar to construct each utterance from scratch. This allows the speaker to devote **attention** to other aspects of the interaction, such as planning ahead. Speakers also use a number of 'tricks' or *production strategies* to convey the illusion of fluency. One such strategy is disguising pauses by filling them, or by repeating a word or phrase.

Some proponents of the **communicative approach** re-defined fluency so as to distinguish it from **accuracy**. Fluency came to mean 'communicative effectiveness', regardless of formal accuracy or speed of delivery. Activities that are communicative, such as information-gap activities, are said to be *fluency-focused*. This is the case even for activities that produce short, halting utterances. Separating accuracy and fluency, and defining the latter as *communicative* language use, is misleading, though. There are many speech events whose communicativeness depends on their accuracy. Air traffic control talk is just one. Moreover, many learners aspire to being more than merely communicative.

Classroom activities that target fluency need to prepare the learner for real-time speech production. Learning and memorizing lexical chunks, including useful conversational gambits, is one approach. **Drills** may help here, as will some types of **communicative activity** that involve repetition. Research has also shown that fluency improves the more times a **task** is repeated. Fluency may also benefit from activities that manage to distract learners' attention away from formal accuracy so that they are not tempted to slow down. (This has been called 'parking their attention'). Some interactive and competitive language **games** have this effect. **Drama** activities, such as roleplays, recreate conditions of real-time language use, and are therefore good for developing fluency. Finally, learners can achieve greater fluency from learning a repertoire of **communication strategies**, ie, techniques for getting around potential problems caused by a lack of the relevant words or structures.

focus on form SLA

When learners focus on form, they direct conscious attention to some formal feature of the language **input**. The feature may be the fact that the past of *has* is *had*, or that *enjoy* is followed by verb forms ending in *-ing*, or that adjectives do not have plural forms in English. The learners' attention may be self-directed, or it may be directed by the teacher or by another learner. Either way, it has been argued that a focus on **form** is a necessary condition for language learning. Simply focusing on the **meaning** of the input is not enough. Focusing on form is, of course, not a new idea: most teaching methods devote a great deal of time to the forms of the language, eg when new grammar items are presented. But the term *focus on form* captures the fact that this focus can, theoretically, occur at any stage in classroom instruction. Thus, **correction**, especially in the form of

negative **feedback**, is a kind of focus on form. In fact, some researchers argue that the most effective form focus is that which arises incidentally, in the context of communication, as when the teacher quickly elicits a correction during a classroom discussion. This incidental approach contrasts with the more traditional and deliberate approach, where teaching is based on a **syllabus** of graded structures (or *forms*), and these are pre-taught in advance of activities designed to practise them. This traditional approach is called – by some researchers – a *focus on formS*.

frequency LINGUISTICS; SLA

The frequency of a word, or other language item, is the number of times the item occurs in a **text** or a **corpus**. Frequency data, derived from large corpora, provide valuable information for syllabus and materials designers. Nowadays, for example, compilers of learner **dictionaries** take frequency into account when deciding which words to include and which meanings of these words to prioritize, and the relative frequency of a word is usually indicated in some way. Word frequency is also a factor in judging the readability of texts. It has been estimated that around eighty per cent of any text consists of the two thousand most frequent words in English. (In this paragraph, for example, the figure is eighty-three per cent). The most frequent words are **function words**, such as *the, of, in, and*, etc. Corpus research also provides frequency information about **grammar** items, but this has made less of an impact on teaching materials than has the research into word frequency. It has been shown, for instance, that simple verb forms are roughly twenty times more frequent than continuous ones (→ **aspect**). Proponents of a form of **lexical approach** argue that frequency should be a major priority when selecting items for a **syllabus**. This is because the most frequent words and structures in the language express its most frequent meanings. Frequency does not always equate with usefulness, however. Travellers know that it is often quite low frequency words, such as *toothbrush* and *bill*, that are of more immediate utility.

The frequency of an item in the input that learners are exposed to may also be a critical factor in the acquisition of that item. It has long been known that the more times a learner encounters a new word the more likely they are to learn it. (One figure quoted by researchers is that at least seven encounters over spaced intervals are necessary → **repetition**.) Now, scholars who subscribe to **usage-based acquisition** theories argue that acquisition is simply the result of exposure, over time, to language data (or 'usage'). From this data, regularities, or patterns, are abstracted using natural human processes of perception, pattern recognition, and association (→ **connectionism**). The more often a pattern occurs in the input, the greater the chance that the pattern will be observed and remembered. Indeed, the more or less fixed **order of acquisition** of grammar structures can be accounted for, at least in part, by the relative frequency of these items in naturally occurring input.

The implications for teaching are that the learning of grammar and vocabulary might be speeded up by using texts that have a high frequency of occurrences of the target items. (The technique is known as *input flood* → **input**.) The 'frequency hypothesis' also justifies frequent recycling of recently taught items (→ **revision**).

function LINGUISTICS

The function of a language item is its communicative purpose. Language is more than simply **forms** and their associated meanings (ie, **usage**). It is also the communicative **uses** to which these forms and meanings are put. These two sentences, for example, share the same forms, but function quite differently:

[in an email] *Thank you for sending me the disk.*
[a notice in a taxi] *Thank you for not smoking.*

The function of the first is *expressing thanks*, while the second is more like a *prohibition*. Likewise, the same function can be expressed by different forms:

[a notice in a taxi] *Thank you for not smoking.*
[a sign in a classroom] *No smoking.*

Thus, there is no one-to-one match between form and function. Assigning a function to a text or an utterance usually requires knowledge of the **context** in which the text is used. The study of how context and function are interrelated is called **pragmatics**.

Communicative functions can be categorized very broadly and also at increasing levels of detail. The 'big' functions, or macrofunctions, describe the way language is used in very general terms. These include the use of language for *expressive* purposes (eg poetry), for *regulatory* purposes (eg for getting people to do things), for *interpersonal* purposes (eg for socializing), and for *representational* purposes (eg to inform). More useful, from the point of view of designing language syllabuses, are microfunctions. These are usually expressed as **speech acts**, such as *agreeing and disagreeing, reporting, warning, apologizing, thanking, greeting*, etc. Such categories form the basis of **functional syllabuses**, a development associated with the **communicative approach**. They often appear as one strand of a coursebook **syllabus**. Functions differ from notions in that the latter describe areas of meaning – such as *ability, duration, quantity, frequency*, etc – rather than the uses to which these meanings are put.

One way to teach functions is to adopt a 'phrasebook' approach, and teach useful ways of expressing common functions (what are called *functional exponents*), such as *Would you like ...?* (*inviting*) and *Could you ..., please?* (*requesting*). More memorable, though, is to teach these expressions in the contexts of **dialogues**, so that the functional exponents are associated not only with common situations in which they are used, but with related functions (such as *accepting* and *refusing*). The term *function*, in contrast to **form**, is also used in linguistics, specifically with regard to the functions of the different elements of a **clause** (such as subject and object).

grammar teaching METHODOLOGY

Like the word **grammar** itself, the topic of grammar teaching is a controversial one, and teachers often take opposing views. Historically, language teaching methods have positioned themselves along a scale from 'zero grammar' to 'total grammar', according to their approach to grammar teaching. Proponents of *natural methods*, who model their approach to teaching second languages on the way that first languages are acquired, reject any explicit teaching of grammar at all. (They may, however, teach according to a grammar **syllabus**, even if no mention of grammar as such is made in the classroom). This implicit approach is common both to the **direct method** and to **audiolingualism**. Through exposure to demonstrations, situations or examples, learners are expected to pick up the rules of grammar by **inductive learning**. At the other end of the spectrum, there are approaches, such as **grammar-translation**, that adopt an explicit and **deductive learning** approach. From the outset, learners are presented with rules which they study and then practise. Occupying a midway point between zero grammar and total grammar is the approach called **consciousness-raising**. Instead of being given rules, learners are presented with language data which challenge them to re-think (and *restructure*) their existing mental grammar. This data might take the form of **input** that has been manipulated in some way. For example, pairs of sentences, such as the following, have to be matched to pictures, forcing learners to discriminate between them, and, in theory, **notice** the difference (→ **noticing**):

The Queen drove to the airport.
The Queen was driven to the airport.

(This is sometimes called a *grammar interpretation task*, or *structured input*.) In order to do the task, learners have to process not just the individual words, but also their grammatical form. That is why this approach to teaching grammar is sometimes called *processing instruction*. There are other researchers who argue that it is by means of manipulating the learner's output, eg through productive practice, that mental restructuring is best effected.

The **communicative approach** accommodates different approaches to grammar teaching. Proponents of **task-based learning**, for example, argue that, if the learner is engaged in solving problems using language, then the mental grammar will develop of its own accord. However, advocates of the weaker version of the communicative approach (and the version that is most widespread) justify a role for the pre-teaching of grammar in advance of production. This view finds support in **cognitive learning theory**, which suggests that conscious attention to grammatical form (called **focus on form**) speeds up language learning, and is a necessary corrective against premature **fossilization**. There is some debate, though, as to whether this form focus should be planned or incidental. Incidental grammar teaching occurs when the teacher deals with grammar issues as and when they come up, eg in the form of **correction**, or task **feedback**. In this way (it is argued) grammar teaching follows the learners' own 'syllabus'. Such an approach attempts to address one of the dilemmas of grammar teaching: the fact that the learner's mental grammar, and the way it develops, bears only an accidental relation to a formal grammar syllabus.

Nevertheless, the research into these different choices is still inconclusive. It may be the case that some items of grammar respond better to explicit teaching, while others are more easily picked up through exposure. There are also different learner types: some prefer learning and applying rules, while others are happier with a more 'deep-end' approach (→ **learning style**). Most current teaching materials hedge their bets on these issues. They offer both deductive and inductive grammar presentations, and opportunities for incidental as well as for planned learning.

learner-centred instruction, learner-centredness
METHODOLOGY

Learner-centred instruction aims to give learners more say in areas that are traditionally considered the domain of the teacher or of the institution. Learner-centred instruction is true to the spirit of progressive education, including the movement towards providing learners with greater **autonomy**. For example, a learner-centred **curriculum** would involve learners in negotiating decisions relating to the choice of syllabus content, of materials, of activity-types, and of assessment procedures. Learner-centredness also describes ways of organizing **classroom interaction** so that the focus is directed away from the teacher, and on to the learners, who perform tasks in pairs or small groups. This contrasts with traditional, teacher-centred, classroom interaction. Some writers believe that the dichotomy between learner-centred (= good) and teacher-centred (= bad) is a false one. It might be more useful to talk about *learning-centred instruction*, ie, instruction which prioritizes sound learning principles. In a learning-centred approach there would be room for both learner-centred *and* teacher-centred interactions.

learning style PSYCHOLOGY

Your learning style is your preferred way of learning. This style may be influenced by biographical factors (such as how you were taught as a child) or by innately endowed factors (such as whether you have a 'good ear' for different sounds). Types of learning style are often presented in the form of polarities (some of which may overlap), such as:

- analytic versus global (or holistic) thinkers, ie, learners who tend to focus on the details, versus learners who tend to see 'the big picture'
- rule-users versus data-gatherers, ie, learners who learn and apply rules, versus those who prefer exposure to lots of examples
- reflective versus impulsive learners
- group-oriented versus solitary learners
- extrovert versus introverted learners
- verbal versus visual learners
- passive versus active learners

Attempts have been made to group these polarities and relate them to brain lateralization. So, a bias towards left-brain processing correlates with analytic, rule-forming and verbal learners, while a bias towards right-brain processing correlates with their opposite. A less binary view of learning style is that proposed by the psychologist Howard Gardner. He identified at least seven distinct intelligences that all individuals possess but to different degrees. These include the *logical/mathematical*, the *verbal/linguistic*, and the *visual/spatial*. Similarly, proponents of **neuro-linguistic programming** distinguish between different sensory orientations, including the *visual*, *aural* and *kinesthetic* (ie, related to movement, touch). So far, though, there is no convincing evidence that any of these dispositions correlates with specific learning behaviours. Nor has it been shown that a preference in one area predicts success in language learning. In fact, it is very difficult to separate learning style from other potentially influential factors, such as personality, intelligence, and previous learning experience. Nor is it clear to what extent learning style can be manipulated, eg through **learner training**. The best that can be said is that, if the learner's preferred learning style is out of synch with the type of instruction on offer, then success is much less likely than if the two are well matched. This supports the case for an **eclectic** approach, on the one hand, and the individualization of learning, on the other.

listening METHODOLOGY

Listening is the skill of understanding spoken language. It is also the name given to classroom activities that are designed to develop this skill – what are also called *listening comprehension* activities – as in 'today we're going to do a listening'. Listening is one of the four language **skills**, and, along with **reading**, was once thought of as being a 'passive' skill. In fact, although receptive, listening is anything but passive. It is a goal-oriented activity, involving not only processing of the incoming speech signals (called *bottom-up processing*) but also the use of prior knowledge, contextual clues, and expectations (*top-down processing*) in order to create meaning. Among the sub-skills of listening are:

- perceiving and discriminating individual sounds
- segmenting the stream of speech into recognizable units such as words and phrases
- using **stress** and **intonation** cues to distinguish given information from new information
- attending to **discourse markers** and using these to predict changes in the direction of the talk
- guessing the meaning of unfamiliar words
- using clues in the text (such as vocabulary) and context clues to predict what is coming
- making inferences about what is not stated
- selecting key information relevant to the purpose for listening
- integrating incoming information into the mental 'picture' (or **schema**) of the speech event so far

Also, since listening is normally interactive, listeners need to be capable of:

- recognizing when speakers have finished their turns, or when it is appropriate to interrupt
- providing ongoing signals of understanding, interest, etc. (*backchannelling*)
- asking for clarification, asking someone to repeat what they have just said, and repairing misunderstandings

These sub-skills exist across languages, so, in theory, learners should be able to transfer them from their first language into their second. In fact, there are a number of reasons why this does not always happen. One is that speakers of different languages process speech signals differently, depending on the phonetic characteristics of the language they are used to. This means that speakers of some languages will find it harder than others to match the spoken word to the way that the word is represented in their mind. They simply do not recognize the word. Another problem is lack of sufficient L2 knowledge, such as vocabulary or grammar. A third problem is that learners may lack the means (and the confidence) to negotiate breakdowns in understanding. Finally, many learners simply lack exposure to spoken language, and therefore have not had sufficient opportunities to experience listening. These problems can be compounded in classrooms because:

- Listening to audio recordings deprives the learners of useful visual information, and allows the learners no opportunity to interact and repair misunderstandings.
- Classroom acoustics are seldom ideal.
- If learners do not know what they are listening for (in the absence, for example, of some pre-set listening task) they may try to process as much information as possible, rather than being selective in their listening. This can lead to listening overload, which in turn can cause inhibiting anxiety.
- Listening texts that have been specially written for classroom use are often simplified. But if this simplification means eliminating a lot of redundant language, such as speaker repetitions, pause fillers and vague language, the density of information that results may make it harder – not easier – to process.

For this reason, the use of audio recordings to develop listening skills needs to be balanced against the advantages of using other media, such as video, and face-to-face interaction with the teacher or another speaker.

Nevertheless, the use of audio recordings is an established part of classroom practice, so it is important to know how to use them to best advantage. The following approach is one that is often recommended:

- Provide some minimum contextual information, eg who is talking to whom about what, and why. This helps to compensate for lack of visual information, and allows learners to activate the relevant mental **schema**, which in turn helps top-down processing, including the sub-skill of prediction.
- Pre-teach key vocabulary: this helps with bottom-up processing, although too much help may mean that learners don't get sufficient practice in guessing from context.
- Set some 'while-listening' questions. Initially, these should focus on the overall *gist* of the text. For example: true/false questions, selecting, ordering or matching pictures, ticking items on a list, following a map
- Play a small section of the recording first, to give learners an opportunity to familiarize themselves with the different voices, and to trigger accurate expectations as to what they will hear.
- Play the recording right through, and then allow learners to consult on the answers to the pre-set task. Check these answers. If necessary, re-play the recording until satisfied that learners have 'got the gist'.
- Set a more demanding task, requiring more intensive listening, such as listening for detail, or inferring speakers' attitudes, intentions, etc. If the recording is a long one, it may pay to stage the intensive listening in sections. Again, allow learners to consult in pairs, before checking the task in open class.
- On the basis of the learners' success with these tasks, identify problem sections of the recording and return to these, playing and re-playing them, and perhaps eliciting a word-by-word transcription and writing this on the board.
- Distribute copies of the transcript of the recording (if available) and re-play the recording while learners read the transcript. This allows the learners to clear up any remaining problems, and also to match what they hear to what they see.

The above approach can be adapted to suit different kinds of recorded texts and different classroom needs. For higher level learners, for example, it may be counter-productive to make listening *too* easy. The approach can also be adapted to the use of video, and even to *live listenings*, such as listening to the teacher or a guest.

meaning LINGUISTICS

Language consists of **forms** that express certain meanings. The study of meaning is called **semantics**. A basic principle in semantics is that the forms of a language are simply *signs* – they are arbitrary and bear no resemblance to the things that are *signified* by them. Thus the word *table* does not look or feel or sound like a table. Any other word, like *Tisch*, or *mesa*, or *tarabeza* (which all translate as *table* in their respective languages), would do as well. Learning a second language, then, is first and foremost a job of matching a whole new set of (arbitrary) forms to existing meanings. The teacher's job is to help in the matching process. In fact, establishing meaning is probably one of the most important functions of a language teacher.

Language teaching methods have evolved different approaches to dealing with meaning. Some, like the **direct method**, relied on visual aids, mime, and gesture, to convey the meanings of words and grammatical structures. Others, like **grammar–translation**, used translation. Either way, meaning is often elusive. The direct method approach, ie, pointing to a real *table* and saying the word *table*, works well with words like table. But it works less well for an expression like *under the table*, as in *The deal was done under the table*. Here, the meaning is not literal but *figurative*, or *metaphorical*. Nor does a direct method approach deal well with the fact that 'table' is *polysemous*, ie, that it has several meanings, one of which is a way of displaying information in rows and lines on a page.

Translation is equally problematic. It is easy enough to translate the literal meaning of words, ie, their *denotations*. But it is less easy to capture a word's associations, often cultural, ie, its **connotations**. For example, the English word *chuffed* translates as *contento* in Spanish, but this does not distinguish it from other words that are translated by *contento*, such as *happy*, *content* and *pleased*. It is not always easy to say what something means, eg by giving a definition. (Dr Johnson famously defined *network* as 'anything reticulated or decussated, at equal distances, with interstices between the intersections'.) For teaching purposes, it is often easier to say what something is *like* (using a **synonym**), what it is a *kind of* (using a **hyponym**), or what it is *not* (using an **antonym**).

motivation PSYCHOLOGY

Motivation is what drives learners to achieve a goal, and is a key factor determining success or failure in language learning. The learner's goal may be a short-term one, such as successfully performing a classroom task, or a long-term one, such as achieving native-like proficiency in the language. With regard to long-term goals, a distinction is often made between *instrumental motivation* and *integrative motivation*. Instrumental motivation is when the learner has a functional objective, such as passing an exam or getting a job. Integrative motivation, on the other hand, is when the learner wants to be identified with the target language community. Intersecting with these two motivational *orientations* are two different *sources* of motivation: *intrinsic* (eg the pleasure of doing a task for its own sake) and *extrinsic* (eg the 'carrot and stick' approach). Another motivational source that has been identified is success: experience of succeeding can result in increased motivation (called *resultative motivation*), which raises the question as to whether motivation is as much a result as a cause of learning.

Various theories of motivation have been proposed. Most of these identify a variety of factors that, in combination, contribute to overall motivation, such as:

- *attitudes*, eg to the target language and to speakers of the language

- *goals*, both long-term and short-term, and the learners' *orientation* to these goals
- how much *value* the learner attaches to achieving the goals, especially as weighed against *expectancy of success*; expectancy of success may come from the learner's assessment of their own abilities, and how they account for previous successes or failures
- *self-esteem*, and the need to achieve and maintain it
- *intrinsic interest*, *pleasure*, *relevance* or *challenge* of the task
- *group dynamic*: is it competitive, collaborative, or individualistic?
- *teacher's attitudes*, eg what expectations does the teacher project about the learners' likelihood of success?

As the last point suggests, teachers can play a key role in motivating learners, not just in terms of choosing activities that are intrinsically motivating, but in the attitudes they project. Two researchers on motivation offer the following advice for teachers:

> Ten commandments for motivating language learners
>
> 1. Set a personal example with your own behaviour
> 2. Create a pleasant, relaxed atmosphere in the classroom.
> 3. Present the tasks properly.
> 4. Develop a good relationship with the learners.
> 5. Increase the learner's linguistic self-confidence.
> 6. Make the language classes interesting.
> 7. Promote learner autonomy.
> 8. Personalise the learning process.
> 9. Increase the learners' goal-orientedness.
> 10. Familiarise learners with the target language culture.

noticing SLA

If you notice a feature of the language that you are exposed to, it attracts your attention and you make a mental note of it. For example, a learner might notice (without necessarily understanding) the sign *Mind the gap*, repeated several times on a railway station platform. That same day, the learner hears the teacher say *would you mind* in the context of making a request in class. A day or two later, the same learner hears someone else say *I don't mind*. Each successive 'noticing' both primes the learner to notice new occurrences of *mind*, and at the same time contributes to a growing understanding of the use and meaning of *mind*. Proponents of **cognitive learning theory** believe that noticing is a prerequisite for learning: without it input would remain as mere 'noise'. The *noticing hypothesis*, then, claims that noticing is a necessary condition for acquisition, although not the only one. Some kind of mental processing of what has been noticed is also necessary before the **input** becomes *intake*, ie before it is moved into long-term **memory**.

Teachers obviously play an important role in helping learners to notice features of the language. They do this when they repeat words or structures, write them on the board, or even drill them. One way of increasing the chance of learners' noticing an item is to include it lots of times in a text, a technique called *input flood*. For example, learners read a text with the word *mind* included several times. They then categorize these examples according to their meaning. A set of **concordance** lines for a particular word can be used in the same way.

There is another type of noticing, called *noticing the gap*. This is when learners are made aware of a gap in their language knowledge. This might happen when they do a **dictation**, for example. When they compare their version with the correct version, they may notice certain differences, such as the lack of past tense endings, that represent a gap in their **interlanguage**. It has been argued that noticing the gap can trigger the **restructuring** of interlanguage. That is, 'minding the gap' leads learners to 'fill the gap'.

personalization METHODOLOGY

When you personalize language you use it to talk about your knowledge, experience and feelings. Personalization of the type *Now write five true sentences about yourself using 'used to'* is often motivated by the need to provide further practice of pre-taught grammar structures. But it is also good preparation for the kinds of situations of genuine language use that learners might encounter outside the classroom. These advantages are lost, though, if the teacher's response is to treat the exercise as *only* an exercise, and correct the learners' errors without responding to the content. The influence of **humanistic approaches** has given a fresh impetus to personalization, both in terms of providing a more coherent rationale and suggesting a broader range of activity types. For a start (it is argued), personalization creates better classroom **dynamics**. This is because groups are more likely to form and bond if the individuals in them know more about one another. And the mental and emotional effort that is involved in finding personal associations with a language item is likely to make that item more memorable. This quality is called cognitive and affective *depth*. Finally, lessons are likely to be more interesting, and hence more motivating, if at least some of the content concerns the people in the room, rather than the characters in coursebooks. On these grounds, some writers have suggested that personalization should not be considered simply as an 'add-on', but should be the principle on which most, if not all, classroom content should be based. One teaching approach that is committed to this view is **community language learning**. In this approach, all the content of the lesson comes from the learners themselves. Personalization is not without risks, though. Teachers need to be sensitive to learner resistance: learners should have the right to 'pass' on questions that they consider too intrusive. And teachers should be authentic in the way that they

respond to learners' personalizations. This means that they should respond to *what* their learners are saying, not just how they say it.

practice METHODOLOGY

If you practise a skill, you experience doing it a number of times in order to gain control of it. The idea that 'practice makes perfect' is fundamental to **cognitive learning theory**. It is through practice that the skill becomes automatic. **Sociocultural learning theory** finds room for practice too. Performing a skill with the assistance of someone who is good at it can help in the **appropriation** of the skill. At issue, then, is not so much whether practice is beneficial, but what form it should take, when, and how much of it is necessary. In addressing these questions, it is customary to distinguish between different kinds of practice, such as *controlled practice* vs *free practice*, *mechanical practice* vs *meaningful/communicative practice*, and *receptive practice* vs *productive practice*.

Controlled practice is associated with the second P of the **PPP** instructional model. Practice can be controlled in at least two senses: *language control* and *interactional control*. In the first, the language that is being practised is restricted to what has just been presented (hence it is also called *restricted practice*). For example, if the first **conditional** has been presented, learners practise this, and only this, structure, and in a repetitive way, eg through a sequence of **drills**. Practice is also said to be controlled if the learners' participation is overtly managed and monitored by the teacher, such as in open-class work, as opposed to closed **pairwork** or **groupwork**. One reason for this degree of control is that it maintains a focus on accuracy, and pre-empts or corrects errors. *Free practice*, on the other hand, allows learners a measure of creativity, and the opportunity to integrate the new item into their existing language 'pool'. It is also less controlled in terms of the interactions, with pairwork and groupwork being favoured. Typical free practice activities might be **games**, **discussions** or **drama**-based activities.

Mechanical practice is a form of controlled practice, where the focus is less on the meaning of an item than on manipulating its component parts. Mechanical practice can be either oral or written: many traditional **exercises** are mechanical in this sense, such as when learners transform sentences from active into passive, or from direct speech into reported speech. The arguments in favour of controlled and mechanical practice have lost their force since the decline of **behaviourism** and its belief that learning is simply habit-formation.

Meaningful practice requires learners to display some understanding of what the item that they are practising actually means. One way of doing this is through **personalization**. *Communicative practice* involves the learners interacting in order to complete some kind of task, such as in an *information gap* activity (→ **communicative activity**). Proponents of a communicative approach argue that it is only this kind of practice that is truly effective. This is because learners are not simply practising language, but are practising the behaviours associated with the language, and this is a pre-condition for long-term behavioural change.

Finally, some practice activities are purely *receptive*. They involve the learners in identifying, selecting, or discriminating between language items, but not actually producing them. Many **consciousness-raising** activities are receptive, on the grounds that learners first need to understand a new structure before they can properly internalize it. Receptive practice is also associated with comprehension-based approaches to teaching. *Productive practice*, on the other hand, requires learners to produce the targeted items (either orally or in writing), and is associated with output-based models of learning.

There is fairly general agreement nowadays that the most effective practice activity combines at least some of the following features:

- It is meaningful, which may mean that is personalized.
- It is communicative, thus it will require learners to interact.
- It involves a degree of repetition – not of the mindless type associated with imitation drills, but of the type associated with many games.
- It is language-rich, ie, learners have to interpret or produce a lot of language.
- Learners can be creative and take risks, but support is at hand if they need it.
- Learners are pushed, at least some of the time, to the limits of their competence
- Learners get **feedback**.

pronunciation teaching PHONOLOGY

Pronunciation is the general term for that part of language classes and courses that deals with aspects of the **phonology** of English. This includes the individual sounds (**phonemes**) of English, sounds in **connected speech**, word and sentence **stress, rhythm** and **intonation**. These components are customarily divided into two groups: the *segmental* features of pronunciation, ie, the individual sounds and the way they combine, and the *suprasegmental* features, ie, stress, rhythm and intonation. **Paralinguistic** features of speech production such as voice quality, tempo and loudness, are also classed as suprasegmental.

Effective pronunciation teaching needs to consider what goals, course design and methodology are most appropriate for the learners in question. The goal of acquiring a native-like **accent** is generally thought to be unachievable for most learners (and perhaps even undesirable). Instead, the goal of **intelligibility** is nowadays considered more realistic, if less easily measurable. It is often claimed that suprasegmental features play a greater role in intelligibility than do segmental ones. Unfortunately, however, some of these suprasegmental features, such as intonation, are considered by many teachers to be unteachable. Moreover, learners intending to interact with native speakers may need to set different goals from those learners whose purpose is to learn **English as an international language (EIL)**. For this latter group,

the so-called **phonological core** is a checklist of those pronunciation features considered critical for intelligibility in EIL.

In terms of the design of course content, a basic choice is whether the pronunciation focus is *integrated* or *segregated*. In an integrated approach, pronunciation is dealt with as part of the teaching of grammar and vocabulary, or of speaking and listening. In a segregated approach it is treated in isolation. A classical segregated exercise is the **minimal pairs** task, in which learners are taught to discriminate and produce two contrasted phonemes (as in *hit* and *heat*). There are doubts as to whether this item-by-item approach to pronunciation reflects the way that the features of pronunciation are interconnected. Nor does it reflect the way that they jointly emerge over time ('as a photo emerges in the darkroom'). A related issue is whether pronunciation teaching should be *pre-emptive* or *reactive*. That is to say, should pronunciation teaching be planned around a syllabus of pre-selected items, or should the focus on pronunciation emerge *out of* practice activities, in the form, for example, of **correction**? There is evidence that the latter approach is more effective than the former.

In 1964 the writer (and former language teacher) Anthony Burgess wrote, 'Nothing is more important than to acquire a set of foreign phonemes that shall be entirely acceptable to your hosts'. However, there is generally less emphasis given to pronunciation teaching nowadays. Indeed, some teachers are sceptical as to the value of teaching pronunciation at all. This view is reinforced by research that suggests that the best predictors of intelligible pronunciation are 'having a good ear' and prolonged residence in an English-speaking country. On the other hand, faulty pronunciation is one of the most common causes of misunderstandings. This is an argument for demanding higher standards than the learners can realistically achieve, in the hope that they will meet you 'halfway'.

reading METHODOLOGY

Reading is a receptive **skill**. But the fact that it is receptive does not mean that it is passive: reading is an active, even interactive, process. Readers bring their own questions to the text, which are based on their background knowledge, and they use these to interrogate the text, modifying their questions and coming up with new ones according to the answers they get. In order to do this, they draw on a range of knowledge bases. They need to be able to decode the letters, words and grammatical structures of the individual sentences – what is called *bottom-up processing*. But they also enlist *top-down processes*, such as drawing on **discourse** and schematic knowledge, as well as on immediate contextual information. Discourse knowledge is knowing how different text-types – such as news reports, recipes or academic papers – are organized. Schematic knowledge is the reader's existing knowledge of the topic. Reading involves an interaction between these different 'levels' of knowledge, where knowledge at one 'level' can compensate for lack of knowledge at another.

Readers also bring their own *purposes* to texts, and these in turn determine the way they go about reading a text. The two main purposes for reading are for *information* (such as when consulting a directory), and for *pleasure* (such as when reading a novel), although these purposes may overlap. Different ways of reading include:

- *skimming* (*skim-reading, reading for gist*): rapidly reading a text in order to get the *gist*, or the main ideas or sense of a text. For example, a reader might skim a film review in order to see if the reviewer liked the film or not.
- *scanning*: reading a text in search of specific information, and ignoring everything else, such as when consulting a bus timetable for a particular time and destination.
- *detailed reading*: reading a text in order to extract the maximum detail from it, such as when following the instructions for installing a household appliance.
- *reading aloud*: such as when reading a prepared speech or lecture, or reading a story aloud, or an extract from the newspaper.

A reader's purpose usually matches the writer's intentions for the text. Readers seldom read telephone books from cover to cover, for example. Nor do they normally skim through a novel looking for names beginning with *Vron* .... In classrooms, however, texts are frequently used for purposes other than those for which they were originally intended. They are often used not so much as vehicles of information or of pleasure, but as 'linguistic objects', that is, as contexts for the study of features of the language. A distinction needs to be made, therefore, between two types of classroom reading: reading as *skills development*, and reading as *language study*. There is no reason why the same text cannot be used for both purposes.

Another distinction that is often made is between *intensive reading* and *extensive reading*. The former applies to the way short texts are subject to close and detailed classroom study. Extensive reading, on the other hand, means the more leisurely reading of longer texts, primarily for pleasure, or in order to accumulate vocabulary, or simply to develop sound habits of reading. This is typically done outside class, using graded **readers**, authentic texts, or literary texts.

A third important distinction is between testing reading and teaching reading. Traditional reading tasks usually involve reading a text and then answering **comprehension questions** about it. This is the testing approach. A teaching approach, on the other hand, aims to help learners to become more effective readers by training them in the *sub-skills* of reading, and by teaching them *reading strategies*. Some of the sub-skills of reading are:

- understanding words and identifying their grammatical function
- recognizing grammar features, such as word endings, and 'unpacking' (or **parsing**) the syntax of sentences
- identifying the topic of the text, and recognizing topic changes
- identifying text-type, text purpose, and text organization, and identifying and understanding **discourse markers** and other cohesive devices
- distinguishing key information from less important information
- identifying and understanding the gist
- inferring the writer's attitude
- following the development of an argument
- following the sequence of a narrative
- paraphrasing the text

Activities designed to develop these sub-skills include: underlining topic-related words; contrasting different text-types; comparing different examples of the same text type and identifying *generic* features; circling and categorizing discourse markers; identifying what the pronouns refer to; predicting the direction the text will take at each discourse marker; choosing the best summary of a text; putting a set of pictures in order; extracting key information on to a grid, writing a summary of the text, etc. *Strategy training* involves training learners in ways of overcoming problems when they are reading. Some useful strategies include:

- using contextual and extra-linguistic information (such as pictures, layout, headlines) to make predictions regarding what the text is about
- brainstorming background (or schematic) knowledge in advance of reading
- skimming a text in advance of a more detailed reading
- keeping the purpose of the text in mind
- guessing the meaning of words from context
- **dictionary** use

There is some argument, however, as to the value of a 'skills and strategies' approach to teaching reading. Most adult learners of English come to English texts with already well-developed reading skills in their own language. They already know how to skim, scan, use context clues, enlist background knowledge, and so on. Theoretically, at least, these skills are transferable. What makes reading difficult is not so much lack of reading skills as lack of *language knowledge*. That is, learners lack sufficient vocabulary and grammar to unpack sentences, and they cannot easily identify the ways that sentences are connected. This can result in 'tunnel vision', with readers becoming distracted by unfamiliar words, at the expense of working out meaning from context. On the other hand, it can also result in an over-reliance on guesswork, and on superficial 'text attack' strategies such as skimming. This suggests that texts needs to be chosen that do not over-stretch learners' ability to read them fluently. At the same time, texts should not be so easy that learners can process them simply by skimming. It also means that tasks need to be chosen that both match the original purpose of the text, and that encourage learners to transfer their first language reading skills. Such tasks are likely to be those that motivate learners to *want* to read the text. This might mean activating interest in the topic of the text, through, for example, a pre-reading quiz. At the same time, classroom reading texts should be exploited, not just for their potential in developing reading skills, but as sources of language input. This will involve, at some point, detailed study of the text's formal features, such as its linking devices, its collocations or its grammar.

speaking METHODOLOGY

Speaking is generally thought to be the most important of the four **skills**. The ability to speak a second language is often equated with proficiency in the language, as in *She speaks excellent French*. Indeed, one frustration commonly voiced by learners is that they have spent years studying English, but still can't speak it. One of the main difficulties, of course, is that speaking usually takes place spontaneously and in real time, which means that planning and production overlap. If too much **attention** is paid to planning, production suffers, and the effect is a loss of **fluency**. On the other hand, if the speaker's attention is directed solely on production, it is likely that **accuracy** will suffer, which could prejudice **intelligibility**. In order to free up attention, therefore, the speaker needs to have achieved a degree of **automaticity** in both planning and production. One way of doing this is to use memorized routines, such as **formulaic language**. Another is to use *production strategies*, such as the use of **pause fillers**, in order to 'buy' planning time. The situation is complicated by the fact that most speaking is interactive. Speakers are jointly having to manage the flow of talk. The management of interaction involves *turn-taking skills*, such as knowing how and when to take, keep, and relinquish speaker turns, and also knowing how to repair misunderstandings.

For language learners these processing demands are magnified through lack of basic knowledge of grammar and vocabulary. For the purposes of most day-to-day talk, however, the grammar that is required is not as complex nor need be as accurate as the grammar that is required for writing. Nor do speakers need an enormous vocabulary, especially if they have developed some **communication strategies** for getting round gaps in their knowledge. A core vocabulary of 1000–1500 high-frequency words and expressions will provide most learners with a solid basis for speaking.

Activating this knowledge, though, requires **practice**. This in turn suggests that the more speaking practice opportunities that learners are given, and the sooner, the easier speaking will become. Speaking practice means more than simply answering the teacher's questions, or repeating sentences, as in grammar practice activities. It means interacting with other speakers, sustaining long turns of talk, speaking spontaneously, and speaking about topics of the learners' choice.

Approaches to teaching speaking vary. Traditionally, speaking was considered to be a by-product of teaching grammar and vocabulary, reinforced with work on **pronunciation**. This view has been replaced by approaches that treat speaking as a skill in its own right. One such approach is to break down the speaking skill into a number of discrete sub-skills, such as *opening and closing conversations, turn-taking, repairing, paraphrasing, interrupting,* etc. Another approach is to focus on the different *purposes* of speaking and their associated **genres**, such as *narrating, obtaining service, giving a presentation, making small talk,* etc. This approach is particularly well suited to learners who have a specific purpose for learning English. A third is to adopt a topic-based approach, where learners are encouraged to speak freely on a range of topics, at least some of which they have chosen themselves. This is the format used in many conversation classes. Typical activity types for the teaching of speaking include: **dialogues**, **drama** activities (including *roleplays* and *simulations*), many **games**, **discussions** and debates, as well as informal classroom chat.

task METHODOLOGY

A task is a classroom activity whose focus is on communicating meaning. The objective of a task may be to reach some consensus on an issue, to solve a problem, to draft a plan, to design something, or to persuade someone to do something. In contrast, practising a pre-selected item of language (such as the present perfect) for its own sake would not be a valid task objective. In the performance of the task, learners are expected to make use of their own language resources. In theory, tasks may be receptive or productive, and may be done individually or in pairs or small groups. However, in practice, most activities that are labelled 'tasks' in coursebooks involve production (either speaking or writing, or both) and require learners to interact with one another.

Tasks are the organizing principle in **task-based learning**. In order to devise a syllabus of tasks it is necessary both to classify tasks, and to identify the factors that make one task more difficult than another. Different criteria for classifying tasks have been suggested. For example, tasks can be *open-ended* or *closed*. An open-ended task is one in which learners know there is no predetermined solution. It might be planning an excursion, or debating a topical issue. A closed task, on the other hand, requires learners to discover the solution to a problem, such as identifying the differences in a *spot-the-difference* task (→ **communicative activity**). Tasks can also be classified according to the kinds of operations they involve, such as *ranking, selecting, sorting, comparing, surveying* and *problem-solving*.

Factors which influence the degree of difficulty of the task, and hence which affect the grading of tasks, include:

- *linguistic factors*: How complex is the language that learners will need to draw on, in order to do the task? How much help, either before, or during the task, will they get with their language needs?
- *cognitive factors*: Does the task require the processing of complex data? Is the task type familiar to learners?
- *performance factors*: Do the learners have to interact in real time in order to do the task? Do they have time to rehearse? Do they have to 'go public'?

The term *task* is now widely accepted as a useful way of labelling certain types of classroom activity, including many which have a thinly disguised grammar agenda. But the concept of task is not without its critics. Some writers feel that the associations of task with 'work' undervalues the more playful – and possibly less authentic or communicative – types of classroom activity, such as games, songs and drama.

vocabulary teaching METHODOLOGY

Vocabulary describes that area of language learning that is concerned with word knowledge. Vocabulary learning is a major goal in most teaching programmes. It hasn't always been so. In methods such as **audiolingualism**, vocabulary was subordinated to the teaching of grammar structures. Words were simply there to fill the slots in the sentence patterns. The move towards *semantic* (ie, meaning-based) **syllabuses** in the 1970s, along with the use of **authentic** materials, saw a revival of interest in vocabulary teaching. Subsequently, developments in **corpus** linguistics and **discourse analysis** started to blur the distinction between vocabulary and grammar. In the 1990s the **lexical approach** ushered in a major re-think regarding the role of vocabulary. This concerned both the *selection* of items (**frequency** being a deciding factor) and the *type* of items: **formulaic language** (or lexical chunks) were recognized as being essential for both **fluency** and **idiomaticity**. These developments have influenced the design of teaching materials. Most contemporary coursebooks incorporate a lexical syllabus alongside the grammar one. Recent developments in lexicography have complemented this trend. There is now a wide range of **dictionaries** available for learners, many of which come with sophisticated software for accessing databases of examples and collocations.

It is now generally agreed that, in terms of goals, learners need a receptive vocabulary of around 3000 high-frequency words (or, better, **word families**) in order to achieve independent user status. This will give them around ninety per cent coverage of normal text. For a productive vocabulary, especially for speaking, they may only need half this number.

Classroom approaches to achieving these goals include dedicated vocabulary lessons. Typically these take the form of teaching *lexical sets* of words (ie, groups of thematically linked words) using a variety of means, including visual **aids**, demonstration, situations, texts and dictionary work. As well as the **meaning** of the items, the **form**, both spoken (ie, **pronunciation**) and written (ie, **spelling**), needs to be dealt with, especially if the words are being taught for productive use. Other aspects of word knowledge that may need to be highlighted include **connotation** and **style**, **collocation**, derived forms, and grammatical features, such as the word's **word class**. Vocabulary is also taught as preparation for listening or reading (*pre-teaching vocabulary*) or as a by-product of these skills.

It would be impossible, in class, to teach all the words that learners need. Learners therefore need opportunities for *incidental* learning, eg through *extensive reading*. They may also benefit from training in how to make the most of these opportunities, eg by means of dictionary use, note-keeping, etc. Some strategies for deducing the meaning of unfamiliar words will also help.

Amassing a fully-functioning vocabulary is essentially a **memory** task, and techniques to help in the memorizing of words can be usefully taught, too. It also helps to provide learners with repeated encounters with new words, eg through the re-reading of texts, or by reading several texts about the same topic. Constant recycling of newly learned words is essential. One simple way of doing this is to have a *word box* (or word bag) in the classroom. New words are written on to small cards and added to the word box. At the beginning of the next lesson, these words can be used as the basis for a review activity. For example, the teacher can take words out of the box and ask learners to define them, provide a translation or put them into a sentence. The words can also form the basis for peer-testing activities, in which learners take a number of word cards and test each other in pairs or small groups.

writing METHODOLOGY

Like speaking, writing is a productive **skill**, and, like other skills, writing involves a hierarchy of *sub-skills*. These range from the most mechanical (such as handwriting or typing legibly) through to the ability to organize the written text and lay it out according to the conventions of the particular text type. Along the way, writers also need to be able to:

- produce grammatically accurate sentences
- connect and punctuate these sentences
- select and maintain an appropriate style
- signal the direction that the message is taking
- anticipate the reader's likely questions so as to be able to structure the message accordingly

In order to enable these skills, writers need an extensive knowledge base, not only at the level of vocabulary and grammar, but at the level of connected discourse. This includes familiarity with a range of different text types, such as *informal letters, instructions, product descriptions*, etc. It follows that if classroom writing is mainly spelling- or grammar-focused, many of the sub-skills of writing will be neglected.

Nevertheless, the teaching of writing has tended to focus on the 'lower-level' features of the skill, such as being able to write sentences that are both accurate and complex, that demonstrate internal cohesion, and that are connected to the sentences next to them. This language-based approach is justified on the grounds that stricter standards of accuracy are usually required in writing than in speaking. Also, writing demands a greater degree of explicitness than speaking, since writers and their readers are separated in time and space. They therefore can't rely on immediate feedback in order to clear up misunderstandings.

By contrast, a text-based approach to teaching writing takes a more 'top-down' view. This approach finds support in **discourse analysis**, which shows that a **text** is more than a series of sentences, however neatly linked. Instead, texts are organized according to larger *macrostructures*, such as problem-solution, or definition-examples. Hence, learners need explicit guidance in how texts are structured. This typically involves analysing and imitating models of particular text types. For example, a business letter might be analysed in terms of its overall layout, the purpose of each of its paragraphs, the grammatical and lexical choices within each paragraph, and the punctuation. Each of these features is then practised in isolation. They are then recombined in tasks aimed first at reproducing the original text and then at producing similar texts incorporating different content.

This approach is called a *product approach* to the teaching of writing, since the focus is exclusively on producing a text (the product) that reproduces the model. By contrast, a *process approach* argues that writers do not in fact start with a clear idea of the finished product. Rather, the text emerges out of a creative process. This process includes: *planning* (*generating ideas*, *goal setting* and *organizing*), *drafting* and *re-drafting*; *reviewing*, including *editing* and *proofreading*, and, finally, '*publishing*'. Advocates of a process approach argue for a more organic sequence of classroom activities, beginning with the brainstorming of ideas, writing preliminary drafts, comparing drafts, re-drafting, and *conferencing*, that is, talking through their draft with the teacher, in order to fine-tune their ideas.

The process approach to writing has a lot in common with the **communicative approach** to language teaching, and each has drawn support from the other. The communicative approach views writing as an act of communication in which the writer interacts with a reader or readers for a particular purpose. The purpose might be to ask for information about a language course, to relay personal news, to complain about being overcharged at a hotel, or simply to entertain and amuse. Thus, advocates of a communicative approach argue that classroom

writing tasks should be motivated by a clear purpose and that writers should have their reader(s) in mind at all stages of the writing process. Such principles are now reflected in the design of writing tasks in public examinations, such as this one, from the Cambridge ESOL First Certificate in English (FCE) paper:

> The school where you learn English has decided to buy some videos in English. You have been asked to write a report to the Principal, suggesting what kinds of videos the school should buy. In your report you should also explain why students at the school will like these videos.
>
> Write your report.

The social purposes of writing are also foregrounded by proponents of a *genre-based approach*. **Genre** analysis attempts to show how the structure of particular text-types are shaped by the purposes they serve in specific social and cultural contexts. Put simply, a business letter is the way it is because of what it does. Advocates of genre-based teaching reject a process approach to teaching writing. They argue that to emphasize self-expression at the expense of teaching the generic structures of texts may in fact disempower learners. Many learners, especially those who are learning English as a *second* language, need a command of those genres – such as writing a CV, or requesting a bank loan – that permit access to the host community. A genre approach to teaching writing is not unlike a product approach, therefore. It starts with model texts that are subjected to analysis and replication. The difference is that these models are closely associated with their contexts of use, and they are analysed in functional terms as much as in linguistic ones. The genre approach has been particularly influential in the teaching of academic writing.

In reality, none of these approaches is entirely incompatible with any other. Resourceful teachers tend to blend elements of each. For example, they may encourage learners to 'discover' what they want to write, using a process approach. They may then give them a model text, both as a source of useful language items, and as a template for the final product. They may also provide exercises in specific sub-skills, such as linking sentences, or using a formal style.

The Common European Framework and *New Inside Out*

The Common European Framework for language learning

Introduction

The Common European Framework (CEF) is a widely used standard created by the Council of Europe. In the classroom, familiarity with the CEF can be of great help to any teacher in identifying students' actual progress and helping them to set their learning priorities.

Students can use the descriptors (description of competences) at any point to get a detailed, articulated, and personal picture of their own individual progress. This is important, as no two language learners progress in the same way, and consequently it's always rather artificial to apply a 'framework level' to a class as a whole, or to a course or coursebook.

The European Language Portfolio is another Council of Europe project, designed to give every learner a structure for keeping a record of their language learning experiences and their progress as described in the CEF. Up-to-date information about developments with the CEF and Portfolio can be found on www.coe.int/portfolio.

The Swiss-based Eurocentres Foundation played a major role in the development of the levels and the descriptors for the CEF and the prototype Portfolio. The CEF descriptors, developed in a Swiss National Research Foundation project, were presented in clearer, simpler, self-assessment form in the prototype (Swiss) Portfolio. There are now dozens of different national versions of the Portfolio for different educational sectors, but the only version for adults is that developed from the Swiss version by EAQUALS (European Association for Quality Language Services) in collaboration with ALTE. The descriptors used in this guide are taken from the EAQUALS/ALTE Portfolio. An electronic version that can be completed on-line can be downloaded in English or French from www.eelp.org. The EAQUALS/ALTE portfolio descriptors have been used in this guide, as they're more concrete and practical than the original CEFR descriptors.

New Inside Out CEF checklists

New Inside Out Upper intermediate is appropriate for students who can already use English in a basic way in a reasonably wide range of situations. They now need to expand their vocabulary, develop good habits of self-monitoring and correction, and practice understanding more challenging texts. By the end of *New Inside Out* Upper intermediate, if the students have had plenty of practice with English outside the classroom, they should feel able to accomplish most things described at the B2 level to a satisfactory extent.

In order to help the teacher and student assess their progress, we've provided a list of B2 descriptors for each unit of *New Inside Out* Upper intermediate. A good ability with the B1 descriptors is presupposed at the start of the book, and most students who have reached that level will already be able to make a fair attempt at some of the things described at B2. The descriptors in these charts allow the teacher to see a typical pattern of language acquisition.

Upper intermediate students can engage fully with the descriptors and begin to assess their own progress autonomously. At the lower levels, it's possible to identify a typical sequence in which the various skills may be acquired. Once the students have mastered the B1 level, the more advanced language competences they still lack are far more global in nature and far more interconnected with one another. For this reason, practice and exposure to a wide range of authentic language become more important than mere study. As a result, the sequence in which individual students will master the abilities identified by the descriptors isn't predictable at all, and certainly shouldn't be prescribed or too rigidly guided. There are more skills to master at this level, but it's seldom possible to trace a student's progress towards an individual descriptor.

Suggested targets for the checklist are provided for each unit. They allow the teacher to identify the key skills focused on in each unit, and so to select supplementary materials or change the emphasis as necessary. They also give the students a checklist of the competences they're working towards, so that they can easily identify their own weak areas and take full responsibility for their own learning. They'll also be able to tell the teacher what they find helpful to spend time on in class. The teacher should make it clear to them that their private study and practice with English is now central to their learning, and will increasingly exploit class time to stimulate students with more challenging examples of language use.

1 Schneider, Günther, & North, Brian (2000): "Fremdsprachen können – was heisst das?" Zürich, Rüegger
   North, Brian (2000): "The Development of a Common Framework Scale of Language Proficiency", New York, Peter Lang

2 EAQUALS is a pan-European language school accreditation body with over 100 full members. ALTE is an association dedicated to raising standards in language testing and encompasses the major European examination providers. Eurocentres provides high quality language teaching in countries where the language concerned is spoken. EAQUALS, ALTE and Eurocentres are the three NGOS advisers for language learning to the Council of Europe and all three implement the CEFR.

CEF Student checklists

Unit 1

Complete the checklist.

1 = I can do this with a lot of help from my teacher
2 = I can do this with a little help
3 = I can do this fairly well
4 = I can do this really well
5 = I can do this almost perfectly

Competences	Page	Your score				
I can understand most radio documentaries delivered in standard language and can identify the speaker's mood, tone, etc.	5, 10	1	2	3	4	5
I can use standard phrases like 'That's a difficult question to answer' to gain time and keep the turn while formulating what to say.	12	1	2	3	4	5
I can produce stretches of language with a fairly even tempo; although I can be hesitant as I search for expressions, there are few noticeably long pauses.	7	1	2	3	4	5
I have sufficient vocabulary to express myself on matters connected to my field and on most general topics.	6, 8, 11	1	2	3	4	5
I can express in a personal letter different feelings and attitudes, and can report the news of the day making clear what in my opinion are the important aspects of an event.	13	1	2	3	4	5

-- ✂

Unit 2

Complete the checklist.

1 = I can do this with a lot of help from my teacher
2 = I can do this with a little help
3 = I can do this fairly well
4 = I can do this really well
5 = I can do this almost perfectly

Competences	Page	Your score				
I can understand in detail what is said to me in standard spoken language even in a noisy environment.	18, 19, 20, 21, 22	1	2	3	4	5
I can help a discussion along on familiar ground confirming comprehension, inviting others in, etc.	14, 18, 20	1	2	3	4	5
I can explain a viewpoint on a topical issue giving the advantages and disadvantages of various options.	21	1	2	3	4	5
I can make a note of 'favourite mistakes' and consciously monitor speech for them.	17	1	2	3	4	5
I can pass on detailed information reliably.	22	1	2	3	4	5

Unit 3

Complete the checklist.

1 = I can do this with a lot of help from my teacher
2 = I can do this with a little help
3 = I can do this fairly well
4 = I can do this really well
5 = I can do this almost perfectly

Competences	Page	Your score				
I can rapidly grasp the content and the significance of news, articles and reports on topics connected with my interests or my job, and decide if a closer reading is worthwhile.	27, 30	1	2	3	4	5
I can understand specialised articles outside my own field if I can occasionally check with a dictionary.	24, 26	1	2	3	4	5
I can initiate, maintain and end discourse naturally with effective turn-taking.	28, 31, 32	1	2	3	4	5
I can speculate about causes, consequence, hypothetical situations.	29	1	2	3	4	5
I can write about events and real or fictional experiences in a detailed and easily readable way.	33	1	2	3	4	5

- ✂

Unit 4

Complete the checklist.

1 = I can do this with a lot of help from my teacher
2 = I can do this with a little help
3 = I can do this fairly well
4 = I can do this really well
5 = I can do this almost perfectly

Competences	Page	Your score				
I can use a variety of strategies to achieve comprehension, including listening for main points, checking comprehension by using contextual clues.	38	1	2	3	4	5
I can understand in detail texts within my field of interest or the area of my academic or professional speciality.	36, 40, 42	1	2	3	4	5
I can convey degrees of emotion and highlight the personal significance of events and experiences.	44	1	2	3	4	5
I have sufficient vocabulary to express myself on matters connected to my field and on most general topics.	36, 38, 40, 43 45	1	2	3	4	5
I can communicate with reasonable accuracy and can correct mistakes if they have led to misunderstandings.	38, 39, 41, 43	1	2	3	4	5

 New Inside Out Upper intermediate Teacher's Book © Macmillan Publishers Limited 2009

Unit 5

Complete the checklist.

1 = I can do this with a lot of help from my teacher
2 = I can do this with a little help
3 = I can do this fairly well
4 = I can do this really well
5 = I can do this almost perfectly

Competences	Page	Your score				
I can understand in detail what is said to me in standard spoken language even in a noisy environment.	48, 51, 53, 54	1	2	3	4	5
I can exchange considerable quantities of detailed factual information on matters within my field of interest.	48, 49, 51	1	2	3	4	5
I have sufficient vocabulary to express myself on matters connected to my field and on most general topics.	46, 48, 50	1	2	3	4	5
I can communicate with reasonable accuracy and can correct mistakes if they have led to misunderstandings.	49, 52, 53	1	2	3	4	5
I can develop an argument systematically in a composition or report, emphasising decisive points and including supporting details.	61	1	2	3	4	5

Unit 6

Complete the checklist.

1 = I can do this with a lot of help from my teacher
2 = I can do this with a little help
3 = I can do this fairly well
4 = I can do this really well
5 = I can do this almost perfectly

Competences	Page	Your score				
I can understand TV documentaries, live interviews, talk shows, plays and the majority of films in standard dialect.	58, 64	1	2	3	4	5
I can read and understand articles and reports on current problems in which the writers express specific attitudes and points of view.	57, 60	1	2	3	4	5
I can understand specialised articles outside my own field if I can occasionally check with a dictionary.	62	1	2	3	4	5
I can engage in extended conversation in a clearly participatory fashion on most general topics.	56, 58, 60, 64	1	2	3	4	5
I have sufficient vocabulary to express myself on matters connected to my field and on most general topics.	57, 58, 60, 63, 64, 65	1	2	3	4	5

Unit 7

Complete the checklist.

1 = I can do this with a lot of help from my teacher
2 = I can do this with a little help
3 = I can do this fairly well
4 = I can do this really well
5 = I can do this almost perfectly

Competences	Page	Your score				
I can follow a lecture or talk within my own field, provided the subject matter is familiar and the presentation straightforward and clearly structured.	71, 74	1	2	3	4	5
I can understand in a narrative or play the motives for the characters' actions and their consequences for the development of the plot.	68, 74	1	2	3	4	5
I can construct a chain of reasoned argument, linking my ideas logically.	74	1	2	3	4	5
I can communicate with reasonable accuracy and can correct mistakes if they have led to misunderstandings.	70, 71, 73, 75, 76	1	2	3	4	5
I can write clear and detailed texts (compositions, reports or texts of presentations) on various topics related to my field of interest.	77	1	2	3	4	5

Unit 8

Complete the checklist.

1 = I can do this with a lot of help from my teacher
2 = I can do this with a little help
3 = I can do this fairly well
4 = I can do this really well
5 = I can do this almost perfectly

Competences	Page	Your score				
I can understand TV documentaries, live interviews, talk shows, plays and the majority of films in standard dialect.	78, 80, 84, 85	1	2	3	4	5
I can read and understand articles and reports on current problems in which the writers express specific attitudes and points of view.	79, 81	1	2	3	4	5
I can give clear, detailed descriptions on a wide range of subjects related to my field of interest.	78, 85	1	2	3	4	5
I can communicate with reasonable accuracy and can correct mistakes if they have led to misunderstandings.	80, 81	1	2	3	4	5
I can discuss a topic in a composition or 'letter to the media', giving reasons for or against a specific point of view.	80	1	2	3	4	5

New Inside Out Upper intermediate Teacher's Book © Macmillan Publishers Limited 2009

Unit 9

Complete the checklist.

1 = I can do this with a lot of help from my teacher
2 = I can do this with a little help
3 = I can do this fairly well
4 = I can do this really well
5 = I can do this almost perfectly

Competences	Page	Your score				
I can understand the main ideas of propositionally and linguistically complex speech on both concrete and abstract topics delivered in a standard dialect, including technical discussions in my field of specialisation.	90, 92, 94	1	2	3	4	5
I can rapidly grasp the content and the significance of news, articles and reports on topics connected with my interests or my job, and decide if a closer reading is worthwhile.	88	1	2	3	4	5
I can quickly look through a manual (for example for a computer program) and find and understand the relevant explanations and help for a specific problem.	96	1	2	3	4	5
I can understand and summarise orally short extracts from news items, interviews or documentaries containing opinions, argument and discussion.	88, 93, 95	1	2	3	4	5
I can speculate about causes, consequence, hypothetical situations.	91	1	2	3	4	5

- ✂

Unit 10

Complete the checklist.

1 = I can do this with a lot of help from my teacher
2 = I can do this with a little help
3 = I can do this fairly well
4 = I can do this really well
5 = I can do this almost perfectly

Competences	Page	Your score				
I can read reviews dealing with the content and criticism of cultural topics (films, theatre, books, concerts) and summarise the main points.	102	1	2	3	4	5
I can convey degrees of emotion and highlight the personal significance of events and experiences.	102, 105, 108	1	2	3	4	5
I can account for and sustain my opinions in discussion by providing relevant explanations, arguments and comments.	104, 108	1	2	3	4	5
I can write summaries of articles on topics of general interest.	106	1	2	3	4	5
I can engage in extended conversation in a clearly participatory fashion on most general topics.	100, 102, 104, 105, 107	1	2	3	4	5

Unit 11

Complete the checklist.

1 = I can do this with a lot of help from my teacher
2 = I can do this with a little help
3 = I can do this fairly well
4 = I can do this really well
5 = I can do this almost perfectly

Competences	Page	Your score				
I can carry out a prepared interview, checking and confirming information, following up interesting replies.	114, 116	1	2	3	4	5
I can give clear, detailed descriptions on a wide range of subjects related to my field of interest.	111, 114, 115	1	2	3	4	5
I can understand and summarise orally the plot and sequence of events in an extract from a film or play.	115	1	2	3	4	5
I can produce stretches of language with a fairly even tempo; although I can be hesitant as I search for expressions, there are few noticeably long pauses.	111, 115, 116	1	2	3	4	5
I can communicate with reasonable accuracy and can correct mistakes if they have led to misunderstandings.	110, 112, 113	1	2	3	4	5

Unit 12

Complete the checklist.

1 = I can do this with a lot of help from my teacher
2 = I can do this with a little help
3 = I can do this fairly well
4 = I can do this really well
5 = I can do this almost perfectly

Competences	Page	Your score				
I can understand in detail texts within my field of interest or the area of my academic or professional speciality.	118, 122	1	2	3	4	5
I can understand in a narrative or play the motives for the characters' actions and their consequences for the development of the plot.	122	1	2	3	4	5
I can initiate, maintain and end discourse naturally with effective turn-taking.	124	1	2	3	4	5
I can speculate about causes, consequence, hypothetical situations.	120, 122	1	2	3	4	5
I have sufficient vocabulary to express myself on matters connected to my field and on most general topics.	118, 120, 122, 125	1	2	3	4	5

 New Inside Out Upper intermediate Teacher's Book © Macmillan Publishers Limited 2009

CEF Student checklists: Answer key

Unit 1

Competences	Page	Your score				
I can understand most radio documentaries delivered in standard language and can identify the speaker's mood, tone, etc.	5, 10	1	2	③	4	5
I can use standard phrases like 'That's a difficult question to answer' to gain time and keep the turn while formulating what to say.	12	1	2	③	4	5
I can produce stretches of language with a fairly even tempo; although I can be hesitant as I search for expressions, there are few noticeably long pauses.	7	1	②	3	4	5
I have sufficient vocabulary to express myself on matters connected to my field and on most general topics.	6, 8, 11	①	2	3	4	5
I can express in a personal letter different feelings and attitudes, and can report the news of the day making clear what in my opinion are the important aspects of an event.	13	1	2	③	4	5

Unit 2

Competences	Page	Your score				
I can understand in detail what is said to me in standard spoken language even in a noisy environment.	18, 19, 20, 21, 22	1	②	3	4	5
I can help a discussion along on familiar ground confirming comprehension, inviting others in, etc.	14, 18, 20	1	2	③	4	5
I can explain a viewpoint on a topical issue giving the advantages and disadvantages of various options.	21	1	2	③	4	5
I can make a note of 'favourite mistakes' and consciously monitor speech for them.	17	1	2	③	4	5
I can pass on detailed information reliably.	22	1	2	③	4	5

Unit 3

Competences	Page	Your score				
I can rapidly grasp the content and the significance of news, articles and reports on topics connected with my interests or my job, and decide if a closer reading is worthwhile.	27, 30	1	②	3	4	5
I can understand specialised articles outside my own field if I can occasionally check with a dictionary.	24, 26	1	②	3	4	5
I can initiate, maintain and end discourse naturally with effective turn-taking.	28, 31, 32	1	②	3	4	5
I can speculate about causes, consequence, hypothetical situations.	29	①	2	3	4	5
I can write about events and real or fictional experiences in a detailed and easily readable way.	33	1	2	③	4	5

Unit 4

Competences	Page	Your score				
I can use a variety of strategies to achieve comprehension, including listening for main points, checking comprehension by using contextual clues.	38	1	2	③	4	5
I can understand in detail texts within my field of interest or the area of my academic or professional speciality.	36, 40, 42	1	②	3	4	5
I can convey degrees of emotion and highlight the personal significance of events and experiences.	44	1	②	3	4	5
I have sufficient vocabulary to express myself on matters connected to my field and on most general topics.	36, 38, 40, 43, 45	1	②	3	4	5
I can communicate with reasonable accuracy and can correct mistakes if they have led to misunderstandings.	38, 39, 41, 43	①	2	3	4	5

Unit 5

Competences	Page	Your score				
I can understand in detail what is said to me in standard spoken language even in a noisy environment.	48, 51, 53, 54	1	2	3	④	5
I can exchange considerable quantities of detailed factual information on matters within my field of interest.	48, 49, 51	1	2	③	4	5
I have sufficient vocabulary to express myself on matters connected to my field and on most general topics.	46, 48, 50	1	2	③	4	5
I can communicate with reasonable accuracy and can correct mistakes if they have led to misunderstandings.	49, 52, 53	1	②	3	4	5
I can develop an argument systematically in a composition or report, emphasising decisive points and including supporting details.	61	1	2	③	4	5

Unit 6

Competences	Page	Your score				
I can understand TV documentaries, live interviews, talk shows, plays and the majority of films in standard dialect.	58, 64	1	②	3	4	5
I can read and understand articles and reports on current problems in which the writers express specific attitudes and points of view.	57, 60	1	②	3	4	5
I can understand specialised articles outside my own field if I can occasionally check with a dictionary.	62	1	2	3	④	5
I can engage in extended conversation in a clearly participatory fashion on most general topics.	56, 58, 60, 64	1	②	3	4	5
I have sufficient vocabulary to express myself on matters connected to my field and on most general topics.	57, 58, 60, 63, 64, 65	1	2	3	④	5

Unit 7

Competences	Page	Your score				
I can follow a lecture or talk within my own field, provided the subject matter is familiar and the presentation straightforward and clearly structured.	71, 74	1	2	③	4	5
I can understand in a narrative or play the motives for the characters' actions and their consequences for the development of the plot.	68, 74	1	②	3	4	5
I can construct a chain of reasoned argument, linking my ideas logically.	74	1	2	③	4	5
I can communicate with reasonable accuracy and can correct mistakes if they have led to misunderstandings.	70, 71, 73, 75, 76	1	2	③	4	5
I can write clear and detailed texts (compositions, reports or texts of presentations) on various topics related to my field of interest.	77	1	2	③	4	5

Unit 8

Competences	Page	Your score				
I can understand TV documentaries, live interviews, talk shows, plays and the majority of films in standard dialect.	78, 80, 84, 85	1	2	3	④	5
I can read and understand articles and reports on current problems in which the writers express specific attitudes and points of view.	79, 81	1	2	3	④	5
I can give clear, detailed descriptions on a wide range of subjects related to my field of interest.	78, 85	1	②	3	4	5
I can communicate with reasonable accuracy and can correct mistakes if they have led to misunderstandings.	80, 81	1	2	3	④	5
I can discuss a topic in a composition or 'letter to the media', giving reasons for or against a specific point of view.	80	1	2	③	4	5

Unit 9

Competences	Page	Your score				
I can understand the main ideas of propositionally and linguistically complex speech on both concrete and abstract topics delivered in a standard dialect, including technical discussions in my field of specialisation.	90, 92, 94	1	2	③	4	5
I can rapidly grasp the content and the significance of news, articles and reports on topics connected with my interests or my job, and decide if a closer reading is worthwhile.	88	1	2	3	④	5
I can quickly look through a manual (for example for a computer program) and find and understand the relevant explanations and help for a specific problem.	96	1	2	③	4	5
I can understand and summarise orally short extracts from news items, interviews or documentaries containing opinions, argument and discussion.	88, 93, 95	1	2	③	4	5
I can speculate about causes, consequence, hypothetical situations.	91	1	2	③	4	5

Unit 10

Competences	Page	Your score				
I can read reviews dealing with the content and criticism of cultural topics (films, theatre, books, concerts) and summarise the main points.	102	1	2	③	4	5
I can convey degrees of emotion and highlight the personal significance of events and experiences.	102, 105, 108	1	2	3	④	5
I can account for and sustain my opinions in discussion by providing relevant explanations, arguments and comments.	104, 108	1	2	③	4	5
I can write summaries of articles on topics of general interest.	106	1	2	③	4	5
I can engage in extended conversation in a clearly participatory fashion on most general topics.	100, 102, 104, 105, 107	1	2	3	④	5

Unit 11

Competences	Page	Your score				
I can carry out a prepared interview, checking and confirming information, following up interesting replies.	114, 116	1	2	③	4	5
I can give clear, detailed descriptions on a wide range of subjects related to my field of interest.	111, 114, 115	1	2	3	④	5
I can understand and summarise orally the plot and sequence of events in an extract from a film or play.	115	1	2	③	4	5
I can produce stretches of language with a fairly even tempo; although I can be hesitant as I search for expressions, there are few noticeably long pauses.	111, 115, 116	1	2	3	④	5
I can communicate with reasonable accuracy and can correct mistakes if they have led to misunderstandings.	110, 112, 113	1	2	3	4	⑤

Unit 12

Competences	Page	Your score				
I can understand in detail texts within my field of interest or the area of my academic or professional speciality.	118, 122	1	2	3	④	5
I can understand in a narrative or play the motives for the characters' actions and their consequences for the development of the plot.	122	1	2	3	④	5
I can initiate, maintain and end discourse naturally with effective turn-taking.	124	1	2	3	④	5
I can speculate about causes, consequence, hypothetical situations.	120, 122	1	2	3	4	⑤
I have sufficient vocabulary to express myself on matters connected to my field and on most general topics.	118, 120, 122, 125	1	2	3	4	⑤

New Inside Out Upper intermediate Teacher's Book © Macmillan Publishers Limited 2009

Impressions *Overview*

Section & Aims	What the students are doing
Speaking SB page 4 Fluency work	Matching photos with events and putting them in chronological order. Writing notes about the events and then discussing them.
🌐 **Listening & Reading SB page 5** Listening for detail Reading for detail	Matching speakers with photos. Completing what people say about events. Writing about memorable events and asking questions about them.
Grammar SB page 5 Verb structures	Underlining appropriate verb structures in sentences. Changing sentences so they are true for them.
Vocabulary SB page 6 Collocation	Talking about first impressions of people. Forming collocations for personal characteristics.
🌐 **Listening page 6** Listening for gist and detail	Listening to a conversation and identifying the context. Completing a table with information from the conversation.
Grammar SB page 7 Auxiliaries (1)	Making sentences with *and so*, *and neither* or *but ...* Writing sentences about themselves and a partner to play a game.
🌐 **Grammar & Pronunciation** **SB page 7** Auxiliaries (2)	Studying question tags. Choosing the correct question tags and practising intonation.
Speaking: anecdote SB page 7 Fluency practice	Talking about a person who made a big impression on them.
Reading SB page 8 Reading for detail	Choosing the best summary of a writer's opinion about Madonna. Matching headings to paragraphs and completing questions.
Vocabulary SB page 8 Word formation	Studying words which can take the prefix *re*. Writing example sentences with words that take *re*.
🌐 **Listening SB page 10** Listening for gist and detail	Looking at photos of men and talking about the image they convey. Listening to the men describing their style, noting down the order they speak, and choosing adjectives to describe the journalist's attitude. Answering questions about the men. Then talking about men they know.
🌐 **Grammar & Speaking SB page 11** Indirect questions	Studying the differences between direct and indirect questions. Completing indirect questions and asking a partner.
Vocabulary SB page 11 Items of clothing	Matching items of clothing to accessories. Choosing alternatives to complete idiomatic expressions.
🌐 **Useful phrases SB page 12** Talking about people's appearance	Listening to conversations and answering questions. Matching useful phrases to functions and expressions to speakers. Completing sentences with useful phrases.
Writing *Extra* SB page 13 Informal letter	Rewriting formal expressions with more suitable informal ones. Writing an introductory letter to a pen friend.
Writing WB page 9	Writing a short biography.

Impressions *Teacher's notes*

Speaking (SB page 4)

1

- Pairwork. Focus the students' attention on the four photos and give them time to discuss in pairs what they can see and to match them with the events in the box.
- Check answers with the class before asking the students to decide in their pairs the chronological order of the events.

> a) Millennium celebrations
> b) First Moon landing
> c) Death of Princess Diana
> d) Beijing Olympics
>
> *Order:* b) 1969, c) 1997, a) 2000, d) 2008

2

- Pairwork. Go through the headings with the class and ask the students for some information about the events pictured in Exercise 1 which could go under these headings.
- Give the pairs a time limit to write as much information as they can about the events under the headings. Emphasise that no piece of information is too small.
- Either conduct feedback with the class or put the students into groups to share their information and discuss the impression the events made on them.

Cultural notes

Millennium celebrations /mɪˈleniəm seləˈbreɪʃ(ə)nz/
The photo shows the millennium celebrations in Sydney, Australia with a spectacular firework display along the waterfront and on Sydney Harbour bridge.

Beijing Olympics /ˈbeɪʒɪŋ əˈlɪmpɪks/
The Beijing Olympics were held in the summer of 2008. Almost 11,000 athletes competed in 28 sports over the two and a half weeks of the competition. The home nation, China, won the most medals followed by the United States.

Princess Diana /prɪnˈses daɪˈænə/
Princess Diana was married to Prince Charles, first in line to the British throne, from 1981 to 1996. The couple had two sons, William (born 1982) and Harry (born 1984). Diana was killed in a car crash in Paris in the early hours of 31st August 1997. Her funeral took place a week later. It's estimated that more than a million people lined the London streets to say goodbye.

The first Moon landing
On 20th July 1969, Americans Neil Armstrong, commander of *Apollo 11*, and Buzz Aldrin, pilot of the Lunar Module, became the first astronauts to set foot on the Moon during America's first attempt at landing a manned vehicle on the Moon.

Listening & Reading (SB page 5)

1 🌐 **1.01–1.04**

Focus attention on the four photos and explain that these people are going to talk about the four events shown on page 4. Ask them to listen and match the people to the events.

> Alec: b) Belinda: c) Chris: a) Dana: d)

> 🌐 **1.01**
>
> Alec
>
> *It made a huge impression on me because, when I was a kid, I always used to think I hope I live long enough to see a man on the Moon. So when it happened – I don't know how old my son was, but I said to him, 'Sit down and watch all of this. This is one of the most momentous things that will ever happen in your life.*

1.02

Belinda

What annoys me is people who think the royal family had something to do with Diana's death. It was a tragic accident. That's what I believe anyway. I was never a big fan of Diana, but she raised a lot of money for charity, and I think she was a good mother to those boys. I just hope the press can leave them alone and not hound them as they hounded their mother.

1.03

Chris

We were standing really close to the Harbour Bridge. We'd decided to get there early to get a good place, so we'd been waiting since six o'clock in the evening. Then, at midnight, the fireworks exploded across the sky. I've never seen anything so spectacular. I felt proud to be an Australian.

1.04

Dana

It was the first time I had visited an Asian country. It was so different. I was amazed at how many people there were. After the Games had finished, we did some sightseeing. The Great Wall was definitely my favourite. It's the most incredible thing I've ever seen.

2

- Go through the instructions with the class and draw their attention to the example in the text by Alex. Ask the students to complete the remaining texts. Allow them to work in pairs if they wish.

- Go round, monitoring and giving help. Check answers with the class, accepting alternative answers that are grammatically correct, and then ask four students to read out the completed texts so that they hear the verbs in context. Then play the recording again for a final check.

Alec	Belinda
1 used to think	1 annoys
2 live (or *'ll live*)	2 believe
3 happened	3 think
4 will ever happen	
Chris	**Dana**
1 were standing	1 had visited
2 'd been waiting	(or *visited*)
3 exploded	2 had finished
4 've never seen	(or *finished*)
(or *'d never seen*)	3 did
5 felt	4 've ever seen

3

- Go through the instructions with the class and ask the students to work individually to choose their three memorable events for each category. Ask them to think about the words they'd need to describe these events and the effect they had on them.

- Put the students into pairs and ask them to take turns to talk to each other about the events they've chosen. Encourage them to ask follow-up questions to find out as much detail as possible about all the events.

- Ask the students to report back to the class on the information they discussed about the events.

Grammar (SB page 5)

Verb structures

1

Do this exercise with the whole class and make sure the students understand the difference between the different structures and their uses. Point out the verbal clues that can help determine which tense to choose. For example, the various time expressions, the use of *for* and *since*, etc.

a) I've known	e) I've been learning
b) I had	f) I've been
c) I was talking	g) I'd already met
d) I like	h) I used to have

Language note

Grammar: verb structures (present and past)
(See Student's Book page 132.)

2

- Go through the instructions with the class and ask the students to work individually to choose their five sentences and change the names. Remind them that the completed sentences must be true.

- Put the students into pairs and ask them to read each other's sentences and to ask follow-up questions to find out more about the people named in them.

- Encourage the students to report back to the class on what they learnt about their partners.

3 Grammar *Extra* 1, Part 1

Ask the students to turn to *Grammar Extra* 1, Part 1 on page 132 of the Student's Book. Here they'll find an explanation of the grammar they've been studying and a further exercise to practise it.

1
a) remember; heard
b) 've seen
c) watched
d) think; was
e) used to; have changed
f) affected
g) 'd never enjoyed; saw

Vocabulary (SB page 6)

1

- Focus the students' attention on the photo and caption. Elicit or explain that a *first impression* is the reaction you have to someone the first time you meet them. The saying *You never get a second chance to make a first impression* emphasises the importance of creating a good impression when you meet people for the first time as it's often only their first impression of you that they remember. If this first impression is bad, then you'll have difficulty making them think better of you in future.
- Go through the ideas in the box with the class. Then put the students into pairs and ask them to discuss which of these things they notice most about people when they meet them for the first time. In a class feedback session, put them in order of importance.

2

- Go through the information about collocations with the class and remind them that a good dictionary will help them with the common collocations of a word.

> a) ~~brand~~   b) ~~shiny~~   c) ~~circular~~   d) ~~pointy~~
> e) ~~strong~~   f) ~~fair~~   g) ~~heated~~   h) ~~profound~~

> **Language note**
>
> **Vocabulary: collocation**
> The examples of collocation in this unit are adjective + noun collocations and focus on ways of describing people's appearance. Although *pointy* and *spiky* mean the same, you'd say someone has *a pointy chin* and *spiky hair* but not ~~pointy hair~~ and ~~a spiky chin~~.

3

- Focus the students' attention on the example. Point out that each set of adjectives can only be matched with one word from the list in Exercise 1, though individual adjectives from each set might also collocate with other words.
- Ask them to match the remaining sets of adjectives with the words in Exercise 1. Allow them to use dictionaries if necessary, then check answers with the class.
- Encourage the students to make sentences using the collocations so that they can hear them in context. For example, you might ask them to use them in sentences describing people they know.
- Finally, put the students into pairs and ask them to discuss which of the characteristics they'd find appealing or unappealing. Encourage them to report back to the class on their thoughts.

> a) handshake   b) face   c) smile   d) eyes
> e) hair   f) voice   g) clothes   h) manner

Listening (SB page 6)

1 🌐 1.05

- Go through the instructions and the questions with the class so that they understand the context of the situation and know what information to listen out for.
- Play the recording and ask the students to answer the questions.

> a) London (Notting Hill)
> b) Working
> c) The conversation stops because the man says something uncomplimentary about Mrs Rivers – the woman's mother.

> 🌐 1.05
>
> (W = Woman; M = Man)
>
> W: *Excuse me, is it OK if I sit here?*
>
> M: *Sure, go ahead.*
>
> W: *Thanks. … Sorry, but you're English, aren't you?*
>
> M: *Yes. How did you know?*
>
> W: *Oh, I heard your accent. … It isn't very busy here today, is it?*
>
> M: *No, it isn't.*
>
> W: *Are you on holiday?*
>
> M: *No, I'm working here for a few months.*
>
> W: *Oh, really? So am I. What do you do?*
>
> M: *I work for the American Central Bank.*
>
> W: *Oh. And do you like it here?*
>
> M: *No. I can't stand it – especially the weather. It was so hot yesterday, wasn't it?*
>
> W: *Oh yeah, you're right: the heat's terrible. But, you know, I love New York.*
>
> M: *How long have you been here?*
>
> W: *Oh, not long – a few weeks. How about you?*
>
> M: *The same. What are you doing here?*
>
> W: *I'm an artist, and I was asked to bring over some of my work to a small gallery just near here. I've just had my first exhibition there.*
>
> M: *Wow – that is impressive.*
>
> W: *Thanks. So where are you from?*
>
> M: *I'm from London – Notting Hill.*
>
> W: *Really? So am I! Don't tell me you went to Atkins School?*
>
> M: *Yes, I did, actually – but I wasn't a very good student.*
>
> W: *Me neither. What year did you leave?*
>
> M   1989.
>
> W: *That's weird – me too. Do you remember Mrs Rivers?*
>
> M: *The maths teacher? Yeah. She was really horrible, wasn't she?*
>
> W: *She's my mum.*
>
> M: *Oh. … Look, I'm sorry. …I didn't mean to…*

2

- Encourage the students to complete as much of the table as they can from memory.
- Play the recording for them to check their answers and complete any gaps. Then check answers with the class.

> a) ✔✔   b) ✗✗   c) ✔✔   d) ✔✗
> e) ✗✔   f) ✗✗   g) ✗✔   h) ✔✔
> i) ✗✗   j) ✔✔

3

- Make sure the students understand the expression 'to put your foot in it', which means to accidentally say something embarrassing or that upsets or annoys someone.
- Put the students into pairs to discuss whether they or anyone they know has ever put their foot in it. You could start them off with an example of your own.
- Encourage them to report back to the class on any interesting stories.

Grammar (SB page 7)

Auxiliaries (1): *so / neither (nor)*

1

- Go through the information in the margin with the class. (See Language notes.) Point out that the ticks and crosses indicate whether the response is agreement or disagreement.
- Pairwork. Put the students into pairs and explain what they have to do. Go through the example with them, pointing out that the second part of the sentence compares the woman with the man, and establishes that the information that the man is English is also true of the woman. As a result you use *so* + an affirmative verb. Write up on the board *The man isn't American* and ask the students about the woman, eliciting *and neither is the woman*. If necessary, do one more example using *but ...*, such as *The man likes New York but the woman doesn't*, before asking them to work in their pairs and complete the exercise.

> a) The man is English and so is the woman.
> b) The man isn't on holiday and neither is the woman.
> c) The man is working in New York and so is the woman.
> d) The man works for a bank but the woman doesn't.
> e) The woman likes New York but the man can't stand it.
> f) The man hasn't been in New York a long time and neither has the woman.
> g) The woman is an artist but the man isn't.
> h) The man is from London and so is the woman.
> i) The man wasn't a good student and neither was the woman.
> j) The man left school in 1989 and so did the woman.

Language notes

Grammar: auxiliaries – *so / neither (nor)*

- When you agree or disagree with someone, you use *so* or *neither (nor)* depending on whether the first person used an affirmative or negative verb. The word *so* is used to agree with an affirmative verb and provides the affirmative idea in the response *So did I*. The word *neither* is used to agree with a negative verb and provides the negative idea in the response *Neither have I* – the verb *have* remains in the affirmative. Note the use of *did* in the responses to the first sentence in which there's no auxiliary verb, and the use of the auxiliary *have* in the responses to the second sentence, which contains the auxiliary *have*.
- For more information see Student's Book page 132.

2

- Establish who is going to work with whom in the pairwork stage of this exercise. Then go through the sentence beginnings with the class and ask them to work individually to write sentences which they believe are true for both themselves and their partner. Don't let them confer.
- Go round monitoring and giving help where needed. Make sure everyone has nine completed sentences.

3

- Ask the students to get into their pairs and to turn to page 128 and follow the instructions there to produce their Bingo cards. Remind them that *so, neither* and *nor* are all used to express agreement and the choice depends on whether the verb used by the original speaker was affirmative or negative. They also need to remember that *do/did* is used in responses to statements that contain no auxiliary, and in the others the auxiliary in the response has to match that used in the original statement.
- As the students play the game, go round checking that they're matching the responses to the statements correctly. In a class feedback session, ask several pairs of students to read out their statements and responses.

Grammar & Pronunciation (SB page 7)

Auxiliaries (2): Question tags

1

- Focus the students' attention on the information in the margin. Point out that the auxiliary used in a question tag matches that used in the original statement, but that a positive statement has a negative tag and vice versa.

- Pairwork. Draw the students' attention to the fact that these sentences come from the conversation between the man and the woman in the *Listening* section on page 6. Point out the intonation arrows on the two example sentences (see Language note below.) Encourage the students to read the examples aloud using the intonation patterns marked so that they can hear the difference. Then ask them in their pairs to match the information in A and B.

A	B
positive statement	asking a real question
negative statement	negative question tag
rising intonation	asking for agreement
falling intonation	positive question tag

Language note

Pronunciation: rising and falling tone on question tags

If you use a question tag to ask for agreement, you'd use a falling tone on the question tag. If you use a question tag to ask a real question, you'd use a rising tone. This distinction is one that students have trouble with and it's always worth giving them as much opportunity to practise as possible.

2 🌐 1.06

- Suggest that the students tackle this in two stages: first identifying the correct question tags and then thinking about the intonation.

- As they work, go round making sure that everyone has chosen the correct question tags. Then ask them to decide which of the questions are asking for information and which are asking for agreement. When they've decided, encourage them to say the questions aloud using the appropriate intonation so that they get a feel for what sounds right.

- Play the recording for the students to check their answers. Play it a second time for them to listen and repeat. When they've done this chorally, ask for individual repetition of the questions and insist on correct pronunciation.

```
a) isn't it? (falling)
b) aren't I? (falling)
c) wasn't it? (falling)
d) have you? (rising – but possibly falling)
e) are they? (rising – but possibly falling)
f) do you? (rising)
```

3 Grammar *Extra* 1, Part 2

Ask the students to turn to *Grammar Extra* 1, Part 2 on page 132 of the Student's Book. Here they'll find an explanation of the grammar they've been studying and further exercises to practise it.

```
2
a) So have I / I haven't
b) So am I / I'm not
c) Neither do I / I do
d) So was I / I wasn't
e) Neither have I / I have
f) So did I / I didn't
g) Neither can I / I can
h) Neither would I / I would
3
a) aren't you        e) mustn't he
b) isn't it          f) have they
c) can she           g) shall we
d) do we             h) will you
```

Speaking: anecdote (SB page 7)

Anecdotes are features that occur regularly in this series. They are extended speaking tasks, where the students tackle a longer piece of discourse on a personal topic. There are questions to guide them. For more information about how to set up, monitor and repeat Anecdotes, see page xx in the Introduction.

- Go through the instructions and the questions with the class. Give the students a minute or two to decide who they're going to talk about. Then ask them to look at the questions and think about their answers to them. Allow them to make notes of what they're going to say and how they're going to say it, but discourage them from writing a paragraph that they can simply read out. Go round, monitoring and giving help where necessary.

- Pairwork. Put the students in pairs and ask them to take turns to tell their partner about the person who made a big impression on them. Encourage them to ask each other follow-up questions to get further information.

- Ask some pairs to report back to the class on what they found out.

Reading (SB page 8)

1

- Focus the students' attention on the photos of Madonna on pages 8 and 9. Ask them to work in pairs and note down everything they know about her.

- Ask them to report back to the class and see how much information the class can pool. Write their ideas on the board. Remind them that thinking in advance about the things they already know about a subject will help them when they come to read a text about it.

2

- Ask the students to read the article on page 9 and ask them also to identify how much of the information they discussed in Exercise 1 was actually in the text.

- Go through the summaries with the class and ask them to choose the one which best fits the writer's opinion of Madonna. Ask them to give reasons to justify their answer.

Cultural notes

Elvis Presley /ˈelvɪs ˈprezli:/ (1935–1977)
Elvis Presley is known as 'The King' (of Rock and Roll). He got his break as a teenager in 1954 in his hometown in Memphis (USA). Over the next two decades Presley became an international star with recordings like *Jailhouse Rock* (1957), *It's Now or Never* (1960) and *Suspicious Minds* (1969). He also starred in 33 films. From 1973, Presley's health declined. In 1977, he died of a heart attack at the age of 42.

Marilyn Monroe /ˈmærəlɪn mənˈrəʊ/ (1926–1962)
Marilyn Monroe was a Hollywood actress and an icon of 1950s America. She starred in such films as *Gentlemen Prefer Blondes* (1953) and *Some Like It Hot* (1959). She was married three times and her love affairs were as famous as her film roles.

Evita /eˈviːtə/ (1996)
Andrew Lloyd Webber and Tim Rice's stage musical *Evita* about the life of Eva Perón was adapted as a film in 1996, starring Madonna and Antonio Banderas and directed by Alan Parker.

Detroit /ˈdiːtrɔɪt/
Detroit city is the largest city in the US state of Michigan. It has a population of just under one million. Detroit is the centre of the US motor industry and is also known as 'Motown' (= Motor + town). The record label Motown, best known for its soul music, was named after, and originally based in, Detroit.

Vanity Fair /ˈvænəti feə/
Vanity Fair is an American society, culture and fashion magazine. It was first published in 1913.

Guy Ritchie /ɡaɪ ˈrɪtʃiː/ (born 1968)
Guy Ritchie is the British film director of *Lock, Stock and Two Smoking Barrels* (1998) and *Snatch* (2000). In 2000, he married singer and actress Madonna. The couple had a son, Rocco, in 2000. They divorced in 2009.

Britney Spears /ˈbrɪtni: ˈspɪəz/ (born 1981)
Britney Spears is an American pop singer. In the late 1990s, she had hits with *Baby One More Time* and *Oops!… I Did It Again*. In 2004, she married dancer Kevin Federline. They had two children but divorced in 2006.

3

Ask the students to read the article again and to match the words in the box to the paragraphs. Explain any unknown vocabulary.

a) Pop icon	d) Motherhood
b) Reinventing the brand	e) Controversy
c) Early life	f) No plans to retire

4

Ask the students to work individually to complete the questions. Check that they've done this correctly and then ask them to think about the answers to the questions. Check answers by getting one student to ask a question and nominate another to answer it. That student then asks a question and nominates another student to answer, and so on.

a) trademark (Her name, Madonna.)
b) on (An ever-evolving look, style and sound.)
c) raised (She was born in Michigan and raised in Detroit.)
d) with (The popular group.)
e) date (An impressive catalogue of albums, world tours, videos, feature films, documentaries and books.)
f) criticism (Because it's thought she used her wealth and fame to speed up the process.)
g) controversy (Because she has shocked people a lot.)
h) gracefully (No.)

5

Ask the students to work in pairs and to discuss their favourite singers or bands. Encourage them to ask each other questions to find out as much information as possible. Then have a class feedback session in which they exchange information about their favourites.

Vocabulary (SB page 8)
Word formation

1

Go through the information in the margin and make sure that the students understand that the implications of the prefix *re* are that something is being done again. Then go through the instructions and ask them to choose the word in each line which cannot form a new verb with *re*. Strong students could try to do this without looking up the answers in the list of verbs in the margin.

a) ~~change~~ b) ~~prepare~~ c) ~~erect~~
d) ~~contemplate~~ e) ~~copy~~ f) ~~find~~

2

Give the students time to look in their dictionaries and find words which they know or can understand easily which have the prefix *re*. Encourage them to list words which take a particular prefix in a special section of their vocabulary notebooks. Go round and check that they're using their chosen words correctly in example sentences and get several students to read out their sentences to the class.

Listening (SB page 10)

1

- Focus the students' attention on the photographs and ask them to think about their answers to the questions.
- In a class feedback session find out how much agreement there is.

> *Possible answers:*
> a) Charles: business-like, cool, fashionable;
>   Rick: casual, quite smart, a bit boring
>   Adam: trendy, fashionable
>   Matt: casual, cool, trendy

2 💿 1.07–1.10

- Explain that the students are going to hear a journalist interviewing the four men about their self image. Ask them to listen and decide in what order she speaks to them. If possible, get them to say what clues in the things the men said led them to make their choices. For example, Matt talks about his trainers; Charles mentions that he's wearing a suit.
- Play the recording again and ask the students to choose the words that best describe the journalist's attitude to the men.

> 1 Rick 2 Matt 3 Charles 4 Adam
>
> The journalist's attitude towards the four men is friendly, polite and respectful.

> 💿 **1.07** (J = Journalist; R= Rick)
>
> 1
> J: *Excuse me.*
> R: *Me?*
> J: *Yes, hi there! I'm working on a feature for* CHAPS *magazine about men's personal style. Do you mind if I ask you some questions?*
> R: *No, I suppose not.*
> J: *Could you tell me what image you're trying to achieve?*
> R: *Image? I don't really have an image. I wear clothes I feel comfortable in – I suppose you'd call it a casual look.*
> J: *Do you think that you're aware of fashion?*
> R: *Er, probably not, no. My style hasn't changed for years.*
>
> 💿 **1.08** (J = Journalist; M = Matt)
>
> 2
> J: *Hello! I'm doing some research for an article about the way men dress. Can I ask you some questions?*
> M: *Yeah, no problem.*
> J: *Do you mind telling me what you wear to go out in the evening?*

> M: *In the evening? You mean clubs and that sort of thing?*
> J: *Yes, when you go clubbing.*
> M: *I dress exactly like this.*
> J: *You don't dress up then?*
> M: *Well, put it this way – I never put a suit on. The clubs I go to don't let men in if they're wearing suits.*
> J: *Really!? How strange. Um, one more question? I'd just like to know if there's an item of clothing you couldn't live without.*
> M: *Trainers. Definitely couldn't live without them. I've got about twenty-five pairs.*

> 💿 **1.09** (J = Journalist; C = Charles)
>
> 3
> J: *Excuse me! Hello.*
> C: *Hello.*
> J: *I work for* CHAPS *magazine and we're doing a survey about men's self-image. Do you mind if I ask you a couple of questions?*
> C: *Oh. No, no go ahead. What do you want to know?*
> J: *Well, I'd like to know what your clothes say about you.*
> C: *What do my clothes say about me!? Gosh – I suppose they say that I'm meeting a client this afternoon, and that means I've got to make the right impression. So I have to wear a suit.*
> J: *Would you say that you care about your image?*
> C: *Oh yes, I think I do. I like to look smart, even when I'm not working. Even when I wear jeans and a T-shirt, I like them to be clean and neat, and I think this says that I care about myself. It says that I've got good self-esteem.*

> 💿 **1.10** (J = Journalist; A = Adam)
>
> 4
> J: *Excuse me, sir. Is it OK if I ask you a couple of questions for an article I'm doing for* CHAPS *magazine?*
> A: *Yes, that's fine. Are you going to take photos?*
> J: *Er, yes, if you don't mind. But first I'd like to know whether your appearance affects your life in any way.*
> A: *Oh yes, totally. The way I dress is my life really. It hasn't really affected my career so far, but I'm hoping it will. Basically, I want to be noticed, and the reason I want to be noticed is that I want to get on television.*
> J: *Ah. And do you know what the last thing you bought was?*
> A: *Oh yes, I adore shopping. Er, that would be a pink shirt I bought yesterday – oh, and a pink and black tie.*

3

- Pairwork. Ask the students to discuss the questions in pairs and to make notes of their answers. Allow them to compare notes with other pairs before you play the recording again for them to check.

- Ask the students to work individually to answer the same questions with the names of men they know. Then ask them to take turns to ask and answer the questions with their partners using the new information. Encourage them to ask follow-up questions to find out more details.

a) Matt	b) Matt	c) Adam	d) Adam
e) Rick	f) Rick	g) Charles	h) Charles

Grammar & Speaking (SB page 11)

Direct questions / Indirect questions

1 🔵 1.11

- Focus the students' attention on the table. Point out that *What image are you trying to achieve?* and *Could you tell me what image you're trying to achieve?* are both correct. They're different ways of asking the same question. (See Language notes below.)

- Ask the students to complete the indirect questions in the right-hand column. Encourage them to do this first without looking up the answers in the recording script.

- Play the recording for them to check their answers. Then play it again for them to listen and repeat. When they've done this chorally, ask for individual repetition of the indirect questions. Encourage them to use a softer tone for these questions than they might for their direct equivalents.

> a) Could you tell me what image you're trying to achieve?
> b) Do you think that you are aware of fashion?
> c) Do you mind telling me what you wear to go out in the evening?
> d) I'd like to know what your clothes say about you.
> e) Would you say that you care about your image?
> f) I'd like to know whether your appearance affects your life.
> g) Do you know what the last thing you bought was?

Language notes

Grammar: indirect questions

- Indirect questions are often used as a way of putting a little (polite) distance between the person who is asking the questions and the person they're asking.

- In indirect questions, you don't put the auxiliary before the subject. The word order (subject + verb) is the same as affirmative sentences.
  Direct question: *When did they meet?*
  Indirect question: *Do you have any idea when they met?*

- In direct questions, the auxiliary verb *do* usually comes before the subject. Verbs like *can, have, be* come before the subject.
  Direct question: *What is your favourite colour?*
  Indirect question: *Could you tell me what your favourite colour is?*

- *Yes/No* questions use *if* or *whether* in indirect questions.
  Direct question: *Are they happy?*
  Indirect question: *Can you tell me if they are happy?*

2

Ask the students to work in pairs and to discuss the main differences between the two styles of question. Ask them to make notes on the four factors listed. Then check answers with the class.

> a) Word order: changes from (auxiliary) verb + subject to (auxiliary) subject + verb (the same as affirmative statements)
> b) *do/does/did*: not used in indirect questions
> c) *if/whether*: used in indirect *yes/no* questions.
> d) Formality: indirect questions are more polite.

3

- Ask the students to work individually to complete the questions. Go round, giving extra help where needed and check answers with the class before moving on to the next stage of the exercise.

- Ask the students to work in pairs and to take turns asking and answering the questions.

- When they've finished, ask them to write three more questions each and then to take turns asking and answering these.

> a) Do you know where the cheapest clothes shop in town is?
> b) Do you think cheap clothes are good value for money?
> c) Where do you think the best place to buy jeans is?
> d) I'd like to know if/whether you've ever sewn a button on a shirt.
> e) Do you mind telling me how much money you would spend on a leather jacket?
> f) Could you tell me how many pairs of trainers you've got?
> g) Would you say (that) clothes and fashion matter to you?

Vocabulary (SB page 11)

1

Put the students into pairs and ask them to look at the list of parts and accessories and note down as many items of clothing as they can think of that have these. Allow them to use dictionaries if necessary.

a) a belt: trousers, a skirt, a dress, a coat, etc.
b) a buckle: shoes, a skirt, a dress, etc.
c) buttons: a shirt, a blouse, a coat, trousers, a jacket, etc.
d) a collar: a shirt, a jacket, etc.
e) cuffs: a shirt, a jacket, etc.
f) a hem: a skirt, a dress, trousers, etc.
g) sleeves: a shirt, a jumper, a coat, etc.
h) a zip: trousers, a skirt, etc.

2

• Ask the students first to work individually to decide what the correct idioms are. Then ask them to discuss their answers in pairs. Tell them to use a dictionary if necessary to check and to find out the meaning of any they don't know.

• Check answers with the class and then ask the pairs to discuss whether they have any similar expressions in their language(s).

• Ask them to take turns saying whether any of the expressions could be used to describe people they know. Encourage them to report back to the class on what they found out.

a) off-the-cuff
b) buckle down
c) as bright as a button
d) collars
e) tighten his belt
f) on her sleeve

Extra activity

Ask the students to think about either the best-dressed or the worst-dressed person they know. Tell them to make notes about who this person is and what they wear. Then put them into pairs and ask them to take turns describing the person they've chosen.

Language note

Vocabulary: idiomatic expressions with clothes
There are many expressions connected with clothes. Clothes are used in similes (*as bright as a button*), in metaphors (*tighten your belt*), as well as countless more idioms. For example, *wear the trousers* (to be the person in a relationship who has the most control and makes most of the decisions); *get / be given the boot* (be told to leave your job); *fill someone's shoes* (do the job that someone used to do).

Useful phrases (SB page 12)

1 🌐 1.12

Focus the students' attention on the illustrations. Go through the questions with the class and tell them to listen to the conversation and find the answers.

a) At a concert (or club).
b) Rose and Ian are probably a couple. Mike is a friend of theirs.
c) Mike's ex-girlfriend.

🌐 1.12 (R = Rose; I = Ian; M = Mike)

R: *Have you got the tickets?*
I: *No, I thought you had them.*
R: *Ian, honestly, I can't trust you to do anything.*
I: *Calm down – they're here.*
R: *Grr – you're so annoying.*
I: *You're so easy to wind up. Hey, look at that woman over there.*
R: *The one in the white jacket?*
I: *Yeah.*
R: *What about her?*
I: *Don't you think she's the spitting image of Gwyneth Paltrow?*
R: *No, she doesn't look anything like Gwyneth Paltrow.*
I: *Yes she does. She's got the same hair.*
R: *What – long and blond?*
I: *Not just that – I'd recognise that smile anywhere.*
R: *How often has Gwyneth Paltrow smiled at you?*
I: *I've seen enough films with her in. She's got a very distinctive smile.*
R: *It can't be her – she wouldn't come here to our local club. And actually, that woman bears absolutely no resemblance to Gwyneth Paltrow.*
I: *Oh.*
…
R: *Hey, there's Mike. Hi Mike – how's it going?*
M: *Very well – you'll never guess who I've been talking to.*
I: *Not Gwyneth Paltrow!*
M: *Gwyneth Paltrow?*
R: *Oh, ignore him – he's obsessed.*
I: *Sorry. You were saying.*
M: *Well, I was just at the bar, and I saw this amazing-looking woman walking towards me. I didn't recognise her until she was right in front of me. She's changed so much!*
R: *Who was it?*
M: *Sally – you know, my ex-girlfriend? Anyway, we …*

2

• Focus attention on the two columns and point out that in column 1 there are some useful phrases from the conversation. Column 2 has a list of their meanings. Ask the students to match the items in the columns.

- Ask the students to try to decide who said each of the expressions without listening to the recording. Then play the recording for them to check their answers.

> a) 2 – Ian d) 5 – Rose
> b) 3 – Rose e) 1 – Mike
> c) 6 – Ian f) 4 – Ian

3

Put the students into pairs and ask them to complete the useful phrases from the conversation, using the words in the box.

> a) that woman f) that smile
> b) in the g) a very
> c) spitting image h) no resemblance
> d) look anything i) looking woman
> e) the same j) changed so

4

- Ask the students to work individually to complete the sentences. Allow them to compare in pairs before checking answers with the class.

- Ask the students to change the sentences to make them true for themselves and their parents. They should then compare them in pairs and discuss their sentences.

> a) the spitting image of him.
> b) got the same eyes.
> c) a very distinctive way of walking.
> d) anything like her/my mother.
> e) absolutely no resemblance to the rest of the family.
> f) was an amazing-looking woman when she was younger.

Writing *Extra* (SB page 13)

Informal letter

1

Ask the students to work in pairs and discuss the questions.

2

Ask the students to read the letter. Give them time to absorb what they read and decide whether the language is appropriate or not.

> The language isn't appropriate as it's an informal letter which contains a lot of formal letter features.

3

- Ask the students to read the letter again and to replace the underlined words and expressions with their less formal equivalents. When checking answers, encourage the students to read the letter aloud so that they get a feel for what sounds right.

- Have a class discussion on anything else they would change in the letter. If you need to give them a hint, ask them to look at the layout of the letter.

> 1 j 2 n 3 k 4 a 5 g 6 c 7 l
> 8 h 9 i 10 p 11 b 12 m 13 o
> 14 f 15 e 16 d
>
> Other things to change to make the letter more informal:
> change the layout so it looks less serious
> delete the recipient's address
> make it handwritten, not typed
> delete the name under the signature

4

The writing could be done at home for homework. Alternatively, set aside class time and go round monitoring and giving help where needed. Point out that when they've written their letters, they'll be exchanging them with another student and replying to the letter they receive. Remind them that they need to show interest in the other person by asking questions.

5

Set up the exchange of letters and ask the students to reply to the one they've received. If they do this in class, go round offering help where necessary. The finished pairs of letters could be displayed in the classroom.

Further practice material

Need more writing practice?

→ Workbook page 9
- Writing a short biography.

Need more classroom practice activities?

→ Photocopiable resource materials pages 151 to 153
  Grammar: *Would you mind telling me …?*
  Vocabulary: *Common ground*
  Communication: *You do, don't you?*
→ Top 10 activities pages xv to xx

Need progress tests?

→ Test CD – *Test Unit 1*

Need more on important teaching concepts?

→ Key concepts in *New Inside Out* pages xxii to xxxv

Need student self-study practice?

→ CD-ROM – Unit 1: *Impressions*

Need student CEF self-evaluation?

→ CEF Checklists pages xxxvii to xliv

Need more information and more ideas?

→ www.insideout.net

2 Generations *Overview*

Section & Aims	What the students are doing
Reading & Vocabulary SB page 14 Reading for detail	Matching ages to stages in life. Reading an article about school exchanges and answering questions. Categorising words and using them to complete comprehension questions. Discussing the advantages of school exchanges and study trips.
Reading SB page 16 Reading for gist and detail	Reading an article about parents with unusual jobs and answering questions.
Grammar & Vocabulary SB page 17 Verb patterns (1)	Categorising verbs from an article according to their patterns. Completing sentences using various verb patterns. Matching sentence halves to make advice for parents with teenagers.
Pronunciation & Vocabulary **SB page 18** Single vowel sounds	Listening to and repeating single vowel sounds. Matching sayings with their meanings.
Speaking & Listening SB page 18 Fluency practice Listening for detail	Discussing what parents look for in their children's future partners. Listening to parents talking about meeting their daughter's boyfriend. Choosing verbs to complete sentences.
Listening SB page 19 Listening for detail	Listening to a boy talking about meeting his girlfriend's parents.
Grammar & Vocabulary SB page 19 Adjective structures	Choosing the correct prepositions to follow adjectives. Completing sentences with appropriate prepositions. Talking about feelings.
Reading & Listening SB page 20 Reading for detail	Choosing expressions to complete conversations. Discussing advice for meeting a boyfriend or girlfriend's parents for the first time.
Listening & Speaking SB page 21 Listening for gist Fluency practice	Listening to someone talking about a school exchange and identifying the gist of what she says. Putting an account of a visit in the correct order. Writing and discussing true sentences with verb + preposition structures.
Speaking: anecdote SB page 21 Fluency practice	Talking about staying in someone's home.
Useful phrases SB page 22 Useful conversational phrases for showing someone around your house	Listening to someone showing a new *au pair* round a house and answering questions. Numbering rooms in the order they're mentioned. Matching the two halves of useful phrases. Practising showing a partner around their home.
Vocabulary *Extra* page 23 Learning about words	Reading a text about word frequency and answering questions. Answering questions on the dictionary entry for *word*. Discussing the meaning of common phrases with *word*.
Writing WB page 15	Writing emails.

2 Generations *Teacher's notes*

Warm up

- Ask the students to write the names of members their own family on pieces of paper and ask and answer questions in groups. For example:

  Who is Annie?
  She's my sister.
  Is she older than you or younger than you?
  She's older than me.
  And who's Bill?
  He's my brother-in-law. He's married to Annie.

- Ask the students which members of their family they consider come from a different generation from themselves. Find out if this is always a question of age or whether they think attitudes play a role in how they define different generations.

Reading & Vocabulary (SB page 14)

1

- Focus attention on the two photos and ask the students to say how old they think the baby and the old woman are.

- Put the students into pairs and ask them to decide what ages correspond to the stages in the chart and to fill them in. Then discuss their answers as a class. Answers may vary, but find out how much consensus there is. Check that the students understand *school exchanges* (see Language note).

- Keep the students in the same pairs and ask them to discuss the remaining tasks. Again, answers will vary (see suggestions below) but see how much consensus there is across the class.

> *Suggested answers:*
> 0–3 infancy: probably associated with first words
> 4–12 childhood: probably associated with learning to swim and school trips or exchanges
> 13–17 adolescence: probably associated with school trips or exchanges
> (You could also talk about 'youth', which might be from adolescence to 40s depending on your vantage point.)
> 18 upwards: adulthood: probably associated with buying a car, changing a baby's nappy, leaving home

> 45/50–about 60/65: middle age: probably associated with retiring, a free bus pass (given at 60 in the UK)
> 70+ old age (getting older all the time!): perhaps get the students to suggest events that they associate with old age

Language note

School exchanges

School exchanges are programmes in which students from a school in one country visit the families of students from another country with a view to improving their language learning. The host students then visit the corresponding families in the other country.

2

Focus the students' attention on the article on page 15. Point out that it was written by a woman called Viv about her experience of school exchanges. Go through the questions with the class to make sure that they know what information to look for when they read the article for the first time.

> a) Three: from Angers, France; from Bremen, Germany; from Salamanca, Spain.
> b) Immersion meant she learnt three languages. Escape from rural life in Somerset. Exoticism of new friends. Host families were amusing.
> c) Frauke got on better with Viv's mother than with her. Viv wasn't cool enough for Amalia. Viv and Axelle grew apart during their university years. Viv never forgave Axelle for making her be a witness at her wedding.

Cultural notes

Angers /ˈɑːndʒeɪ/, **France**
An ancient city in north-western France dating back to before Roman times. It has a population of 160,000 and is famous for growing and selling flowers. The orange liqueur Cointreau is produced there.

Bremen /ˈbreɪmən/, **Germany**
A medieval port city on the north-western coast of Germany. It has a population of 550,000 and is famous as the home of Beck's beer and aircraft manufacturer Airbus.

Salamanca /ˌsælə'mænkə/, **Spain**
A city in western Spain with a population of 350,000. The city was founded by Celts and was occupied by the Romans and then the Moors. These days Salamanca is a popular tourist destination and is famous for its university.

Somerset /'sʌməset/, **England**
A county in south-west England. Somerset was famously the home of the mythical King Arthur and the small town of Glastonbury was an important religious centre from 700 A.D. It's better known these days as the venue of one of world's largest rock festivals.

3

Ask the students to look at the highlighted words in the article and put them in the table under the correct headings.

Language learning	Relationships	Describing people
pen friend	doted on	sporty
fluency	soured	earnest
aptitude	grew apart	cool
immersion	barely	hip
rusty	speaking	urban
	in touch	

4

- Do the first question with the class as an example and then ask them to complete the remaining questions with words from Exercise 3.

- Make sure all the students have completed the questions correctly before getting them to answer them.

a) aptitude	d) hip; urban
b) rusty	e) barely speaking
c) doted on	f) in touch

a) She'll send them on exchange trips because she thinks it's the best way to learn a language.
b) Spanish and German.
c) The German student's parents.
d) They were used to going out till much later. The nightclub available was horrible.
e) Because Viv was annoyed that Axelle had held her to a promise, made when they were thirteen, to be a witness at her wedding.
f) Axelle and Frauke.

5

Put the students into small groups to discuss the questions. Encourage them to report back to the class on what they found out.

Reading (SB page 16)

1

- Pairwork. Focus the students' attention on the three photos and ask them to discuss the two questions with a partner.

- Play the recording and ask the students to listen and read the article. Then ask them to discuss as a class which of the parents they'd least like to have. Extend the discussion to situations in which they find their own parents embarrassing.

2

- Go through the questions with the class. Make sure that everyone understands them. Then ask them to work individually to re-read the article and find the answers.

- Put the students into pairs to discuss anyone they know who has an unusual job or hobby. Encourage them to report back to the class.

a) Gina's mum.	d) Kayleigh's mum.
b) Alex's dad.	e) Kayleigh.
c) Gina.	f) Alex.

Grammar & Vocabulary (SB page 17)

Verb patterns (1)

1

- Go through the advice on verb patterns with the class. Make sure everyone understands the abbreviations: *sb* = somebody; *sth* = something.

- Focus attention on the verb patterns in the boxes and ask the students to look back at the underlined words in the article and Exercise 2 on page 16. Ask them to record these verb patterns in the correct boxes.

a) **verb + *to*-infinitive:** get to do sth, love to do sth, try to do sth, manage to do sth, attempt to do sth
b) **verb + object + *to*-infinitive:** want sb to do sth, force sb to do sth
c) **verb + gerund:** love doing sth, can't stand doing sth, enjoy doing sth, hate doing sth

d) **verb + object + gerund:** dread sb doing sth
e) **verb + object + infinitive without *to*:** made sb do sth

Language note
Grammar: verb patterns
(See Student's Book page 132.)

2

- Go through the instructions with the class. Do one or two as an example. Then put the students into pairs and ask them to categorise the remaining verbs and verb phrases in the box. Allow them to use dictionaries if they wish.
- Check answers with the class. Ask the students if they can make example sentences using these verb patterns.

> a) **verb + *to*-infinitive:** aim, arrange, ask, can't afford, decide, expect, help, hope, offer
> b) **verb + object + *to*-infinitive:** allow, ask, expect, encourage, help, teach, tell, urge, warn (not)
> c) **verb + gerund:** avoid, finish, not mind, spend time
> d) **verb + object + gerund:** avoid, not mind
> e) **verb + object + infinitive without *to*:** let

3

- Ask the students to complete the sentences with the correct form of the verb in brackets. When checking the answers, get the students to read out the whole sentence so that they hear each word in context.
- Put the students into pairs and ask them to discuss which of the sentences are true for them.

a) talking	e) stay out
b) to save	f) studying
c) lending	g) sitting; watching
d) to drive	h) to start

4

- Pairwork. Ask the students to work in pairs to match up the sentence halves. Remind them that the advice should be sensible.
- When you've checked the answers, ask the pairs to discuss what advice their parents gave them when they were teenagers. Encourage them to report back to the class on what they found out.

> *Expected answers:*
> a) You should help them to do well at school.
> b) You shouldn't let them smoke.
> c) You should make them keep their rooms tidy.
> d) You should tell them not to believe everything they hear.
> e) You should warn them not to take drugs.

f) You should encourage them to keep fit.
g) You should ask them not to play their music too loud.
h) You should expect them to respect their elders.

Extra activity
Put the students into small groups. Ask them to prepare a list of eight children's rules for parents. These could be general rules or rules aimed at limiting the embarrassment they cause their children.

5 Grammar *Extra* 2

Ask the students to turn to *Grammar Extra* 2 on page 132 of the Student's Book. Here they'll find an explanation of the grammar they've been studying and further exercises to practise it.

1	
1 to get	5 looking
2 to rush	6 coming
3 to go	7 to do
4 to buy	8 make

2	
a) to cook	e) obey; do; getting
b) living; to move	f) to get; have
c) going	g) to follow
d) to have	

Pronunciation & Vocabulary
(SB page 18)
Single vowel sounds

1 🌐 1.13

Focus the students' attention on the phonemic symbols and example words in the margin. Play the recording and ask the students to listen and repeat. Point out the different spellings which can represent the vowel sounds.

Language note
Pronunciation: single vowel sounds
Single vowel sounds can be broken into two types: long and short. The phonemic symbol for long single vowel sounds contains /ː/, which shows that the vowel sound is intended to be drawn out (e.g. /griːn/ = green, as compared to /grɪn/ = grin).

2 🌐 1.14

- Play the recording and ask the students to listen and repeat.
- They should then write the phonemic symbol which represents the vowel sound in each underlined syllable.

a) /æ/, /ɪ/	d) /ɜ:/, /e/, /ɒ/
b) /ʌ/, /ɔ:/	e) /u:/, /i:/
c) /ɑ:/	f) /ʊ/, /ə/

3

Point out that all the sentences in Exercise 2 are English sayings. Go through the meanings with the class and ask them to match them to the sayings.

| 1 f) | 2 d) | 3 a) | 4 e) | 5 c) | 6 b) |

4

- Put the students into pairs to discuss which of the sayings they like best and whether there are any similar sayings in their own language(s). Encourage them to report back to the class.

- Point out that although there are many sayings and proverbs like these in the English language, they are very seldom used and are probably best avoided by non-native speakers in conversation. These sayings most often occur in writing and are often alluded to in part rather than used in their entirety.

Speaking & Listening (SB page 18)

1

- Groupwork. Go through the points with the class and make sure that everyone understands them. Then ask the groups to discuss which they think parents would consider important or not important.

- In a class feedback session find out whether there is general agreement across the groups. Then discuss as a class whether it makes a difference whether the child is a son or a daughter.

2 🌐 1.15

- Ask the students to look at the photos. Tell them that Andy is Sarah's new boyfriend and ask them to speculate on whether or not they think Sarah's parents will like Andy.

- Go through the instructions and the statements with the class. Then play the recording and ask the students to mark the statements true or false.

- Check answers and ask the students to correct the false statements.

| a) False. They've heard a lot about him. |
| b) True. |
| c) False. They've only met some of them – about half a dozen. |
| d) True. |
| e) False. It was because her parents *did* like him. |
| f) False. They think she's too young and she isn't ready for anything serious yet. |

🌐 **1.15** (I = Interviewer; M = Mum; D = Dad)

I: *You're going to meet Sarah's boyfriend tomorrow.*

M&D: *That's right.*

I: *How do you feel about that?*

M: *Well, we're looking forward to meeting Andy at last – we've heard a lot about him, because Sarah's been going out with him for a while now. Several weeks, I believe.*

I: *Does Sarah usually bring her boyfriends home to meet you?*

D: *Well, it's difficult to know with Sarah really – she changes boyfriends like other people change their socks. We've met some of them.*

M: *Yes, I'd say we've met half a dozen over the years.*

I: *Have you liked most of her boyfriends?*

M: *No, not really. I'm always amazed at how awful they are. She goes for very strange types. There was just one we liked, wasn't there?*

D: *Oh, yes – you mean Jeremy. Lovely chap. We were impressed with him.*

M: *But he didn't last long. As soon as we told her we liked him, she dropped him.*

I: *What sort of person would you like Sarah to go out with?*

M: *Well, I think it's essential for him to come from the same kind of background.*

D: *Yes, and it's very important for him to have some kind of qualifications – you know, some ambition.*

M: *He needs to be a strong character to stand up to Sarah – she'd soon go off somebody who lets her do what she wants all the time.*

D: *Oh anyway, we're not going to take it too seriously. She's far too young to get married or engaged or anything like that. And the poor chap is unlikely to last very long.*

3

- Ask the students to work individually to choose the correct verb forms to complete the sentences. Remind them of the work they've done on verb patterns.

- Allow the students to compare their sentences in pairs before playing the recording for them to check their answers.

a) meeting	d) to have
b) to know	e) to be
c) to come	f) to last

Listening (SB page 19)

1 🔘 1.16

- Remind the students that in the last section they heard Sarah's parents talking about meeting her new boyfriend, Andy. Now they're going to listen to him talking about how he feels about meeting them.
- Play the recording and ask the students to say what reason Andy gives for meeting Sarah's parents.

> He's meeting them because Sarah fancies going to London for the day and she wants to have Sunday lunch at her parents' house (and he always does what Sarah wants).

> 🔘 1.16 (I = Interviewer; A = Andy)
>
> I: *How do you feel about meeting Sarah's parents?*
>
> A: *A bit nervous. I'm worried about making a bad impression because I'm quite shy. So I find it difficult to get on with people straight away.*
>
> I: *But you're a DJ, aren't you?*
>
> A: *Yes, but it's easy for me to hide behind my music decks at work. I'm not very good at making conversation, especially with older people.*
>
> I: *What are you most nervous about?*
>
> A: *Well, I gave up studying to become a DJ, and I don't think Sarah's parents will be very impressed with that. Also, I dyed my hair red last week, and they'll probably be a bit shocked by that.*
>
> I: *How are you going to try to make a good impression?*
>
> A: *Well, I'm going to wear clean clothes – not a suit or anything. I haven't got one. And I'll take her mum some flowers.*
>
> I: *Why are you going to meet Sarah's parents?*
>
> A: *Because Sarah fancies going to London for the day, and she feels like having Sunday lunch at home. And I always do what she wants.*

2

- Go through the items in the box and ask the students to underline the ones that Andy says might make a bad impression on Sarah' parents.
- Play the recording for them to check their answers; then ask what Andy is planning to do to make a good impression on Sarah's parents.

> his shyness, his conversation skills, his job, his education, his red hair
>
> By wearing clean clothes and taking some flowers.

Grammar & Vocabulary (SB page 19)

Adjective structures

1

- Focus the students' attention on the information on the three adjective structures and the example sentences in the margin.
- Ask them to read the three extracts from the interviews with Sarah's parents and with Andy, and to underline the correct prepositions.
- When you check their answers, get them to identify who says each of these extracts.

> a) at (Sarah's mum)
> b) with (Sarah's dad)
> c) about (Andy)

Language notes

Grammar: adjective structures

Adjective + *to*-infinitive

This is a very common structure when using adjectives describing degrees of difficulty (*It's **easy to do** / I find it **hard to imagine***) or feelings (*It's so **irritating to do** what she wants all the time*).

Adjective + *for* + object + *to*-infinitive

An extension of the previous structure allows the speaker to apply the phrase to a third party (*It's **easy for you to do** / It's **hard for her to imagine***).

Adjective + prepositions

Other adjectives commonly followed by prepositions are: *embarrassed about, proud of, good at, worried about, satisfied with, excited about, scared of*.

2

- Ask the students to work individually to complete the sentences. As they work, go round giving extra help if necessary.
- Check answers with the class, then put the students into pairs to take turns asking and answering the questions.

> a) at   b) for   c) on   d) of   e) to
> f) in   g) with   h) about

3

Ask the students to look at the table. Point out that the two example sentences have been formed by taking different elements from the table. Ask the students to write three facts about their feelings on a piece of paper. Point out that they can form these from the elements of the table or they can use their own ideas.

4

- Collect all the pieces of paper from the students, then go through the instructions with the class. Use the question structure to elicit further examples of possible questions.

- Shuffle the pieces of paper and distribute them at random. Make sure that no one has received their own piece of paper. Then ask the students to mingle and ask questions to find out who wrote the sentences on the piece of paper they've received.

Reading & Listening (SB page 20)

1 🌐 1.17–1.18

- Focus attention on the two conversations. Point out that they're similar in that both involve people arriving at someone else's home. Ask the students to say what's likely to be the difference between them. If they're unsure, ask them what the relationships are between the people arriving and the people whose home it is, and how well they know each other. Get the students to predict that the conversation at Sarah's parents' house is likely to be more formal as Andy hasn't met her parents before, they're from an older generation and he wants to make a good impression.

- Ask the students to work individually to choose the most appropriate options to complete the two conversations.

- Allow them to compare their answers in pairs before playing the recording for them to check. Ask the students to predict how long Andy and Sarah will continue going out together and encourage them to give reasons for their predictions.

Conversation 1
1 a) The door's open!
2 c) cheers – that's great
3 b) how's it going
4 a) totally shattered
5 a) What've you been up to
6 c) chill out
7 a) Do you want
8 b) Whatever
9 c) No idea
10 b) on its last legs

Conversation 2
1 b) Do come in.
2 a) thank you – that's very kind of you
3 c) how are you
4 b) absolutely exhausted
5 c) What's the matter
6 b) relax
7 b) Would you prefer
8 c) I don't mind
9 b) I'm afraid I don't know
10 a) rather old

🌐 **1.17**

Conversation 1 (S = Sarah; A = Andy)
S: Hello!
A: Hiya. The door's open!
S: Here, I remembered to bring you that CD.
A: Oh, cheers – that's great!
S: So, how's it going?
A: All right, but I'm totally shattered.
S: Why? What've you been up to?
A: Nothing – it's just that I didn't finish work until five o'clock this morning.
S: Oh right. Well, you'd better just chill out this evening. Do you want to watch TV, or shall I go and get a DVD?
A: Whatever.
S: Do you know what's on TV tonight?
A: Oh, no idea. Rubbish as usual, I should think.
S: Oh dear, you are in a bad mood. You're not nervous about meeting my parents, are you?
A: No – why should I be? But I am a bit worried about the long drive – my car's on its last legs.
S: Oh well, let's worry about that tomorrow. Come on – make me a nice cup of tea.

🌐 **1.18**

Conversation 2 (M = Mum; D = Dad; S = Sarah; A = Andy)
M: Hello, welcome. Do come in.
S: Mum, Dad, this is Andy.
M&D: Nice to meet you.
A: Nice to meet you. These are for you – Sarah says they're your favourites.
M: Oh, thank you – that's very kind of you. And how are you, darling?
S: I'm absolutely exhausted, actually.
M: Oh dear. What's the matter? Have you been working too hard?
S: Oh no, nothing like that – it's just a long drive, isn't it?
M: Yes, of course. You must sit down and relax, both of you. Would you prefer coffee or tea, Andy?
A: I don't mind. Whatever's easiest.
D: How many miles is it exactly?
A: Oh, I'm afraid I don't know. The journey's taken us five and a half hours, but my car is rather old.
D: Oh yes, I always take the M4, followed by the A34, except during the summer when I tend to avoid motorways and go through Winchester on the backroads.
M: Well, we're not going to talk about roads all day, are we? Now Andy, what exactly do you do? Sarah tells us you're in the music industry …

Language notes

Vocabulary: social register
This section deals with the different ways you talk to people depending on how well you know them. In many languages, there's a formal and an informal way of addressing people. The same applies in English, although it's the choice of

phrase rather than a formal/informal way of saying 'you' that makes the difference. Colloquial language like *chill out* is acceptable when speaking to friends, but in more formal circumstances *relax* would be the appropriate choice. On the other hand, it would sound strange if you said to a friend: *Do help yourself to coffee* as this is a formal way of trying to put someone at ease in your home. *You know where the coffee is – I'll have one too, please* is a more likely way of speaking to a friend.

2

Groupwork. Go through the situation with the class, then ask the students to discuss in their groups the kind of advice they might give and to make a list. Get the groups to report back to the class on what they decided.

Listening & Speaking (SB page 21)

1

- Pairwork. Ask the students to discuss the question in pairs and to make a list of the things they'd expect.
- In a class feedback session, get each pair to present their list to the class.

2 🌐 1.19

- Focus attention on the photo and explain that it shows Nora, a young woman from Colombia who lived with an English family as an *au pair*. If necessary, explain that an *au pair* is someone who lives in a host family's house and helps with the children and the housework in return for food, lodging and a small salary. Go through the statements with the class.
- Play the recording and ask the students to mark the statements true or false. When checking the answers, ask the students to correct the false statements.

a) True.
b) False. She was excited about trying out new things
c) False. She hates hot summers.
d) False. They were happy to talk about them.
e) True.

🌐 1.19

I knew there were lots of things I would have to get used to when I decided to go to England and stay with a family. But I was looking forward to experiencing a new culture. I'm not difficult when it comes to food, so I was excited about trying new things, especially fish and chips! Also, I hate hot summers, so I was dreaming of the typical English grey days. I was a bit worried about the reserved British character. I'd heard that British people objected to talking about anything personal, but insisted on talking about the weather all the time. So I was surprised when I met my English family for the first time and they gave me a big hug and then asked me about my family, my work and

even my boyfriend. The other surprise was the weather – I think global warming has succeeded in turning England into a hot country! I had problems with the language at first – I couldn't understand anything! But the family made me feel at home, and it was definitely the best way to improve my English. In a family situation, you have to sink or swim. It's as simple as that.

3

- Ask the students to put the sentences in order. Then to compare in pairs before checking with the class.
- Point out the used of verb + preposition structures in Nora's account of her stay in England.

Correct order: 1, 8, 4, 2, 5, 11, 6, 12, 10, 3, 7, 9

4

- Go through the sentences stems with the class and make sure everyone understands them. Then ask them to work individually to complete the sentences so that they are true for them.
- Tell the students to discuss their sentences in pairs, asking follow-up questions to find out more details.

Speaking: anecdote (SB page 21)

For more information about how to set up, monitor and repeat Anecdotes, see page xx in the Introduction.

- Go through the instructions and the questions with the class. Give the students a minute or two to decide what they're going to talk about. Then ask them to look at the questions and think about their answers to them. Allow them to make notes of what they're going to say and how they're going to say it, but discourage them from writing a paragraph that they can simply read out. Go round, monitoring and giving help where necessary.
- Pairwork. Put the students in pairs and ask them to take turns to tell their partner about the time they stayed in somebody's home. Encourage them to ask each other follow-up questions to get further information. Then ask some pairs to report back to the class about what they found out.

Useful phrases (SB page 22)

1 🌐 1.20

- Focus the students' attention on the picture and ask them to say what they think is happening.
- Go through the instructions and the questions with the class and ask them to listen to the recording and note down their answers.

a) Two.
b) The kitchen.
c) Pink.

🔘 **1.20** (J = Jill; M = Marie; B = Ben; K = Katy)

J: Hello, Marie, come in. Did you have a pleasant journey?

M: Pleasant journey?

J: A good trip?

M: Oh yes, thank you. Very good.

J: Well, welcome to our home. I hope you'll be happy here. It's not very big, but I think you'll have everything you need.

M: Yes, thank you. It's very nice.

J: Oh good, I'm glad you like it. Let me introduce you to the rest of the family, and then I'll show you around.

M: OK, thank you Mrs Brown.

J: Oh, you must call me Jill. Now, this is Benjie – he's thirteen.

B: Nearly fourteen, actually. And it's Ben.

M: Hello, Ben.

J: And this is Katy – she's eleven.

M: Hello, Katy.

K: Hello.

J: And this is Max – he's a baby so he can be a bit excited. … Down, Max. Sorry. I hope you don't mind dogs.

M: No, I love dogs.

J: Oh good. So this is the kitchen – we usually eat breakfast in here. Help yourself to tea and coffee. The fridge is here, look – and the cups and saucers are in this cupboard here. I'm afraid the microwave is broken, but we seem to manage without.

M: It's a lovely kitchen.

J: Yes, it's my favourite room actually. Now, this is the living room – excuse the mess, but Benjie and Katy have lots of friends around. This is the dining room – Max isn't allowed in here, are you Max? … Down boy! … Now, if you'd like to leave your bags here for a minute, I'll show you the upstairs.

M: Thank you.

J: Here's the bathroom. Sorry about the pink walls – that was Katy's idea.

M: Oh, I like pink. My bedroom walls are pink.

J: Really? How funny. OK, this is Katy's bedroom – we're not allowed to go into Benjie's room, but it's probably just as well. And this is your room. It's quiet in here because the window looks out on the garden.

M: Oh it's lovely – thank you.

J: Now, you make yourself at home, and if there's anything you need, just give me a shout, OK?

M: OK.

J: Oh, by the way, Benjie's vegetarian, so we don't usually eat meat because he gets upset. Is that OK with you?

M: Yes, I like vegetables.

2

- Go through the rooms in the box and make sure everyone understands them. Play the recording again. Ask the students to number the rooms in the order that Jill shows them to Marie.
- Check their answers and ask them to identify the three rooms that Jill doesn't show her.

1 the kitchen	4 the bathroom
2 the living room	5 Katy's bedroom
3 the dining room	6 Marie's bedroom

She doesn't show Marie her own bedroom (Jill's bedroom), Ben's bedroom or the study.

3

Go through the instructions with the class and ask if anyone can remember what Jill was referring to in each case. Play the recording again for them to check.

a) The house.	d) The living room.
b) Her dog Max.	e) The bathroom.
c) The microwave.	

4 🔘 **1.21**

- Ask the students to work individually to match the two halves of the useful phrases. Then allow them to compare in pairs.
- Play the recording for the students to check their answers. Play it a second time for them to listen and repeat. When they've done this chorally, ask for individual repetition of the useful phrases.

a) 4	b) 3	c) 7	d) 2	e) 8	f) 5
g) 6	h) 1				

🔘 **1.21**

a) Did you have a pleasant journey?
b) Welcome to our home.
c) Let me introduce you to the rest of the family.
d) Then I'll show you around.
e) You must call me Jill.
f) Help yourself to tea and coffee.
g) Make yourself at home.
h) If there's anything you need, just give me a shout.

5

Ask the students to work individually to decide which options are inappropriate. Then allow them to compare in pairs before checking answers with the class.

a) ~~entertain you~~	d) ~~my money~~
b) ~~surprise~~	e) ~~get up at 6.30 a.m~~
c) ~~scarce~~	

6

- Give the students time to draw their plans, but point out that they don't have to be very elaborate. Tell them to mark in the positions of any members of the family or pets that they'll be introducing to their partner, together with any features that they'd like to point out.
- Put the students into pairs and ask them to take turns to show each other around their homes. Go round giving help where needed and taking note of any particularly good examples which could be performed later for the class.

Vocabulary *Extra* (SB page 23)

Learning about words

1

Pairwork. Ask the students to discuss the questions quickly in pairs. Have a quick class feedback session to find out their answers.

2

Ask the students' to read the information about word frequency, look at the graph and discuss the questions.

a) *the*	c) 80%.
b) Around 45%.	d) 7,500.

3

Ask the students to look at the dictionary extract for *word* and to answer the questions.

> a) five
> b) a short conversation or discussion, usually without other people listening
> c) news or information about someone or something
> d) 24
> e) Students' own answers.

4

Pairwork. Put the students into pairs and ask them to discuss the situations or contexts in which they might hear the sentences. Ask them to compare their ideas in small groups before having a class feedback session.

> *Possible answers:*
> a) When they are asking a witness to a crime or accident for information.
> b) When someone can't remember the lyrics to a song.
> c) When someone is about to give a speech.
> d) When someone, particularly in a work situation, would like to have a confidential chat with a colleague.
> e) When someone is asking the other person to keep information secret.

5

- Ask the students to make their choices without referring to the dictionary extract if they can. When they've finished allow them to check their answers and the meaning of the phrases in the extract.
- Check answers with the class and see if the students can use the phrases in mini-conversations.

a) say	b) keep	c) hear	d) put
e) Take	f) fail		

6

- Ask the students to look at their own dictionaries and compare the way it presents the entry for *word* with the extract on the Student's Book page. Then ask them to report back to the class on what they found.
- Ask the students to choose five useful phrases which include *word* to learn. Encourage them to record them in their vocabulary notebooks in example sentences.

Further practice material

Need more writing practice?

→ Workbook page 15
- Writing emails.

Need more classroom practice activities?

→ Photocopiable resource materials pages 154 to 156
  Grammar: *Tell me something about yourself*
  Vocabulary: *Vince's bike*
  Communication: *Single vowel dominoes*
→ Top 10 activities pages xv to xx

Need DVD material?

→ DVD – Programme 2: *Meet the folks*

Need progress tests?

→ Test CD – *Test Unit 2*

Need more on important teaching concepts?

→ Key concepts in *New Inside Out* pages xxii to xxxv

Need student self-study practice?

→ CD-ROM – Unit 2: *Generations*

Need student CEF self-evaluation?

→ CEF Checklists pages xxxvii to xliv

Need more information and more ideas?

→ www.insideout.net

3 Gold *Overview*

Section & Aims	What the students are doing
Reading SB page 24 Reading for specific information	Reading a text about the California gold rush. Describing people.
Listening SB page 25 Listening for specific information	Connecting items in a photo with the story of a gold rush millionnaire. Completing sentences to retell the story they've heard.
Vocabulary SB page 25 Collocations with *have, make* and *take*	Completing collocations from the reading text. Completing more collocations with *have, make* and *take*. Completing sentences with nouns and writing example sentences.
Vocabulary SB page 26 Metaphor Reading for detail	Studying the use of metaphors involving movement. Completing extracts from the reading text with metaphors. Reading a conversation and completing metaphors. Completing a table with metaphors.
Reading & Grammar SB page 27 Reading for gist Reported speech	Reading about a teenager who sold his mother's car. Rewriting reported speech as direct speech. Identifying how to change direct speech into reported speech.
Pronunciation SB page 28 The schwa sound	Completing a paragraph about the schwa sound. Underlining vowel sounds pronounced using a schwa.
Listening & Vocabulary SB page 28 Listening for gist Money expressions	Discussing questions about money. Listening to people talking about their attitudes to money. Identifying expressions connected with money.
Grammar SB page 29 Unreal conditionals	Matching clauses to make conditional sentences. Discussing the structure and meaning of conditional sentences. Discussing hypothetical situations. Completing conditional sentences.
Reading & Vocabulary SB page 30 Reading for gist	Reading about a man who sold his life on eBay. Identifying true and false sentences. Matching words and meanings. Talking about a possession they'd never sell.
Listening SB page 31 Listening for gist	Matching possessions with notes on the stories about them. Reconstructing the stories from notes.
Speaking: anecdote SB page 31 Fluency practice	Talking about their most treasured possession.
Useful phrases SB page 32 Shopping – money expressions; explaining what you want	Listening to a conversation about shopping and answering questions. Matching useful phrases to meanings. Rewriting requests in less direct language. Talking about buying expensive items.
Writing *Extra* SB page 33 Description	Completing a text about an imaginary perfect day with linking words. Adding their own details to the text. Writing an account of their own perfect day.
Writing WB page 21	Writing a story from pictures.

Gold *Teacher's notes*

Warm up

Ask the class if they know why the population of California increased dramatically around 160 years ago. If anyone mentions the gold rush, find out what they know about it.

Reading (SB page 24)

1

Focus the students' attention on the picture that goes with the text and ask them what they think the text will be about. Then go through the items in lists a), b) and c) with the class, and ask them to read the article and find what the links are between the items in each list.

> a) John Sutter came to California to build his own private empire. When the Forty-Niners came, his dream turned to disillusion.
> b) James Marshall was building a sawmill on the American River when he saw a piece of gold half the size and shape of a pea.
> c) President James Polk's statement to Congress in 1848 started the gold rush. Hundreds of thousands of people journeyed to the west to look for gold. They were called the 'Forty-Niners' because they left home in 1849.

Cultural notes

San Francisco /sæn frənˈsɪskəʊ/
San Francisco was founded in 1776 by Spanish settlers. It experienced rapid growth during the California Gold Rush in 1848. In 1906 an earthquake devastated the city, but it was quickly rebuilt, and has become a popular tourist destination as well as being home to 750,000 residents.

President James Polk /ˈprezɪdənt dʒeɪmz pɒlk/ (1795–1849)
James Polk was the 11th president of the United States. He served from 1845 to 1849.

2

• Go through the words in the box with the class and make sure that everyone understands them. Explain that *dreamer* and *visionary* are similar in meaning, although *dreamer* tends to have negative connotations and *visionary* positive ones. Similarly, someone who might be praised by some people as an *entrepreneur* might be criticised by others as an *opportunist*.

• Ask the students to work in pairs and decide which words they'd use to describe John Sutter and one of the Forty-Niners. Then ask them to discuss whether they could use any of the words to describe people they know.

> a) **John Sutter:** businessman, conservative, dreamer, entrepreneur, farmer, visionary.
> b) **One of the Forty-Niners:** dreamer, entrepreneur, opportunist, risk-taker.

Listening (SB page 25)

1 🔊 **1.22**

• Focus the students' attention on the photo of Sam Brannan and tell them that he was the first person to become a millionaire in the California gold rush. Ask them to look at the photo of the Forty-Niner and identify the objects mentioned in the caption. Tell them that there's a connection between these items and Sam Brannan's fortune and that they're going to listen to the recording and find out what that connection is. With strong classes, ask the students to speculate on this connection before they listen.

• You may need to play the recording more than once. Encourage them to write brief notes as they listen.

> During the gold rush, Sam Brannan made his fortune by selling these items and others to the gold diggers. He had the only store between San Francisco (Yerba Buena) and the gold fields. He bought up all the mining tools he could find and then he sold them to the Forty-Niners and made a lot of money. In the end he lost his fortune because of drink (liquor).

> 🔊 **1.22**
>
> *During the gold rush, Sam Brannan became one of the most successful businessmen in California. He arrived in California in 1846, when San Francisco (then called Yerba Buena) was just a small community of a few hundred people.*
>
> *When gold was discovered on John Sutter's land in 1848, Sam Brannan was running the only store between San Francisco and the gold fields. Quickly recognising a gap in the market, he bought up all the picks, shovels and pans he could find, and then ran up and down the streets of San Francisco shouting, 'Gold, gold on the American River!'* ➤

*He had no intention of digging for gold! No, he was
planning to sell shovels. And having cornered the
market, he ended up with a lot more gold than the
person who had to dig for it.*

*This was a man who keenly understood the laws
of supply and demand. A metal pan that sold for
twenty cents a few days earlier, was now available
from Brannan for fifteen dollars. In just nine weeks
he made $36,000. Within a few years he had became
the first gold rush millionaire.*

*In the end, though, Sam Brannan lost his fortune
and his health, as did many of those who first
benefited from the gold rush. Alcoholism finally led
to his downfall, and California's first millionaire died
an unnoticed death.*

2

• Pairwork. Go through the instructions with the class,
  then ask the students to work in pairs to complete the
  sentences. Encourage them to try to do this without
  looking at the sentence endings.

• Play the recording again for them to check their
  answers.

a) 3   b) 6   c) 8   d) 1   e) 10   f) 4
g) 2   h) 9   i) 5   j) 7

Vocabulary (SB page 25)

1

Ask the students to look through the article on page 24
and find the extracts and the words that complete them.
When checking answers, explain that *he had no idea* is a
strong way of saying *he didn't know*.

a) idea   b) statement   c) chance

Language note
Vocabulary: collocations
Many words in English exist as part of a group
of words which commonly occur together in a
certain order. Verbs like *have*, *make* and *take* are
all commonly used in collocations. *Have breakfast*
is much more natural than *eat breakfast*; you
make a mistake, you don't ~~do a mistake~~; you *take a
photograph*, you don't ~~make a photograph~~.

2

• Focus the students' attention on the table. Ask them
  to complete it by adding *have*, *make* and *take*.

• Put the students into pairs and ask them to tick the
  collocations in the list that they already know. In
  a class feedback session encourage the students to
  teach the collocations that they know to students who
  don't know them.

a) make   b) take   c) have

3

• Ask the students to complete the sentences and to
  think about which ones are true for them.

• When you've checked and discussed their answers,
  ask them each to choose five collocations from
  Exercise 2 that they think will be useful for them and
  to write example sentences. As they do this, go round
  monitoring and helping where necessary. Encourage
  the students to read out their sentences to the class.

a) mess   b) sense   c) office
d) difficulty   e) sugar   f) right

Vocabulary (SB page 26)

Metaphor

1

Focus the students' attention on the dictionary
definitions. Read them aloud or get a student to read
them. Ask for suggestions on what the words have in
common. Explain that these are all metaphors and that a
metaphor is a way of describing something by comparing
it to something else that has similar qualities. (See
Language notes below.)

They all have something to do with both water and
movement.

Language notes
Vocabulary: metaphor
• A metaphor is a word or phrase that means one
  thing and is used for referring to another thing
  in order to emphasise their similar qualities.

• In this unit, movement (of people, mainly) is
  compared to water through metaphor. A *trickle*
  is a small flow of water, whereas *flood* and *deluge*
  are the opposite. Using metaphor in this way
  gives the text a more literary sense.

2

• Pairwork. Put the students into pairs and ask them
  to use words from dictionary definitions to complete
  the extracts. Encourage them to do this first without
  looking back at the article on page 24.

• Go round, giving help and encouragement. Then
  allow them to check their answers in the article on
  page 24.

a) trickle, flood, deluge
b) drifted
c) streamed

3 1.23

- Go through the instructions with the class and allow the students plenty of time to read the conversation. Ask them what the difference is between Martha's and her dad's attitudes to Martha's idea (Martha is enthusiastic, her father dismissive), and how her dad's attitude changes towards the end of the conversation (he begins to see that the idea is a good one). This will help them with the meaning of the metaphors they have to complete.

- Play the recording for the students to check their answers.

> 1 spare   2 precious   3 worth   4 wasting
> 5 profitably   6 half-baked   7 chewing
> 8 food   9 digest   10 running out   11 spend

> 1.23 (M = Martha; D = Dad)
>
> M: Morning!
>
> D: You're in a good mood today. Any particular reason?
>
> M: Yes, there is actually. I've decided to become a millionaire.
>
> D: You've decided to become a millionaire. I see. And how exactly do you propose to do that?
>
> M: Well, if you can spare a couple of minutes, I'll tell you.
>
> D: Martha, you know how precious my time is …
>
> M: Dad, I promise you it will be worth your while.
>
> D: Oh, OK – but just five minutes or else I'll be late for work.
>
> M: Right. I've got this idea for a website …
>
> D: Oh come on, you're wasting your time if you think you can make money out of the internet. All the best ideas have been used up. You should be using your time more profitably, getting a proper job …
>
> M: I promise you it's not some half-baked idea. It's something I've been chewing over for the last few weeks. Please just have a look at these plans, then tell me what you think.
>
> D: Hm, yes, interesting. There's certainly food for thought here. How are you going to find the money to do it?
>
> M: Ah, well, I was rather hoping you might help me. Will you?
>
> D: Well, I can't tell you until I've had time to digest all this information. But you've certainly got a good idea. Very original.
>
> M: But we're running out of time. If we don't do it very soon, somebody else will.
>
> D: Yes, you could be right. Look, I've got to go now, but as soon as I get back from work I'll spend the rest of the evening looking at it. Have you told anybody else your idea?
>
> M: No, not yet.
>
> D: Well, don't … I think you've really got something here.

4

- Ask the students to to put the metaphors from the conversation in Exercise 3 into the table. Allow them to compare their answers in pairs.

- Check answers and make sure everyone understands all the metaphors. Then ask them to discuss whether they have similar metaphors in their own language(s).

> **Time = money**
> to spare a couple of minutes
> to know how precious sb's time is
> to be worth sb's while
> to waste sb's time
> to use sb's time profitably
> to run out of time
> to spend time
>
> **Ideas = food**
> a half-baked idea
> to chew sth over
> to be food for thought
> to digest all the information

5

- Ask the students to complete the sentences.
- Check answers and then put the students into pairs to discuss whether they agree or disagree with them.

> a) chew   b) run   c) waste   d) food
> e) spend

Reading & Grammar (SB page 27)

Reported speech

1

- Pairwork. Ask the students to discuss the questions in pairs. You may need to explain *extravagant* (spending a lot of money on something that isn't really necessary).

- Ask the pairs to report back to the class on what they found out about each other.

2

- Ask the students to look at the photo of Christopher Townsend and his mother. Ask them how they think Christopher and his mother feel about each other.

- Go through the instructions with the class and ask them to speculate on why they think Christopher had to pay his mother £68.70. Accept any ideas and don't confirm or deny anything. Then ask the students to read the article and find out the truth. (Note: Wiltshire is a county in south-west England.)

> Because he had stolen his mother's car and sold it. £68.70 was the amount she'd had to spend on public transport since she'd been without the car.

3

- Focus attention on the sentences in the margin. Point out that these are examples of reported speech, i.e. when you say what one person said to another without using their actual words.

- Ask the students to look through the article again and to underline any examples of reported speech. Then check their answers.

- Go through the example with the class. Point out that there are differences between direct speech and indirect speech. Ask them to think about what the actual words were most likely to have been.

Direct speech
a) 'My mother's gone abroad. She asked me to sell the car.'
b) 'I've arranged a surprise for your birthday. We're going to Paris next weekend. I've booked a luxury suite in a five-star hotel.'
c) 'How can you afford it?'
d) 'I/I've inherited a sum of money from my grandfather. He died a few months ago.'
e) 'He's apologised, but I still have no idea why he did it.'

Language note

Grammar: reported speech
(See Student's Book page 134.)

4

Go through the list of changes which occur when speech is reported with the class. Then ask the students to work in pairs and to find examples of each in the article. You could also ask them to look back at the sentences in the margin and to say what the actual words were.

---

a) Tense changes, e.g. *has gone abroad* ➔ *had gone abroad*; *asked him* ➔ *had asked him*; *have a surprise* ➔ *had a surprise*; *are going to Paris* ➔ *were going to Paris*, etc.
b) Word order changes, e.g. *how can you afford it?* ➔ *how he could afford it*
c) Pronoun changes, e.g. *I* ➔ *he*; *I* ➔ *she*; *your* ➔ *her*, etc.
d) Time reference changes, e.g. *next weekend* ➔ *the following weekend*; *a few months ago* ➔ *a few months previously*

---

5 Grammar *Extra* 3, Part 1

Ask the students to turn to *Grammar Extra* 3, Part 1 on page 134 of the Student's Book. Here they'll find an explanation of the grammar they've been studying and a further exercise to practise it.

1
a) He said that he was just thinking about me.
b) She told us that they'd been to Paris a few days previously.
c) He said that when he got his bonus, he was going to spend it wisely.
d) He asked us how we managed to live on so little money.
e) She asked him what would happen to them the following day.
f) My manager told me that my work was excellent.
g) I asked her if we could afford a holiday that year.

Pronunciation (SB page 28)

1

- Ask the students to read the explanation and underline the correct words to complete it.

- Then ask a student to read the explanation out loud, making sure that they're pronouncing the short words correctly.

---

1 vowel   2 unstressed   3 never

Language note

Pronunciation: the schwa
The schwa /ə/ is a neutral, unstressed single vowel sound. It is the most common vowel sound in English. Getting the schwa sound right is a good way for your students to make their pronunciation sound natural. Students should always focus on the (phonetic) pronunciation of a word rather the way it's spelt. For example, in these words the schwa sound is: the *a* in *about* /əbaʊt/, the *e* in *given* /gɪvən/, the *i* in *pencil* /pensəl/, the *o* in *melody* /melədi/ and the *u* in *survive* /səvaɪv/.

---

2 🌐 **1.24**

- Encourage the students to read the sayings aloud so they can hear which vowel sounds are pronounced using a schwa. They could do this in pairs, taking turns to read out a saying and identifying the schwa sounds.

- Play the recording for them to check their answers, then play it again for them to listen and repeat. When they've done this chorally, ask for individual repetition of the sayings and make sure they're pronouncing the schwa correctly.

---

a) Money makes th<u>e</u> world go round.
b) There's no such thing <u>as</u> <u>a</u> free lunch.
c) Put y<u>ou</u>r money where y<u>ou</u>r mouth is.
d) In f<u>or</u> <u>a</u> penny, in f<u>or</u> <u>a</u> pound.
e) Watch th<u>e</u> pennies, <u>an</u>d th<u>e</u> pounds take care <u>of</u> th<u>e</u>mselves.
f) Th<u>e</u> love <u>of</u> money is th<u>e</u> root <u>of</u> all ev<u>i</u>l.

3

- Ask the students to discuss the sayings with a partner. Get them to report back to the class on which, if any, they like and whether similar sayings exist in their own language(s). (See Language note below.)
- As with those in Unit 2 (Student's Book page 18), it would be wise to warn the students that these sayings are very little used in everyday life and that they are probably best avoided by non-native speakers, certainly in conversation.

Language notes

Vocabulary: money expressions

a) *Money makes the world go round.* = Money is powerful and the world relies on it.

b) *There's no such thing as a free lunch.* = Be suspicious of people who give you something free, as they'll probably expect something in return.

c) *Put your money where your mouth is.* = Make your actions match your words.

d) *In for a penny, in for a pound.* = If you're going to take a risk, you might as well make it big.

e) *Watch the pennies, and the pounds take care of themselves.* = If you are careful with small amounts of money, you won't need to worry about money.

f) *The love of money is the root of all evil.* = People do evil things to get rich.

There are a lot of expressions where money is compared metaphorically to food: *bring home the bacon* (earn the money), *chicken feed* (small money), *breadwinner* (money earner); money is related metaphorically to clothes (see page 11): *tighten your belt, lose your shirt, live on a shoestring*, and money is related to the sea: *splash out, push the boat out* (see Student's Book page 32).

Listening & Vocabulary (SB page 28)

1

- Groupwork. Go through the questions with the class and ask them to think about their answers.
- Put them into small groups and ask them to discuss their answers. Encourage each group to appoint a spokesperson to report back to the class.

2 🌐 1.25

- Tell the students that they're going to listen to three people talking about their answers to the questions in Exercise 1. Go through the list of items and ask them to listen and identify who talks about each one.
- Play the recording. You may need to pause after each speaker to allow the students to note down the speaker's initial next to the relevant items.

| 1 Patti | 2 Lee | 3 Lee | 4 Patti | 5 Eric |
| 6 Eric | | | | |

🌐 **1.25** (I = Interviewer; P = Patti; E = Eric; L = Lee)

I: *It's impossible to have too much money – do you agree with that, Patti?*

P: *Yes. If you have dreams, money makes them possible. Personally, I can't imagine having too much money. I'm always broke. Anyway, if I ever felt I had too much money, I'd give it away to charity.*

I: *And Patti, would you prefer fame or fortune?*

P: *Being practical, I'd say fortune, but if I were single with no kids and no responsibilities, I'd go for fame.*

I: *Eric, were you given or did you earn pocket money as a child?*

E: *I was given two shillings a week by my father, but on condition that I behaved myself. If I didn't behave well, I didn't receive it. Parents were much stricter in those days.*

I: *And Eric, what was the first thing you saved up for and bought yourself?*

E: *A set of toy soldiers. Not the plastic ones you get nowadays, but little metal ones, beautifully hand-painted. It took me nearly a year to save up for them. If I'd known that they would become valuable antiques, I would've kept them. They'd probably be worth a fortune now.*

I: *Tell me, Lee, if you could buy yourself a skill or a talent, what would it be?*

L: *Well, there are lots of things I'd like to be better at, but if I had to choose one, it would have to be football – I'd like to be a brilliant football player!*

I: *And finally Lee, what can't money buy?*

L: *Happiness. I tend to think that once I have enough money to buy some new clothes or get a better car, then I'll be happy. But it never works out like that.*

---

3 🌐 1.26

- Go through the instructions with the class and make sure they understand that they first have to choose the correct alternative to make common money expressions, and then decide who gave each answer.
- Play the recording for the students to check their answers, then focus on the money expressions and make sure everyone understands them (see Language notes on page 28).
- Finally, put the students into pairs and ask them to discuss what their own answers to the two questions would be. Encourage them to report back to the class.

Question 1	Question 2
a) living – Eric	a) rainy; overdraft;
b) breadwinner;	out – Patti
loaded – Lee	b) blow – Lee
c) Patti	c) peanuts – Eric

1.26 (I = Interviewer; P = Patti; E = Eric; L = Lee)

Question 1

I: *Does it matter if a wife earns more than her husband? How would you handle it?*

P: *It wouldn't matter to me, but it might matter to my husband. It shouldn't matter, but human nature being what it is, it probably would.*

E: *I would feel like a failure if my wife earned more than I did. It's a man's job to earn a living, and a woman's place is in the home.*

L: *It wouldn't worry me. I know lots of couples where the woman is the main breadwinner. In fact, it would be really good to have a wife who was loaded.*

Question 2

I: *If you were given £1,000 to save, spend or invest, what would you do?*

P: *Um, the sensible thing to do would be to save it for a rainy day or pay off my overdraft, but I think I'd rather splash out on a family holiday. We need it.*

E: *I think I'd be tempted to buy a new computer. Mine's getting a bit slow. You can get them for peanuts these days you know, so with £1,000 I should be able to buy a really good one.*

L: *Well, I certainly wouldn't save or invest it – I'd probably blow it on a new music system and some massive speakers.*

Language notes

Vocabulary

- *Loaded* is a slang expression for *rich*.
- *To save something for a rainy day* is to save some money so that you can use it at a time when you don't have much.
- *Splash out* means to buy something expensive.
- *To blow money on* means to spend all your money on something.
- *Peanuts* is a slang expression for a small amount of money.

Grammar (SB page 29)

Unreal conditionals

1

- Focus the students' attention on the example in the margin. Read it out and ask them if the speaker used his or her credit card to buy the thing (no). Ask if he or she is still paying for it now (no). Point out that in this sentence you're using an unreal conditional to talk about the likely results of some action that in fact never happened.

- Ask the students to match the two halves of the other conditional sentences. Check answers with the class before putting the students into pairs to analyse the sentences and answer questions a) to d).

---

a) 5   b) 3   c) 1   d) 4   e) 2

a) Two. Yes.
b) Real situations: a, c
c) Hypothetical situations: b, d, e
d) *would*

Language note

Grammar: unreal conditionals
(See Student's Book page 134.)

2

- Focus the students' attention on the photo and the caption. Point out that the caption underneath the photo is the beginning of an unreal or hypothetical conditional sentence. The man is talking about what his life would be like if his circumstances were different.

- Ask the students to look at the table and read the real situations and the hypothetical ones. Ask them to say what happens to the verb form when you move from a real situation to a hypothetical one.

- Go through the list of *if*-clauses and ask the students which one isn't acceptable in modern English.

> The verb moves one step back into the past. (It backshifts.)
> Clause e) is considered incorrect. It should be *If I were you, …*

3

Groupwork. Go through the instructions and ask the students to discuss the questions in small groups. As they work, go round making sure they're using unreal conditionals correctly. Ask each group to appoint a spokesperson who can report back to the class on the decisions they make.

4

- Ask the students to work individually to complete the sentences so that they are true for them. Go round offering help with vocabulary where necessary.

- Put the students into pairs and tell them to discuss their sentences.

5 Grammar *Extra* 3, Part 2

Ask the students to turn to *Grammar Extra* 3, Part 2 on page 134 of the Student's Book. Here they'll find an explanation of the grammar they've been studying and further exercises to practise it.

> 2
> a) If you could speak English fluently, what would you do?
> b) If you had won the lottery, what would you have bought?
> c) If you were rich, where would you go?

d) If you could afford an expensive car, what would you choose?

e) If you hadn't arrived on time this morning, what would have happened?

f) If you were the president of your country, what would you change?

g) If it hadn't rained yesterday, what would you have done?

h) If you hadn't had to work last weekend, where would you have gone?

3

a) If I could speak English fluently, I'd become a teacher.

b) If I had won the lottery, I'd …

c) If I was/were rich, I'd go …

d) If I could afford an expensive car, I'd choose …

e) If I hadn't arrived on time this morning, I'd / I wouldn't …

f) If I was/were president of my country, I'd …

g) If it hadn't rained yesterday, I'd have …

h) If I hadn't had to work last weekend, I'd have gone …

Reading & Vocabulary (SB page 30)

1

- Make sure the students are familiar with eBay (see Language notes below.) Go through the questions with the class and make sure they understand them.

- Ask the students to read the article and compare their own answers with those given in the text. Ask them if they're surprised that anyone bid for Usher's life. Help them with any difficult vocabulary.

> a) A seperation.
> b) A house, car, kite-surfing gear, hammock, spa, motorbike, jet ski, BBQ, DVDs, job, PlayStation, friends.
> c) about £190,000 or €250,000.

Language notes

Vocabulary: eBay
An online auction and shopping website, where people and companies place their products and consumers bid for them or buy them outright. Founded in the US in 1995, eBay now operates in more than 30 countries around the world.

Vocabulary: hammock
A long piece of cloth tied at each end to a post or tree to form a bed.

Vocabulary: PlayStation
PlayStation is a video game produced by Sony.

2

- Ask the students to mark the sentences true or false, checking back in the article if necessary. Ask them to correct the false sentences. Then check answers with the class before moving on to the next stage.

- Focus the students' attention on the underlined words in the sentences. Ask them to look back at the article to find words or phrases with the same meaning.

> a) True.
> b) False. They were included.
> c) True.
> d) False. He has no idea.
> e) True.
> f) True.
> g) True.
> h) False. He sold it all together.
>
> a) … but Ian Usher <u>went through with it</u>.
> b) … included in <u>the deal</u>.
> c) He <u>walked off</u> with only …
> d) … what <u>the future holds</u> for him.
> e) … <u>at the root</u> of his decision …
> f) … attempt to <u>start afresh</u>.
> g) … he is <u>after</u> a book …
> h) … rather than <u>as a job lot</u>

3

- Give the students time to think of their answers before putting them into pairs to discuss the question.

- In a class feedback session, find out what was the most popular answer.

Listening (SB page 31)

1 🌐 1.27–1.29

Focus the students' attention on the photos, the list of items and the notes, and explain that they're going to hear these three people talking about their most treasured possessions. Play the recording and ask them to match the notes to the possessions.

> a) 2   b) 1   c) 3

> 🌐 **1.27**
>
> a) Chris
> *I suppose you'd call it a vintage camera now. It's a Zeiss Contaflex and I bought it in South Africa 50 years ago. It cost £50, which was a lot of money for me then, but it was still a lot less than I would have paid back home in England. So I was delighted – it was the best camera you could get at the time and it was a bargain. Unfortunately, I had to pay nearly $40 in tax at customs when I arrived back in the UK, so in the end it was less of a bargain. But I've certainly had my money's worth out of it. It's been everywhere with me and all our family photographs were taken on this camera. Last year, for my 70th birthday, my children bought me a wonderful, and very modern, digital camera. It takes much better photographs than my old Zeiss, but I can't use it I'm afraid. I'm too old-fashioned.*

b) Katie

I know it sounds a bit stupid, but this is the thing I would least like to lose. It's not because it's worth anything, although it is quite an expensive one because it's got GPS – you know, satellite navigation – on it too. But the main thing is that if I lost this, I'd lose the addresses and numbers of practically everybody I know. It contains the details of about three hundred people.

🎵 1.29

c) Heather

This is my most precious possession because it saved my life when I got caught in an avalanche in Johnson Pass in Alaska's Chugach Mountain Range. It had been snowing for four days, and the temperature rose that morning – perfect avalanche conditions. When the first person in our group of snowboarders leaped off the cornice, the rest of us decided to follow his tracks – no traversing and no hard turns, so as to not disturb the snow. When it was my turn, I made it down the first pitch safely and thought I was out of danger. But the person behind me started before I was at a safe distance and nervously made a hard right turn. I heard a loud crack, and then WHOMPH! The snow hit me really fast in the back of the neck. I pushed my neck-warmer over my face, which kept the snow out of my mouth and nose, allowing me to breathe as the avalanche swept me up. I began frantically swimming and tried to stay aware of which way was up. When the snow finally settled, I had managed to get part of my glove up through the surface. It took the others a few minutes to find me, but I knew they would. Luckily, my neck-warmer allowed me the extra air to wait out those few minutes.

2

- Put the students into pairs and ask them to use the notes to try to reconstruct the stories. Ask several pairs to tell their stories to the class.
- Play the recording again for the students to check.

a) Chris' camera is a vintage Zeiss Contraflex which he bought in South Africa 50 years ago. It was a bargain compared with the price in England, but in the end he had to pay nearly £40 in tax at the UK customs. All his family photographs were taken on this camera. For his 70th birthday, his children bought him a digital camera, but he prefers his old camera.

b) Katie's mobile phone is quite an expensive one because it's got GPS on it. But the main reason Katie doesn't want to lose it is that she'd lose the addresses and numbers of the people she knows. Her phone contains the details of about three hundred people.

c) Heather's neckwarmer saved her life when she got caught in an avalanche. She pushed the neckwarmer over her face, which kept the snow out of her mouth and her nose. This allowed her to breathe until she was rescued.

Ask the students to think of two possessions they would save if their house was on fire. What would they choose and why.

Speaking: anecdote (SB page 31)

For more information about how to set up, monitor and repeat Anecdotes, see page xx in the Introduction.

- Go through the instructions and the questions with the class. Give the students a minute or two to decide what they're going to talk about. Then ask them to look at the questions and think about their answers to them. Allow them to make notes of what they're going to say and how they're going to say it, but discourage them from writing a paragraph that they can simply read out. Go round, monitoring and giving help where necessary.
- Pairwork. Put the students in pairs and ask them to take turns to tell their partner about their most treasured possession. Encourage them to ask each other follow-up questions to get further information. Ask some pairs to report back to the class about what they found out.

Useful phrases (SB page 32)

1 🎵 1.30

- Focus the students' attention on the picture and ask them to describe the situation (a man is buying an engagement ring for his fiancée in a jeweller's shop; a female friend is helping him). Tell them that they're going to listen to conversations between the man and woman in the picture, and two shop assistants.
- Go through the questions with the class before you play the recording so that they know what information to listen out for.

a) Julia is John's fiancée.
b) Two or three hundred pounds.
c) £950.

🎵 1.30 (J = John; C = Cara; SA1 = Ship assistant 1; SA2 = Shop assistant 2)

J: *Thanks for doing this. I really don't know where to start.*

C: *Right, first you need to tell me what you're looking for. Do you have any ideas?*

J: *Well, diamonds are always good.*

C: *OK. And do you prefer gold or silver or platinum or white gold?*

J: *Whoa, hang on. Say that again.*

C: *Does Julia wear more gold or more silver?*

J: *Gold, I think.*

C: *And what's your budget?*

J: *My budget? I don't know. This is only the second time I've done this.*

C: What? You were engaged before?

J: Yes, it was a mistake. We were too young.

C: And did she keep the ring?

J: Yeah, but it wasn't worth much – I was really hard up at the time so I just got something cheap and cheerful.

C: Well, you have to be prepared to splash out this time. It's a once in a lifetime thing. Well, twice in a lifetime for you, I suppose.

J: OK – my budget is … two or three hundred pounds.

C: Hmm. OK, well, you may have to revise that figure.

J: What do you mean?

C: You'll see. Come on. Let's go.

…

SA1 Good morning, sir, madam. Are you looking for something special?

J: Yes, um, a diamond engagement ring, please.

SA1 I see – our diamond rings are over here, sir. If you'd like to browse and then ask me to show you anything you particularly like.

J: Thanks …. Have you seen the price?

C: I told you …

SA1 Is there something you'd like to see?

J: Um, they're lovely, but they're a little out of my price range.

SA1 Sorry we can't help you, sir. Goodbye.

…

J: Right, let's go somewhere less exclusive, shall we?

C: OK, but you're going to have to pay a bit more.

J: I'm not made of money!

C: No, I know, but this is a time when you have to push the boat out.

…

SA2 Can I help you with anything today?

J: Er, yes, I'm looking for a very simple engagement ring – perhaps one diamond?

SA2 And what are you looking to pay?

J: Well, around £500?

SA2 OK, this is £560– it's a six carat diamond.

J: It's small, isn't it?

C: You get what you pay for.

J: OK, I was hoping for something slightly more sparkly. How much is this one, for example?

SA2 That one's £1,400.

J: Right. I suppose, I was thinking of something a little less pricey.

SA2 What's your budget?

J: I suppose I could stretch to £1,000.

SA2 OK. This one costs £950.

J: What do you think?

C: I think it's lovely, and I think Julia would love it.

J: I should certainly hope so. This is definitely the last time I'm doing this. …

2

- Ask the students to match the pairs of useful phrases to their meanings.

- Check answers before playing the recording again and asking the students to number the phrases in the order in which they hear them.

> a) and b): 4   e) and f): 2
> c) and d): 1   g) and h): 3
> 1 a   2 c   3 b   4 e   5 g   6 d   7 f
> 8 h

3 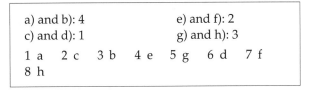 **1.31**

- Do the first part with the whole class and explain that in English you often use *a little* when you mean a lot. This sort of indirect expression is used for reasons of politeness and to soften a hard fact – in this case that the rings are much too expensive for John.

- Focus attention on the other statements where John uses less direct language and ask the students to put the words in order.

- Play the recording for them to check their answers.

> a) They're much too expensive.
>
> (See answers for 1 and 2 which are underlined in the audioscript below.)

> 🌐 **1.31**
> 1 I was hoping for <u>something slightly more sparkly</u>.
> 2 I suppose I was thinking of <u>something a little less pricey</u>.

4 🌐 **1.32**

- Do the first one as an example with the class and then ask the students to rewrite the remaining requests in less direct language.

- Play the recording for them to check their answers. Then play it again for the students to listen and repeat. When they've done this chorally, ask for individual repetition of the requests.

> (See answers in audioscript below.)

> 🌐 **1.32**
> a) I was looking for something a little less tight.
> b) I'd prefer slightly more comfortable trousers.
> c) I'm looking for something slightly more fashionable.
> d) I'd like something a little more formal.
> e) I was looking for a slightly smarter pair of shoes.
> f) I was wondering if you might have a slightly less colourful jacket.

5

Pairwork. Put the students into pairs and ask them to take turns to talk about the three items. Encourage them to ask follow-up questions and to report back to the class on what they found out.

Writing *Extra* (SB page 33)

Description

> ### Extra activity
> Ask the students to look at the photo of the woman. Get them to describe her and predict how she would spend a typical day.

1

Focus the students' attention on the text and photo and tell them it's an account of an imaginary day in this woman's life. Ask them to complete it using the linking words and expressions in the box. Tell them that they can only use each word or expression once, but some can go in more than one place. As they work, go round giving help where necessary and making sure everyone understands the meaning and function of the linking words.

1	when / as soon as	6	until
2	Then	7	During
3	while	8	As soon as / When
4	After	9	By the time
5	As / Just as	10	Just as / As

2

- Ask the students to decide where in the text to insert the adjectives. Remind them that they should appear in the same order as in the box.

- Ask them to compare their answers with a partner. Then check with the class. There may be more than one way to do this, so accept any other answers that make sense.

> *Possible answers:*
> breathtaking view; vigorous exercise; luxurious bath; extremely efficient secretary; huge parcel; a light lunch; close friend; latest film; absolutely starving

3

- Go through the instructions with the class, then ask the students to work individually to decide what details to add to the account. They will need plenty of time to think of ideas, and you could ask them to write out the whole text including their new details.

- When they've finished, put them into pairs and ask them to take turns to read their accounts to each other. As they work, go round monitoring and take note of any particularly good versions which could be repeated later for the class.

4

This writing exercise could be done for homework. Remind the students that they should use linking words to make their texts flow well and should include adverbs and adjectives to make them more interesting.

5

You could ask the students to swap their accounts in pairs or small groups and read each other's. Alternatively, the finished accounts could be displayed in the classroom for everyone to read. This would make it easier to take a class vote on which is the best.

> ### Further practice material
> **Need more writing practice?**
> → Workbook page 21
> • Writing a story from pictures.
>
> **Need more classroom practice activities?**
> → Photocopiable resource materials pages 157 to 159
> **Grammar:** *Reported speech*
> **Vocabulary:** *Money talks*
> **Communication:** *Life is a journey*
> → Top 10 activities pages xv to xx
>
> **Need progress tests?**
> → Test CD – *Test Unit 3*
>
> **Need more on important teaching concepts?**
> → Key concepts in *New Inside Out* pages xxii to xxxv
>
> **Need student self-study practice?**
> → CD-ROM – Unit 3: *Gold*
>
> **Need student CEF self-evaluation?**
> → CEF Checklists pages xxxvii to xliv
>
> **Need more information and more ideas?**
> → www.insideout.net

Review A *Teacher's notes*

These exercises act as a check of the grammar and vocabulary that the students have learnt in the first three units. Use them to find any problems that students are having, or anything that they haven't understood and which will need further work.

Grammar (SB page 34)

Remind the students of the grammar explanations they read and the exercises they did in the *Grammar Extra* on pages 132 to 135.

1

This exercise reviews verb structures from Unit 1. Remind the students to look for time expressions and other clues that will help them decide which verb form is needed.

1 've had	7 was expecting
2 've been working	8 had been
3 've met	9 were
4 have travelled	10 were
5 was	11 had to
6 were living	12 had never seen

2

This exercise reviews responses with *so* and *neither* from Unit 1. Remind the students that they need to look at whether the verb in the initial sentence is in the affirmative or the negative as this will determine whether the agreement response requires *so* or *neither*. Check answers with the class before putting the students into pairs to compare their own responses to the questions.

a) 2   b) 6   c) 5   d) 4   e) 1   f) 3

a) Neither am I. / I am
b) So can I. / I can't.
c) So did I. / I didn't.
d) Neither have I. / I have.
e) So have I. / I haven't.
f) So would I. / I wouldn't.

Cultural note

James Bond /dʒeɪmz bɒnd/
James Bond is a fictional British spy, codenamed 007. The first Bond novel *Casino Royale* was written by Ian Fleming in 1953. The first Bond film *Dr No* was shown in 1962. Bond has been played by six actors including Sean Connery; Roger Moore, Pierce Brosnan and Daniel Craig.

3

This exercise reviews question tags from Unit 1. Remind the students that positive statements take negative question tags and vice versa. Check answers before asking the students to give their own true responses to the questions.

a) isn't (Yes, it is. / No, it isn't.)
b) don't (Yes, I do. / No, I don't.)
c) aren't (Yes, I am. / No, I'm not.)
d) do (Yes, I do. / No, I don't.)
e) have (Yes, I have. / No, I haven't.)
f) shall (*Possible answers:* Yes, OK. / No, I can't.)

4

This exercise reviews indirect questions from Unit 1.

a) Could you tell me what time it is?
b) Do you know where the station is?
c) Do you think it's going to rain today?
d) Do you know whether I can buy a sandwich here?
e) Where do you think the best place to have a coffee is?

5

This exercise reviews verb patterns with gerunds and infinitives with *to* from Unit 2.

1 helping	6 to lend
2 to go	7 to buy
3 to have	8 lending
4 to spend	9 to pay
5 working	

6

This exercise reviews reported speech from Unit 3. Remind students that they may need to make changes to tenses, word order, pronouns and time expressions when changing direct speech to reported speech.

a) he had an idea to make some money.
b) he'd been thinking about it for a long time.
c) he wanted to open a shop.
d) he could borrow some money.
e) he would pay me back within five years.

7

This exercise reviews conditional sentences from Unit 3.

a) was/were; 'd buy
b) borrow; 'll be
c) won; wouldn't keep; 'd give
d) didn't have; wouldn't buy
e) had known; wouldn't have married
f) were; 'd get

Vocabulary (SB page 35)

1

This exercise reviews adjective and noun collocations from Unit 1.

a) 6   b) 2   c) 5   d) 3   e) 4   f) 1

2

This exercise reviews clothing vocabulary from Unit 1.

a) collar   b) button   c) sleeve   d) cuff
e) belt   f) buckle   g) zip   h) hem

3

This exercise reviews verbs that can take the prefix
re- from Unit 1.

a) rearrange   b) reconsider   c) reword
d) reconstruct   e) relocate

4

This exercise reviews vocabulary from Unit 2.

a) rusty   d) dotes on
b) aptitude   e) in touch with
c) pen friend   f) barely speaking

5

This exercise reviews collocations with *have, make* and
take from Unit 3.

1 having   2 making   3 making   4 take
5 have   6 taking   7 have   8 took
9 is making

6

This exercise reviews money expressions from Unit 3.

a) loaded   b) rainy   c) breadwinner
d) peanuts   e) blown

Pronunciation (SB page 35)

1

Explain to the students that the boxes show the syllables
of a word and the large boxes indicate the stressed
syllables. Here they're being asked to classify words
according to how many syllables they have and where
the main stress falls. Encourage them to say each word
aloud to get a feeling for what sounds right.

2 ⊕ 1.33

Ask the students to underline the stressed syllables in
the words in the table. Then play the recording for them
to check their answers. Play it a second time for them to
listen and repeat.

1 and 2		
A: □□□	**B:** □□□	**C:** □□□□
ap<u>pear</u>ance	<u>busi</u>nessman	ad<u>van</u>tages
de<u>ci</u>sion	<u>Eve</u>rything	em<u>bar</u>rassing
de<u>sign</u>er	<u>Me</u>morable	re<u>la</u>tionship
im<u>pres</u>sion	<u>tal</u>ented	spec<u>ta</u>cular

4 Challenge *Overview*

Section & Aims	What the students are doing
Reading & Vocabulary SB page 36 Reading for detail Word formation: *self-* and *able/ible*	Speculating about the activities of a polar explorer. Matching missing sentences to the appropriate places in an article. Marking statements true or false. Studying the prefix *self-* and suffixes *able/ible*.
Listening & Vocabulary SB page 38 Listening for detail Collocations	Identifying true and false facts about polar bears. Answering questions about an account of meeting a polar bear. Identifying tenses used in the story. Completing collocations from the story.
Grammar SB page 39 Narrative tenses	Matching sentence endings with meanings and naming tenses. Choosing the correct endings to sentences.
Speaking: anecdote SB page 39 Fluency practice	Talking about doing something challenging.
Reading SB page 40 Reading for gist	Matching headings to sections of an article. Choosing correct collocations and answering the questions. Talking about raising money for good causes.
Grammar SB page 41 Future continuous and future perfect	Completing a table with future forms from the reading text. Writing sentences in the future continuous and in the future perfect. Making questions using *How many ...?* and *How much ...?*
Listening & Vocabulary SB page 41 Listening for detail	Discussing excuses for not doing exercise. Listening to people talking about why they don't exercise. Finding out about classmates' exercise habits.
Reading SB page 42 Reading for detail	Talking about giving up smoking. Reading an article and identifying the writer's views.
Vocabulary SB page 43 Phrasal verbs	Reading information and advice about phrasal verbs. Replacing phrases with phrasal verbs in sentences. Completing sentences by putting object pronouns in the correct position.
Speaking SB page 43 Fluency practice	Talking about health using phrasal verbs.
Useful phrases & Pronunciation SB page 44 Common ailments; showing sympathy; recommendations	Listening to conversations and matching them to ailments. Completing conversations with advice. Identifying whether speakers are sympathetic or unsympathetic, and practising the stress and intonation of the useful phrases. Describing problems, reacting to them and giving advice.
Vocabulary *Extra* SB page 45 Phrasal verbs	Studying phrasal verbs and writing definitions for them. Completing phrasal verbs with verbs and particles. Matching phrasal verbs with their definition. Replacing words and phrases with phrasal verbs in sentences.
Writing WB page 27	Writing an article.

Warm up

Ask the students to say what they understand by the word *challenge*. What kinds of things do they think are challenging? Do they see challenge simply in terms of things like extreme sports or do they think the word can be applied to everyday events and personal relationships?

Reading & Vocabulary (SB page 36)

1

- Focus attention on the photo and ask the students what sort of a person they think Ben Saunders is and what words they might expect people to use to describe him. Go through the questions with the class and then ask them to discuss them in pairs.

- Ask the class for their ideas before asking the students to read the article on page 37. Check answers and find out how accurate their guesses were. Get their reactions to the text. Would any of them think about doing something like this?

> a) Polar/Mountain expeditions.
> b) Freezing cold; getting lost; running out of food; getting ill; getting attacked; getting injured, etc.
> c) To break a record. To test some equipment. To compete in a race.

Cultural notes

Richard Branson /ˈrɪtʃəd ˈbrænsən/ (born 1950)
A British businessman who started up Virgin Records when he was 20 years old. In 1984, the Virgin brand grew when he formed Virgin Atlantic Airways.

Ellen MacArthur /ˈelən məˈkɑːθə/ (born 1976)
Ellen MacArthur is a solo long-distance yachtswoman who, on 7th February 2005, broke the world record for the fastest solo circumnavigation of the globe.

2

Go through the sentences with the class and make sure everyone understands them. Explain that these sentences have been removed from the article on page 37. Ask the students to match them to the appropriate places in the article. Check answers with the class.

3

- Ask the students to read the sentences and decide if they are true or false.

- Check answers before asking the students to identify the words and phrases in the article that have the same meaning as those underlined in the sentences.

> a) False: imminent return
> b) False: obscenely rich
> c) True: shambolic
> d) True: media interest
> e) False: book deal
> f) True: genuine belief
> g) True: doable / feasible / possible
> h) False: particularly gifted

4

- Go through the instructions and read out the information in the margin to the class. Ask them to complete the sentences using words from the margin.

- Check answers before asking the students to say whether any of the sentences are true for them.

> a) self-conscious   d) reasonable
> b) self-employed   e) enjoyable
> c) self-esteem   f) unbearable

Language notes

Vocabulary: word formation

- The prefix *self-* relates to yourself. Other examples include: *self-indulgent, self-righteous, self-assured, self-confessed* and *self-destructive*. It's usually paired with words of English or Latin origin. The prefix *auto-* also relates to yourself, but pairs with other words, usually of Greek origin, to make new words. In many cases the words are not hyphenated, e.g. *autograph, autobiography, autonomy*, etc.

- The suffixes *-able* and *-ible* can be used with adjectives to indicate something that can be done. *-able* is more common than *-ible*, but there's no magic formula for deciding which suffix to use.

5

- Ask the students to use their dictionaries to look up the words which take the prefix *self-*. They should tick the ones they already know or can understand easily.

- Ask them to choose three more to learn and to write example sentences for these. As they work, go round monitoring and helping where necessary.

Listening & Vocabulary (SB page 38)

1 🌐 **1.35**

- Focus attention on the photo of the polar bear. Encourage the students to suggest words that could be used to describe it.

- Put the students into pairs and ask them to read the list of statements about polar bears and decide whether or not they think they are true.

- Play the recording and ask them to check their answers according to what Ben Saunders says. Note that this is a recording of an authentic text and that authentic English is sometimes ungrammatical. For example, the speaker says 'swang' rather than 'swung'. Although the speaker says that the polar bears have been hibernating, it's only the breeding females that stay inside a den in winter, and they don't hibernate in the true sense of the word because they don't sleep, and their body temperature doesn't fall.

> a) True.
> b) False. (They normally eat seals.)
> c) True.
> d) False. (You have to make yourself look as big as possible.)
> e) True.

> 🌐 **1.35**
>
> *It was day two of my first ever North Pole expedition back in 2001. I was twenty-three years old. There were two people on this expedition: me and a guy called Pen Hadow, who was very experienced, so he was really teaching me how to survive in the Arctic, and it was the morning of day two. We'd just taken down our tent and started skiing. Pen was in front, navigating, and I was following his tracks, dragging my sledge and I started getting a very strange feeling that something was wrong and I wasn't sure to start with. It felt like I'd forgotten something important. I couldn't quite figure out what wasn't right and I stopped and turned around and looked behind me. Looked back along our tracks and saw a polar bear, walking towards us.*
>
> *Now, early in the spring, at the very start of the expedition, and this was very early March, 2001, polar bears have been hibernating through the winter so they are hungry. They've just woken up, they are looking for breakfast and we are wearing black clothing. We probably look a bit like seals, which is what bears normally eat. Bears are also the largest land-based carnivore in the world, so they are quite big, scary predators.*

> *And I turned around and shouted at Pen, who was in front. Luckily he heard me, and our bear drill swang into action. Now we'd practised what to do once in the car park of a café just before we left the UK, and the theory is that we had to stay where we were and try and convince the polar bear that we were bigger and scarier than, than it was.*
>
> *As I have said, they are big creatures – the heaviest adult male ever recorded was, I think, just over a thousand kilos, so a tonne. They can move at nearly fifty kilometres per hour if they want to. Now our top speed, pulling sledges, was about three kilometres per hour, so we knew there was no way we could outrun the bear, so we had to stay where we were, try and look big, and scare it away.*
>
> *Pen was in charge of the gun. We had a shotgun that we'd bought in Russia. That was his job. My job was to look big and to take off my skis, hold the skis in the air, make lots of noise, try and frighten away the bear. And Pen loaded the gun with two cartridges. There are two barrels in the gun; closed the barrels, pulled the triggers – there are two triggers, one for each barrel of the gun – click, click, and he said, 'The gun's jammed.' And I looked at him. He reloaded the gun – two more cartridges, pulled the triggers, click, click. He said, 'The gun's still jammed,' and everything went into slow motion.*

2

Pairwork. Ask the students to discuss the questions based on what they can remember. Then play the recording again for them to check their answers.

> a) Two. Pen Hadow was navigating.
> b) He had a strange feeling that something was wrong. He thought he'd forgotten something important.
> c) March.
> d) In a café car park in the UK.
> e) They intended to stay where they were and convince the polar bear that they were bigger and scarier than it was.
> f) It didn't go off.

3 🌐 **1.36**

Pairwork. Ask the students to discuss what they think happened next. Let them pool their ideas as a class and take a vote before playing the recording for them to find out what really happened.

> a) He continued pulling the trigger. He walked towards the polar bear.
> b) Nothing.
> c) It turned around and walked off.

🔊 1.36

The bear is walking towards us. Pen is reloading the gun again with a fifth and sixth cartridge. We had twelve cartridges to last eight weeks, so Pen is now halfway through our supply of ammunition. He pulls the first trigger, click, and then he walks around his sledge towards the bear, and I remember thinking, 'Wow, Pen's gone mad, completely. He's going to get eaten. What do I do?'

And I couldn't – I felt quite calm and I couldn't quite think what to do. I thought maybe I could throw a ski at it or try and stab it with a ski pole or something, and then the bear stopped. Pen stopped. Bang. The gun, the gun goes off in the air. Big cloud of smoke, and I think it surprised Pen and me more than it surprised the bear. The bear looked up, looked down, turned around and walked off, and Pen turned round and said, 'Quick, get the camera and take a photograph,' and that was when suddenly I felt really scared and nervous. I couldn't even undo the zip on the sledge.

That was the morning of the second day of this expedition. We were out there for two months – fifty-nine days, but we never saw another bear that close.

One of the surprising things I've seen and one of the ways the Arctic is changing – certainly in my experience – is that there is less and less evidence of polar bears being there at all. In 2001 we saw many, many sets, dozens of sets of polar bear footprints – of tracks in the snow in that expedition which lasted two months. Three years later I went back to exactly the same point – I followed the same route and I saw three or four sets, where three years before we had seen thirty or forty sets. So there is a lot less evidence of bears being around, which is tragic.

4

Play the recording again and ask the students to read the extracts as they listen and note the tenses used. Discuss as a class why these tenses are used.

The bear **is walking** towards us. Pen **is reloading** the gun … so Pen **is** now half way through our supply of ammunition. He **pulls** the first trigger … he **walks** around his sledge … I **remember** thinking, 'Wow, Pen's gone mad … He's going to get eaten. What **do I do**?'

Present simple and continuous – for dramatic effect (the story sounds more vivid/immediate).

5

- Ask the students to complete the collocations from memory, if they can.

- Ask them to turn to page 147 to check their answers. Get them to choose the three most useful expressions and to write their own example sentences.

---

a) figure   b) action   c) way   d) charge
e) loaded   f) jammed   g) slow   h) undo

Grammar (SB page 39)
Narrative tenses

1

- Focus the students' attention on the information in the margin. Read out the example sentences or get a student to read them. Explain that these tenses are all commonly used to tell stories or describe past events.

- Read out the sentence beginning in the exercise and focus the students' attention on the possible endings. Point out that each ending gives the sentence a slightly different meaning. Ask them to match the endings to their meanings.

- Ask the students to name the tenses and to write the negative and question forms. Check answers before moving on to the next stage.

- Ask the students to make their own sentences about different situations when they got home yesterday, using each of the tenses. Go round, giving help where necessary. Then put the students into pairs and ask them to tell each other their sentences.

---

a) 2   b) 3   c) 1   d) 4

a) Past simple: He didn't make dinner. Did he make dinner?
b) Past continuous: He wasn't making dinner. Was he making dinner?
c) Past perfect simple: He hadn't made dinner. Had he made dinner?
d) Past perfect continuous: He hadn't been making dinner. Had he been making dinner?

Language note

Grammar: narrative tenses
(See Student's Book page 134.)

2

Pairwork. Focus the students' attention on the sentence beginnings. Ask them to discuss the possible endings and choose the one that best fits the facts of the story.

---

a) 1   b) 1   c) 2   d) 1   e) 2

---

3 Grammar *Extra* 4, Part 1

Ask the students to turn to *Grammar Extra* 4, Part 1 on page 134 of the Student's Book. Here they'll find an explanation of the grammar they've been studying and a further exercise to practise it.

1
1 was climbing	9 ate
2 had	10 had never experienced
3 set off	11 arrived
4 were following	12 had travelled
5 had taken	13 had been keeping
6 had advised	14 published
7 was	15 had faced
8 wore	

Speaking: anecdote (SB page 39)

For more information about how to set up, monitor and repeat Anecdotes, see page xx in the Introduction.

1

Pairwork. Focus the students' attention on the list of challenges and make sure they understand all of them. Ask them to discuss in pairs which ones they think are most daunting (difficult or frightening) and which, if any, they've had to face. Encourage them to report back to the class on what they discussed.

2

- Go through the instructions and the questions with the class. Give the students a minute or two to decide what they're going to talk about. Then ask them to look at the questions and think about their answers to them. Allow them to make notes of what they're going to say and how they're going to say it, but discourage them from writing a paragraph that they can simply read out. Go round, monitoring and giving help where necessary.
- Pairwork. Put the students in pairs (if possible, not with the same people they worked with in Exercise 1) and ask them to take turns to tell their partner about a time when they did something challenging. Encourage them to ask each other follow-up questions to get further information. Then ask some pairs to report back to the class about what they found out.

Reading (SB page 40)

1

- Focus the students' attention on the photo and ask them what they think the text will be about (a woman doing a sponsored walk to raise money for charity).
- Ask them to read the text and match the headings to the sections.

a) MoonWalk?	d) Clothing
b) Fitness and training	e) The mind
c) Nutrition	

Cultural note

Hyde Park /haɪd pɑːk/, **London**
Hyde Park is one of the largest parks in central London and is situated between Knightsbridge and Marble Arch. Famous landmarks within the park include Speaker's Corner, and the Serpentine (lake).

2

- Encourage the students to try to identify the correct collocations without looking back at the text.
- When they've finished, ask them to look back at the text to check their answers. Explain any unknown vocabulary. Then ask them to answer the questions.

- Put the students into pairs and ask them to discuss whether they've ever done anything to raise money for a good cause, or if they know anybody else who has. Encourage them to report back to the class.

a) raise	b) fitness	c) diet	d) regular
e) pair	f) mind		

a) Breast cancer.
b) Going to the gym four times a week.
c) With protein drinks and vitamins.
d) To maintain blood sugar levels.
e) To get the right support for her feet and ankles.
f) That she's doing it for a very good cause.

Grammar (SB page 41)

Future continuous and future perfect

1

- Focus the students' attention on the example sentences in the margin. Then get them to look at the headings of the table in Exercise 1 and the example in the first column. Ask them to look back at the article on page 40 and find more examples of the future continuous and the future perfect to add to the table. As they do this, go round offering help and making sure that they're putting their sentences in the correct columns.
- When you've checked answers with the class, get them to answer questions a) and b).

Things *she'll* be doing to prepare for the MoonWalk	Things *she'll* be doing during the MoonWalk	Something *she'll* have done when she's completed the MoonWalk
She'll be working on her stamina and general fitness levels. She'll be going to the gym. She'll be supplementing her diet. She'll be investing in a good pair of trainers.	She'll be eating energy bars, bananas and other fruit snacks. She'll be drinking plenty of water. She'll be wearing a hat and a decorated bra.	She'll have contributed a sum of money to a good cause.

a) Future continuous
b) Future perfect

Language note

Grammar: future continuous and perfect
(See Student's Book page 141.)

2

Go through the instructions with the class. Then ask the students to work individually to complete the sentences. Check answers by getting several students to read out their sentences.

3

- Go through the example with the class, then ask the students to work individually to write sentences using the prompts. Go round making sure that everyone is forming the future perfect correctly. Then check answers by getting several students to read their sentences to the class.

- Look at the example question under the prompts with the class and ask them for a few more examples of questions they could ask with *How many ...?* and *How much ...?* With weaker classes, get the students to write all the questions and then check that they've formed them correctly.

- Put the students into pairs and ask them to take turns asking and answering questions about the things they'll have done by the end of today.

> a) By the end of the day how much money will you have spent?
> b) ... how many text messages will you have sent?
> c) ... how many people will you have spoken to?
> d) ... how many shops will you have been into?
> e) ... how much exercise will you have done?
> f) ... how many kilometres will you have driven?
> f) ... how much chocolate will you have eaten?
> g) ... how much time will you have spent online?
> h) ... how many times will you have said *sorry*?

4 Grammar *Extra* 4, Part 2

Ask the students to turn to *Grammar Extra* 4, Part 2 on page 134 of the Student's Book. Here they'll find an explanation of the grammar they've been studying and a further exercise to practise it.

> 2 (Students' own answers.)

Listening & Vocabulary (SB page 41)

1

- Focus the students' attention on the list of reasons people give for not doing exercise. Explain any difficult vocabulary (e.g. *lycra* is the stretchy fabric used to make sports and fitness clothing).

- Put the students into pairs and ask them to discuss the questions. Encourage them to report back to the class on their discussion and find out whether the class as a whole is keen on doing exercise or not.

2 🕐 1.37–1.40

- Focus attention on the photos and ask the class to speculate on whether these people enjoy doing exercise.

- Tell the students that they're going to listen to the four people in the photos answering the questions in Exercise 1. Ask them to listen and make notes of the reasons they give for not doing exercise.

> Steve – 5: he's too tired after work.
> Maria – 4: bad weather, which means she can't go running.
> Sam – 8: she doesn't have time because she's got three kids under five.
> Tim – 7: nothing usually. He only doesn't do exercise, if he's pulled a muscle or something, and it hurts.

> 🕐 1.37 (I = Interviewer; S = Steve)
>
> I: *A recent survey by the British heart foundation has revealed that only 38% of us would be motivated to do more exercise if our life depended on it. In other words, six out of ten of us would rather die than exercise!*
>
> *We went out on the streets of London to find out how much exercise people are really doing, and if they're not doing it, what exactly is stopping them?*
> *...*
> *How much exercise do you do?*
>
> S: *Oh dear, not as much as I should. I used to have an expensive gym membership, but I only went twice so I cancelled it. I'm not very sporty so I don't do any team sports like football or anything. I do love football, but strictly as a spectator, not as a participant. I have noticed that it's harder to keep the weight off than when I was younger though, so I've started cycling into work. That's about forty minutes of exercise every day. Better than nothing.*
>
> I: *What stops you?*
>
> S: *I'm just so tired after work – I get home, sit on the sofa and do nothing.*
>
> 🕐 1.38 (I = Interviewer; M = Maria)
>
> I: *How much exercise do you do?*
>
> M: *I'm revising for exams at the moment so I go running quite a lot, just to get some fresh air. There's nothing worse than being stuck inside all day. I think it helps if you have someone to go with – it's a quite hard to motivate yourself, but if you arrange to go running with a friend, you feel you can't let them down, and that forces you to go.*
>
> I: *What stops you?*
>
> M: *The weather! If it's raining, or really cold, I can usually talk myself out of it.*

I: *How much exercise do you do?*

S: *I run up the stairs, and that's it. Well, at the weekends I do a few hours of housework – I should think that burns off a few calories. I hope so anyway, because when I've finished I sit down with a cup of tea and a packet of biscuits. I certainly don't go to the gym if that's what you mean. Can you imagine me in lycra? Ha ha.*

I: *Is that what stops you going to the gym?*

S: *Er, not really. It's finding time to fit it in around everything else I have to do. I've got three kids under five, so there's no way I have time to go to the gym or anything like that. But I reckon I run a marathon every day just running around after the children!*

1.40 (I = Interviewer; T = Tim)

I: *How much exercise do you do?*

T: *I go swimming and I work out at the gym. I try to do some kind of aerobic exercise for about thirty minutes three times a week, and I do weights a couple of times a week. At the weekends I often go for a brisk walk in the country, and my girlfriend's trying to get me to go to salsa classes – she says it's a really good workout.*

I: *What stops you?*

T: *Nothing really – unless I've pulled a muscle or something, and it hurts. I love it. I sit at a desk all day long, and if I don't do some physical exercise at least three or four times a week, I feel really out of shape. But it isn't just about weight loss – exercise gives me a general feeling of wellbeing.*

3

- Pairwork. Ask the students to turn to page 128 and follow the instructions. As they work, go round giving extra help where needed. Allow them to consult the recordings on page 147, if necessary.

- Check answers with the class before asking the students to mingle and find out who does or has done the activities.

> burns off calories by cycling to work
> does team sports
> feels out of shape
> gets plenty of fresh air
> goes running
> goes for a brisk walk at the weekend
> has cancelled a gym membership
> is stuck inside all day
> wears lycra gear at the gym
> works out at the gym

Reading (SB page 42)

1

- Find out how many of the class smoke. If so, ask them if they've ever tried to give it up and, how difficult they found it. Is there anyone who would like to give up, but is unable to?

- Go through the items with the class and write their ideas on the board.

> *Possible answers:*
> a) It's bad for your health. It's expensive. It makes your breath/clothes smell terrible.
> b) It's addictive. It's calming. It's sociable.
> c) Nicotine replacement patches / chewing gum / hypnosis.

2

- Ask the students to read the article and note down the reasons the writer gives for wanting to give up smoking, the reason why he smokes and the method he has used to try to give up.

- Check their answers and answer any questions about the text. Then have a class discussion on whether they think the writer is likely to give up smoking and to give reasons for their opinions.

- Widen the discussion on smoking if the students are interested in the topic.

> a) He's getting old. Health reasons. He's hooked.
> b) It's never let him down, never abandoned him. It clears his head, helps him to think. It helps start conversations, drives away annoying people. It helps celebrate victories, get over losses, comfort the comfortless. It chases away the mosquitoes.
> c) He's been to see a man (Shubentsov), who uses healing energy.
>
> Probably not. He isn't serious about giving up.

Vocabulary (SB page 43)

Phrasal verbs

1

- Remind the students that phrasal verbs are verbs that consist of more than one word, often a verb + one or two particles. They are sometimes known as multi-word verbs.

- Put students in pairs to discuss the questions. Then check their answers as a class.

- Ask the students to underline all the phrasal verbs in the article on page 42 and discuss with their partner what type of phrasal verbs they are.

a) *pick a book up* is literal, i.e. you understand the meaning from the verb and particle.
pick a language up is idiomatic, i.e. you don't necessarily understand the meaning from the verb and particle. Here *pick* means 'to learn'.
b) *I gave in* is intransitive. It doesn't take an object. The meaning (to stop arguing or competing) is idiomatic.
I gave my homework in is transitive. The object is 'homework'. The meaning is literal.
c) ~~I looked up it~~ is not possible. When a phrasal verb is separable (i.e. the particle is an adverb) and the object is a pronoun, the pronoun always goes between the verb and the particle.
d) ~~I looked the matter into~~ and ~~I looked it into~~ are not possible. When a phrasal verb is not separable (i.e. the particle is a preposition) the object always comes after the particle.

Phrasal verbs from the article:
hop down from – literal – intransitive – not separable
pick sth up – literal – transitive – separable
pick sth up – idiomatic (= to learn) – transitive – separable
let sb down – idiomatic (= to make sb disappointed) – transitive – separable
drive sb away – idiomatic (= make sb stop wanting to be with you) – transitive – separable
get over sth – idiomatic (= recover from) – transitive – not separable
chase sth away – literal – transitive – separable
give up – idiomatic (= quit) – intransitive (can be transitive)
light up – idiomatic (= light a cigarette) – intransitive with this specific meaning
call sb back – literal – transitive – separable
put sth down – literal – transitive – separable

Language notes

Vocabulary: phrasal verbs
- Like other words, each phrasal verb can have several different meanings. For example: *go off* = decompose; *go off* = explode, etc.
- Sometimes the meaning is literal and you can guess it from the verb and the particle. For example *go off* = leave; *take off* = remove, etc.
- Mostly, the meaning is abstract, and you can only guess it from the context. For example, *go off* = take place/happen; *take off* = start flying, etc.
- When your students encounter a phrasal verb in a text, tell them to try to guess the meaning from the context. This will help if they then look it up in a dictionary. A good dictionary will tell you if the verb needs an object (transitive) or doesn't (intransitive). These are often marked [I] and [T].

- There are two types of transitive phrasal verbs, separable and non-separable.
  In separable phrasal verbs the object can separate the phrasal verb or come after it:
  ***Throw** the banana skin **away**. / **Throw away** the banana skin.*
  But if the object is a pronoun, it must separate the phrasal verb:
  ***Throw** it **away**.*
  In non-separable phrasal verbs the object always comes after it:
  *Could you **deal with** the problem? / Could you **deal with** it?*
- If a phrasal verb has two particles (*get on with*), the object always comes after it:
  *My husband **gets on with** my parents. / He **gets on with** them.*

2
- Ask students to use a phrasal verb from the article to replace the underlined phrases in the sentences.

> a) he picked them up
> b) he picked it up
> c) they've never let him down
> d) it helps you get over them
> e) it says call me back

3
- Ask the students to look at the sentences and decide where the object pronoun, given in brackets, should go in each one. Check answers with the class, getting the students to say the sentences aloud so that they get a feel for what sounds right.
- Have a class discussion of whether any of the sentences are true for any of the students.

> a) It really put <u>me</u> off.
> b) … I always seem to come down with <u>it</u>.
> c) … it usually takes me ages to shake <u>it</u> off.
> d) It's a pity I don't take after <u>him</u>.
> e) I just don't feel up to <u>it</u>.
> f) … my kids wear <u>me</u> out.

Speaking (SB page 43)

1

Ask the students to find and underline all the phrasal verbs in the statements. Encourage them to use dictionaries to look up the meaning of any that they don't know.

> a) keep up with sth/sb; come out
> b) put sth off
> c) do without sth
> d) come up with sth
> e) cut down on sth
> f) take sth up; take up sth

2

- Put the students into groups and ask them to discuss which of the statements they relate to most.
- Encourage them to report back to the class on their discussion.

Useful phrases & Pronunciation

(SB page 44)

1

- Ask the students to look at the illustrations and go through the list of ailments in the box, making sure everyone understands them. Then ask the students to read the six conversations and match an ailment to each one.
- When you've checked their answers, give help with any difficult vocabulary or expressions (e.g. *you look like death warmed up* is a slang expression for 'you look terrible'; *I didn't sleep a wink* means 'I didn't sleep at all'; *it's killing me* means 'it's really painful').

a) difficulty sleeping	d) sunburn
b) a twisted ankle	e) a splitting headache
c) a sore throat	f) hay fever

2 🔘 1.41

- Pairwork. Point out that the conversations all end where one of the speakers is about to give some advice. Ask the students to think about what advice they'd give in the circumstances and to note this down. As they work, go round monitoring, encouraging and giving help where needed.
- Play the recording for the students to compare their advice with the original conversations. Then find out how close the students' advice was to the original.

(See answers underlined in the audio script below.)

🔘 1.41

a)
A: *Oh dear – you look like death warmed up. Late night last night?*
B: *No, not really. But I couldn't sleep. I don't think I slept a wink and now I feel exhausted.*
A: *Oh, it's horrible when that happens. <u>You should try listening to soft music. That usually works for me.</u>*

b)
C: *Oh dear! What's happened?*
D: *I've done something to my ankle. It's killing me!*
C: *Oh dear, you poor thing! It looks really swollen.*
D: *I know, and it's getting worse.*
C: *<u>If you ask me, you need to lie down and put some ice on it.</u>*

c)
E: *Ugh! I can't swallow anything.*
F: *Oh yes. I know what you mean. I was the same last week. I could only eat ice cream!*
E: *So, what did you do?*
F: *<u>Well, you could try this. Chop up some ginger and put it in boiling water with some honey and lemon. Drink it as hot as you can.</u>*
E: *Does it work?*
F: *Well, it makes you feel better, but it's probably a good idea to take some aspirin too.*

d)
G: *Don't touch my back!*
H: *Why? What's up?*
G: *I wanted to get a tan quickly so I didn't bother to put any sunblock on.*
H: *Oh well, it serves you right then, doesn't it?*
G: *It really stings.*
H: *<u>Have you tried putting some cream on it?</u>*
G: *I can't reach my back.*
H: *OK, take your shirt off. I'll do it for you.*

e)
I: *When did it start?*
J: *After I'd been playing computer games for a few hours. I feel as if my head's going to explode!*
I: *Oh well, you've only got yourself to blame, haven't you?*
J: *I know, I know. But I've taken aspirin, and it hasn't worked.*
I: *<u>Well, you could try putting your hands over your eyes and leaving them there for about five minutes. That usually works for me.</u>*

f)
K: *Have you got a cold?*
L: *No, I'm all right – I always get a streaming nose and red eyes at this time of the year.*
K: *That must be awful. <u>If I were you, I'd try acupuncture.</u> My sister used to suffer terribly, but then she had three sessions of acupuncture, and that was it.*
L: *Really? Can you find out who she saw?*

3 🔘 1.42

- Ask the students to look at the highlighted expressions in the conversations and listen to the recording. Tell them to make a note of whether they think the speaker sounds sympathetic or unsympathetic. Point out that stress and intonation can affect the impression given by a speaker.
- Put the students into pairs and ask them to practise saying the useful phrases to each other, using the same stress and intonation as the recording.

a) Sympathetic.	d) Unsympathetic.
b) Sympathetic.	e) Unsympathetic.
c) Sympathetic.	f) Sympathetic.

Language note

Pronunciation: stress and intonation
Note how the speaker's tone is softer and the tonal range more varied when being sympathetic, whereas it's harder and more monotonous when being unsympathetic.

4

Put the students into pairs and tell them who will be Student A and who will be Student B. Ask them to turn to their respective pages and follow the instructions. As they do the exercise, go round monitoring and giving help. Take note of any errors which may need particular attention later, and also any examples of good language use which you can praise.

Vocabulary *Extra* (SB page 45)

Phrasal verbs

1

- Pairwork. Ask the students to look at the diagrams. Point out that the words in the centre can be combined with the particles around the outside to form phrasal verbs.
- Ask them to follow the instructions. Go round as they work, offering help and encouragement. Check answers with the class.

2

Ask the students to work individually to complete the questions. Check answers with the class, then put the students into pairs to ask and answer the questions.

a) get   b) take   c) get   d) take   e) get
f) get

3

Focus the students' attention on the 'meaning menus' (A–F). Ask them to read each one and decide which phrasal verb is being defined in each case. Go through the example with the class first, demonstrating that *come up* has all eleven meanings in menu A. Use example sentences if the students need convincing.

A) come up   B) get on   C) go on
D) put up   E) set off   F) take on

4

Ask the students to replace the underlined phrases with the correct phrasal verbs. As they work, go round giving extra help where needed.

a) going on   b) set off   c) come up
d) get on   e) take on   f) put people up

5

- Do the first one as an example with the class, then ask them to complete the remaining sentences. Allow them to use dictionaries if necessary.
- Check answers with the class before asking the students to say what the situation or context might be in which someone would say these sentences.

a) with (Possible situation: boss addressing an employee; a teacher talking to a pupil.)
b) for (Possible situation: when someone thinks their insurance or tax disc needs renewing.)
c) with (Possible situation: parent to child when feeling impatient.)
d) at (Possible situation: teenager to parent when feeling exasperated.)
e) with (Possible situation: parent to teenager when they feel angry.)
f) on (Possible situation: responding to a friend's offer of help or holiday accommodation.)

6

- Ask the students to look in their own dictionaries to find out how phrasal verbs are presented.
- Ask the students to choose five new phrasal verbs to learn. Encourage them to record them in their vocabulary notebooks in example sentences.

Further practice material

Need more writing practice?

→ Workbook page 27
- Writing an article.

Need more classroom practice activities?

→ Photocopiable resource materials pages 161 to 163
   Grammar: *A dangerous adventure*
   Vocabulary: *Phrasal verb crossword*
   Communication: *Storytellers*
→ Top 10 activities pages xv to xx

Need DVD material?

→ DVD – Programme 4: *Good health*

Need progress tests?

→ Test CD – *Test Unit 4*

Need more on important teaching concepts?

→ Key concepts in *New Inside Out* pages xxii to xxxv

Need student self-study practice?

→ CD-ROM – Unit 4: *Challenge*

Need student CEF self-evaluation?

→ CEF Checklists pages xxxvii to xliv

Need more information and more ideas?

→ www.insideout.net

5 Ritual *Overview*

Section & Aims	What the students are doing
Reading SB page 46 Reading for detail	Reading an article and matching objects to famous people. Completing a sentence about rituals with possible endings.
Vocabulary SB page 46 Guessing from context	Looking at how the context can give clues to the meaning of a word. Completing a glossary with words and phrases from the article.
Speaking SB page 48 Fluency work	Talking about personal rituals.
Listening & Vocabulary SB page 48 Listening for detail Collocations	Listening to a woman talking about her father and identifying true and false statements. Making collocations and using them to describe the relationship.
Vocabulary SB page 48 Expressions with *go* (noun)	Completing sentences with *go* as a noun. Writing more example sentences.
Grammar SB page 49 Present and past habits	Studying verb structures for talking about habits. Writing about their own routines. Completing statements with *used to, will* and *would*.
Speaking SB page 49 Fluency work	Writing sentences about their lives ten years ago compared to today. Guessing which of their partner's sentences are false.
Reading & Vocabulary SB page 50 Reading for specific information Weddings	Reading about an unusual wedding. Identifying whether statements are true or false. Then matching words from the text with others with similar meanings.
Listening & Vocabulary SB page 51 Listening for specific information Weddings	Looking at various wedding rituals. Matching speakers to rituals and explaining their meaning. Studying vocabulary for talking about weddings.
Speaking: anecdote SB page 51 Fluency practice	Talking about a wedding they've been to.
Reading & Vocabulary SB page 52 Reading for gist; marriage	Reading quotations and discussing the secrets of a successful marriage. Completing and comparing the different views of a married couple.
Vocabulary & Grammar SB page 53 Verb patterns (2)	Studying verb patterns with a *to*-infinitive or a gerund. Underlining the correct structures in sentences.
Listening SB page 53 Listening for gist	Listening to people talking and deciding how romantic they are. Completing sentences about being romantic and putting them in a table.
Useful phrases & Pronunciation **SB page 54** Talking about annoying habits	Completing descriptions with correct verb structure. Practising the useful phrases with the correct intonation. Completing a table with more phrases and saying what annoys them.
Writing *Extra* SB page 55 Expressing an opinion	Reading an article and choosing the best title. Organising the article into five paragraphs. Writing an article giving opinions on a given topic.
Writing WB page 33	Writing a letter of complaint.

5 Ritual *Teacher's notes*

Reading (SB page 46)

1

- Focus the students' attention on the list of famous people and the objects. Ask the students what the connection between them might be and which celebrity they think has a connection with which object. When the students have decided on the connections, put them into pairs to compare their answers and discuss them. Then ask the students to read the article on page 47 to find the answers.

- In a class feedback session, get the students' reactions to the text and ask them if they know of any further examples of rituals performed by celebrities or people they know. Don't answer any questions about the words in the article as this would pre-empt the work the students will do in the next section. If anyone asks about these words, just say that you will be looking at their meanings later.

> a) 3 – She has to tie them up the same way.
> b) 5 – She doesn't like to walk on white lines.
> c) 4 – He wears his underwear inside out to protect himself from curses.
> d) 2 – He has to have it all straight.
> e) 1 – He has to eat a bowl of his favourite popcorn before performing.

Cultural notes

Serena Williams /səˈriːnə ˈwɪljəms/ (born 1981) American tennis player Serena Williams has won more prize money than any other female sports star. She's held a number one ranking on more than four occasions.

Ana Ivanovic /ˈænə iːˈvænɒvɪtʃ/ (born 1987) Champion Serbian tennis player Ana Ivanovic turned professional when she was 16. She won several singles titles before winning her first Grand Slam at the age of 20.

Adrian Mutu /ˈeɪdrɪən ˈmuːtuː/ (born 1979) Mutu is a professional footballer who has played for Arges Pitesti, Dinamo Bucharest, Inter Milan, Chelsea, Juventus, Fiorentina and his national team, Romania.

David Beckham /ˈdeɪvɪd bekəm/ (born 1975) English footballer who has played for Manchester United (1992–2003), Real Madrid (2003–2007), LA Galaxy and AC Milan. He captained the England football team on 58 occasions. He married ex-Spice Girls singer Victoria Adams in 1999.

Michael Jackson /ˈmaɪkəl ˈdʒæksən/ (1958–2009) American pop singer whose hits included *Beat it*, *Billie Jean* and *Thriller*. Michael Jackson's private life was the source of much public speculation. He died of a heart attack at the age of 50, just before embarking on the final tour of his career.

Prince /prɪns/ (born 1957) Prince is a singer, songwriter and musician. As well as enjoying success with hits like *Purple Rain* (1984) and *Raspberry Beret* (1985), Prince has also written hits for many other artists.

2

- Read out the sentences beginning to the class and ask them to choose and underline five possible endings from the list.

- Check answers by asking the students to read out their completed sentences. Then find out what their opinions are about which is the strangest ritual.

> b), c), e), h), i)

Vocabulary (SB page 46)

1

- Ask student to go through the article on page 47 and underline all the words and phrases they don't know. Then ask them to answer the questions.

- Ask the students if the strategies given helped them to guess the meaning of the words and expressions they didn't know.

2

- Ask the students to complete the glossary with the correct words from the article. Ask them to discuss their ideas in pairs before checking with the class.

- Finally, ask the students to write glossary definitions for any other words or phrases from the article that they didn't know that haven't been covered.

1	stride	8	curse
2	derive	9	jinx
3	thrash	10	renowned
4	rituals	11	uneven
5	the upper hand	12	outfit
6	come across	13	rife
7	loopy	14	immune

Speaking (SB page 48)

1

Go through the list of situations with the class. Then ask the students to think of examples of personal rituals that might be performed in these situations.

2

Pairwork. Ask the students to discuss their own rituals or those of people they know.

Listening & Vocabulary (SB page 48)

1 ⊛ 2.01

- Explain that the students are going to hear a woman talking about her father and his car. Teach the words *obsessed with/by* and *obsession* and tell them that the woman thinks her father is obsessed with his car. Ask them what other things people can be obsessed with. Ask them if they think these people would agree that they're obsessed or whether it's just the opinion of other people who don't share their interests.

- Go through the statements with the class first. Then play the recording and ask them to say whether the statements are true or false. Encourage strong classes to correct the false statements.

- Check answers before asking whether or not Laura is sympathetic to her father's ritual.

a) True.
b) False. (They only went out on rare occasions, and only then if the bus wasn't running.)
c) False. (Their father made them wear plastic bags on their feet just in case they vandalised the seats with their shoes.)
d) True.
e) False. (He backs out of the drive at breakneck speed.)
f) True.

⊛ 2.01

My dad is the most ritualistic person I know, and many of his rituals involve his car.

We've never kept domestic animals in our house, but my father's car is as close as you'll get to the family pet. In fact, to be honest, the car probably gets better treatment and more affection than a pet would.

Each night, the car is tucked up in its garage under a cosy blanket. Nobody – but nobody – is allowed in the garage in case they accidentally brush against 'the precious one', causing who knows what damage.

When we were children, on the rare occasions when my dad would get the car out of the garage (for births, deaths, marriages and national disasters – and then only if the buses weren't running), we would have to wear plastic bags on our feet in case we had a sudden urge to vandalise the seats with our school shoes.

We would never be allowed to shut the car doors ourselves … in case we slammed them too hard, I suppose. I mean, three, five and seven-year-old girls can do untold damage to a car by slamming the door shut.

Nowadays, we don't have to wear plastic bags on our feet, but the 'Starting the car and setting off' ritual has never changed.

He'll start the engine and then sit there for at least five minutes with the engine turning. As repulsive fumes pump out into the fresh country air, he'll take out his pipe, and start tapping out his last smoke. Then he'll take a pinch of Players Medium Navy Cut (no other tobacco will do), stuff it in the bowl and spend a minute or two patting it down. Next, he'll get out his box of matches and give it a shake. He always gives his matchbox a shake. The pipe won't light first go – he'll have several goes at it, and finally, when the tobacco takes, he'll puff and puff until the car is full of smoke. With visibility dangerously reduced and a car full of choking passengers, he'll take the hand-brake off and reverse out of the drive at breakneck speed.

It isn't pleasant being a passenger, but we've always let him get away with this strange behaviour because he's the boss. None of us would dare to complain.

My father used to be a pilot in the Royal Air Force, and I often wonder whether he would indulge in this kind of ritual before take-off and whether his crew would let him get away with it because he was the boss. Probably.

2

- Ask the students to match the words to make collocations from the recording. Encourage them to do this from memory.

- Play the recording again for the students to check their answers. Then ask them to work in pairs to talk about the relationship between Laura's father and his car, using these collocations. As they work, go round taking note of any particularly good descriptions, which can be repeated to the class.

a) domestic animals   e) a box of matches
b) a cosy blanket   f) first go
c) a sudden urge   g) at breakneck speed
d) slam the door   h) Royal Air Force

a) He treats his car better than a domestic animal.
b) He covers his car with a cosy blanket in the garage.
c) He seems to think his daughters might get a sudden urge to damage the car.
d) The children weren't allowed to shut the car doors in case they slammed them.
e) He always gave his box of matches a shake.
f) His pipe never lit first go.
g) He would reverse out of the drive at breakneck speed.
h) He was a pilot in the Royal Air Force.

3

Pairwork. Ask the students to discuss anyone they know who has a strong attachment to a car or other piece of machinery or equipment. Encourage them to report back to the class on their discussion.

Vocabulary (SB page 48)

Expressions with *go* (noun)

1

- Focus the students' attention on the expressions in the margin. Explain, or get the students to identify, that in these expressions *go* is a noun. Ask them to think about what these expressions might mean.

- Go through the instructions with the class and ask them if they can say the sentence *Laura's father has several goes at lighting his pipe* in other words (perhaps *Laura's father has several attempts at …* or *Laura's father has several tries at …*). Ask them to use the expressions from the box in the margin to complete the sentences.

- Check answers and make sure everyone understands the meaning of the expressions. Get students who do to paraphrase them for the rest of the class.

a) have a go on   d) have a go at
b) in one go   e) on the go
c) give it a go   f) make a go of it

2

- Ask the students to say if any of the sentences in Exercise 1 are true for them.

- Ask them to make new sentences using the expressions with *go*. You could ask them to make these sentences which are true for them. Then put the students into pairs to compare their sentences.

Grammar (SB page 49)

Present and past habits

1

- Focus the students' attention on the example sentences in the margin and explain that they are both talking about habits, the first a present habit, the second a past habit.

- Read out the extracts from the listening on page 48 or get a student to read them out. Point out that these extracts are also talking about habits. Ask the students to discuss the questions underneath in pairs.

- Check answers with the class and make sure that everyone is clear about the use of *will* + verb for present habits. Get them to look again at the examples in the margin and point out that you use *would* + verb for past habits.

a) *will*   c) A repeated action.
b) Present habits.   d) Characteristic.

2

- Read the text in its present form to the class, or get a student to read it. Explain that there's nothing wrong with the text as it stands. However, there are places where you could use *will* + verb to emphasise the habitual nature of the actions.

- Either ask the students to work individually to decide which verbs can be replaced with *will* + verb or do it as a class, taking one sentence at a time. Make sure they realise that not all the verbs can be changed. When checking answers, make sure that the students understand that you use this structure to talk about habitual actions, but not when describing states, such as *He is never late* or *She likes to take her time*.

```
1   'll get up
2   –
3   'll have
4   –
5   won't usually get ready
6   –
7   –
8   'll always leave
9   'll vary
10  'll usually depend
```

```
1
a) My father will insist on smoking in the car.
   I hate it!
b) My family and I used to live in a large house.
c) During the school holidays I'd spend all my
   time with my friends.
d) I didn't use to have dark hair when I was
   young.
e) During the week I won't go to bed until after
   midnight.
f) At school I'd take a lucky charm into the exams
   with me.
g) My partner will speak for hours on the phone.
   It drives me crazy!
```

3

- Ask the students to write similar accounts of their own families' morning routines. As they work, go round giving extra help where needed and encouraging them to use *will* + verb where possible.
- Put the students into pairs. Ask them to take turns to read out their texts and see how their routines differ.

4

- Remind the students that you use *would* + verb to talk about past habits. Ask them to think about life when they were twelve years old and to complete the sentences in the left-hand column about their daily routines. You might like to give them an example or two of your own memories to start them off.
- Get several students to read out their sentences describing their daily routines.
- Focus attention on the right-hand column. Point out that this is headed 'My thoughts and feelings' and get the students to identify that the structure you use to talk about past thoughts and feelings is *used to* + verb. Before asking them to complete these sentences, give them a couple of examples from your own past.
- Check answers by getting several students to read out their sentences.

Language note
Grammar: presnt and past habits – *will, would*
and *used to*
(See Student's Book page 136.)

5

Ask the students to work individually to complete the statements. If anyone is struggling, remind them to look at the sentences they've just written and those in the earlier exercises to find the answers.

```
a) will    b) would    c) used to
```

6 Grammar *Extra* 5, Part 1

Ask the students to turn to *Grammar Extra* 5, Part 1 on page 136 of the Student's Book. Here they'll find an explanation of the grammar they've been studying and a further exercise to practise it.

Speaking (SB page 49)

1

- Remind the students of the structures for talking about past habits and past states, which they studied in the previous section.
- Go through the examples with the class and then ask the students to work individually to write four true sentences and one false sentence about ways in which their lives were different ten years ago. Remind them not to consult other students about their sentences. As they work, go round giving help where needed and make sure they're using *used to* + verb and *would* + verb correctly.

2

Pairwork. Put the students into pairs, preferably with people they don't know very well. Ask them to take turns to read out their sentences and guess which one of their partner's sentences is false. Encourage them to report back to the class about what they found out.

Extra activity
Follow up this exercise with a piece of written work for homework, in which the students write an account of how life was different in the past.

Reading & Vocabulary (SB page 50)

1

- Ask the students where weddings normally take place in their country. Is it possible for them to get married in other locations, such as in a garden or on a beach or in an exotic location such as underwater, while parachuting or in a helicopter?
- Put the students into pairs. Tell them to look at the photo and decide if it represents their ideal setting for a wedding. Give them plenty of time to look at the photo and discuss their answers. Then ask them to discuss what they think is the best location for a wedding and to describe it. Get the pairs to report back to the class on what they decided.

2

- Go through the questions with the class so that they know what information to look out for as they read the text. Give them plenty of time to read the text and find the answers to the questions.

- When you check their answers, encourage them to give their response to the text. Would they want a wedding like the one described?

> a) Las Vegas in June.
> b) Hank – father of the groom. Mat – groom. Rebecca – bride. Ron DeCar – 'Elvis' (person who married them).
> c) Because they were Elvis' favourite colours.

Cultural notes

Hank Wangford
Hank Wangford is a well-known English country and western singer.

Elvis Presley
(See notes about Elvis Presley on page 7.)

The King and I
The King and I is the name of a 1956 film musical, starring Yul Brynner and Deborah Kerr about a widow who takes a job as governess to the King of Siam's children.

Virgin Atlantic /'vɜːdʒɪn ətˈlæntɪk/
Airline started by British businessman Richard Branson in 1984. It's now co-owned by Branson and Singapore Airlines.

Las Vegas /'læs 'veɪɡəs/
Las Vegas is in the US state of Nevada. It's nicknamed 'Sin City' because of its gambling and bright lights.

Noel Gallagher /'nəʊəl 'ɡæləhə/ (born 1967)
Noel Gallagher is a British songwriter and musician. In 1991, he formed the band Oasis with his younger brother Liam. The band's first album, *Definitely Maybe* (1994), launched them onto the music scene.

3

- Ask the students to read the sentences, then look back at the text to decide whether they are true or false. Tell them to ignore the underlining for the present. Ask them to rewrite any false sentences to make them true. Then check answers with the class before moving on to the next stage of the activity.

- Focus attention on the underlined expressions in the sentences. Ask the students to look through the text to find words or phrases with the same meaning. Take the opportunity to discuss any other vocabulary in the text that the students found difficult.

> a) False – 'Elvis' conducted it.
> b) True.
> c) False – They chose a white Vegas flared 'Elvis'.
> d) True.
> e) False – Hank did.
> f) True.
> g) True.

> a) ceremony = service
> b) bride and groom = happy couple
> c) chose = went for; suitable = apt
> d) short practice = run through
> e) accompanied = walked with
> f) sunglasses = shades
> g) declared = pronounced

Listening & Vocabulary (SB page 51)

1

Go through the rituals with the class and have a discussion on whether any of them are common in the students' country or countries. Encourage them to add any further information that they can about any of the rituals that are familiar to them and to describe any wedding rituals they know of that aren't in the list.

2 🔊 2.02–2.05

- Ask the students to look at the photos and flags and identify where the people are from (Spain, Taiwan, Turkey, Morocco). Explain that they're going to hear these people talking about wedding rituals from their countries. Ask the students to listen and match one ritual from the list in Exercise 1 to each of the speakers. Check answers before moving on to the next stage of the activity.

- Ask the students to explain the meaning of each ritual. You may need to play the recording more than once to enable them to do this.

> 1 b: to show that the bride and groom will share everything
> 2 f: to protect the bride from the evil spirits (and prevent bad luck)
> 3 d: to help set the bride and groom up with money for their new life
> 4 c: to show that the bride and groom will be prosperous and the bride doesn't have to do any housework until the henna wears off

> 🔊 2.02 (I = Interviewer; J=Jorge)
>
> 1
> I: *Tell me about weddings in your country.*
> J: *Well, in Spain, where I'm from, there is this ritual that happens after the rings have been exchanged between the groom and the bride. It is called 'las arras', and it consists of thirteen gold coins which the groom puts in the bride's hands. It symbolises their intention of sharing everything: all the worldly goods they are going to receive together.*

2.03 (I = Interviewer; S = Sandra)

2

I: *Tell me about weddings in your country.*

S: *Well in Taiwan we use a black umbrella to cover the bride's head, because we believe it can protect the bride from the evil spirits. So normally there will be an elder person to hold the umbrella when she leaves her house to go to the groom's house.*

I: *And will this bring her good luck as well?*

S: *Yes, it will prevent bad luck.*

2.04 (I = Interviewer; Il = Ilhan)

3

I: *Tell me about wedding traditions in Turkey.*

Il: *Weddings in Turkey are quite different to how they are in the UK. There are a lot of people at the wedding. There are sometimes as many as four or five hundred guests, and one of the most interesting things, I think, about Turkish weddings is the fact that the guests at the wedding pin gold, money, banknotes, on the bride's and groom's costumes, on the bridegroom's suit and on the bride's dress. I think, from what I can understand, that this money and gold is used by the bride and groom to set themselves up for their new life together, living in their new house, their new home, to buy things like a fridge, and other things they might need for their future life together.*

2.05 (I = Interviewer; L = Laila)

4

I: *Tell me about wedding traditions in Morocco.*

L: *Oh, Moroccan weddings are elaborate affairs. Preparations take weeks, and the whole community is involved! The bride gets lots of attention in the days leading up to the wedding – a group of women, usually older than the bride, but connected to her in some way, give her a sort of milk bath, which is supposed to purify her. Then she has her hands and feet decorated in henna. This ritual symbolises prosperity. It looks beautiful, and there's another custom which says that the bride isn't supposed to do any housework until the henna wears off.*

Extra activity

Ask the students to discuss what they think the remaining rituals in the list might mean.

a) This symbolises the couple's commitment to working together through their married life.

e) Rice symbolises prosperity and fertility. It's supposed to bring the bride and groom good luck and ensure they have children.

g) It's believed that the person (usually a woman) who catches the bouquet will be the next one to get married.

h) Speeches from the bride's father and the groom cement the relationship between the two families. The best man thanks the bridesmaids and traditionally makes a humorous speech about the groom's past.

3

- Ask the students to read the words and phrases in the box and to work individually to complete the task. While they're doing the exercise, go round, monitoring and giving help.

- When they've finished writing their descriptions, put them into pairs and ask them to exchange their texts and read and comment on the one they've received.

> b) aisle, best man, bouquet of flowers, bridesmaid, church, confetti, honeymoon, photographer, priest, propose a toast, reception, rice, ring, speech, veil, vows, wedding cake, wedding presents

Speaking: anecdote (SB page 51)

For more information about how to set up, monitor and repeat Anecdotes, see page xx in the Introduction.

- Go through the instructions and the questions with the class. Give the students a minute or two to decide which wedding they're going to talk about. Then ask them to look at the questions and think about their answers to them. Allow them to make notes of what they're going to say and how they're going to say it, but discourage them from writing a paragraph that they can simply read out. Go round, monitoring and giving help where necessary. If any of your students have never been to a wedding, then you'll need to substitute some other ceremony. If you do this, remind the students that they'll need to change the questions to make them applicable to this event.

- Pairwork. Put the students in pairs and ask them to take turns to tell their partner about a wedding they've been to. Encourage them to ask each other follow-up questions to get further information. Then ask some pairs to report back to the class about what they found out.

Reading & Vocabulary (SB page 52)

1

- Pairwork. Put the students into pairs and ask them to discuss the quotations about marriage. Ask them to report back to the class on the one they like best.

- Ask the students to discuss what they think is the secret of a successful marriage. In a class feedback session, find out how much agreement there is across the class.

Cultural notes

Rodney Dangerfield /ˈrɒdni ˈdeɪndʒəfiːld/ (1921–2004) Husky-voiced American comedian and actor, best known for his pessimistic outlook on life.

Zsa Zsa Gabor /zɑː zɑː gəˈbɔː/ (born 1917) Hungarian-American actress, most famous for having been married nine times. Many of her humorous comments refer to her marriages and how she gained materially from each.

Ritual   UNIT **5**   **51**

2

- Pairwork. Ask the students to look at the photo of
  Chris and Shirley and go through the instructions
  with the class. Remind any students who have
  forgotten of the difference in meaning between
  the *to*-infinitive and the gerund with some verbs,
  e.g. *I remembered to buy her some flowers* (= I didn't
  forget) and *I remembered buying her flowers* (= I could
  remember an occasion when I bought her flowers).
  This will be covered in more detail in the next section.

- Put the students into pairs and ask them to decide
  who will be Student A and who Student B. Tell them
  to follow the instructions and complete their person's
  thoughts.

- When they've completed their accounts, ask them to
  compare them and discuss their answers. Don't give
  the correct answers at this stage.

1	bringing; to bring	6	practising; to buy
2	telling; to tell	7	to attract; looking
3	looking; to find	8	driving; to drive
4	to have; having	9	going; to go
5	spending; to spend	10	being; to be

3 🌐 2.06

Play the recording for the students to check their
answers. Then have a class discussion on the main
differences between Chris and Shirley's state of mind.

> Chris is romantic, ready for a good time, wanting
> to celebrate.
> Shirley is worried about the children, tired, wants
> to go home.

🌐 2.06 (C = Chris; S = Shirley)

C: *I remember bringing Shirley here for our third date –
it must be nearly ten years ago …*

S: *Oh dear, I hope I've remembered to bring the mobile
phone. Oh good, here it is.*

C: *Yes, that was the evening I couldn't help telling her
that I loved her.*

S: *Oh no, I think I forgot to tell the babysitter what the
number is. What if the kids wake up …?*

C: *I'll never forget looking at Shirley that evening and
thinking, 'This is the woman I want to marry'.*

S: *Calm down – she knows the name of the restaurant so
she'll manage to find the number.*

C: *We both work so hard – we deserve to have a break.*

S: *We both work so hard – I don't like having so little
time to play with the children.*

C: *Maybe we should try spending a romantic weekend
in Paris, just the two of us. My mother will have
the children.*

S: *From now on, I intend to spend more time with them.
I'm going to stop working. Chris will understand.*

C: *Yes – Paris. Good idea. I'll enjoy practising my
French.*

S: *We must stop to buy milk on the way home –
I haven't got anything for breakfast.*

C: *I've tried to attract the waitress's attention but she
won't look this way! I want to get a nice bottle of
wine.*

S: *He'd better stop looking at that waitress. Otherwise
I'm going home!*

C: *Mm, this wine's lovely. I regret driving here now –
we should have got a taxi.*

S: *I hope he doesn't expect me to drive the babysitter
home.*

C: *I fancy going to a club later – we haven't been
dancing together for ages.*

S: *I'm tired and I want to go home. I wish he'd finish
his wine.*

C: *I can't stand being at home all the time – we must
do this more often.*

S: *I'd just like to be at home relaxing in front of the
television.*

Vocabulary & Grammar (SB page 53)

Verb patterns (2)

1

Ask the students to look back at the text on page 52
and find the four verbs that can be followed by either
a *to*-infinitive or a gerund. They may find it helpful to
underline the sentences in which these occur.

> remember, forget, try, stop

2

- Focus attention on the table and go through the
  examples with the class. Make sure they understand
  the difference in meaning between *remember + to-
  infinitive* and *remember + gerund*.

- Ask them to complete the table with the four verbs
  they identified in Exercise 1 and the example
  sentences from the text on page 52.

> a) remember doing sth: 1 – I remember bringing
>   Shirley here.
> b) remember to do sth: 2 – I hope I've
>   remembered to bring the mobile.
> c) (never) forget doing: 3 – I'll never forget
>   looking at Shirley that evening and thinking
>   'This is the woman I want to marry'.

d) forget to do sth: 4 – I forgot to tell the babysitter what the number is.

e) stop doing sth: 5 – he'd better stop looking at that waitress.

f) stop to do sth: 6 – we must stop to buy milk on the way home – I haven't got any for breakfast.

g) try doing sth: 7 – we should try spending (or *try to spend*) a romantic weekend in Paris, just the two of us.

h) try to do sth: 8 – I've tried to attract the waitress's attention, but she won't look this way.

Language note

Grammar: verb patterns – *to*-infinitive or gerund
(See Student's Book page 136.)

3

- Ask the students to choose the correct verb structures in the sentences. Allow them to compare in pairs before checking answers with the class. Point out that the difference between *try doing* and *try to do* is very subtle, and in many cases they can be used interchangeably.

- Ask the students to tick any of the sentences that are true for them. They should then rewrite the others to make them true and compare with a partner.

a) buying	e) to have
b) to bring	f) sleeping
c) travelling	g) coming
d) to pack	h) to take

4 Grammar *Extra* 5, Part 2

Ask the students to turn to *Grammar Extra* 5, Part 2 on page 136 of the Student's Book. Here they'll find an explanation of the grammar they've been studying and a further exercise to practise it.

2	
1 to get on with	5 having
2 flirting	6 to bring
3 seeing	7 to get
4 arguing	8 to buy

Listening (SB page 53)

1 🌐 2.07

- Write the word *romantic* on the board and brainstorm a few things that the students associate with being romantic. They'll discuss this later, so don't spend too much time on it at this stage.

- Focus attention on the photos and tell the students that they're going to listen to these people's answers to the question *Do you think you're romantic?* Ask them to listen and number the people in order from most romantic to least romantic.

---

1 b   2 a   3 c   4 d

🌐 2.07

a)
Well, I try to remember my wife's birthday every year, and on the way home yesterday I stopped to buy her some flowers – I think that's romantic, but she just thought I'd done something wrong.

b)
I'm very romantic, but I think most women are. I remember meeting my boyfriend for the first time. It was in a club and I remember seeing him across the room and thinking, 'He's nice.' He was wearing a black T-shirt and really nice jeans. I even remember what he said to me – he said 'Do you want to dance?' When I asked him recently if he remembered meeting me for the first time, he had no idea.

c)
I don't know. I don't think my partner would say I'm romantic because I always forget to buy him presents or say nice things to him. But deep down I think I am romantic. Since I met my partner, I've stopped looking at other men. Well, I haven't stopped looking, but I have stopped fancying them.

d)
No, I don't think I'm romantic really. I don't like all that romantic nonsense. Women expect you to buy them presents and remember their birthdays. And they try to make you give up football and all those things I enjoy. I can't be bothered with all that. Maybe that's why I haven't managed to find a girlfriend!

Cultural note

You may need to explain that in Britain men sometimes buy flowers to apologise or make up to their wives or girlfriends for something that they did wrong. So, if it's unusual for the man to buy flowers, his wife or girlfriend may be suspicious about his motive for buying her flowers.

2

- Pairwork. Ask the students to work together to complete the sentences. Then ask them to decide whether they are Dos or Don'ts for being romantic and to put them into the correct column on the table.

- Check answers before asking the students to suggest other dos and don'ts which can be added to the table.

a) Try to remember: DO
b) Stop to buy: DO
c) Remember meeting: DO
d) Forget to say: DON'T
e) Stop looking: DO
f) Try to make: DON'T

Useful phrases & Pronunciation

(SB page 54)

1 🌐 2.08

- Focus the students' attention on the illustration and give them time to take in what they can see. Tell them that they're going to read and listen to six people talking about things that really annoy them. Play the recording and ask the students to read the texts. Then ask them to match one of the people to the illustration.

- Check answers and then ask the students to discuss which of the habits mentioned they'd find most annoying.

---

6 Martin

🌐 2.08

1 Naomi

*I hate it when men wear too much aftershave.
My brother-in-law, for example. He will insist on
covering himself in this really strong aftershave – it
makes me sneeze.*

2 Kevin

*Oh dear, there are so many things that annoy me!
But I think the thing that annoys me most is when
I watch a film with my girlfriend. She's always
asking me questions about what's happening: 'Who's
this? What happened there? Why did he do that?'
Argh. That really gets on my nerves.*

3 Roz

*It really winds me up when people talk about how fat
they are when they are stick thin! I've got this friend
who's really slim – much slimmer than me. But she
will go on about being fat. It's so annoying.*

4 Dan

*It really annoys me when my brother and his
girlfriend are together. They're forever hugging and
kissing in front of me. Urgh – it makes me sick!*

5 Sally

*I can't stand it when people say they haven't done
any work for an exam, and then they get the highest
marks. One of my friends is like that. She's always
telling us how worried she is because she hasn't done
any work, but then she gets 90%.*

6 Martin

*I find it irritating when people keep losing things.
For example, my mum's always losing her glasses.
Why doesn't she put them on a chain? Or get a spare
pair? She drives me mad.*

2

Ask the students to listen again and to complete the descriptions with the correct verb structures. Play the recording and then check answers with the class.

---

1 will insist on
2 's always asking
3 will go on about
4 're forever hugging and kissing
5 's always telling
6 's always losing

---

3 🌐 2.09

- Play the recording for the students to listen and repeat the phrases. After they've done this chorally, ask several students to repeat the phrases individually, and check that everyone is pronouncing the words correctly.

- Ask them to mark the stressed words and play the recording again for them to check and to note the speakers' intonation. They should then practise the phrases again. Tell them to try to imitate as closely as possible the stressed-timed phrases to achieve their maximum effect.

---

1 He <u>will</u> in<u>sist</u> on <u>covering</u> him<u>self</u> in this <u>really</u> strong <u>aftershave</u>.
2 She's <u>always</u> <u>asking</u> me <u>questions</u> about what's <u>happening</u>.
3 She <u>will</u> go on about <u>being</u> fat.
4 They're for<u>ever</u> <u>hugging</u> and <u>kissing</u> in front of me.
5 She's <u>always</u> <u>telling</u> us how <u>worried</u> she is.
6 My <u>mum's</u> <u>always</u> <u>losing</u> her <u>glasses</u>.

4

Ask the students to work individually to complete the phrases in the table. Allow them to compare their results in pairs before checking with the class.

---

a) hate   b) annoys   c) winds   d) annoys
e) can't   f) find   g) gets   h) annoying
i) makes   j) drives

5

- Ask the students to work individually to make lists of things that annoy them. Go round, giving help with vocabulary where needed.
- Put them into pairs and ask them to discuss their lists, asking each other questions to find out more details about the things that annoy them.

Writing *Extra* (SB page 55)

Article: expressing an opinion

1

Focus the students' attention on the photo and get them to identify that it shows a wedding on a beach. Ask them to read the article and choose the best title.

> b) Weddings are for the family

Cultural notes

The Little White Wedding Chapel
The Little White Wedding Chapel was established in 1951 in Las Vegas. It's famous for its 'quickie' weddings, where people can turn up and get married shortly afterwards. Famous brides and grooms who have married in the chapel include Frank Sinatra, Bruce Willis and Britney Spears.

Britney Spears
(See notes about Britney Spears on page 7.)

Renée Zellweger /rəˈneɪ ˈzelveɪɡə/ (born 1969)
Renée Zellweger is an American actress who starred in the films *Bridget Jones's Diary* (2001) and *Cold Mountain* (2004). She also played Roxie Hart in the musical *Chicago* (2002), which won the Academy Award for Best Picture.

Mauritius /məˈrɪʃəs/
Mauritius is an island in the south-west Indian Ocean with a population of 1.3 million. It was the only known habitat of the now extinct dodo. The official language of Mauritius is English.

2

- Remind the students that dividing your writing into paragraphs makes it easier for people to read. New paragraphs often begin where there is a change of function or a change of idea. Go through the paragraph plan with the class. Then ask them to read the article again and use this plan to divide up the paragraphs.
- When they've finished, ask them to compare their answers with a partner. Then check with the class.

> Paragraph 2 begins at line 4: *But are they making a terrible mistake?*
> Paragraph 3 begins at line 11: *Celebrities are renowned …*
> Paragraph 4 begins at line 18: *It is worth considering …*
> Paragraph 5 begins at line 24: *In my opinion …*

3

Focus attention on the highlighted sections of the article and ask the students to work individually to find the things in the list. Allow them to compare their answers in pairs before checking with the class.

> a) in my view; in my opinion
> b) for instance
> c) But are they making a terrible mistake?
> d) Understandably; not surprisingly; personally
> e) First and foremost; it is worth considering; what strikes me is that

4

This writing exercise could be done for homework. Remind the students that they should use linking words to make their articles flow well and should use paragraphs to divide the different sections. With weaker classes, work out a paragraph plan on the board similar to the one in Exercise 2 for one of the subjects first. It's a good idea to recommend that the students always start with a paragraph plan.

Further practice material

Need more writing practice?
→ Workbook page 33
- Writing a letter of complaint.

Need more classroom practice activities?
→ Photocopiable resource materials pages 164 to 166
   Grammar: *Keep talking*
   Vocabulary: *Wedding message*
   Communication: *Old habits die hard*
→ Top 10 activities pages xv to xx

Need DVD material?
→ DVD – Programme 5: *Wedding bells*

Need progress tests?
→ Test CD – *Test Unit 5*

Need more on important teaching concepts?
→ Key concepts in *New Inside Out* pages xxii to xxxv

Need student self-study practice?
→ CD-ROM – Unit 5: *Ritual*

Need student CEF self-evaluation?
→ CEF Checklists pages xxxvii to xliv

Need more information and more ideas?
→ www.insideout.net

6 Eat *Overview*

Section & Aims	What the students are doing
Reading & Speaking SB page 56 Reading for specific information Fluency work	Reading about a bad experience in a restaurant. Talking about restaurant experiences.
Reading & Vocabulary SB page 57 Reading for specific information Collocations with parts of the body	Reading a text about sign language in restaurants. Choosing words that collocate. Performing actions and gestures.
Listening & Vocabulary SB page 58 Listening for specific information Food collocations	Listening to an interview and identifying true and false statements. Making collocations with food words. Talking about the best and worst restaurants in their area.
Speaking: anecdote SB page 58 Fluency practice	Talking about their favourite restaurant.
Grammar SB page 59 Present perfect simple and continuous	Studying the form and use of the present perfect simple and continuous. Describing pictures using the present perfect continuous. Discussing when continuous forms are incorrect or sound strange.
Reading & Vocabulary SB page 60 Reading for gist Guessing meaning from context	Listing the advantages and disadvantages of more people becoming vegetarian and reading an article to find out which points it mentions. Completing a glossary by guessing meaning from context. Discussing arguments for becoming a vegetarian.
Vocabulary & Writing SB page 61 Linkers	Completing a summary of an article using linking words. Categorising linkers by their function. Choosing the correct linkers in a text.
Reading SB page 62 Reading for specific information	Guessing the correct statistics to complete sentences about food waste in the UK. Then reading an article to check their ideas. Discussing food waste.
Grammar SB page 63 Passives review	Completing sentences with information from an article, then rewriting them in the passive. Reading a film review and identifying why it sounds unnatural. Rewriting the review with passives so it reads more naturally.
Pronunciation & Vocabulary SB page 63 Numbers review	Studying different types of numbers. Practising reading different types of numbers. Looking at different ways of pronouncing *0*.
Useful phrases SB page 64 Food idioms and expressions	Matching words to things people complain about in restaurants. Listening to people complaining and completing useful phrases. Replacing phrases with idioms. Completing more idioms involving food.
Vocabulary *Extra* SB page 65 Exploring synonyms	Ordering expressions from least hungry to most hungry. Choosing the correct collocations and talking about food and eating. Completing a table with synonyms, then describing people with them.
Writing WB page 39	Writing a discursive essay.

Eat *Teacher's notes*

Warm up

Ask the students how often they eat out in restaurants. Do they have 'takeaways' in their country (cooked food that you buy from a restaurant but take home to eat)? What kinds of restaurants do they prefer?

Reading & Speaking (SB page 56)

1 🌐 2.10

- Tell the students that they're going to read and listen to a text about a bad experience in a restaurant. Ask them what kind of things this might constitute.

- Play the recording and ask them to listen and read the text at the same time. Then ask them how many potatoes the customer eventually ordered.

> Two spoonfuls.

2

- Focus attention on the questions. Ask the students to think about their answers. Give them time to do this and allow them to make brief notes if they wish.

- Put the students into pairs and ask them to compare their answers. Encourage them to ask each other follow-up questions to find out more details and to report back to the class on what they've found out.

Reading & Vocabulary (SB page 57)

1

Go through the questions with the class so that they know what information to look out for as they read the text. Then check answers and ask the students whether they think the article is serious or humorous (humorous) before moving on to the next exercise. Also see how many of them can make the gesture described.

> a) World Restaurant International Sign Technique
> b) No. (It was made up by this writer.)

Cultural note

Brasserie /ˈbræsəri/
A brasserie is a café/restaurant. The setting is usually less formal than a normal restaurant.

2 🌐 2.11

- Pairwork. Ask the students to work in pairs to read the next part of the article and to try to make the gestures described. They should also guess the meaning of these gestures and complete the gaps.

- Get several students to make the gestures in front of the class and to say what they think they mean. Play the recording for them to check their answers.

> | 1 an espresso | 3 bottle of wine |
> |---|---|
> | 2 dinner date | 4 bill; your bill |

> 🌐 2.11
>
> *Other common forms of WRIST include the following.*
>
> **1**
>
> *Raise your right hand in front of your mouth, then squeeze your thumb and index finger together as if squashing a bee. Then make your whole hand tremble, as if the bee had just given you an electric shock. This means, 'Waiter, an espresso, please.'*
>
> **2**
>
> *Using both hands, mimic the tying of a knot at the side of your neck, then raise one hand high, as if you are still holding one end of this imaginary tie or ligature. Now stick your tongue out and make your eyes bulge. This alerts everyone in the restaurant to the fact that you are finding your dinner date a bit of a bore.*
>
> **3**
>
> *Lift the empty wine bottle out of your ice bucket. Hold it up, point to it with your free hand, then make a roll-over motion with this hand. This means, 'Can we have another bottle of wine, please?'*
>
> **4**
>
> *Perhaps the most famous WRIST gesture is when customers take it upon themselves to sign an invisible cheque in the air. For centuries this has meant, 'Can I have the bill?' These days this action is so archaic it's almost amusing. In the UK, the correct WRIST for requesting your bill now means holding your hands apart, as if you are requesting a parrot-sized coffin. Now stab the palm of your hand four times with a finger, simulating the act of punching in your PIN number.*

3

- Ask the students to to choose the noun in each list that doesn't usually collocate with the verb. Allow them to compare in pairs and then check answers.

- Put the students into pairs to test each other on the collocations by taking turns to ask their partner to do some of the actions.

---

a) ~~hair~~   b) ~~ear~~   c) ~~toes~~   d) ~~eyes~~
e) ~~shoulders~~   f) ~~tongue~~

Language note

Vocabulary: collocation

Note that although *clench* means *close tightly*, it's only used with certain nouns. You might *clench your teeth* or *clench your fists* if you were angry, but you wouldn't ~~clench your eyes~~.

Listening & Vocabulary (SB page 58)

1 🔘 **2.12**

- Make sure the students understand that a restaurant critic is a journalist who writes restaurant reviews. Ask them to think about what Jean Crowshaw's job involves and write their suggestions on the board.

- Pairwork. Go through the statements with the class and ask them to discuss in pairs whether they think they are true or false. Then play the recording for the students to check their answers.

(Answers for Exercise 2 are in brackets.)

a) False. (She eats out two or three times a week.)
b) False. (She takes three friends with her. Everyone orders something different and she tastes about two bites of each dish.)
c) False. (She doesn't write anything down. She takes mental notes.)
d) False. (She doesn't wear any disguise.)
e) True.
f) False. (The newspaper pays.)
g) False. (She really hates that. They should know by the look on the customer's face.)
h) False. (She can't stand them.)
i) False (It was in a very rural place in Umbria, Italy.)

🔘 **2.12** (I = Interviewer; JC = Jean Crowshaw)

I: *How did you become a restaurant critic?*

JC: *Well, I've been working for newspapers for more than twenty years. I started out as a journalist when I was twenty-three, and I've worked for several newspapers since then including this one. Then, when the last restaurant critic retired, I was asked to take his place. And I've been doing it for the last thirteen years.*

I: *How can you do this job and stay so slim?*

JC: *Yeah, that's a good question. I mean, I eat out two or three times a week. But as a matter of fact, to write about a restaurant and its cuisine, I need to taste the food, but I don't need to clean my plate. When I'm covering a restaurant, I always take three friends with me. Everyone has to order a different dish. So then I taste about two bites of everything on their plates, and then I eat the same amount of food on my plate. Then I stop eating. And that's not just so that I stay slim, it's so that I can remember all the different flavours.*

I: *Do you take notes?*

JC: *No, I don't write anything down because I don't want to draw attention to myself. So while I'm eating, I'm making mental notes about the restaurant. How does the room look? Is the lighting too dim, too bright? Is the service efficient or is it slow? How is the food presented? Are the waiters doing their job well? Do the customers look happy? Then, as soon as I get home, no matter how late it is or how tired I am, I write down my impressions – I write pages and pages of notes.*

I: *You must be pretty well-known on the restaurant circuit. Do you wear a disguise?*

JC: *What, like a wig? Ha ha, no, I couldn't do that. Like I said, I've been working around the Manchester area for some thirteen years now, so inevitably, I do sometimes get recognised, but by that time it's too late for the management to call in another chef or change the serving staff.*

I: *Do people get upset if you give them a bad review?*

JC: *Oh yes, but the bad reviews are the most fun to write! Once, a restaurant owner called my editor and threatened to come in with a gun – I don't think he did in the end.*

I: *Who pays for your meals?*

JC: *The newspaper pays for the meals. No food is accepted for free.*

I: *Have you had any particularly good or bad experiences that stand out in your memory?*

JC: *There was the waitress who tripped and poured my son's dessert and a glass of wine in my lap. I wasn't too pleased at the time, but I managed to see the funny side of it later. But there's one thing I really hate and that's when the waiter keeps asking 'Is everything all right?' Good, experienced waiters never ask that – they don't need to because they can tell if everything's all right just by looking at the customers' faces.*

I: *Have you met any rude waiters or waitresses?*

JC: *I've experienced every kind of waiter and waitress – rude and moody, chatty and enthusiastic, flirtatious and over-familiar. The best waiters are those who are attentive but not intrusive. I can't stand those waiters who squat down beside you to take your order, and then proceed to tell you their favourite items on the menu, because they ate it on their holidays in Greece ... this kind of invasion of your privacy is totally unacceptable.*

> I: What's the best meal you've ever eaten?
>
> JC: It was in Italy, in Umbria. I was travelling with my husband, and we stopped in a very rural place where we had the meal I'll remember for the rest of my days. Olive oil pressed from the restaurant's own trees, lamb with so much flavour that it defines what the meat should taste like – wonderful bread, handmade pasta, local wines. It wasn't a formal restaurant, but I've never forgotten it and I've never enjoyed a meal more.

2

Ask the students to correct the false statements. Play the recording again for them to check their answers.

> (See answers in brackets in Exercise 1.)

3

- Make sure the students understand the words in the box. Ask them to think about which one collocates with all the items in each list. Point out that while individual items from each list may collocate with more than one word from the box, only one word from the box collocates with all the items in each list.

- Check answers with the class before asking the students to circle the collocations that they don't know. They can then look these up in a dictionary and write example sentences for them.

> a) food   b) meal   c) dish   d) plate
> e) flavour   f) menu

4

Pairwork. Put the students into pairs and ask them to decide which is the best and worst restaurant in your area. This could be in the area where you are now or about their hometown. Ask the pairs to report back to the class, giving reasons for their choices.

Speaking: anecdote (SB page 58)

For more information about how to set up, monitor and repeat Anecdotes, see page xx in the Introduction.

- Go through the instructions and the questions with the class. Give the students a minute or two to decide which restaurant they're going to talk about. Then ask them to look at the questions and think about their answers to them. Allow them to make notes of what they're going to say and how they're going to say it, but discourage them from writing a paragraph that they can simply read out. Go round, monitoring and giving help where necessary.

- Pairwork. Put the students in pairs and ask them to take turns to tell their partner about their favourite restaurant. Encourage them to ask each other follow-up questions to get further information. Then ask some pairs to report back to the class about what they found out.

Grammar (SB page 59)
Present perfect simple and continuous

1

- Focus the students' attention on the information in the margin. Make sure they understand the difference between actions and states.

- Ask the students to look at the extract from the interview. Point out the words in bold and ask them to name the tenses and match each to one of the descriptions.

> I've been working: present perfect continuous – c
> I started out: past simple – a
> I've worked: present perfect simple – b

2

- Go through the example with the class, then ask the students to work individually to write their three sentences. Remind them that they must use the three tenses in the given sequence and that one of their sentences should be false. As they work, go round giving extra help where needed and making sure that the students are all forming their sentences correctly.

- Put the students into pairs and ask them to take turns to read their sentences out. Their partner should try to guess which sentence is false. Encourage them to report back to the class on what they found out.

3

- Do the first one as an example with the class, then ask the students to choose the most appropriate forms.

- Put the students into pairs to discuss their answers before checking with the class.

> 1 a) learnt   b) been learning
> 2 a) read   b) been reading
> 3 a) been eating   b) eaten
> 4 a) worked   b) been working

4

Go through the explanation and instructions with the class. Then focus attention on the first picture and ask the students to say what the man has been doing (he's been chopping onions). Ask them to make similar sentences about the remaining pictures.

a) He's been chopping onions.
b) He's been eating his dinner.
c) She's been cleaning/mopping the floor.
d) He's been putting up shelves / doing some DIY.

5

- Read the sentences with the class, then ask them to think about why they sound strange or wrong. Remind them to think about the difference between states and actions. Then check answers.

- As the students rewrite the sentences, go round giving extra help where needed. After checking their answers, ask if any of the statements are true for them. If you have time, ask them to change the statements so that they are true.

a) *hate* describes a state: it isn't an action. So the continuous form is wrong.
b) *stop* describes a single action: you do it once. It isn't normally possible to repeat it.
c) *decide* describes a single action. You do it once. It isn't normally possible to repeat it.
d) *cut* describes a single action: you do it once. Repeating it would be considered 'self-harm'.
e) *have* describes a state: it isn't an action. So the continuous form is wrong.
f) *understand* describes a state: it isn't an action. So the continuous form is wrong.

a) I've always hated … d) I've cut myself …
b) I've stopped …   e) I've had …
c) I've decided …   f) I've never understood …

6 Grammar *Extra* 6, Part 1

Ask the students to turn to *Grammar Extra* 6 Part 1 on page 136 of the Student's Book. Here they'll find an explanation of the grammar they've been studying and further exercises to practise it.

1
a) I've been learning English for six years.
b) I've known my best friend since I was a child.
c) I'm exhausted. I've been working hard all day.
d) I haven't seen my parents for ages.
e) I'm tired. I haven't been feeling well lately.
f) I haven't done any housework for weeks.
g) I've been sitting here for more than an hour.
h) I've been thinking about changing my job recently.

2
a) since   b) for   c) since   d) for   e) since
f) for   g) since

Reading & Vocabulary (SB page 60)

1

- Ask the students to work individually to make lists of what they ate yesterday. Tell them to be specific about the food items and not just to put the names of meals or vague descriptions of dishes.

- Put the students into groups and ask them to compare their lists. Then ask them to discuss the questions and report back to the class on their answers.

2

- Make sure the students understand *vegetarian* (someone who doesn't eat meat or fish) and the distinction between a *vegetarian* and a *vegan* (a vegetarian who also doesn't eat animal products, such as eggs, milk and cheese). Have a class discussion on the advantages and disadvantages of more people become vegetarian. Write their suggestions on the board under the headings of *health*, *animal welfare* and *the environment*.

- Ask the students to read the article and see how many of the points they thought of are mentioned in it.

Health
Advantages: Improve health. Reduce the risk of heart disease, cancer, etc. Feel better.
Disadvantages: Friends treat me like an eccentric. No decent food available.

Animal welfare
Advantages: Reduce cruelty to animals. Reduce spread of disease.

Environment
Advantages: Reduce greenhouse gases. Helps feed the poor and hungry.

3

- Focus attention on the words in the article that are highlighted in yellow (tell them to ignore the ones highlighted in blue; these will be dealt with in the next section). Remind the students of the work they did on guessing meaning from context on page 46. Get them to say what strategies they used there.

- Ask the students to work out the meanings of the highlighted words from their context and to complete the glossary. When checking answers, ask them to say which strategy they used for each word.

a) cram   g) fin
b) lapse   h) stroke
c) shun   i) fussy
d) skip   j) soggy
e) slaughter   k) do my bit
f) crop   l) retain the moral high-ground

4

Have a class discussion of the arguments in the article and see if anyone finds them convincing.

Vocabulary & Writing (SB page 61)

1

- Focus the students' attention on the table of linkers. Draw their attention to the headings and point out that different linkers perform different functions in a text. (See Language note below.)

- Ask the students to use the linkers in the table to complete the summary of the article on page 60.

> 1 so (or consequently)
> 2 Consequently (or so)
> 3 However
> 4 Even though (or Although)
> 5 Furthermore
> 6 Although (or Even though)
> 7 To sum up

Language note

Vocabulary: linkers

These discourse markers provide us with a logical sequence (organising ideas / adding more information / concluding) to the text and show us how the different parts of the text relate to each other (showing contrast / demonstrating cause and effect).

2

- Ask the students to look back at the article on page 60 and find the ten highlighted linkers within it. Ask them to put them in the correct column on the table.

- Allow the students to compare their tables with a partner before checking answers with the class.

> **Organising ideas**
> The first … reason why, Secondly, Finally
>
> **Adding more information**
> In fact, In other words, What is more
>
> **Connecting contrasting ideas**
> and yet, but
>
> **Showing cause and effect**
> As a result
>
> **Concluding**
> On balance

3

- Ask the students to read the text about bottled water. Tell them to ignore the choices in bold for the time being. This will give them an idea of the overall structure and content of the text. Then ask them to go back through the text and choose the correct linkers. Remind the students that they need to think about the function of the linker in each place and choose the appropriate one for that function.

- Check answers with the class before having a class discussion on how much bottled water they drink every day.

> 1 However
> 2 The first reason why
> 3 As a result,
> 4 What is more
> 5 In other words
> 6 Secondly
> 7 In fact
> 8 Finally
> 9 Furthermore
> 10 Consequently,
> 11 To sum up

Reading (SB page 62)

1

- Pairwork. Ask the students to read the five statistics about food waste in the UK and to discuss in pairs which number they think is correct for each one. Ask the pairs to report back to the class on their choices and see how much agreement there is.

- Ask the students to read the article and check their ideas. Ask them if they find the information surprising or not.

> 1 c) 60%   2 c) £9 billion   3 c) 27%
> 4 c) 5,500   5 c) 1.3 million

2

Groupwork. Go through the questions with the class and make sure that everyone understands them. Put the students into groups and ask them to discuss the questions. Go round monitoring and offering help with vocabulary where needed. Then ask the groups to report back to the class on their discussions.

Grammar (SB page 63)

Passives review

1

- Focus the students' attention on the words in the box. Ask them to use these words to complete the sentences underneath, according to the information they read in the text on page 62. Tell them to ignore the underlined words for the moment. Check answers before moving on to the next stage of the activity.

- Focus attention on the information and the examples in the margin. Ask the students to rewrite the sentences in the exercise, using passive forms for the underlined verbs. Encourage them to do this without looking back at the article. When they've finished, allow them to look back and check their answers. Then ask them to say why passive structures have been used in the article rather than active ones.

> a) bread   b) year   c) plate   d) date   e) day
>
> a) Salad, fruit and bread were most commonly wasted.
> b) £9 billion of avoidable food waste in England and Wales was disposed of each year.
> c) Most of the food could have been consumed if it had been stored or managed better, or had not been left uneaten on a plate.

d) Nearly a quarter of the food was disposed of because the 'use by' or 'best before' date had expired.

e) 5,500 whole chickens were thrown away each day.

The passive is preferred because the article is about food waste. So you want 'food' or 'food waste' (the object of the active verb) to be the topic of each sentence. The subject of the active verb ('people') is obvious in the context.

Language note
Grammar: passive review
(See Student's Book page 136.)

2

Find out if any of the students have seen the film *Wall-E* and if they enjoyed it. Ask them to read the film review and identify why is reads unnaturally.

It reads unnaturally because the subject of many of the active verbs is 'somebody'. Since we don't know or need to know who this 'somebody' is, it would read better if the active verbs were in the passive.

3

Ask the students to rewrite the review so it reads more naturally. Go through the two instructions that they should follow first and make sure they understand what they have to do. Check answers by getting the students to read out their new texts.

The film *Wall-E* was produced by Pixar Animation Studios and directed by Andrew Stanton. It follows the story of a robot called Wall–E (Waste Allocation Load Lifter Earth-Class), who has been programmed to clean up the polluted planet. Earth has been so overrun by rubbish that the planet's population has been forced to take a vacation on a holiday resort spaceship, where everything is done for them. The holiday resort is run by the corporation Buy n Large. Into this scenario pops Eve, another robot who's been sent to Earth to find plant life. Wall-E falls in love, but at first his feelings aren't reciprocated because she has no feelings. *Wall-E* has been aimed at children, but adults won't be disappointed.

4 Grammar *Extra* 6, Part 2

Ask the students to turn to *Grammar Extra* 6, Part 2 on page 136 of the Student's Book. Here they'll find an explanation of the grammar they've been studying and a further exercise to practise it.

3

a) That chair was made by my brother.
b) We were introduced yesterday.
c) More than 80% of our waste could be recycled.
d) Your application is being processed now.
e) The telephone was invented by Alexander Graham Bell.
f) English is spoken as a first language by 400 million people.
g) A man has been arrested in connection with the robbery.
h) An announcement will be made later on in the week.

Pronunciation & Vocabulary
(SB page 63)
Numbers review

1 🎧 2.13

- Focus the students' attention on the information in the margin. Point out that numbers can take many forms and that they can be pronounced in different ways. Ask the students to say the numbers in the box and to put them in the correct columns in the table.

- Play the recording for them to check their answers. Then play it again for them to repeat the numbers. When they've done this chorally, ask for individual repetition of the numbers.

1 and 2

Cardinal numbers	Ordinal numbers	Fractions
246,813,579	53rd	$4/5$
1,234,567	75th	$5/6$

Decimals	Dates	Telephone numbers
99.9	01/01/1901	020 7278 2332
0.25	27/07/2012	020 7782 43356

🎧 2.13

Cardinal number: two hundred and forty-six million, eight hundred and thirteen thousand, five hundred and seventy-nine

Ordinal numbers: fifty-third

Fraction: four fifths

Decimal: ninety-nine point nine

Date: the first of January nineteen oh one

Telephone number: oh two oh, seven two seven eight, two double three two

Language notes

Vocabulary

Numbers

- Number *0* is often pronounced like the letter 'O' when saying numbers one figure at a time, e.g. for a telephone number. It can also be pronounced *zero* or *nil* in a sports score (except tennis, where it's *love*).

- British English: always put *and* before the tens in a number, e.g. *six hundred and twenty*. In American English, it's *six hundred twenty*.

- You write a comma after the thousands, but if the number has just four figures, you can write the number without a comma, e.g. *1,500* or *1500*.

- You don't use the comma to indicate decimals. You use the full stop as the decimal point.

Fractions

It's usual to use *a/an* (/ə/ /ən/) rather than *one* when saying any fraction that has number '1' in the top half (1/8, ¼ , 1/3, ½, etc), e.g. *'a third'* is more common than *'one third'*, while *'one half'* is never said.

Dates

In standard British English, you write *10th May*, but you say *the tenth of May*. When you write the date in figures, you write, e.g. *10/5/2007*. In American English, you write *May 10*, and you say *May tenth*. Because you say the month first, you write, e.g. *5/10/2007*.

2 🔊 2.14

Ask the students to listen to five more numbers on the recording and put them in the correct column of the table in Exercise 1. They then practise saying them.

> (See answers in Exercise 1.)

> 🔊 2.14
>
> *nought point two five*
>
> *one million, two hundred and thirty-four thousand, five hundred and sixty-seven*
>
> *seventy-fifth*
>
> *oh two oh, double seven eight two, four double three five six*
>
> *five sixths*
>
> *the twenty-seventh of July, twenty twelve*

3 🔊 2.15

- Ask the students to write the letters a) to e) on a piece of paper. Tell them they're going to hear five different ways of saying the number *0*. Ask them to write these down as they hear them.

- Check answers with the class before asking them to match each way of saying *0* to one of the situations.

> a) 3–0 – 2   b) 2–0 – 5   c) 1908 – 3
> d) 10° – 1   e) 0.7 – 4

> 🔊 2.15
>
> a) *Manchester United won three nil.*
> b) *Rafael Nadal is winning two sets to love.*
> c) *My grandfather was born in nineteen oh eight.*

> d) *It's really cold – ten degrees below zero.*
> e) *Nought point seven seconds – it's a new world record!*

Useful phrases (SB page 64)

1 🔊 2.16

- Get students to discuss the first question and write their suggestions on the board. Then ask them to match the items in the box with the list of things that people might complain about.

- Play the recording for them to see how many of their suggestions are mentioned.

> a) The service – (un)helpful, rude, slow
> b) The lighting – bright, dark
> c) The wine – (not) chilled, corked, off
> d) The food – bland, off, over-cooked, over-done
> e) The other customers – noisy, (rude), slow
>
> (See complaints underlined in the audioscript below.)

> 🔊 2.16
>
> (W1 = Waiter; W2 = Waitress; M = Man; Wom = Woman)
>
> W1:   *Busy tonight, isn't it?*
>
> W2:   *Yeah. Who's the man on table 4? He looks familiar.*
>
> W1:   *Oh, that's Burt Sinclair. He's a big cheese in the hotel industry, so if you butter him up, he'll give you a nice big tip.*
>
> W2:   *Oh right – I could do with a bit of extra cash.*
>
> M: *Excuse me! Excuse me!*
>
> W2:   *Yes, sir. Can I help you?*
>
> M: *Yes, you can. <u>The service in here is very slow</u> this evening. We've been sitting here for ten minutes and we haven't even seen the menu yet.*
>
> W2:   *Oh I'm terribly sorry, sir. We're very busy tonight. I'll get you the menus immediately.*
>
> W1:   *How are you getting on with the big cheese on table 4?*
>
> W2:   *Well, he obviously thinks he's the best thing since sliced bread, and so does the woman with him.*
>
> W1:   *That's his wife.*
>
> W2:   *His wife! I thought it was his daughter.*
>
> M: *Excuse me!*
>
> W2:   *Yes, sir. Are you ready to order?*
>
> M: *I'm afraid not. <u>It's so dark in here that we can't read the menu.</u>*

W2:	Oh, one moment, sir. I'll bring you a bigger candle. There, is that OK?
M:	Yes, yes, that's fine.
W2:	Would you like a few more minutes, sir?
M:	No, no. I'll have the steak.
W2:	Right, and how would you like it, sir?
M:	Medium rare.
Wom:	And I'll have seafood pasta and a green salad.
W2:	That's one steak, medium rare and one seafood pasta. And to drink?
M:	The Chablis.
W2:	Who would like to taste the wine?
Wom:	I will. Hm. <u>It could do with being a bit colder. Can we have the wine chilled, please?</u>
W2:	That's no problem – I'll just fetch an ice bucket.
W1:	Everything OK with table 4?
W2:	They're tricky customers. I feel like I'm walking on eggshells.
W1:	Just remember the tip.
M:	Excuse me!
W2:	Yes, sir.
M:	<u>I think the wine is corked</u>. It certainly tastes very strange.
W2:	Oh, I'm terribly sorry, sir. I'll bring you a new one immediately.
W1:	Big cheese doesn't look too pleased. What's up?
W2:	Oh dear, it's all going pear-shaped now. The service is slow. The restaurant's too dark, and now the wine's corked.
W1:	Calm down. You have to take it all with a pinch of salt. If you start taking it personally, you've had it. …
M:	Excuse me!
W2:	Yes, sir?
M:	I'm afraid <u>this steak is overcooked</u>. I asked for medium rare.
W2:	I'm sorry, sir.
M:	And there's another problem.
Wom:	It's my seafood pasta – I think <u>the prawns are off</u>.
W2:	Oh dear. I'm very sorry. I'll talk to the chef.
W1:	It's not looking very good for the tip, is it?
W2:	That's not funny.
M:	Excuse me!
W2:	Grrr.

Language note

Vocabulary

- *Corked* is a rather specialised word which you may need to explain. If wine is corked, it tastes bad because the cork used to close the bottle has decayed and allowed air into the wine.

- *Off* can refer to the quality of the food having deteriorated to the point where it's unpleasant or dangerous to eat and it's generally used for things like fish and seafood, which can deteriorate quickly. *The prawns are off* means that the prawns are inedible. You can also use *off* to describe a wine that is corked.
  Off is also used in a restaurant to say that a dish advertised on the menu is no longer available, usually because it has sold out. *The roast lamb is off* means that it is no longer available.

2 🌐 2.17

- Ask the students to complete the useful phrases. Ask them to compare in pairs, then check with the class.
- Play the recording for the students to listen and repeat. When they've done this chorally, ask for individual repetition of the useful phrases.
- Put the students into pairs and ask them to discuss their own experiences of complaining in restaurants.

a) slow	b) dark	c) chilled
d) over-cooked		e) off

> 🌐 2.17
>
> a) The service is slow this evening.
> b) It's so dark in here that we can't read the menu.
> c) Can we have the wine chilled, please?
> d) I'm afraid this steak is overcooked.
> e) I think the prawns are off.

3

Draw the students' attention to the list of idioms 1–6. Remind them that they heard them all in the conversation in Exercise 1. Ask them to use the idioms to replace the underlined phrases in the sentences. Tell them to do this without looking at the recording script on page 149, but allow them to look at it to check their answers.

a) 5	b) 1	c) 4	d) 3	e) 6	f) 2

4 🌐 2.18

- Pairwork. Put the students into pairs and ask them read the conversation and choose the best words to complete the idioms.
- Play the recording for them to check their answers. Then ask them to say what the idioms mean.

> 1 recipe (= a situation which is likely to end badly)
> 2 lemon (= to feel foolish)
> 3 beetroot (= to blush/go red in the face with embarrassment)
> 4 pie (= to be very pleasant)
> 5 beans (= tell me all the gossip)
> 6 peanuts (= low wages)
> 7 cookie (= clever)

H: *How was work tonight?*

W: *Mad as usual. Over-booked with two waiters off sick.*

H: *Oh no, sounds like a recipe for disaster.*

W: *Exactly. Then I dropped a whole tray of glasses.*

H: *Oh, poor you. I bet you felt a real lemon.*

W: *I did. I went as red as a beetroot.*

H: *Was Chef his usual bad-tempered self?*

W: *No, actually he was as nice as pie. I think he's got a new girlfriend.*

H: *Oh, come on, spill the beans. Who is she?*

W: *Well, there's this new waitress. She's just finished university and wants to earn some money to go travelling.*

H: *Well, she'll have to earn some good tips because the restaurant pays peanuts.*

W: *I know – but she's a smart cookie. She'll be fine. Anyway, last week …*

5

Put the students into pairs to discuss people and situations where these idioms are appropriate. Then ask them to report back to the class on what they found out.

Vocabulary Extra (SB page 65)

Exploring synonyms

1

Pairwork. Ask the students to look at the sentences and put them in order as indicated. Then ask them to read the dictionary extract to check their answers.

1 'I'm a bit peckish.'
2 'I'm hungry.'
3 'I'm really starving.'
4 'I'm famished.'
5 'I'm absolutely ravenous.'

2

- Go through the instructions with the class, then ask the students to work individually to form the collocations. When they've finished, ask them to check in the dictionary extract.

- Check answers with the class, then ask the students to find out how the other verbs are used. Ask them to identify which verb suggests you have only a short time to eat.

c) *grab* and d) *have*
Grab suggests you only have a short time to eat.

3

Ask the students to go through the list and note down their answers. Then ask them to compare their ideas with a partner.

4

Focus attention on the table and point out that there are different ways of saying *fat* and *thin*. (Some are more polite than others.) Ask them to read the two dictionary extracts on *fat* and *thin* and to complete the table.

FAT		THIN	
positive	negative	positive	negative
plump	big, large	slim	skinny
chubby	dumpy	slender	anorexic
	overweight	lean	emaciated
	obese	trim	gaunt
			bony

5

Pairwork. Ask the students to discuss in pairs which words they would use to descibe the people listed.

a) chubby   b) anorexic   c) trim   d) emaciated

6

Ask the students to look in their own dictionaries to find out what synonyms are given for *hungry*, *eat*, *fat* and *thin*. Then ask the students to find all the different ways of saying *cook* (e.g. *roast*, *boil*, *grill*, etc.). Encourage them to record them in their vocabulary notebooks in example sentences to show the difference in meaning.

Further practice material

Need more writing practice?

→ Workbook page 39
- Writing a discursive essay.

Need more classroom practice activities?

→ Photocopiable resource materials pages 167 to 169
   Grammar: *What have I been doing?*
   Vocabulary: *Food fight*
   Communication: *Make the question*
→ Top 10 activities pages xv to xx

Need progress tests?

→ Test CD – *Test Unit 6*

Need more on important teaching concepts?

→ Key concepts in *New Inside Out* pages xxii to xxxv

Need student self-study practice?

→ CD-ROM – Unit 6: *Eat*

Need student CEF self-evaluation?

→ CEF Checklists pages xxxvii to xliv

Need more information and more ideas?

→ www.insideout.net

Review B *Teacher's notes*

These exercises act as a check of the grammar and vocabulary that the students have learnt in the Units 4–6. Use them to find any problems that students are having, or anything that they haven't understood and which will need further work.

Grammar (SB page 66)

Remind the students of the grammar explanations they read and the exercises they did in the *Grammar Extra* on pages 134 to 137.

1

This exercise reviews narrative tenses from Unit 4.

1	decided	7	heard
2	had travelled	8	was coming
3	were counting	9	looked
4	had been living	10	had been putting
5	picked	11	heard
6	was cutting	12	saw

2

This exercise reviews the future continuous from Unit 4.

3

This exercise reviews the future perfect from Unit 4. Check the students' answers by asking them to read out their sentences. Then put them into pairs and ask them to compare with a partner and see how many of the sentences they wrote for this exercise and the previous one are the same.

4

This exercise reviews *will*, *would* and *used to* for habits from Unit 5. Check answers before asking the students to discuss in pairs which sentences are true for them.

a) ✔
b) ✗ Change *'d* to *used to*. (*would* can only be used for past actions, not states.)
c) ✗ Change *used to* to *will*. Or change *used to work* to *work*. (*used to* can only be used for past actions or states, not present ones.)
d) ✔
e) ✗ Change *'ll like* to *like*. (*will* can only be used for present habits, not states.)
f) ✔

5

This exercise reviews verbs with *to*-infinitive or gerund from Unit 5. Check answers before asking the students to tick the sentences which are true for them.

a) seeing	d) eating
b) to buy	e) loving
c) to call	f) to pass

Cultural note

Elvis Presley
(See notes about Elvis Presley on page 7.)

6

This exercise reviews the present perfect simple and continuous from Unit 6.

1	Correct.	7	I've had
2	I've worked	8	I've always loved
3	Correct.	9	Correct.
4	has happened	10	Correct.
5	I've cut	11	I've enjoyed
6	Correct.		

7

This exercise reviews the passive from Unit 6.

a) was used as payment for work.
b) are eaten every year.
c) has been produced for 2,000 years.
d) is eaten by half the world's population.
e) are being thrown away right now.

Vocabulary (SB page 67)

1

This exercise reviews the prefix *self-* and the suffix *ible/able* from Unit 4.

a) self-conscious	e) doable
b) reasonable	f) unbearable
c) self-employed	g) self-discipline
d) visible	h) edible

2

This exercise reviews phrasal verbs from Unit 4.

a) get   b) let   c) take   d) call
e) picked   f) keep

3

This exercise reviews expressions with *go* from Unit 5.

a) I'd love to have a go on a Harley-Davidson.
b) I'd love to have a go at surfing.
c) I'm on the go from 9–6 every day. / I'm on the go every day from 9–6.
d) I wouldn't mind giving yoga a go.
e) I couldn't drink a glass of whisky in one go.

Cultural note

Harley-Davidson /'hɑːli 'deɪvɪdsən/
Harley-Davidson Motor Company is a motorcycle manufacturer based in Milwaukee, Wisconsin, USA. It was founded in 1903 by William S Harley and Arthur Davidson (and Arthur's brothers Walter and Will). Harley-Davidsons are used by many US police forces. It was once the world's largest motorcycle manufacturer. The average age of a Harley rider these days is 47 years old.

4

This exercise reviews wedding vocabulary from Unit 5.

a) bride   g) bridesmaid
b) groom   h) vows
c) best man   i) propose a toast
d) confetti   j) wedding cake
e) veil   k) bouquet of flowers
f) honeymoon

5

This exercise reviews collocations involving body parts from Unit 6.

a) Stick   b) Hold   c) Bend   d) Shake
e) Clench   f) Raise

6

This exercise reviews collocations involving food from Unit 6.

a) three-course   d) fast
b) hard   e) organic
c) unmistakable

7

This exercise reviews different types of numbers from Unit 6. When they've completed their lists, put the students into pairs to read them out to each other.

(Answers will vary according to the students' personal circumstances.)

Pronunciation (SB page 67)

1

Remind the students that the boxes show the syllables of a word and the large boxes indicate the stressed syllables. Here they're being asked to classify words according to how many syllables they have and where the main stress falls. Encourage them to say each word aloud to get a feeling for what sounds right.

1 and 2		
A: ☐☐☐	**B:** ☐☐☐	**C:** ☐☐☐☐
candlelight	however	competition
hazardous	organic	expedition
neighbourhood	reception	invitation
organised	tomato	superstitious

2 🔊 2.19

Ask the students to underline the stressed syllables in the words in the table. Then play the recording for them to check their answers. Play it a second time for them to listen and repeat.

(See answers underlined in Exercise 1.)

Further practice material

Need more classroom practice activities?
→ Photocopiable resource materials page 170
   🔊 2.20 **Song:** *Big Yellow Taxi*
→ TOP 10 activities pages xv to xx

Need progress tests?
→ Test CD – *Test Review B*

Need more on important teaching concepts?
→ Key concepts in *New Inside Out* pages xxii to xxxv

Need student self-study practice?
→ CD-ROM – *Review B*

Need more information and more ideas?
→ www.insideout.net

7 Escape *Overview*

Section & Aims	What the students are doing
Reading & Vocabulary SB page 68 Reading for gist; scanning Beach activities	Talking about beach holidays and comparing their ideas with a text. Marking statements true or false. Scanning the text for vocabulary items to complete definitions.
Vocabulary & Grammar SB page 70 Reporting verbs	Putting a summary in order. Studying the use of reporting verbs.
Speaking: anecdote SB page 70 Fluency practice	Talking about a family holiday they went on as a child.
Listening & Grammar SB page 71 Listening for gist Past modals of obligation	Discussing potential holiday problems. Then listening to accounts of the holidays to find out went wrong. Studying the use of modal verbs to talk about past obligation. Talking about recent travel experiences.
Reading SB page 72 Reading for gist	Talking about writing and receiving postcards. Matching character types to postcards according to a text. Talking about people they know who fit the character types.
Vocabulary SB page 73 Word formation: *ful*, *ish* and *less*	Underlining the suffixes *ful*, *less* and *ish* in the reading text. Forming adjectives with suffixes. Then writing example sentences. Completing a table with adjectives. Completing a text by modifying words.
Listening & Speaking SB page 74 Listening for specific information Fluency practice	Talking about relationships formed on holiday. Then listening to someone talking about a holiday romance and answering questions. Completing extracts from the recording. Matching discourse markers with interpretations. Underlining appropriate discourse markers in a dialogue. Writing and practising conversations about a holiday romance.
Reading & Grammar SB page 75 Reading for gist Articles	Completing a story with articles and identifying the moral. Finding examples in the text for rules on using articles. Writing three interesting generalisations using given words.
Pronunciation SB page 75 Pronunciation of articles in place names	Listening and repeating place names. Then identifying the different ways in which *the* is pronounced. Adding more examples of place names with *the*.
Useful phrases SB page 76 Advice and recommendations	Talking about things to see in Paris. Then listening to a conversation and finding how many museums are mentioned. Matching sentence halves. Completing travel tips and matching them to the correct cities. Writing travel tips for their own city.
Writing *Extra* SB page 77 Travel guide	Matching paragraphs with the correct city and writing headings. Matching words with their synonyms. Replacing the word *very* with adverb + adjective combinations. Writing a travel guide for their own city.
Writing WB page 45	Writing a description of a place.

7 Escape *Teacher's notes*

Reading & Vocabulary (SB page 68)

1

- Focus the students' attention on the photo at the bottom of the page. Ask them if this is the sort of beach they like to go to when they have a holiday.

- Go through the questions with the class. Then put the students into small groups to discuss them. Appoint a representative of each group to report back to the class. Make sure they keep a written list of their ideas for things that might spoil a day at the seaside.

- Ask the students to read the text and see how many of the things they put on their list are mentioned. Find out if any of these things have ever happened to anyone in the class. If so, ask them to explain what happened.

> c) The author mentions:
> - Seeing people taking their shirt off in public.
> - Getting sand in everything.
> - Getting sunburned and windburned.
> - Cold water.
> - Traffic jams.
> - Children misbehaving.
> - No toilets on beach.
> - Stray dogs.
> - Losing things.
> - Getting tar in hair.

Cultural notes

Maine /meɪn/
A state in New England, in the north-east of the United States famous for its pine trees, snowy winters and craggy, dramatic coastline.

Kennebunkport /kenɪˈbʌnkpɔːt/
Kennebunkport (population 4000) is a town in the south of Maine. During the summer months, Kennebunkport and the beaches along the coast near the town are popular with wealthy tourists, and in autumn many come to see the flame-red maples.

2

Ask the students to decide if the statements are true or false. Then allow them to compare notes with a partner. When checking answers, ask them to correct the false statements, using evidence from the text to support their answers.

> a)
> 1 False. ('Frankly, I have never understood the British attachment to the seaside.')
> 2 True.
> 3 False. ('I managed to get so sunburned that a dermatologist invited me to a convention in Cleveland the following weekend as an exhibit.')
> b)
> 1 True.
> 2 False. ('I put my foot down and said, "Never – absolutely not," which is of course why we ended up, three hours later, at Kennebunk Beach in Maine.')
> 3 True.
> c)
> 1 True.
> 2 False. ('I'll call him Jimmy in case he should one day become a lawyer.')
> 3 True.

3

- Focus the students' attention on the definitions. Ask them if they can complete any of them without looking back through the text. When they've done this, they can check with the text and find the remaining ones.

- Check answers before asking the students to write their own example sentences.

> a) paddle   b) foot down   c) scene
> d) dinghy   e) nibble   f) nap

4

Pairwork. Put the students into pairs and ask them to discuss the question. Encourage them to report back to the class and take a class vote to find out who sides with the author and who with the author's wife.

Vocabulary & Grammar (SB page 70)

1

Read the first two lines of the summary to the class and then go round the class, student by student, establishing the correct order for the remaining lines in the summary.

> *Correct order:* 8, 1, 4, 6, 3, 2, 7, 10, 9, 5

2

Elicit examples from the students which demonstrate the difference between *tell* and *say* before they categorise the highlighted verbs from Exercise 1.

> **2 and 3**
> A: reassured me that, informed me that, persuade me to
> B: Mentioned that, announced that, insisted on (+ gerund), explained that, suggested that / (+ gerund)

Language notes

Vocabulary & Grammar: reporting verbs

- *Say, tell* and *ask* are the most common reporting verbs.

- *Tell, reassure, inform, advise, assure, convince, encourage, persuade* and *warn* are usually followed by an object pronoun (*me, him/her*, etc.), e.g. *He told me he wanted to go home.*

- *Say, mention, confirm, claim, admit, announce, insist, explain* and *suggest* aren't necessarily followed by an object pronoun, but can be followed by an optional *that*, e.g. *She mentioned to me (that) she was on a diet.* Or *She mentioned (that) she was on a diet.*

---

3 🌐 2.21

- Ask the students to think about which column the verbs should go in before they turn to their dictionaries to check the patterns.

- Play the recording for the students to listen to five people talking about their favourite beaches and to confirm their answers.

> A: advise sb that / sb to; assure sb that; convince sb that; encourage sb to
> B: admit that; claim that; confirm that

> 🌐 2.21
>
> 1
> *My favourite beach is in Cape Town. It's called Camps Beach, and I love it, because the location is spectacular. But if you want to swim there, I'd advise you to wear a wetsuit because the water is freezing.*

2
My favourite beach is in the south of France, but nobody knows about it. It took a while to convince my girlfriend that it was worth climbing down a very dangerous cliff to get there, but she had to admit that it was worth it.

3
My favourite beach is in Sardinia. I've travelled to hundreds of beaches in different countries, and I can now confirm that the best beach in the world is Cala del Morto.

4
Holiday brochures claim that the best beaches are in far away places like the Caribbean or the Indian Ocean, but I can assure you that there are wonderful beaches nearer home. For example, my favourite beach is in Cornwall, and I can drive there in a day.

5
My favourite beach is the man-made beach along the river Seine in Paris. In summer, they import a load of sand and encourage people to go there to sunbathe and relax. I think it's great for families who can't afford to go away on holiday.

Speaking: anecdote (SB page 70)

For more information about how to set up, monitor and repeat Anecdotes, see page xx in the Introduction.

- Go through the instructions and the questions with the class. Give the students a minute or two to decide what they're going to talk about. Then ask them to look at the questions and think about their answers to them. Allow them to make notes of what they're going to say and how they're going to say it, but discourage them from writing a paragraph that they can simply read out. Go round, monitoring and giving help where necessary.

- Pairwork. Put the students in pairs and ask them to take turns to tell their partner about a family holiday they went on as a child. Encourage them to ask each other follow-up questions to get further information. Then ask some pairs to report back to the class about what they found out.

Listening & Grammar (SB page 71)

Past modals

1 🌐 2.22–2.24

- Pairwork. Put the students into pairs and ask them to look at the photos and discuss what sort of things might go wrong on holidays like these. Encourage them to make a list for each one and to report back to the class on their ideas.

- Go through the instructions and the three questions with the class, then play the recording for them to listen, compare their ideas with what happened on each holiday and find the answers to the questions.

> a) Rachel.
> b) Sarah and Paul.
> c) Amy and Josh.

🔵 2.22

Paul

We decided to do something really special for Christmas. We both love skiing so we managed to book ten days in a small ski resort in the French Alps. When we arrived there, though, we found out that the temperatures had been unseasonably warm. Basically, there was no snow. Well, there were a few centimetres of snow very high up on the black pistes, but we weren't allowed to go there, because it was too high and too dangerous. So we had to find other ways to entertain ourselves, and in the end, this was really good because we were forced to relax. We didn't have to get up early to go skiing, so we could go out until late at night and sleep in the morning. We read books, had long lunches, went for walks and drank lots of hot chocolate. At the end of the holiday, we felt completely relaxed.

🔵 2.23

Amy

When I was 18, I was desperate to go to Guatemala to see the volcanoes but I wasn't allowed to go there alone – my parents thought I was too young. So my brother agreed to come with me, and we carefully planned a three-week tour. We set off from London, and our destination was the Guatemalan city of Antigua, but we had to stop over at Miami for a few hours. Anyway, we finally took off from Miami, and during the flight, my brother asked a fellow passenger if he'd been to Antigua before. He replied that he had, and it was one of the most beautiful islands he'd ever come across. At that point, we realised we were on the wrong plane, going to the wrong holiday. Obviously we couldn't get off the plane there and then, so we had to carry on and then sort ourselves out when we landed. There were no direct flights from the Caribbean island of Antigua to the Guatemalan city of Antigua, so we had to go back to North America and start again. We lost a week of our holiday, but in the end it just made us appreciate Guatemala all the more.

🔵 2.24

Rachel

When I told my friends I was going on a cycling holiday in Andalucia, they thought I was joking. But I thought it would be fine. OK, I don't actually own a bicycle, but I do go to the gym twice a week. I even go on the exercise bike sometimes. In preparation, I went to a specialist bike shop to buy some cycling gear. The helmet was compulsory, so I got one of those, but I didn't think I needed to bother with the padded cycling shorts. The man in the shop recommended them, but I thought they looked stupid, so I didn't get them. I should have listened to the man. As soon as I met the other people I knew I was in trouble. One man had recently cycled from London to Edinburgh – for fun! Our Spanish tour leader looked like she was about to set off on the Tour de France. I made a big effort to keep up on the first day, but by the evening my bottom was in agony, and I couldn't sit down. Fortunately, we didn't have to carry anything – there was a car that took all our baggage from one place to the next. But I have to admit that I got a lift in the baggage car a couple of times. I never realised that Andalucia was so hilly.

2

• Pairwork. Go through the instructions with the class and make sure they understand that two phrases are appropriate in each list. Ask the students to discuss in pairs which answer isn't appropriate in each case.

• Play the recording again for them to check. Ask them to tick the modal verb or phrase that each speaker actually uses.

1 a and b	4 a and c
2 b and c	5 b and c
3 a and b	6 a and b

The modal verbs actually used in the recordings:
1 b)   2 b)   3 a)   4 c)   5 c)   6 a)

3

Go through the example sentences in the margin and ask the students to match each one with the functions listed in the exercise. Then do the exercise with the class.

a) I had to / needed to
b) I didn't have to / didn't need to
c) I could / was allowed to
d) I couldn't / wasn't allowed to
e) I shouldn't have done
f) I should have done / ought to have

4

• Go through the instructions with the class and make sure they understand that they should make as many true sentences as they can using the prompts.

• Put the students into pairs and ask them to tell each other their sentences.

5 Grammar *Extra* 7, Part 1

Ask the students to turn to *Grammar Extra* 7, Part 1 on page 138 of the Student's Book. Here they'll find an explanation of the grammar they've been studying and a further exercise to practise it.

1	
a) didn't have to	e) shouldn't have
b) didn't need to	f) had to
c) ought to have	g) couldn't
d) wasn't allowed to	h) should have

Reading (SB page 72)

1

- Pairwork. Focus attention on the postcards and ask the students when they last received a postcard, who it was from and what it said. Ask them to say what kind of things they normally write on postcards.

- Go through the questions with the class and ask the students to discuss them in pairs. Encourage the pairs to report back to the class on their discussion.

2

Give the students time to read the article carefully and to match the character types to the postcards. They can check their answers at the end of the article.

A 3   B 4   C 5   D 2   E 1

3

Pairwork. Ask the students to discuss the five character types described in the article and to say if they know anyone who fits the descriptions.

Vocabulary (SB page 73)

Word formation

1

Go through the instructions with the class, then ask them to turn back to the article on page 72 and underline all the adjectives they can find with the three suffixes. Check answers before getting the students to say which suffix has which meaning.

> tasteful, bookish, humourless, cheerful, thoughtful, stylish, snobbish, tasteless
>
> 1 ful or ish
> 2 less

2

- Make sure the students understand that for each list they have to decide which suffix combines with all the words (individual words within a list may also combine with the other suffixes).

- Ask the students to check their answers by looking in the Word formation panel in the margin. This gives more examples of words which have the three suffixes. Ask them to tick the ones they know and to choose three more to learn.

a) less   b) ish   c) ful

3

- Focus attention on the prefixes in the table and point out that these prefixes give a negative meaning to the words they combine with. Ask the students to look back through the article on page 72 and find ten negative adjectives with these prefixes. They should write these in the correct columns of the table. Check answers before moving on to the next stage.

- Ask the students to form negative adjectives from those in the box and add them to the table.

dis	il	im
dissatisfied	illegible	impatient
dishonest	illegal	immature
disloyal	illiterate	immoral
disobedient	illogical	impolite

in	ir	un
indecisive	irresistible	unadventurous
incapable		uninteresting
		unusual
		unself-conscious
inadequate	irrational	undivided
inappropriate	irrelevant	unwilling
	irresponsible	

4 🌐 2.25

Paper 3: Use of English Part 3 Word Formation

- Point out that the students will need to modify the words at the ends of the lines to make them fit the gaps. This could mean adding a prefix or a suffix or both, making the word negative, etc. The words needed are all ones which have been looked at in this section. The students may need help with the final gap, where the writer is being sarcastic. If they fail to grasp this, they may try to complete it with *unhelpful*.

- Play the recording for the students to check their answers.

1 unwilling	2 irresistible	3 relentless
4 disobedient	5 devilish	6 undivided
7 stressful	8 irresponsible	9 careful
10 hellish	11 tearful	12 helpful

5

Pairwork. Ask the students to discuss the question in pairs and to report back to the class any surprising or amusing things they find out.

Listening & Speaking (SB page 74)

1

Get students to discuss this question as a class. The listening text in the next exercise is about a holiday romance. If your students prefer, talk about simple friendships that have developed during a holiday.

2 🌐 2.26

Tell the students that they're going to listen to a woman talking about a holiday romance. Go through the questions with the class first, then play the recording.

> a) She was travelling around Australia.
> b) Her visa ran out.
> c) Amsterdam.

🌐 2.26
(F = Frank; A = Angela)

F: *Have you ever had a holiday romance, Angela?*

A: *I have actually … many years ago!! When I was twenty, I went travelling to Australia – I went to Sydney – and while I was there I met Brad.*

F: *Brad?!!!*

A: *Yes, I know. Come to think of it, he did look a bit like a film star, with his blond hair, and lovely white teeth. Anyway, we met through a mutual friend, and she arranged our first date. And that was it – the beginning of a lovely relationship!*

F: *Ahh!*

A: *We got on so well together. In fact, I really thought I'd met my soulmate. Do you know what I mean? I thought we may end up together.*

F: *Yeah – I know what you mean. So, what happened next?*

A: *Well, eventually my visa ran out and I returned to London. We then spent six months on the phone, swapping letters and parcels. But long-distance relationships are really difficult, and neither of us wanted to give up our lives and move to the other side of the world. Basically, our relationship wasn't strong enough to survive the distance.*

F: *What happened?*

A: *Well, in the end, he met somebody else.*

F: *Ah.*

A: *And to be honest, I was relieved.*

F: *So have you ever heard from him again?*

A: *No, but the funny thing is that I heard through our mutual friend that he met a Dutch girl and ended up moving to Amsterdam!*

3

Give the students time to look through the extracts so that they know what to listen out for. Play the recording again and ask the students to write in the missing words.

a) ago	b) star	c) friend	d) soulmate
e) together	f) enough	g) else	h) relieved

4

Focus attention on the words in bold in Exercise 3. Explain that these are known as *discourse markers*. Go through the list of eight interpretations and ask them to match them to the discourse markers.

1 g)	2 e)	3 a)	4 b)	5 d)	6 c)	7 h)
8 f)						

Language note

Vocabulary: spoken discourse markers
These discourse markers are either spoken or found in informal writing such as an email or a letter to a friend. During a conversation many of them are signals to provide the listener with the information they need to react. *Actually* can be used as a way of contradicting someone, e.g. *You aren't the type to have a holiday romance, are you? – Actually, I am.* If you've strayed from the topic you were discussing, *Anyway*, is the perfect way of saying, e.g. *Let's get back to what we were talking about.*

5 🌐 2.27

- Tell the students they're going to read about another holiday romance. Tell them to read it carefully and decide which discourse marker is the most appropriate for each choice.

- Play the recording for the students to check their answers. Then ask them to practise the conversation with a partner, taking turns to be Gill and Tony. Play it again if they need help with intonation. Ask a confident pair to perform the conversation for the class.

1	Actually	5	Basically
2	come to think of it	6	to be honest
3	Anyway	7	In fact
4	Do you know what I mean	8	in the end

6

- Pairwork. Put the students into pairs and ask them to write a similar conversation about meeting someone on holiday, using as many discourse markers as they can.

- When they've finished, ask them to practise their conversations. Take note of any particularly good ones, which could be performed for the class.

Reading & Grammar (SB page 75)

Articles

1 🌐 2.28

- Ask the students to look quickly through the story and ask a confident student to give a quick summary of what it's about. Then ask them to read it more carefully and to decide which articles need to be added to the story.

- Play the recording for them to check their answers. Ask them what they think the moral of the story is.

---

1 A   2 –   3 the   4 a   5 –   6 a   7 an
8 a   9 The   10 the   11 the   12 The
13 a   14 The   15 –   16 The   17 the
18 a   19 a   20 a   21 –   22 a   23 –
24 the   25 the   26 a   27 the   28 the

The moral of the story: Be satisfied with who you are and with what you have. More money/ success won't necessarily make your life better.

🌐 2.28

Gone fishing

A tourist in Africa was walking by the sea when he saw a man in simple clothes dozing in a fishing boat. It was an idyllic picture, so he decided to take a photograph. The click of the camera woke the man up. The tourist offered him a cigarette.

'The weather is great. There are plenty of fish. Why are you lying around instead of going out and catching more?'

The fisherman replied, 'Because I caught enough this morning.'

'But just imagine,' the tourist said, 'If you went out there three times every day, you'd catch three times as much. After about a year you could buy yourself a motor-boat. After a few more years of hard work, you could have a fleet of boats working for you. And then …'

'And then?' asked the fisherman.

'And then,' the tourist continued triumphantly, 'you could be calmly sitting on the beach, dozing in the sun and looking at the beautiful ocean.'

2

- Go through the rules with the class and then ask them to find an example of each in the text in Exercise 1.

- When you've checked answers, ask them to look at the information about articles in the box in the margin.

Rule a): 1, 4, 6, 7, 8, 13, 18, 19, 20, 22
Rule b): 5, 15, 21, 23
Rule c): 11, 12, 16, 17, 24, 25, 26
Rule d): 3, 9, 10
Rule e): 14, 27, 28
Rule f): 2

Language note

Grammar: articles
(See Student's Book page 138.)

3

- Go through the instructions and make sure everyone understands the concept of 'things in general'. Point out that in the first example, the speaker is talking about travel in general, not one particular journey; the second example is about men and women in general, not one particular man or woman.

- As the students write their own generalisations, go round giving extra help where needed. Then put the students into pairs to discuss their sentences. Finally, have a class feedback session in which all the generalisations are shared.

4 Grammar *Extra* 7, Part 2

Ask the students to turn to *Grammar Extra* 7, Part 2 on page 138 of the Student's Book. Here they'll find an explanation of the grammar they've been studying and further exercises to practise it.

2
a) the   b) –, –   c) –, –   d) –, –   e) –, –
f) –, –   g) –, –   h) –, –   i) the, the
j) the, the   k) the, the   l) the, the
3
1 An   2 the   3 –   4 a   5 a   6 a   7 a
8 –   9 The   10 the   11 the   12 a   13 the
14 a   15 the   16 the   17 The   18 –   19 –

Pronunciation (SB page 75)

1 🌐 2.29

Play the recording and ask the students to listen and repeat the place names, paying particular attention to the pronunciation of *the*. Ask them what the difference is between A and B.

In list A *the* is pronounced /ðə/.
In list B *the* is pronounced /ði/.

The difference is because the items in list B all begin with a vowel sound.

Cultural notes

The Danube /ðə ˈdænuːb/
The Danube is the second longest river in Europe after the Volga. It flows for 2,850km through ten countries (Austria, Bulgaria, Croatia, Germany, Hungary, Moldova, Romania, Serbia, Slovakia and Ukraine).

The Dead Sea /ðə ded sɪː/
The Dead Sea is a lake which lies between Israel/ The West Bank (to the west) and Jordan (to the east). It's famous for its high salt content, which gives bathers much more buoyancy than sea water.

The Himalayas /ðə hɪməˈleɪjəs/
The Himalaya Range sits between Bhutan, India, Nepal and the Tibetan region of China. Its highest point is Mount Everest (8,874m), the highest point on Earth.

The Thames /ðə temz/
The River Thames is 350km long. It's the second-longest river in the UK – the longest is the River Severn. It flows through Oxford and London before running into the sea at Southend-on-Sea.

The Urals /ðə ˈjɔːrəls/
The Urals are a mountain range running 2,500km from north-western Russia to south-western Russia, forming a natural border between Europe and Asia.

The Andes /ði: jænˈdiːz/
The Andes are the longest mountain range in the world, running along the length of the western side of South America for 7,000km through Argentina, Bolivia, Chile, Colombia, Ecuador, Peru and Venezuela. The average height of the range is 4,000m.

The Eiffel Tower /ði: ˈjaɪfəl ˈtaʊə/
The Eiffel Tower was constructed in central Paris under the supervision of Gustave Eiffel for the Grand Exposition of 1889. At 243m high, it was the tallest building in the world and remained so until 1930.

The Empire State Building /ði: ˈempaɪə steɪt ˈbɪldɪŋ/
The Empire State Building is 102 storeys high and was the world's tallest building from 1931 to 1972. Now that the Word Trade Center has been destroyed, it's once again the tallest building in New York City.

The Indian Ocean /ði: ˈɪndɪən ˈəʊʃən/
The Indian Ocean sits between Africa (to the west) and Indonesia/Australia (to the east), India (to the north) and Antarctica (to the south). It covers about one-fifth of the Earth's water surface and is the third largest ocean.

The Orinoco /ði: ɒrɪnˈnəʊkəʊ/
The Orinoco is a South American river running for more than 2,000km through Colombia and Venezuela.

Language notes

Pronunciation: *the*
When pronouncing place names starting with a consonant or the vowel *u* pronounced /juː/, *the* is pronounced /ðə/, e.g. *The Danube* /ðə dænjuːb/, *The USA* /ðə juːeseɪ/. For names starting with any other vowel sound, *the* is pronounced /ðiː/, e.g. *The Andes* /ði: jændiːz/, *The Eiffel Tower* /ði: jaɪfəltaʊə/. Note that there's an intrusive /j/ sound between a word that ends with a vowel sound, e.g. *the* /ðiː/, and a word that follows which begins with a vowel sound, e.g. *Andes* /ændiːz/, so that you say the /j/ Andes.

2

Ask the students to think about the question and add any more examples that they can think of to the table, when they've checked the pronunciation in a dictionary.

Useful phrases (SB page 76)

1 🌐 2.30

- Pairwork. Focus the students' attention on the picture and ask them to identify the place the woman is dreaming about (Paris). Ask them to discuss with their partner the sights they'd want to see on a first visit to Paris.

- Play the recording and ask the students to listen and find out how many museums are mentioned.

> Three museums are mentioned: the Louvre, the Musée d'Orsay and the Picasso Museum.

> 🌐 2.30 (T = Tim; S = Sal)
>
> T: *What are you doing for the long weekend?*
> S: *I'm off to Paris.*
> T: *Oh great – I love Paris.*
> S: *Oh yes, you know it pretty well, don't you? Can you believe this is my first time there? Do you have any tips?*
> T: *Well, there's so much to see. I'd definitely recommend the Eiffel Tower. Take the glass-sided lift – when it comes out into the daylight, the views are spectacular.*
> S: *That sounds like a must. What about museums?*
> T: *Well, of course the most famous museum is the Louvre, but it's probably best to avoid it because of the queues, but make sure you go to the Musée d'Orsay. It's one of the best museums in the world. You'll have to queue there too, but it's well worth the effort. Where are you staying?*
> S: *In a little hotel in the 3rd arrondissement.*
> T: *Oh, that's a really nice area. While you're there, make sure you walk around the backstreets because there are some lovely little shops – oh, and while you're there you should go to the Picasso museum. You won't be disappointed.*

Escape UNIT **7** **75**

S: Oh, I love Picasso. And how should we get around? What are the taxis like?

T: Um, I think it's probably best to avoid taxis, because the traffic can be very slow. If I were you, I'd use the buses or the metro. They're very good.

S: Wow, that sounds great.

T: And whatever you do, don't leave Paris without tasting the oysters at Bofinger.

S: Bofinger?

T: Yes, it's a restaurant in Rue de la Bastille. It's the best place for seafood, and the décor is fantastic.

S: I think I need to write this down. How do you spell Bofinger?

2 🌐 2.31

- Point out that matching the sentence halves produces useful phrases for giving advice about places to visit.
- Play the recording for the students to check their answers. Then play it again for them to repeat.

a) 6   b) 9   c) 10   d) 1   e) 3   f) 5
g) 8   h) 2   i) 7   j) 11   k) 4

🌐 2.31

a   I'd definitely recommend the Eiffel Tower.
b   The views are spectacular.
c   That sounds like a must.
d   It's probably best to avoid the Louvre.
e   Make sure you go to the Musée d'Orsay.
f   It's well worth the effort.
g   You should go to the Picasso Museum.
h   You won't be disappointed.
i   If I were you, I'd use the buses or the metro.
j   Whatever you do, don't leave Paris without tasting the oysters.
k   It's the best place for seafood.

Cultural notes

The Louvre /ðə ˈluːvrə/
The Louvre is one of the largest museums in the world. Among the thousands of famous paintings housed there is Leonardo da Vinci's *Mona Lisa*.

The Musée d'Orsay /ðə muːˈseɪ dɔːˈseɪ/
Once a railway station, the Musée d'Orsay was converted into a museum in 1986. It now houses 19th-century French art and design, including a large collection of French Impressionist paintings.

The Eiffel Tower
(See notes about the Eiffel Tower on page 75.)

The Picasso Museum /ðə pɪˈkæsəʊ mjuːˈziːəm/
The Picasso Museum in Paris has 3,000 works by Pablo Picasso as well as work by other artists including Degas, Matisse and Seurat, from Picasso's private collection.

- Ask the students to complete the tips using the useful phrases.
- Check answers before asking the students to match each tip to one of the cities in the box.

a) if … were; views … spectacular
b) you; don't … without
c) best … for; should
d) make … you; won't … disappointed
e) best … avoid
f) a; well … the
a) Cape Town   b) Barcelona   c) Bangkok
d) Sydney   e) New York   f) Mexico City

Cultural notes

Table Mountain
A flat sandstone mountain (1,086m) overlooking the city of Cape Town, South Africa.

Antoni Gaudi /ænˈtɒni ˈɡaʊdi/ (1852–1926)
Antoni Gaudi was a Catalan architect who worked in the Spanish city of Barcelona. He was influenced by gothic and Catalan architecture, but developed his own unique and eccentric style.

Bondi Beach /ˈbɒndaɪ biːtʃ/
The name of a famous beach and suburban area close to the centre of Sydney, Australia.

Coogee /kuːˈgi/
A suburb on the south-east coast of Sydney, Australia.

Central Park /ˈsentrəl pɑːk/
Central Park is an 843-acre public park in the middle of New York City. It was created in 1853. It includes several artificial lakes, two ice-skating rinks and a sports area.

Teotihuacan /teɪəʊtiwæˈkæn/
Teotihuacan is an ancient city in central Mexico. Between 300 and 650 A.D. Teotihuacan controlled a wide area. It was destroyed in about 750.

4

- Pairwork. Put the students into pairs and ask them to write some tips for their own city. If they don't come from the same place, get them to write tips for the city they are in at present or a place that they both know.
- Go round, giving help and making sure they're using the useful phrases wherever possible. Ask several pairs to read out their tips to the class.

Writing *Extra* (SB page 77)

Travel guide

1

- Pairwork. Focus the students' attention on the photos and tell them to discuss the questions in pairs.
- Find out how much the students can say about the different cities and make notes of their ideas on the board.

2

Ask the students to match the paragraphs in the guide to the cities shown in the photos. When they've finished, ask them to compare their answers with a partner. Then check with the class. Ask them what details helped them decide on the answers (e.g. *famous canals* number 1).

> 1) Amsterdam   2) Madrid   3) Dublin
> 4) Buenos Aires   5) Sydney

> **Cultural notes**
>
> **Guinness** /ˈgɪnɪs/
> Guinness is a dry stout beer from Dublin, Republic of Ireland, first brewed in 1759. Its characteristics are a deep black body with a creamy white head of froth.
>
> **The Blue Mountains**
> A mountain range and popular tourist destination in New South Wales, Australia.

3

Point out that guidebooks often have questions as headings for different sections. These are the sorts of questions that tourists visiting the places described might want to ask. Ask the students to think of suitable questions to use as headings for the paragraphs of the guide. When they've finished, put them into pairs and ask them to compare the headings they've thought of.

> *Possible questions:*
> 2 How hot does it get in the summer?
> 3 What's the best drink in the city?
> 4 Where can I find the best steak?

4

Focus attention on the highlighted words in the guide and ask the students to match them with the synonyms in the table. Allow them to compare their answers in pairs before checking with the class.

> **Saying how things usually are**
> is sometimes = can be
> normally = in general
> most = the majority of
> are usually = tend to be
>
> **Linking words**
> owing to = because of
> Despite this = However
> Even though = In spite of the fact that
> Or else = Alternatively

5

Point out that there are many different ways of saying *very*. Draw the students' attention to the example: *extortionately expensive*. Ask them first to underline all the instances of *very* in the guide, then to replace each one with an appropriate alternative from the box. Remind them to use each one only once.

> Paragraph 1: extortionately expensive
> Paragraph 2: extremely hot; bitterly cold
> Paragraph 3: particularly chilly
> Paragraph 4: surprisingly popular; totally addictive
> Paragraph 5: dazzlingly white

6

- This writing exercise could be done for homework. Remind the students to use linking words to make their texts flow well and to include adverb + adjective combinations to make them more interesting.

- You could ask the students to swap their accounts in pairs or small groups and read each other's. Alternatively, they could be displayed in the classroom for everyone to read and enjoy.

> **Further practice material**
>
> **Need more writing practice?**
> → Workbook page 45
> • Writing a description of a place
>
> **Need more classroom practice activities?**
> → Photocopiable resource materials pages 171 to 173
>   **Grammar:** *Pleasure and pain*
>   **Vocabulary:** *Word formation*
>   **Communication:** *Pronunciation review*
> → Top 10 activities pages xv to xx
>
> **Need DVD material?**
> → DVD – Programme 7: *Cindy Jackson*
>
> **Need progress tests?**
> → Test CD – *Test Unit 1*
>
> **Need more on important teaching concepts?**
> → Key concepts in *New Inside Out* pages xxii to xxxv
>
> **Need student self-study practice?**
> → CD-ROM – Unit 7: *Escape*
>
> **Need student CEF self-evaluation?**
> → CEF Checklists pages xxxvii to xliv
>
> **Need more information and more ideas?**
> → www.insideout.net

8 Attraction *Overview*

Section & Aims	What the students are doing
Listening & Vocabulary SB page 78 Listening for gist Facial features	Completing collocations about facial features. Listening to people talking about features they find attractive. Talking about computer-generated 'perfect' male and female faces.
Reading SB page 79 Scanning for information Guessing meaning from context	Agreeing or disagreeing with statements about the nature of beauty. Scanning a text to find if statements are true. Guessing the meaning of unknown words and compiling a glossary.
Grammar SB page 80 Passive report structures	Studying the use of passive reporting in written texts. Completing passive reporting sentences. Rewriting statements in a more informal style.
Listening SB page 80 Listening for gist	Matching people with opinions on plastic surgery. Completing extracts from a radio debate.
Reading & Grammar SB page 81 *have/get something done*	Completing a text about what a woman has had done to her face. Identifying when you use *have/get* + object + past participle. Putting sentences in order. Talking about the best places to *get/have* things done.
Reading & Speaking SB page 82 Reading for detail; fluency practice	Discussing being attracted to someone. Reading an article and completing a table
Vocabulary SB page 82 Character adjectives	Deciding whether adjectives are positive or negative. Replacing words in sentences with others of similar meaning.
Pronunciation SB page 82 Stress in character adjectives	Marking the stress on adjectives describing character. Identifying changes of stress when adjectives are turned into nouns.
Reading & Speaking SB page 84 Reading for gist; fluency practice	Reading the synopsis of a DVD to see if they would like to watch it. Discussing sayings.
Listening SB page 84 Listening for specific information	Listening to a radio programme and answering questions. Discussing the ideas presented in the programme.
Grammar SB page 85 Unreal conditional structures	Completing hypothetical questions with *would* and *were*. Then underlining the alternatives to *if* in the questions. Completing questions and interviewing other people.
Speaking: anecdote SB page 85 Fluency practice	Talking about the most positive or negative person they know.
Useful phrases SB page 86 Body idioms	Listening to a conversation and identifying phrases that are different. Matching useful phrases to those they've underlined. Then writing example sentences using the useful phrases. Writing and practising a conversation using body idioms.
Vocabulary *Extra* page 87 Metaphor	Looking at some common metaphors to describe people's emotions. Using these metaphors to describe personal experiences.
Writing WB page 51	Writing a description of a person.

8 Attraction *Teacher's notes*

Listening & Vocabulary (SB page 78)

1

Groupwork. Put the students into small groups and ask them to discuss the questions. Ask them to make a group decision on the most handsome man and most beautiful woman, and encourage them to go into detail about what it is that makes them more attractive than other men and women. Then different groups present their ideas to the class.

2 🔘 **2.32**

- Ask the students to work individually to decide how to complete the collocations.

- Allow them to compare their answers in pairs before playing the recording for them to check. Then ask the students to discuss the opinions they heard and whether or not they agree with them.

a) skin	g) lips
b) bone structure	h) smile
c) teeth	i) nose
d) eyes	j) cheekbones
e) jaw	k) eyebrows
f) eyes	l) in the cheeks

🔘 **2.32** (I = Interviewer; W = woman; M = Man)

1
I: *What do you think makes a face attractive?*
W1: *For a woman, smooth skin and good bone structure.*
I: *And for a man?*
W1: *Um, nice white teeth, sparkling eyes and a square jaw. That's what I like anyway.*

2
I: *What do you think makes a face attractive?*
M1: *Big eyes, full lips and a big smile.*
I: *Like Julia Roberts?*
M1: *Exactly.*

3
I: *What do you think makes a face attractive?*
W2: *It's probably easier to say what I don't like. On a man, I don't like a small nose – it doesn't have to be enormous, but a little turned-up nose on a man looks silly.*
I: *So you don't like Brad Pitt then?*
W2: *Well, I like everything about him except his nose!*

4
I: *What do you think makes a face attractive?*
M2: *High cheekbones, especially on a woman. Like Marlena Dietrich. She's my ideal woman. I love her arched eyebrows.*

5
I: *What do you think makes a face attractive?*
W3: *I love dimples.*
I: *Do you mean a dimple in the chin?*
W3: *Yeah, I quite like that, but I meant dimples in the cheeks when somebody smiles – it's so cute.*

3

- Focus attention on the photographs and read out the text, or get a student to read it. Make sure everyone understands that these computer-generated images are supposed to represent perfect faces.

- Put the students into pairs and ask them to discuss what they like and dislike about the faces. Encourage them to report back to the class on their opinions.

4

Pairwork. Put the students into pairs and ask them to think about people they know with interesting faces. When they're ready, ask them to take turns to describe these people to their partners. Encourage them to use as many of the collocations from Exercise 2 as they can. As they work, go round listening and helping where necessary. Encourage students who produce particularly good descriptions to repeat them for the class.

Reading (SB page 79)

1

- Go through the statements with the class and make sure everyone understands them. Explain that 'Beauty is in the eye of the beholder' is an old-fashioned saying meaning that everyone has their own idea of what constitutes beauty; whether people or things are beautiful or not depends on the attitude of the person looking at them.

- Put the students into pairs and ask them to decide whether they agree with the statements or not. Ask them for their opinions on this before moving on to the next stage of the activity.

- Ask the students to read the article and mark the statements true or false according to the research reported in it.

> a) False.   b) False.   c) True.   d) True.
> e) False.   f) False.

Cultural notes

Betty Boop /ˈbeti buːp/
A cartoon character produced by Max Fleischer. She made her first appearance in 1930 and was a composite of several real-life sex symbols of the era.

Aladdin /əˈlædɪn/
A character from the book *One Thousand and One Nights*, a collection of folk and fairy tales from around the world. Aladdin discovers a lamp which, when rubbed, releases a genie who does the bidding of the keeper of the lamp.

Bambi /ˈbæmbi/
The central character in the full-length animated Disney film *Bambi* (1942). Bambi is a deer, the son of the Great Prince of the Forest.

Julia Roberts /ˈdʒuːlijə ˈrɒbɜːts/ (born 1967)
The American actress Julia Roberts has appeared in a number of romantic comedies, such as *Pretty Woman* (1990), *My Best Friend's Wedding* (1997) and *Notting Hill* (1999). She won the Best Actress Academy Award for the title role in *Erin Brockovich* (2000).

Leonardo DiCaprio /lɪjɒˈnaːdəʊ dɪˈkæprɪjəʊ/ (born 1974)
Leonardo DiCaprio started acting when he was 14. He's starred in a number of successful films, such as *Romeo and Juliet* (1995), *Titanic* (1996), *Gangs of New York* (2002), *The Aviator* (2005) and *Revolutionary Road* (2008). He's also greatly involved in environmental work in the US.

Jude Law /dʒuːd lɔː/ (born 1972)
Jude Law is an English actor who starred with Matt Damon in the film *The Talented Mr Ripley* (1999). He then moved to Hollywood and has starred in many films since, such as *Cold Mountain* (2003), *Closer* (2004) and *The Holiday* (2006).

2

- Remind the students of the work they did on guessing the meaning of unknown words from context in Unit 5. Then ask them to underline any words and phrases in the article that they don't know and to try to work out their likely meaning from the context.

- Get them to complete the glossary and add to it any other words that they underlined. Encourage them to try to write their own definitions before turning to a dictionary to check.

> a) beholder   e) irresistible
> b) rank   f) trustworthy
> c) at first glance g) subtle
> d) adage   h) prominant

Grammar (SB page 80)

Passive report structures

1

Ask the students to look at the two versions of each sentence and discuss the questions with the class. Focus the students' attention on the information and the examples in the margin.

> a) passive   b) passive   c) passive

Language notes

Grammar: passive report structures

- When reporting what people consider(ed) to be true, it's often easier to drop the 'people', especially if you don't know or you don't care which people, and use a passive report structure. If you're writing or submitting a formal spoken report, it's more appropriate.

- The most common reporting verbs are: *say, think, consider, believe* and *assume*.

- The two ways of presenting a passive report structure are:

  1) subject + *is/was/are/were* + past participle of reporting verb + infinitive, e.g. *Chocolate is thought to be bad for your skin.*

  2) *It* + *is/was* + past participle of reporting verb + *that* + subject phrase, e.g. *It's said that reading in a dim light can damage your eyes.*

2

Ask the students to work individually to put the words in the correct places in the sentences. Allow them to compare in pairs before checking with the class.

a) Chocolate is thought to be bad for your skin.

b) It has been suggested that you should drink at least two litres of water a day.

c) It used to be assumed that carrots were good for your eyesight.

d) It is said that reading in a dim light can damage your eyes.

e) Shaving body hair is widely believed to make it grow back thicker and faster.

f) It is often said that we only use 10% of our brains.

3

- Ask the students to rewrite the statements in a more informal style. As they do this, go round checking that everyone is manipulating the structures correctly.

- Put the students into pairs and ask them to discuss whether people believe the same things in their country or countries.

a) People think that chocolate is bad for your skin.

b) Some doctors have suggested that you should drink at least two litres of water a day.

c) People used to assume that carrots were good for your eyesight.

d) They say that reading in a dim light can damage your eyes.

e) Many people believe that shaving body hair will make it grow back thicker and faster.

f) They often say that we only use 10% of our brains.

Listening (SB page 80)

1 🌐 2.33

- Focus the students' attention on the photos and ask them to discuss in pairs what sort of people they think they are. Read out the opinions and ask them to match each person with one of the opinions.

- Play the recording for the students to check their ideas.

a) Rita   b) Michael   c) Jean

🌐 **2.33** (JO = Jean Oldham; RT = Rita Taylor; MH = Michael Hirst)

JO: *Personally, I'm dead against cosmetic surgery of any kind. I work on a women's magazine, so you can imagine how many beautiful models I've met. But I'm also in daily contact with women who are not physically perfect, and I have to say that the most beautiful women I know are not models – they are the intelligent, interesting women whose life experience shows on their faces. I believe that true beauty comes from within, and no amount of cosmetic surgery can give you that.*

RT: *Yes, I agree with you, Jean, but not everybody has the confidence to let their inner beauty shine out. Plastic surgery can actually give people that confidence. I really don't think there's anything wrong with trying to improve on what nature has given us.*

MH: *Ah well, that's where I disagree with you, Rita. I think we should be grateful for what God has given us. The point is, it's selfish and indulgent of people to spend vast amounts of money on superficial improvements when there is so much poverty and sickness in the world.*

RT: *Actually, it's not that expensive, you know, Michael. I mean you could have your nose done for the price of a holiday, and quite frankly, cosmetic surgery can do more for you than a holiday, because the benefits last longer.*

MH: *Are you saying I need a nose job?*

RT: *No, of course not. I suppose what I'm trying to say is that plastic surgery nowadays is almost as routine as going on holiday. Basically, it's here to stay, and I'm afraid you just have to accept it.*

JO: *Well, I don't go along with that at all. Growing old is a natural part of life and if you ask me, what we need to accept is that we can't look young forever.*

RT: *Well, I would disagree with that, but let's leave it there.*

2

- Ask the students to try to complete the extracts without listening to the recording again. Then play it for them to check their answers. Point out that the expressions they've completed are common ways of expressing strong opinions in debates and discussions.

- Put the students into pairs and ask them to discuss whether or not they think cosmetic surgery is a good thing. Encourage them to use the highlighted expressions to give their opinions.

a) have   b) believe   c) point   d) frankly
e) trying   f) ask

3

- Go through the topics in the box and make sure that everyone understands them. (Botox is a substance that can be injected under the skin to reduce wrinkles or increase the size of the lips.)

- Give the students time to think about the topics and decide what their opinions are. Tell them that they can choose their own topics if they prefer. When they're ready, put them into pairs and ask them to take turns expressing their opinions on the topics they feel strongly about. Go round offering help and encouragement. Ask any students who express their opinions particularly well to repeat them to the class.

Reading & Grammar (SB page 81)

have/get something done

1

- Ask the students if they've ever owned a Barbie or Sindy doll. If so, ask them to look at the photo of Cindy Jackson and say if they think she looks like one of these dolls. Explain that she's had a lot of cosmetic surgery done on her face and invite them to say what they think she's had done. Give the students time to read the text and find out if they were right.

- Focus attention on the gaps in the text and ask the students to complete them with *had*, *have* or *having*.

- Finally, get their reaction to the text and have a class discussion of the questions underneath it.

---

eyes, nose, chin, lips, cheeks

1 had   2 Having   3 have   4 had
5 had   6 had   7 having   8 had   9 had

The main change is that now she gets lots of attention.

Cultural notes

Barbie /ˈbɑːbi/ **and Sindy** /ˈsɪndi/
Barbie is a fashion doll for girls, launched in the US by Mattel in 1959. Sindy is the British version of Barbie and was first launched four years later, in 1963. While Barbie has been successfully re-styled over the years, Sindy has fared less well and has lost her share of the market.

2

Focus the students' attention on the two sentences and get them to identify that you use *have/get* + object + past participle to talk about things you get other people to do for you rather than things you do for yourself. Draw their attention to the further examples in the margin.

I did my hair = I did it myself.
I had my hair done = somebody else did my hair.

You use it when we're talking about services you ask (and usually pay) people to do for you.

Language note

Grammar: *have / get something done*
(See Student's Book page 138.)

3

- Ask the students to put the words in order to make sentences. Check answers with the class before asking them to use the sentences to make questions.

- Again, check answers with the class before moving on to the next stage of the activity.

- Put the students into pairs and ask them to take turns asking and answering their questions.

---

a) I get my car serviced every six months.
b) I had my house redecorated four years ago.
c) I get my hair cut once a month.
d) I've had a burglar alarm installed.
e) I had my blood pressure checked last month.
f) I've never had my nails done.

a) How often do you get your car serviced?
b) When was the last time you had your house redecorated?
c) How often do you get your hair cut?
d) Have you ever had a burglar alarm installed?
e) When was the last time you had your blood pressure checked?
f) Have you ever had your nails done?

4

Pairwork. Go through the example question with the class, then ask them to make questions with the other prompts and take turns to ask and answer them. Point out that they can also use their own ideas if they wish. As they work, go round checking that they're using the target structures correctly.

5 Grammar *Extra* 8, Part 1

Ask the students to turn to *Grammar Extra* 8, Part 1 on page 138 of the Student's Book. Here they'll find an explanation of the grammar they've been studying and a further exercise to practise it.

1
a) Would you ever get your head shaved?
b) Would you ever have/get your teeth whitened?
c) Would you ever have/get your hair coloured?
d) Would you ever have/get a tattoo done?
e) Would you ever have/get your legs waxed?
f) Would you ever have/get your ears pierced?
g) Would you ever have/get your teeth straightened?

Reading & Speaking (SB page 82)

1

Groupwork. Put the students into small groups. Ask them to discuss the questions and to be prepared to report back to the class on what they decided. If dating is a sensitive issue with your students, they could have the same discussion about making friends with people in general.

2

- Ask the students if they are familiar with the idea of speed dating. (It's explained in the first paragraph of the text.) Give them plenty of time to read the article and take in the information in it. As they note down their answers, go round checking and giving help where needed.

- When you've checked the answers, put the students into pairs and ask them to discuss their reactions to the idea of speed dating and whether they've ever tried it or would be interested in trying it.

> a) Most popular: Mark. Least popular: Tony.
> b) Most popular: Sindy. Least popular: Erica and Lara.
> c) Kevin and Tony.
> d) Tony and Sindy.

Vocabulary (SB page 82)

1
- Ask the students to look at all the words in the list, which all describe a person's character, and to decide whether they think they are usually positive or negative.
- Ask them to find and underline the words in the article on page 83 and check their answers.

> a) Negative.
> b) Positive (sometimes negative).
> c) Positive.
> d) Positive.
> e) Negative.
> f) Positive (sometimes negative).
> g) Positive.
> h) Positive.
> i) Negative.
> j) Positive.
> k) Positive (sometimes negative).

Language notes
Vocabulary: describing character
- It's always important for your students to note whether an adjective carries a positive, negative or neutral connotation. Sometimes a neutral word like *sensible* can be given a negative charge by preceding it with *too* (*too sensible* makes a person sound a bit safe and a bit boring). Similarly, a positive word can be made negative by adding the prefix *over-* (*over-optimistic* makes a person sound almost gullible).
- The compound adjectives listed on this page all require a hyphen between their separate parts to show that the elements are connected to form one meaning. Other examples include: *small-minded*, *loud-mouthed* and *big-headed*.

2
- Ask the students to find the words in the list in Exercise 1 which are closest in meaning to those in bold in the sentences.
- Check answers. Then put the students into pairs and ask them if they can identify with any of the sentences.

> a) sensitive; trustworthy
> b) sensible
> c) laid-back
> d) stand-offish
> e) straight; open-minded
> f) mature
> g) enigmatic
> h) down-to-earth
> i) self-centred

Pronunciation (SB page 82)

1 🌐 2.34
- Focus the students' attention on the adjectives in the box and ask them to decide where the stress should be in each one. Encourage them to say the words out loud as they try to underline the stress so that they get a feel for what sounds right.
- Play the recording for the students to check their answers. Then play it again for them to listen and repeat. When they've done this chorally, ask for individual repetition of the words and make sure everyone is putting the stress in the correct place.

> com<u>pa</u>tible   <u>flex</u>ible   <u>friend</u>ly   <u>gen</u>erous
> <u>happy</u>   <u>live</u>ly   ma<u>ture</u>   <u>sad</u>   <u>sen</u>sitive
> <u>sexy</u>   <u>weak</u>

2 🌐 2.35
- Point out that each of the adjectives in the box in Exercise 1 can be made into a noun by adding either the suffix *ity* or *ness*. Do the first one (*compatibility*) with the class as an example. Then ask them to change the remaining adjectives into nouns.
- Play the recording for them to check their answers and repeat the words.

> compati<u>bil</u>ity   flexi<u>bil</u>ity   <u>friend</u>liness
> gene<u>ros</u>ity   <u>happi</u>ness   <u>live</u>liness   ma<u>tur</u>ity
> <u>sad</u>ness   sensi<u>tiv</u>ity   <u>sexi</u>ness   <u>weak</u>ness

3
- Play the recording again and ask the students to pay attention to the stress in the nouns. Ask if this is in a different place from where it was in the adjectives and if there's a difference between those ending in *ity* and those ending in *ness*.
- Play the recording once more. Ask for individual repetition of the adjectives and their nouns. Make sure everyone is putting the stress in the correct places.

> *ity* = stress moves to syllable before the suffix
> *ness* = no change in stress

Language note
Pronunciation: word stress
- Adjectives which change to nouns ending in *ity* keep the stress on the third from last syllable, so *compatible* (□□□□) becomes *compatibility* (□□□□□□). The stress within the word changes, but the end pattern remains the same.
- Adjectives ending in *ness* keep the stress in the same place, so *happy* (□□) becomes *happiness* (□□□). The stress within the word stays in the same place even though an extra (unstressed) syllable is added to the end of the word.

Attraction   UNIT 8   83

Reading & Speaking (SB page 84)

1

Ask the students to look at the DVD cover and read the description. Find out how many of them think they'd like to see it. Ask if they are familiar with the genre of self-help books and films, which claim to offer people ways in which they can improve their lives. Do the students believe any of them actually work?

2

Read the sayings to the class, or ask a student to read them. Ask the students to discuss the questions in pairs and report their answers to the class.

> a) *Possible answers:*
> 1 People who have similar outlooks are drawn to each other.
> 2 You can't change the way you are.
> 3 Something that looks valuable may not be.
> 4 Your actions will have consequences.
> 5 You can't get something if it's not there to begin with.
> 6 Take care that the things you want in life are really those that will benefit you rather than harm you.
> c) 1, 3 and 6

Listening (SB page 84)

1 🌐 2.36

Point out the genie illustrated on the page. Make sure the students know what one is (a mythical creature that is supposed to be able to make your wishes come true). Ask them to listen to the radio programme and note down how the 'Law of attraction' is like a genie, according to Dr Hudson.

> It can give you whatever you want.

🌐 2.36 (P = Presenter; DrH = Dr Hudson)

P: *Now, you may or may not have read the best-selling self-help book,* The Secret, *but almost two million people have, and the movie version on DVD has sold one and a half million copies to date. To tell us what all the fuss is about, we have with us in the studio today psychologist and expert in the 'Law of attraction', Dr Rick Hudson. Welcome.*

DrH: *Thank you – I'm pleased to be here.*

P: *Dr Hudson,* The Secret *is based on the 'Law of attraction', the idea that like attracts like. This isn't a new phenomenon is it?*

DrH: *No, no, not at all. The theory behind the 'Law of attraction' has been around for ages. But it is the recent success of* The Secret *that has brought it to the attention of so many people around the world.*

P: *What exactly is the 'Law of attraction'?*

DrH: *Well, put simply, the 'Law of attraction' is all about positive thinking. We attract things we want and we also attract things we don't want. So, if you were the sort of person who was always cheerful and optimistic, you would give off good vibrations, and these good vibes would in turn attract positive energy, and good things would happen to you. Similarly, a stressed out sort of person would put out stressed vibes, and they would attract more stress into their lives. Whatever you are thinking and feeling at any given time is basically your request to the universe for more of the same.*

P: *Hmm. So how can you apply this theory, this positive thinking, to your every day life?*

DrH: *You can use it to make some very positive changes in your life. It depends what you want.*

P: *Where do I start?*

DrH: *Ha ha. Well, let me give you a very simple example – OK, let's suppose you're on your way to the supermarket on a Saturday morning, so you're arriving pretty much at the same time as several hundred other shoppers! The one thing that would improve your life at that moment is a parking space. So you start focusing on that space. You visualise the ideal parking space, right near to the supermarket entrance, and you imagine yourself swinging into the space as you arrive.*

P: *OK, I like that image.*

DrH: *And to make the positive vibrations really work for you, you need to imagine how you would feel if you already had that space.*

P: *I see.*

DrH: *Imagine that you already had that space – how would you be feeling?*

P: *Um, amazed?*

DrH: *Right, so you're still in your car on the way to the supermarket, but you're saying to yourself, 'I'm so happy I found a space. I'm delighted and grateful that I found a parking space so close to the entrance.' It works. Try it.*

P: *I must say, it sounds a bit too good to be true. Supposing I really, really wanted a ten million dollar house with a swimming pool – would I just think about it, and hey presto it would materialise?*

DrH: *Well, if you wanted to start living your life according to the 'Law of attraction', you'd have to learn a few simple techniques, and these are explained in* The Secret. *But basically, if that's what you really want, then yes, you can make it happen.*

P: *But don't you think it encourages people to be more materialistic. I mean, I don't need a house with a swimming pool. Isn't that just being plain greedy?*

DrH: *Listen, I'll give you another example. Imagine that a genie appeared in front of you and offered to grant your wishes. Would you ask for something small? Say a new bicycle? No. You'd be asking for bigger things. A business, a soul mate, a million dollars. The 'Law of attraction' is like a genie.*

> P: Hmm.
>
> DrH: And here's why it's important to think big. There is so much that can be improved in the world. There is much more you can contribute. But you cannot do this by being mediocre. You owe it not just to yourself – but also to the world – to THINK BIG.
>
> P: Well, thank you, Dr Hudson. For more information, read The Secret or watch the DVD. I'm going to start visualising a Gucci handbag.

2

FCE Exam Practice

Paper 4: Listening Part 4 Multiple choice

- Give the students time to read the questions and the options through before you play the recording again. This will give them a chance to identify the sort of information that they should be listening for.

- Check answers before putting the students into pairs and asking them to discuss whether they believe in the 'Law of attraction' or not. Ask several pairs to report back to the class on their views.

1 b	2 a	3 c	4 a	5 b	6 b	7 c

Grammar (SB page 85)

Unreal conditional structures

1

- Remind the students that they studied unreal conditionals in Unit 2 and that the sentences they looked at had an *if*-clause and a result clause. Tell them that they're now going to look at how to talk about hypothetical situations without using *if*. Give the students time to read the questions and complete them with *would* or *were*.

- Check the answers with the class and then put the students into pairs and ask them to underline the words you can use instead of *if*. Tell them to try making similar questions starting with *if*, if this helps.

- Again, check answers with the class before moving on to the next stage of the activity. Draw their attention to the information in the margin and point out that unreal conditions without *if* follow the same structure as those with *if*: the main clause uses the past simple and the result clause uses *would*.

- Give the students a few minutes to think about their own answers to the questions. When they've done this, ask them to compare their answers with their partner and see how similar they are.

a) were; would	d) would
b) were; would; would	e) were; would
c) were; would	f) were; would

Words you can use instead of *if*: Suppose, Imagine, Supposing, Assuming

---

Language note

Grammar: unreal conditional structures
(See Student's Book page 138.)

2

Pairwork. Ask the students to work in pairs to complete the questions. Check their questions before asking them to go around the class interviewing people. Ask them to keep a note of the replies and to report back to the class on what they found out.

Cultural note

President Barack Obama /ˈprezɪdənt bəˈræk əʊˈbɑːmə/ (born 1961)
Barack Obama became the 44th President of the United States on January 20, 2009. He's the first African-American US President.

3 Grammar *Extra* 8, Part 2

Ask the students to turn to *Grammar Extra* 8, Part 2 on page 138 of the Student's Book. Here they'll find an explanation of the grammar they've been studying and a further exercise to practise it.

> 2
> a) Supposing you could take a year off work, what would you do?
> b) Imagine you could have dinner with anyone in the world, who would you choose?
> c) Assuming you were a millionaire, what would you spend most of your money on?
> d) Supposing someone was late for your first date, how long would you wait?
> e) Assuming your first date went well, how long would you wait before phoning him/her again?
> f) Imagine that you had a different job, what do you think you'd have chosen to do?
> g) Supposing that you hadn't gone to bed until 3.00 a.m., how do you think you'd be feeling now?
> h) Imagine that you could change one aspect of your character, what would it be?

Speaking: anecdote (SB page 85)

For more information about how to set up, monitor and repeat Anecdotes, see page xx in the Introduction.

- Go through the instructions and the questions with the class. Make sure they understand that they can choose to talk about either a very positive person or a very negative person. Give the students a minute or two to decide who they're going to talk about. Then ask them to look at the questions and think about their answers to them. Allow them to make notes of what they're going to say and how they're going to say it, but discourage them from writing a paragraph that they can simply read out. Go round, monitoring and giving help where necessary.

- Pairwork. Put the students in pairs and ask them to take turns to tell their partner about the most positive (or negative) person they know. Encourage them to ask each other follow-up questions to get further information. Then ask some pairs to report back to the class about what they found out.

Useful phrases (SB page 86)

1 🌐 2.37

- Focus the students' attention on the picture and ask them what they think is happening. Explain that the people in the picture, Laura and Phil, have met by chance in the street. Ask them to read the conversation as they listen to the recording and underline eight phrases that are different.

- When checking answers, ask if anyone can remember what the speakers actually said.

> *Answers to Exercises 1 and 2:*
> 1 extremely busy (e)
> 2 say something to make you feel worse (a)
> 3 talk about it (d)
> 4 around here (f)
> 5 be involved in a lot of things (h)
> 6 decided yet (g)
> 7 see how I feel at the time (b)
> 8 someone to talk to (c)

> 🌐 2.37 [L = Laura; P = Phil]
> L: *Hey, Phil, how are you doing?*
> P: *Oh hi, Laura – not too bad thanks. How are you?*
> L: *Oh, up to my eyes in work as usual. I'm on my way to my third meeting today. How's that lovely girlfriend of yours?*
> P: *Oh, we split up three weeks ago. She's on holiday with her new boyfriend.*
> L: *Oh no – trust me to put my foot in it. I'm really sorry.*
> P: *No, it's OK. I need to get it off my chest.*
> L: *Who's her new boyfriend?*
> P: *You wouldn't know him. He's not from this neck of the woods.*
> L: *How did she meet him?*
> P: *Through work I think. He's one of those people who seems to have his fingers in a lot of pies. He owns several companies, including the one Mandy was working for.*
> L: *Oh, Phil, I don't know what to say.*
> P: *Yeah – it's hard. I mean, we were supposed to be going on holiday together in a couple of weeks.*
> L: *So, what are you going to do?*
> P: *I don't know – I haven't made my mind up yet. I might go anyway, or I might not feel like it when the time comes. I don't know. I'll just have to play it by ear.*

> L: *Look Phil, I'm afraid I've got to run – but if you need a shoulder to cry on, you know where to find me.*
> P: *Thanks, Laura – I'll be fine.*

2

- Pairwork. Ask the students to work together to match the useful phrases to the expressions they underlined in Exercise 1. Point out that these phrases are all idioms involving parts of the body.

- Play the recording for them to check their answers. Then ask them to choose at least three phrases and write example sentences using them. Put them in pairs to compare their sentences.

> (See answers to Exercise 1.)

3

- Pairwork. Ask the students to work in pairs and to look in a dictionary to find six useful phrases using the body parts in the box. As they do this, go round giving help and making sure they choose suitable phrases. Remind them that these have to be worked into a conversation and must convey the appropriate meaning.

- Allow time for the pairs of students to practise their conversations and for each one to be performed to the class. You could ask the listening students to identify the body idioms used and to say what they think they mean.

Vocabulary *Extra* (SB page 87)

Metaphor

1

- Ask the students to look at the sentences and match each one with one of the adjectives from the box.

> a) happy   d) busy
> b) sad   e) nervous
> c) angry   f) losing your temper

2

- Go through the instructions and the example with the class, then ask the students to work individually to underline the correct words.

> 1 flared up
> 2 blew his top
> 3 snowed under
> 4 on top of the world
> 5 feels really down
> 6 wound up

3

Ask the students to match the emotions from Exercise 1 to the lists of words. They should then find example sentences from the dictionary boxes. Check answers and ask them to choose one phrase for each metaphor that they'd like to learn.

a) busy	d) happy
b) nervous	e) losing your temper
c) angry	f) sad

4

- Ask the students to work individually to make their choices. They should then compare their answers in pairs and check them in the metaphor boxes.

- Encourage the pairs to discuss whether they agree or not with the statements and to report back to the class.

a) row	b) gloomy	c) inundated
d) let	e) up; bright	

5

Pairwork. Ask the students to take turns to ask and answer the questions. Encourage them to report back to the class on what they found out.

6

Ask the students to look in their own dictionaries to find out what information they give on metaphors and how this is shown.

Further practice material

Need more writing practice?

→ Workbook page 51
- Writing a description of a person.

Need more classroom practice activities?

→ Photocopiable resource materials pages 174 to 176
  Grammar: *Have you no samples?*
  Vocabulary: *Character search*
  Communication: *Face to face*
→ Top 10 activities pages xv to xx

Need DVD material?

→ DVD – Programme 8: *Like clockwork*

Need progress tests?

→ Test CD – *Test Unit 8*

Need more on important teaching concepts?

→ Key concepts in *New Inside Out* pages xxii to xxxv

Need student self-study practice?

→ CD-ROM – Unit 8: *Attraction*

Need student CEF self-evaluation?

→ CEF Checklists pages xxxvii to xliv

Need more information and more ideas?

→ www.insideout.net

9 Genius *Overview*

Section & Aims	What the students are doing
Reading & Vocabulary SB page 88 Scanning; reading for detail Describing places	Naming people who are geniuses in various fields. Scanning an article to find the adjectives used to describe things. Explaining the connections between things in the article. Replacing words and phrases in sentences with ones used in the article.
🔊 **Listening & Vocabulary SB page 90** Listening for detail Describing places	Listening to information about Stonehenge and answering questions. Matching synonyms. Then talking about the oldest building they've visited.
🔊 **Grammar SB page 91** Past modals of deduction	Studying ways of talking about certainty and uncertainty. Completing sentences about the construction and purpose of ancient monuments. Then discussing theories about other ancient ruins.
Speaking: anecdote SB page 91 Fluency practice	Talking about their favourite historic place.
🔊 **Grammar & Listening SB page 92** *look*, *seem* and *appear* Listening for gist and detail	Discussing the story behind three paintings by Frida Kahlo. Then listening to a museum guide to compare descriptions. Matching sentences to the paintings. Finding examples of the use of *look*, *seem* and *appear* in the recording script.
Reading & Vocabulary SB page 93 Reading for detail Time expressions	Comparing events in Frida Kahlo's life with elements in her paintings. Matching time expressions with similar meaning. Writing about the life of a famous person.
🔊 **Speaking & Listening SB page 94** Fluency practice Listening for specific information	Discussing and evaluating inventions. Listening to an interview and putting questions in order. Matching responses to questions.
Vocabulary SB page 94 Collocations	Matching verbs with the nouns they collocate with. Putting stages of production of a new invention into a logical order.
Reading SB page 95 Reading for detail	Completing a text with suitable words. Discussing the clockwork radio and appliances they would miss if there were no electricity.
🔊 **Vocabulary & Pronunciation** **SB page 95** Word families	Completing a table with words in the same family. Completing extracts from newspaper reports with appropriate collocations.
🔊 **Useful phrases SB page 96** Explaining how something works	Listening to a conversation and matching objects with functions. Completing useful phrases with *it*. Comparing written and spoken instructions for a coffee machine. Using informal language to explain how to use a machine or gadget.
Writing *Extra* SB page 97 Narrative	Completing a text with time expressions. Choosing appropriate verb structures to complete a description. Writing a story about an innovation by expanding notes.
Writing WB page 57	Writing a story.

9 Genius *Teacher's notes*

Warm up

Write *a genius* on the board and ask the students what it means (someone who possesses exceptional mental or creative ability). Ask them for the names of a couple of people that they consider to be geniuses and ask what these people have done to deserve the name *genius*.

Reading & Vocabulary (SB page 88)

1

- Pairwork. Put the students into pairs. Go through the categories with the class and ask them if they can think of someone (alive or dead) whom they regard as a genius for each of these categories.

- Ask the pairs to report back to the class on the names they've chosen and see how much agreement there is.

2

- Ask the students to look at the photo on page 89 and decide which words in the box they'd use to describe the Guggenheim Museum. Draw their attention to the information about Frank Gehry in the margin.

- Tell the students to read the article and see if the words used in it match their choices. Find out if they like the building or not. Then ask them to classify the words as outlined in the instructions.

> *Possible answers:*
> contemporary, eccentric, important, metallic, post-modern, shiny, space-age
> a) metallic, post-modern, space-age, shiny, important, contemporary
> b) 19th century, tough, sprawling, eccentric
> c) hideous, urban, semi-derelict, run-down

Cultural notes

The Pompidou Centre /ðə ˈpɒmpɪduː ˈsentə/
The Pompidou Centre was built between 1971 and 1977 in the Beaubourg area of central Paris, on the edge of a densely populated medieval quarter. The museum was designed by architects Richard Rogers and Renzo Piano.

The Sydney Opera House /ðə ˈsɪdni ˈɒp(ə)rə haʊs/
The Sydney Opera House was opened in 1973 . It's situated in Sydney Harbour, next to the bridge. It was designed by Jøern Utzon in 1955. It became a UNESCO World Heritage Site in 2007.

3

Pairwork. Put the students into pairs. Ask them to try to remember what the connections are and to decide how they could explain them, before they look back at the text. Check answers by getting several pairs to give their explanations.

> a) Thomas Krens discovered the site for the museum while he was out jogging.
> b) The museum is surrounded by run-down derelict buildings – urban sprawl.
> c) The Basque government wanted an art museum in order to strengthen Bilbao's growing global reputation.
> d) The Bibao city council had chosen a former wine-bottling warehouse in the centre of town as the site for the new art museum. (Thomas Krens saw at once that this site had no chance of succeeding.)
> e) Thomas Krens took the Pompidou Centre and the Sydney Opera house as examples for the kind of space he wanted to create for the Guggenheim Museum.
> f) Frank Gehry loved the city and didn't want to change anything about the waterfront site.

4

- Ask the students to look back through the article and find words and phrases with the same meaning as those underlined in the sentences.

- Check answers with the class before putting the students into pairs. Ask them to adapt each sentence so that it describes their own city or one they know well.

> a) wind   e) ideal site
> b) can be glimpsed   f) dominates
> c) hideous urban sprawl g) is well worth
> d) commissioned

Listening & Vocabulary (SB page 90)

1 🔊 3.01

- Pairwork. Focus attention on the pictures of Stonehenge and ask if anyone has visited the site (in England). Then put the students into pairs and ask them to read the questions and try to guess the correct answers.

- Play the recording for them to check.

🌀 **3.01** (OB: Oliver Bridge; RJ: Richard Jones)

OB: *It's a cold, grey morning. The sky is overcast and it's drizzling. For me, these are ideal conditions to visit the mysterious and ancient Stonehenge, my favourite place.*

As a child, when I first visited the stone circle, it was the sense of mystery that fascinated me – what are the stones for? How did they get here and what sort of ceremonies and events went on here? As an adult, what I love about Stonehenge is that it's been standing there for 5,000 years – and it endures. I love the fact that after so many millennia, it remains such an enigmatic and enchanting place.

It's a bit difficult to picture exactly how it was all that time ago, with only sixty odd stones left and half of those fallen down, but when it was complete, there would have been over 160 stones carefully laid out as a circle with a horseshoe in the centre. Two types of stone were used – sarsen and bluestone. The huge upright stones are sarsens weighing up to forty tonnes each. Then the inner circle is made up of bluestones, and they weigh a mere four tonnes each. The bluestones are so-called because they turn blue when they get wet.

Stonehenge is, without a doubt, one of the greatest engineering achievements of pre-historic times. The stones were huge, and not a single one can be found locally. One can only marvel at the phenomenal effort involved in bringing the stones here.

I'm joined by Richard Jones, an expert in Stonehenge history, to tell us about the latest theories about how the stones got here, and why they bothered.

Richard, these huge upright stones, the sarsens – I suppose they were dragged across the land.

RJ: *They would have been dragged, yes, from the Marlborough Downs, about twenty miles away to the north of here.*

OB: *And the bluestones, they were, they came from Wales, is that right?*

RJ: *From South West Wales, from the sunny mountains of South West Wales. Yes, a good 250 miles away from here.*

OB: *So there must have been some really powerful reason for them to situate it here.*

RJ: *Yes, there must have been a very good reason to bring them all the way here. It can't have been easy to get these stones in place – they didn't have the wheel at that time. In fact, it must have taken them years.*

OB: *But the reason why it's located here remains a mystery.*

RJ: *Absolutely. Something was such an important draw that they had to bring all these materials to here, to this place. Why they brought them here, no idea. And you know, if you put twelve archeologists in one room, you'll have twelve different theories – but we will never know for sure because Stonehenge was built before written history began. So we don't have any written evidence of a motive, a reason for why Stonehenge is here.*

OB: *All we can do is speculate. No one really knows what went on here, and I've got a feeling that Stonehenge will always keep some of its secrets.*

2

- Go through the instructions with the class and make sure they understand that they have to find two synonyms for each underlined word or phrase.

- Play the recording again for the students to identify which word was actually used in the documentary.

- Put the students into pairs and ask them to tell each other about the oldest building they've ever visited. Encourage them to give as many details as possible. Tell the listening partner to ask follow-up questions in order to find out as much information as possible.

> a) <u>drizzling</u>; spitting   d) just; <u>a mere</u>
> b) <u>endures</u>; survives   e) <u>draw</u>; incentive
> c) <u>enigmatic</u>; intriguing
>   alluring; <u>enchanting</u>
>
> The words underlined above are those actually used in the recording.

Grammar (SB page 91)

Past modals of deduction

1 🌀 **3.02**

- Tell the students that they're going to listen to five people talking about what they think Stonehenge was built for. Go through the list of suggestions with the class, then play the recording and ask the students to decide how certain each speaker is. When checking answers, ask them for the reasons for their choices. Was it the speaker's tone of voice or the words they used that influenced their decision?

- Go through the information in the margin, then ask the students to complete the sentences.

> a) almost certain   d) uncertain
> b) almost certain   e) almost certain
> c) uncertain
>
> 1) It must have happened.
> 2) It can't have happened.
> 3) It might have happened. / It may have happened. / It could have happened.

🌐 3.02

a)

The big stones look like a doorway. The shape is very similar to those found in Japan at the entrance of some of our temples. I think it must have been a kind of temple, a religious place.

b)

Well, apparently, the stones are aligned with the sun and the moon at certain times of the year – the solstices and the equinoxes. So I think it might have been a sort of prehistoric calendar. But it can't have only been a calendar. It was more important than that. I think Stonehenge must have been a place where people worshipped the sun and the moon.

c)

I think it might have been a place where important ceremonies took place. It probably had a roof on it originally – if you think about it, it makes sense. It was obviously an important place, and it rains a lot round here.

d)

We don't know do we? It could have been a landing site for spacecraft from other planets for all we know. Some people believe it was. Personally, I think it's just a bunch of stones in a field.

e)

Well, it's a mystery, isn't it? Even the archaeologists can't agree. There's one lot who have dug up bones, and they reckon they can prove that it must have been a cemetery. Then there's another group of archaeologists who think that the bluestones may have had special properties, and that's why they brought them all the way from Wales. Personally, I think it may have been a kind of healing place.

Language note

Grammar: past modals of deduction
(See Student's Book page 140.)

2

FCE Exam Practice

Paper 3: Use of English Part 4 Transformations

- Do the first one with the class as an example. Remind the students that they must use only two to five words including the word given to complete the second sentence. Ask them to complete the remaining sentences and allow them to compare their answers in pairs before checking with the class.

- Put the students into pairs and ask them to discuss any other theories they know about the origin of the places mentioned, or other ancient ruins that they know about.

---

a) might have been moved
b) must have been transported
c) could have involved
d) may have been
e) can't have come
f) must have been built

Cultural notes

The Great Sphinx of Giza /ðə greɪt sfɪŋks əv ˈɡiːzə/
The sphinx is a mythological creature with a lion's body and a human head. The Sphinx at Giza dates back to the 3rd millennium B.C. and is the oldest sculpture in the world.

The Nile /ðə ˈnaɪəl/
The Nile is the longest river in Africa and possibly the longest river in the world (6,650 km). It flows south to north through ten African countries (Burundi, Congo, Egypt, Eritrea, Ethiopia, Kenya, Rwanda, Sudan, Tanzania and Uganda).

The Great Pyramid of Giza /ðə greɪt ˈpɪrɪmɪd əv ˈɡiːzə/
The pyramids at Giza were built 4,500 years ago. The Great Pyramid is the only one of the Seven Wonders of the World still standing.

The Nazca Lines /ðə ˈnæzkə laɪnz/
The Nazca Lines are a series of lines and images drawn in the soil in the Nazca Desert in Peru. The full force of the designs can be seen from the air. They're believed to have been drawn up to 2,500 years ago. Why the lines exist isn't known, but some speculate they were for religious purposes.

Easter Island /ˈiːstə ˈaɪlənd/
Easter Island is a Polynesian island in the southeastern Pacific Ocean. It's famous for the huge statues (called 'moai') and is a World Heritage Site.

Machu Picchu /ˈmætʃuː ˈpiːtʃuː/
Machu Picchu is a pre-Columbian Inca ruin set on a high mountain ridge in Peru. It was built in about 1440, and was inhabited until the Spanish conquest of Peru in 1532. After that time it wasn't widely known about for centuries until it was rediscovered in 1911. It was designated a UNESCO World Heritage Site in 1983.

3 Grammar *Extra* 9 Part 1

Ask the students to turn to *Grammar Extra* 9 Part 1 on page 140 of the Student's Book. Here they'll find an explanation of the grammar they've been studying and a further exercise to practise it.

1

a) Albert Einstein may have been born in Austria.
b) U.S. astronauts can't have seen the Great Wall of China from the Moon.
c) Picasso must have produced more than 5,000 paintings in his lifetime.
d) Shakespeare may/might not have died on his birthday.
e) Mozart can't have been very well known when he died.
f) Walt Disney must have won more Oscars than any other entertainer.
g) Leonardo da Vinci could/may/might have had an affair with Mona Lisa.

Speaking: anecdote (SB page 91)

For more information about how to set up, monitor and repeat Anecdotes, see page xx in the Introduction.

- Go through the instructions and the questions with the class. Give the students a minute or two to decide which place they're going to talk about. Then ask them to look at the questions and think about their answers to them. Allow them to make notes of what they're going to say and how they're going to say it, but discourage them from writing a paragraph that they can simply read out.

- Pairwork. Put the students in pairs and ask them to take turns to tell their partner about their favourite historic place. Encourage them to ask each other follow-up questions to get further information. Then ask some pairs to report back to the class about what they found out.

Grammar & Listening (SB page 92)

look, seem, appear

Warmer

Groupwork. Ask the students to brainstorm all the words they know to do with art. Write their suggestions on the board and leave them there as a vocabulary bank for them to use as they talk about their attitudes to art.

1 🌐 3.03

- Pairwork. Put the students into pairs and ask them if they know of the painter Frida Kahlo and are familiar with her paintings. (Don't go into any details as they'll be reading a text on her later.) Then ask them to look closely at the paintings in the Student's Book and to discuss what they think the story might be behind them. (Discourage any students who know these paintings from giving the answer to this.) Ask the students say what they can see in each picture, whether they like the paintings, what they think the people in the paintings might be thinking or feeling, etc.

- Tell the students that they're going to listen to a museum guide describing the paintings. Ask them to listen and see how the ideas mentioned compare to their own. (See audioscript below.)

🌐 3.03

The double portrait, Frida and Diego Rivera, was completed in 1931 and was probably based on a wedding photograph. When they were first married in 1929, Diego was forty-three years old, and Frida was twenty-two. He was a celebrated artist; she was an unknown art student.

The physical difference between the couple is striking in this portrait – he is tall with enormous legs rooted to the ground by heavy work boots. By contrast, she is tiny and wearing doll-like shoes. She almost looks as if she's floating next to her larger-than-life husband.

With his palette and paint-brushes in his right hand, Diego Rivera is portrayed as an artist. In fact, at the time Frida painted this portrait, Rivera was the most famous artist in the Americas. The couple are holding hands, but you can see in the way Frida is tilting her head towards her husband that she seems to be deferring to him and giving him a place of importance in the portrait.

Diego is wearing a blue work-shirt, thus defining him as a working class craftsman. Frida is dressed in traditional Mexican clothes, wearing a long green dress and a red shawl. These are in fact the colours of the Mexican flag.

A bird holds a ribbon above their heads, and on the ribbon are written the words: 'Here you see us, me, Frida Kahlo with my adored husband, Diego Rivera.'

…

Let's move on to the second exhibit, Self-portrait with Cropped Hair.

The relationship between Frida and Diego was a stormy one. Self-portrait with Cropped Hair was painted shortly after they had separated, following Diego's affair with Frida's sister. In this portrait, she looks like a man with her heavy single eyebrow and cropped hair. She's wearing a man's shirt and a baggy suit, which looks as if it might have belonged to her former-husband. She's sitting on a wooden chair with strands of her hair lying all around her. Diego loved her long hair and traditional Mexican dresses, so Frida painted this portrait as a sort of revenge for her husband's affair.

…

Finally, we have Roots, a portrait painted later on in 1943. In Roots, Frida is wearing an orange dress and lying on a dry barren landscape with roots and leaves growing out of her body. With her elbow resting on a pillow, she looks quite comfortable. In fact, in this painting, Frida does not appear to be anguished as in many of her self-portraits. She often goes back to the theme of nature, and here she seems to be nourishing the Mexican earth. This painting was completed after Frida remarried Diego Rivera. The couple were unable to have children, and Roots expresses Kahlo's desire for fertility and to be a part of the life cycle.

2

- Focus the students' attention on the sentences beginnings and endings and ask them to match them. Then focus their attention on the information in the margin about *look*, *seem* and *appear*.

- Check answers before asking the students to match each sentence to one of the paintings by Frida Kahlo.

---

a) She looks like a man.
b) She looks quite comfortable.
c) She looks as if she's floating next to her husband.

a) *Self-portrait with cropped hair*, 1940
b) *Roots*, 1943
c) *Frida and Diego Rivera*, 1931

3

Ask the students to turn to page 152 and read the script as they listen to the recording again. Ask them to underline any sentences that include examples of *look*, *seem* and *appear*. Check answers and make sure the students are aware of the various structures used with *look*, *seem* and *appear*.

> (See answers underlined in the tapescript on page 92.)

4 Grammar *Extra* 9 Part 2

Ask the students to turn to *Grammar Extra* 9, Part 2 on page 140 of the Student's Book. Here they'll find an explanation of the grammar they've been studying and a further exercise to practise it.

> 2 (Students' own answers.)

5

Ask the students to look at the paintings for 30 seconds and try to remember as many details as they can. When the 30 seconds is up, ask them to turn to page 128 and answer as many questions as they can. Don't let them turn back to the paintings until they've answered all the questions. In a class feedback session, find out who got the most correct answers.

> *Frida and Diego Rivera*, 1931
> a) Frida's wearing traditional Mexican clothes: a long green dress, a red shawl and doll-like shoes.
> b) She's wearing a necklace.
> c) Diego is holding some paint-brushes and a palette.
> d) There's a dove holding a ribbon in its beak.
> e) It's blue.
>
> *Self-portrait with Cropped Hair*, 1940
> a) It's serious/stern.
> b) She's wearing a man's shirt and a baggy suit.
> c) She's holding a pair of scissors.
> d) It's made of wood.
> e) There's some writing and some musical notes.
>
> *Roots*, 1943
> a) A dry, barren (empty) landscape.
> b) She's leaning on a pillow.
> c) Her hair is loose.
> d) It's coming out of her stomach.
> e) They're green

Reading & Vocabulary (SB page 93)

1

Focus attention on the text and the photo. Ask the students to read about Frida Kahlo's life and to discuss in pairs what aspects of her life they think are depicted in the paintings on page 92. Remind them that the museum guide in the listening text gave some links between the paintings and Kahlo's life.

Cultural notes

Leon Trotsky /ˈliːɒn ˈtrɒtski/ (1879–1940) Russian revolutionary and Marxist theorist. Trotsky rose under Lenin to be the second most powerful person in Russia. However, he lost a power struggle with Stalin, went into exile and was finally assassinated in Mexico in 1940.

Pablo Picasso /ˈpæbləʊ pɪˈkæsəʊ/ (1881–1973) Spanish painter, sculptor and co-founder (with Georges Braque) of the Cubist movement. Picasso lived for most of his life in France.

2

- Focus attention on the underlined time expressions in the text. Go through the instructions with the class and make sure they understand that only one option in each pair is correct and has a similar meaning to the expression underlined in the text.

- Ask the students to work individually to identify the correct expressions. Allow them to compare in pairs before checking answers with the class.

> a) At the age of six
> b) After that
> c) During her life
> d) during her convalescence
> e) previously
> f) as soon as she returned
> g) while she was separated
> h) just two weeks

Language note

Vocabulary: time expressions
These discourse markers provide us with a logical sequence to the text. There are several phrase types that can be adapted to suit individual circumstances and lengths of time (*while he/she/ they was/were -ing, when he/she was* (age), *during/ throughout his/her/their* (long-term event), etc.).

3

- Go through the instructions with the class and give them a few minutes to think about who they're going to write about and to decide what information they know about this person. As the students write their sentences, go round making sure they haven't named the person and that they're using time expressions from Exercise 2.

- Put the students into pairs. Ask them to take turns guessing who their partner's sentences are describing.

Speaking & Listening (SB page 94)

1

- Groupwork. Focus the students' attention on the photos of products invented in the last five hundred years. Ask them to decide on the order in which they were invented and to guess a date for each one.

- Ask the students to turn to page 129 to check their answers. Find out which group got closest to the correct order and dates. Then ask the students to remain in the same groups and to discuss the questions. Get them to report back to the class on their ideas.

1	f) toothbrush (1498)	4	a) contact lens (1887)
2	b) toilet (1597)	5	e) safety razor (1901)
3	d) false teeth (1770)	6	c) zip (1913)

2 🌐 3.04

- Focus attention on the photo and the information. Ask the students to suggest circumstances in which a clockwork radio would be a good idea.

- Tell the students that they're going to listen to an interview with Trevor Baylis. Go through the questions with the class, and then ask them to listen and number the questions in the order they are asked.

> *The correct order:* d, e, b, f, a, c

🌐 3.04

Interview with Trevor Baylis

I: *Trevor, let me start by asking you what gave you the idea for the clockwork radio?*

TB: *Well I was sitting where I am now looking at that television over there, and I was um actually watching a programme about the spread of AIDS in Africa, and they said the only way they could stop this dreadful disease cutting its way through Africa was with the power of information and education. But there was a problem. Most of Africa doesn't have electricity. The only form of electricity available to them was in the form of batteries, which were horrendously expensive. And so I said to myself, hang on, hang on. Now, this is where dreams play an important part in everybody's life. Um. The beautiful thing about a dream is you can do anything you like in your dreams, right? Now why I am saying this to you is because I could see myself listening to some raunchy number by Dame Nellie Melba on my wind-up gramophone, mmm? And then I am thinking to myself, blimey, if you can get all that noise by dragging a rusty nail around a piece of old bakelite using a spring, surely there's enough power in that spring to drive a small dynamo which in turn will drive my radio, and so I was stirred enough to get off my backside and go to my shed, and actually find enough parts to actually start doing those first primitive experiments …*

I: *And, um, how long did it take you to design a prototype from the idea?*

TB: *Well, from the actual, from the concept to, er, having the first in-a-box model out there it would have taken me two to three months, I guess, so yes, it took about two or three months.*

I: *So you got, you got the prototype, how easy was it from that point on? How easy was it to find a backer and set up production?*

TB: *Well first things first. I did know that there are these thieves about that will steal your idea. So I found a lady called Jackie Needle, a patent attorney, and I said to her 'Jackie, I want to write up a patent, can you help me?' So we did a search and couldn't find any clockwork radios of the kind that I had done, and she filed for a patent to me, for me, and therefore then I had a starting date, as it were. Now I knew that nobody pays you for a good idea, but they could pay you for that piece of paper, so then I went round every British company I could think of with a confidentiality agreement, and they all talked down to me. 'Oh yes, I think we're, I think that we are working on something like this, aren't we, Johnny?' You know all that old sausage. Um, I mean it was so humiliating … and in the end, quite frankly after about three or four years of this, I thought, I have had enough of this. Why do I need this? I was fifty-six or something when this happened. So I was given a chance through the BBC World Service to meet up with the guys from the BBC Tomorrow's World programme, and they said, 'Come on, we'll do the story.'*

I: *So the whole thing got off the ground. How long was it then before the production of them started?*

TB: *Well, the important thing was funding. The Tomorrow's World programme was seen by a fellow in South Africa, a chap from a company called Liberty Life. He came to my house here, and we sat out there, and he said, 'Look, um, we can help you make this happen, provided we can share in its success.' I said of course, and so we formed a company called Baygen, Baylis Generators, and he wrote a cheque for three-quarters of a million pounds whilst I was in this room.*

I: *And how many radios are produced each month?*

TB: *Well, I'm sure they might tell me differently, but I'm sure they must be doing 200,000 a month.*

I: *And finally what advice would you give to someone who had a good idea?*

TB: *Don't go down the pub and tell everybody about it. That's the first thing, right? Get on to the Patent Office. Get their literature, and read all about it, right? Nobody pays you for a good idea, but they might pay you for a piece of paper which says you own that idea. But remember, somebody might already own that idea, so you must do a search first. There's no excuse afterwards.*

3

- Ask the students to match the replies to the questions.
- Play the recording a second time for them to check their answers.

> 1 c)   2 e)   3 a)   4 d)   5 f)   6 b)

Vocabulary (SB page 94)

1

Focus the students' attention on the collocations. Ask them to decide which verb from the brackets also collocates with the noun to give a similar meaning. Allow the students to discuss their ideas in pairs or small groups and to use their dictionaries to check their answers.

> a) set up   e) begin
> b) carry out   f) develop
> c) come up with   g) conduct
> d) apply for

2

Pairwork. Ask the students to discuss in pairs what they think is the most logical order for the stages in Exercise 1. Get them to report back to the class on their decisions.

> *Probably:* c, b, f, g, d, a, e

Reading (SB page 95)

1

Pairwork. Ask the students to take turns to tell each other all they can remember about the story of Trevor Baylis which they heard in the interview in the previous section. Then ask them to work together to complete the summary.

> 1) epidemic   2) spread   3) electricity
> 4) dream   5) prototype 6) patent   7) set
> 8) yourself

2

Do this as a class activity, but give them time to think of ideas to contribute to the discussion. Encourage any students who give ideas for the second question to say why these products are the most important or useful to them.

Vocabulary & Pronunciation

(SB page 95)

1 🌐 3.05

- Focus the students' attention on table and explain that some words come in families, i.e. from the same root there can be one or more nouns, adjectives and verbs. Do the first line of the table with the class, eliciting the words *biology*, *biologist* and *biological* and pointing out that the words collocate with the noun.

- Ask the students to complete the table and then to decide where the stress should go on each word. Encourage them to say the words aloud as they do this so that they get a feel for what sounds right. They should then practise saying the words.

- Play the recording for them to check their answers. Play it a second time for them to listen and repeat.

1 Noun (subject)	2 Noun (person)	3 Adjective	+ example collocations
a) biology	biologist	biological	weapons
b) chemistry	chemist	chemical	reactions / weapons
c) economy / economics	economist	economic	growth / research
d) genetics	geneticist	genetic	engineering
e) maths	mathematician	mathematical	equations / research
f) science	scientist	scientific	advances / research
g) technology	technologist	technological	advances / research

2

Tell the students to read the newspaper extracts and decide which adjective + noun collocation best fits each gap. Allow them to compare answers in pairs before checking with the class.

> 1) mathematical equations
> 2) scientific research
> 3) genetic engineering
> 4) Economic growth
> 5) biological weapons
> 6) Technological advances
> 7) chemical reactions

3

Ask the students to look in their dictionaries and find other noun collocates for each of the adjectives in the table in Exercise 1. Then tell them to write an example sentence for five collocations that are new to them.

Useful phrases (SB page 96)

1 🌐 **3.06**

• Focus attention on the picture and tell the students that they're going to listen to a conversation between these women. Explain that Brigit is going to stay at Alice's house while Alice is away. Go through the objects and functions with the class so that they know what to listen out for. Then play the recording and ask them to match the objects with the functions.

• Check answers with the class and ask them to say what surprise Brigit gets at the end.

---

a) 3   b) 6   c) 1   d) 5   e) 4   f) 2

Brigit is surprised to learn that she has to look after Molly, the dog.

🌐 **3.06** (A =Alice; B = Brigit)

A: *Oh, I'm so pleased you can stay here while we're away and keep an eye on the place.*

B: *No problem. It'll be nice to have a change of scenery for a couple of weeks.*

A: *Now, there are a few things I need to tell you. Did you get the keys in the post?*

B: *Yes, I've got them here.*

A: *OK, to open the front door, you need the small key.*

B: *Right.*

A: *You need to turn it twice anti-clockwise.*

B: *OK. And I suppose the big key is for the back door?*

A: *Exactly. Now, if you need the heating on, you just need to turn up the thermostat.*

B: *OK, and where do I do that?*

A: *There's a dial in the hallway, between the sitting room and the kitchen. Just turn it until it clicks.*

B: *Right.*

A: *And then make sure you turn it down again before you go to bed.*

B: *Of course.*

A: *Right – the TV's in the sitting room, and you use the silver remote control to switch it on and off, and the smaller black one for changing channels. Are you likely to watch a DVD?*

B: *Er, no it's OK.*

A: *Now, what else. The smoke alarms are always going off in our house. The best thing to do is to have the fan on when you're cooking – just press the red button above the cooker to turn it on. You can't miss it. And if the smoke alarm goes off, just stand under it and wave your arms.*

B: *OK. Is there anything else?*

A: *Oh yes, I know what I haven't told you. Do you like coffee?*

B: *Yes, I love it.*

A: *Well, there's a coffee machine next to the cooker. It's very easy to use. Basically, plug it in at the wall, and the on/off switch is at the back of the machine. Then you put a filter into the filter holder and put the coffee into the filter. Put water into the thing above it, and make sure the lid's on tight. Then put a cup under the place where the coffee comes out. The machine will warm the water up to the right temperature, so you just have to wait a few seconds. When the cup's full, take it off and your coffee's ready. Anyway, I'll leave you the proper instructions.*

B: *Oh good, thanks.*

A: *That's it then. Oh, and Molly needs a walk twice a day, and don't forget to let her out before you go to bed – we wouldn't like her to have an accident.*

B: *Molly? You didn't mention …*

A: *Oh didn't I? She's no trouble, are you? Yes … oh yes … you're lovely … down girl, down.*

2

• Go through the example with the class, then ask the students to decide where to insert *it* in each sentence.

• Ask the students to decide what *it* refers to in each sentence. Play the recording again for them to check.

---

a) You need to turn <u>it</u> twice anti-clockwise.
b) You turn <u>it</u> until it clicks.
c) Make sure you turn <u>it</u> down again.
d) You use the silver remote control to switch <u>it</u> on and off.
e) Press the red button above the cooker to turn <u>it</u> on.
f) Plug <u>it</u> in at the wall.
g) Put water into the thing above <u>it</u>.

a) The front door key	d) The TV
b) The dial for the thermostat	e) The cooker fan
c) The thermostat	f) The coffee machine
	g) The coffee filter

3

Ask the students which they think is likely to be in more formal language, the written instructions or Alice's spoken instructions. Ask them to read both texts and underline the formal equivalents of the highlighted words and phrases. Ask them if the spoken and written forms of their own language have similar differences.

Spoken	Written
put	insert
put	place
put; thing above it	pour; water tank
make sure; on tight	ensure; secure
put; the place where the coffee comes out	place; the spout
warm up; right	heat; correct
take off	remove

4

- Give the students time to decide which machine or gadget they're going to talk about. Allow them to make brief notes if they wish, but don't allow them to write full sentences to read out.

- Put the students into pairs and ask them to take turns giving their spoken instructions. Ask the listening partner each time to say whether they'd now feel confident about using the machine or gadget.

Writing *Extra* (SB page 97)

Narrative

1

- Focus the students' attention on the first text and get them to identify the illustration (a pad of Post-it notes). Ask them to read the text and complete it with the time expressions from the box.

- Check answers with the class and then elicit their reactions to the text. Did they know of the origins of the Post-it note? Do they think that many inventions are basically very simple ideas or come from things that were initially regarded as failures?

1) In 1977	4) a few months previously
2) Each Sunday	5) The following day
3) One Sunday	

2

Tell the students that they're going to read about another invention which was discovered almost by accident. Ask them to read the article and choose the most appropriate verb structures. When they've finished, ask them to compare their answers with a partner. Then check with the class.

1) was working	4) had heard
2) felt	5) had been installed
3) had been affected	

3

- Focus attention on the notes and the photo of Mark Zuckerberg, the founder of Facebook. Ask the students whether they use Facebook and if they know anything about its origins. Ask them to read the notes, and explain anything they don't understand.

- Go through the frame with the class and then ask them to use it to write an article about how Zuckerberg developed Facebook.

Mark Zuckerberg founded Facebook while studying psychology at Harvard University. He had already developed a number of social-networking sites for fellow students, including Facemash, a site for rating people's attractiveness.

In February 2004 he launched 'The Facebook'. Within 24 hours, 1,200 students had signed up and after one month, half the student population of Harvard had set up profiles on the site.

The site became 'Facebook' in August 2005 when Zuckerberg purchased the name 'facebook.com' for $200,000. Previously the site was only available to university students, but since September 2006 it's been available to anyone over thirteen.

In 2007, rumours that Prince William had signed up circulated, but this was not true. In 2008, four years after three Harvard classmates accused Zuckerberg of stealing the idea for Facebook, he settled out of court.

Today, Zuckerberg is one of the youngest billionaires in the world.

Cultural notes

Prince William /prɪns ˈwɪljəm/ (born 1982)
Eldest son of Prince Charles and Princess Diana, Prince William is second in line to the British throne.

Harvard University /ˈhɑːvəd juːnɪˈvɜːsəti/
A private college in Massachusetts, which was founded in 1636, making it the oldest college of its kind in the USA. Only excellent academics or members of the social elite are regarded as eligible as students.

Further practice material

Need more writing practice?

→ Workbook page 57
- Writing a story.

Need more classroom practice activities?

→ Photocopiable resource materials pages 177 to 179
  Grammar: *Why would a person do this?*
  Vocabulary: *Word families*
  Communication: *Compare pictures*
→ Top 10 activities pages xv to xx

Need DVD material?

→ DVD – Programme 9: *Fact or fiction?*

Need progress tests?

→ Test CD – *Test Unit 9*

Need more on important teaching concepts?

→ Key concepts in *New Inside Out* pages xxii to xxxv

Need student self-study practice?

→ CD-ROM – Unit 9: *Genius*

Need student CEF self-evaluation?

→ CEF Checklists pages xxxvii to xliv

Need more information and more ideas?

→ www.insideout.net

Review C *Teacher's notes*

These exercises act as a check of the grammar and vocabulary that the students have learnt in Units 7–9. Use them to find any problems that students are having, or anything that they haven't understood and which will need further work.

Grammar (SB page 98)

Remind the students of the grammar explanations they read and the exercises they did in the *Grammar Extra* on pages 138 to 141.

1

This exercise reviews reporting verbs from Unit 7. Remind the students of the two different patterns: with the hearer as direct object and where the hearer isn't the direct object.

1 announced	5 inform you
2 assure you	6 explain
3 confirm	7 suggest
4 admit	

2

This exercise reviews past modals of obligation from Unit 7.

1 need 2 had 3 allowed 4 didn't	
5 ought 6 should	

3

This exercise reviews articles from Unit 7. Check answers with the class before asking the students to say which of the sentences are true for them.

a) –   b) an   c) the   d) –   e) a   f) the
g) –

4

This exercise reviews passive reporting structures from Unit 8.

a) The rate of inflation is expected to rise sharply.
b) It is thought the Prime Minister will resign soon.
c) It is said that the world's climate will become more extreme.
d) Vast oil reserves are thought to exist under the Arctic ice cap.
e) It used to be thought that the Earth was the centre of the universe.
f) It is said that the Mafia were involved in the assassination of JFK.

5

This exercise reviews unreal conditionals from Unit 8. Check answers with the class before asking the students to answer the questions for themselves and then compare with a partner.

a) If you won £10 million, would you keep it all?
b) Supposing you could be someone famous, who would it be?
c) Imagine you were able to do your dream job, what would you do?
d) Assuming time were no object, what new skill would you like to learn?

6

This exercise reviews past modals of deduction from Unit 9.

Possible answers:
a) Amy might have woken up late.
b) Will must have had too much to drink last night.
c) Daniela must have gone out.
d) Kenji must have had an accident.
e) Paula can't have slept well last night.
f) Sam might have had some good news.

7

This exercise reviews *looks, looks like, looks as if / though* and *seems to be* from Unit 9. Remind the students that they may have to change some of the forms. Check answers with the class. Then ask the students to decide which sentences are true for them and to discuss them with a partner.

a) looks	d) seemed
b) looked like	e) as if
c) though	f) to be

Vocabulary (SB page 99)

1

This exercise reviews word formation from Unit 7.

a) bullish	b) cheerful	c) endless
d) foolish	e) homeless	f) relentless
g) selfish	h) stressful	i) tearful

2

This exercise reviews word formation from Unit 7.

dis-	il-	im-
dishonest	illegal	immature
disloyal	illegible	immoral
disobedient	illiterate	impatient
dissatisfied	illogical	impolite

in-	ir-	un-
inadequate	irrational	unadventurous
inappropriate	irrelevant	undivided
incapable	irresistible	unusual
indecisive	irresponsible	unwilling

3

This exercise review the words to describe personal appearance from Unit 8. Check answers with the class before putting the students into pairs to discuss which features they think make a person attractive.

1 mouth	2 lips	3 cheekbones	4 skin
5 teeth	6 eyes	7 dimples	8 jaw

4

This exercise reviews useful adjectives for describing a person's character from Unit 8. Check answers, then ask the students to work individually to choose three adjectives to describe themselves. They should then compare their choices with a partner.

a) 2	b) 5	c) 8	d) 10	e) 11	f) 3
g) 7	h) 4	i) 1	j) 6	k) 9	

5

This exercise reviews words for describing places from Unit 9.

a) contemporary	f) run-down
b) eccentric	g) semi-derelict
c) hideous	h) space-age
d) metallic	i) sprawling
e) post-modern	

6

This exercise reviews time expressions from Unit 9. Ask the students if they've seen any films starring Audrey Hepburn. They may know *Roman Holiday*.

1) When	2) During	3) After	4) While
5) Soon	6) As	7) Barely	

Pronunciation (SB page 99)

1

Remind the students that the boxes show the syllables of a word and the large boxes indicate the stressed syllables. Here they are being asked to classify words according to how many syllables they have and where the main stress falls. Encourage them to say each word aloud to get a feeling for what sounds right.

2 3.07

Ask the students to underline the stressed syllable in each word. Then play the recording for them to check their answers. Play it a second time for them to listen and repeat.

1 and 2

A: ■□	B: □■□	C: ■□□
drizzle	attractive	company
lively	cosmetics	genius
physics	encourage	genuine
urban	meander	traveller

Further practice material

Need more classroom practice activities?

→ Photocopiable resource materials page 180
  3.08 **Song:** *Mozambique*
→ TOP 10 activities pages xv to xx

Need progress tests?

→ Test CD – *Test Review C*

Need more on important teaching concepts?

→ Key concepts in *New Inside Out* pages xxii to xxxv

Need student self-study practice?

→ CD-ROM – *Review C*

Need more information and more ideas?

→ www.insideout.net

Before the next lesson

Ask the students to bring some advertisements from magazines and newspapers to the next lesson. Alternatively, bring in a selection of adverts yourself.

10 Sell Overview

Section & Aims	What the students are doing
Reading & Vocabulary SB page 100 Reading for gist *see* and *look at*	Discussing logos and branded goods. Reading an extract from a book about living without designer brands. Underling the correct phrases to complete a description.
Listening & Vocabulary **SB page 101** Listening for gist	Listening to a marketing executive and a head teacher talking about children and advertising. Then matching opinions to speakers.
Reading & Vocabulary SB page 102 Reading for detail Sales and marketing collocations	Reading about a popular TV commercial and matching paragraphs to parts of a photo. Finding the significance of names and numbers in the text. Completing a glossary with words and phrases from the text.
Grammar SB page 102 Relative clauses	Studying the functions and punctuation of relative clauses. Matching sentences with suitable follow-ups. Studying relative clauses and relative pronouns.
Listening & Speaking SB page 104 Listening for gist and for detail Fluency practice – agreeing and disagreeing	Discussing celebrity magazines. Listening to a radio programme and explaining the issues discussed. Reading sentences from the listening and identifying who said what. Then replacing highlighted words with what was actually said. Categorising phrases used by the speakers according to their function.
Grammar SB page 105 Emphasis (cleft sentences)	Changing emphasis by using cleft sentences. Correcting statements about celebrities using cleft sentences.
Pronunciation SB page 105 Stress in cleft sentences	Practising stress in cleft sentences.
Reading & Vocabulary SB page 106 Reading for detail	Reading a text about product placement in Bond films. Replacing missing sentences in the text. Putting a summary of the text in the correct order. Talking about a favourite movie character.
Speaking: anecdote SB page 107 Fluency practice	Talking about a blockbuster movie they've seen.
Useful phrases SB page 108 Using emotive language	Listening to people talking about going to see a film and identifying which film it is. Completing useful phrases for describing people's feelings. Then identifying incorrect collocations. Listening to people and identifying their general reaction to a film. Using the useful phrases to discuss the worst films, TV programmes, concerts, etc. that they've seen recently.
Vocabulary *Extra* SB page 109 Collocations	Identifying collocations and categorising them. Rewriting a text using alternative collocations. Studying noun-verb collocations and noun-adjective collocations.
Writing WB page 63	Writing a film review.

10 Sell *Teacher's notes*

Reading & Vocabulary (SB page 100)

1

Pairwork. Ask the students to look at the six sets of logos, identify the companies that own them and decide which is the correct one in each case. They can check their answers on page 129.

1a (Head)   2b (Nike)   3a (Adidas) 4c (Speedo)   5c (Slazenger)   6b (Kappa)

2

- Pairwork. Ask the students to discuss the questions and try drawing brands for their partners to identify.

- In a class feedback session, display the various logos that the students have drawn and see if the rest of the class can identify them.

3

- Go through the instructions with the class so that they know what information to look out for in the text. When the students have identified the three objects (encourage them to give details about what the objects looked like), give them time to read the text more closely before asking them to discuss in pairs whether they were the same as or different from Neil Boorman when they were at junior school.

- In a class feedback session, encourage the students to give their reactions to Neil Boorman's later decision to destroy all the branded goods he owned.

a 1 trainers: specifically, the ticks and stripes on the sides of the other boys' trainers compared with his blue sports shoes 2 T-shirts: they all had crocodiles, eagles and tigers on the breast 3 school bags: a blue plastic holdall with a leaping puma in silver on the side.

4

- Focus the students' attention on the different ways of saying *look at* and *see*. (See Language note below.)

- Ask the students to look through the text on page 101 and to find four more examples to complete the columns. Remind them to use the infinitive form.

LOOK AT: glance at, eye up SEE: notice, catch sight of

Language notes

Vocabulary: *look at* and *see*

- The verbs *look at*, *gaze at*, *stare at*, *glance at* and *eye up* all suggest the action is deliberate.

- The verbs *see*, *spot*, *make out*, *notice* and *catch sight of* all suggest a more random, unpremeditated event.

5

- Ask the students to choose the right words to complete the description. Allow them to compare answers in pairs before checking with the class.

- Encourage the students to give their reactions to the text and then to discuss with a partner their own attitude towards brands and designer labels.

1 gazing at	5 stare at
2 eyeing up	6 noticed
3 spot	7 catch sight of
4 glance at	

Listening & Vocabulary (SB page 101)

1 🔊 3.09–3.10

- Focus the students' attention on the photos and point out that Joe is a marketing executive and Sally a head teacher. Tell them that they're going to hear Joe and Sally giving their opinions about children and advertising. Go through the statements with the class, making sure they understand all of them, then ask them to predict which person made each statement.

- Play the recording and ask the students to listen and check their answers. Check answers with the class before putting the students into pairs to discuss whether or not they agree with the statements. Encourage them to report back to the class on their opinions, giving their reasons.

a) Sally   b) Joe   c) Sally   d) Joe   e) Joe
f) Sally

🌐 3.09

Joe Smedley, marketing executive

Children are much easier to reach with advertising than adults are – they like it and they pick up on it really fast. So, it's the advertiser's job to capitalise on this.

We have a term 'pester-power', which means the marketing potential of children nagging their parents to spend money. And I'm not just talking about toys here – our aim is getting children to pester parents to buy something for the whole family, like a holiday or a car. What we try to do is to produce adverts that appeal to both children and adults.

Another key concept for advertisers is the 'playground pound'. Children want what their friends have – playground credibility is very important. In other words, brands give children a sense of identity and help them fit in with a peer group.

So you can see children are a very important market for us, and in return, we like to promote education. This is something that's already happening in America. Companies donate free computers and in exchange they can advertise their brands on book covers and posters. I think it's fantastic – the kids benefit and the companies get brand loyalty from a very early age.

I'd love to be a child today. They really know what they want and they have so many more choices. Advertisers respect children's opinions.

🌐 3.10

Sally McIlveen, headteacher

Basically, children are being brainwashed by all the advertising that goes on around them. Quite honestly, if the children in my school remembered any of their schoolwork as well as they remember the advertising jingles they hear on television, my job would be a pleasure.

Usually the pupils at our school wear uniforms, but Friday is a non-uniform day, and that's when you really see the power of advertising. The kids are dressed from head to toe in labels, mainly sports stuff like Adidas, Nike, that sort of thing. And they all look the same!

There's a great deal of pressure on parents to buy children all these labels and gadgets, and I feel so sorry for the families who don't have much money because the pressure is just the same.

I really believe it's time the government put a stop to all this aggressive television advertising.

Mind you, it's worse in America apparently. Schools are actually being subsidised by companies like McDonald's and Pepsi. OK, the school gets free equipment from these big companies, but then the children have to add up burgers or multiply cans of Pepsi in their maths lessons. It's terrible to think that the schools end up promoting a product that's not even good for the children.

What I think is really sad is that children are being forced to be consumers from such an early age. I don't think all this choice is liberating for children – it just means that they're encouraged to be materialistic instead of focusing on more important basic values such as kindness and respect for others.

2

- Pairwork. Put the students in pairs and tell them who will be Student A and who will be Student B. Then ask them to turn to their respective pages and to follow the instructions there.

- Ask each student to find a word from the box which collocates with each list, using their dictionaries if necessary. Then tell them to check their answers with their partner.

- Ask the students to write example sentences for six of the collocations from the list.

Student A: a) consumer   b) price
c) advertising
Student B: a) sales   b) brand   c) market

Extra activity

Ask the students, who have children themselves, if their children pester them to buy certain brands. If they don't, ask if they pestered their own parents when they were children to buy things for them.

Reading & Vocabulary (SB page 102)

1

- Focus attention on the picture on page 103. Explain that it's taken from a famous TV advert which was made in the 1980s and that it regularly comes high up in lists of people's favourite TV adverts of all time.

- Go through the questions and ask the students to give their ideas. Then ask them to read the first paragraph of the article on page 103 to check their answers.

- Give the students time to read the whole article in detail and ask them to match each paragraph to one of the numbered parts of the picture.

a) jeans
b) USA, 1950s
A 1   B 4   C 5   D 2   E 3

Language note

Vocabulary: *commercial* or *advert*?
In the US, advertisements which are shown on TV are known as *commercials*. There are usually several *commercial breaks* during a TV show. In the UK, they're called *TV advertisements*, *adverts* or, more commonly, *ads*.

Marlon Brando /'maːlən 'brændəʊ/ (1924–2004)
Marlon Brando was an Academy award-winning
American actor. His most famous films include
On the Waterfront (1954), *The Godfather* (1972) and
Apocalypse Now (1979).

James Dean /dʒeɪmz diːn/ (1931–1955)
James Dean was an American film actor and
cultural icon of the 1950s. He played the roles
of a troubled teenager in the films *East of Eden*
(1955), *Rebel Without a Cause* (1955) and *Giant*
(1956). His death at an early age in a road accident
guaranteed him legendary status. He received two
posthumous Academy acting awards.

Elvis Presley
(See notes about Elvis Presley on page 7.)

Marvin Gaye /'maːvɪn geɪ/ (1939–1984)
American soul singer famous for songs such as
I Heard It Through the Grapevine (1968), *Let's Get It
On* (1973) and *Sexual Healing* (1982). His life was
cut tragically short when his father shot him dead
during an argument.

Nick Kamen /nɪk 'keɪmən/ (Born 1962)
British-born actor and musician. He became
famous in the 1985 Levi's commercial on British
TV. After that Kamen enjoyed limited success in
the pop world before returning to obscurity.

Madonna /mə'dɒnə/ (born 1958)
(See information about Madonna in the Student's
Book, Unit 1, page 9.)

2

Pairwork. Encourage the students to discuss the names
and numbers and try to remember their significance
without looking back at the article. When they've
finished, allow them to read it again to check their
answers.

> 501 = brand of jeans
> 1985 = when the advert was made
> Marlon Brando = iconic 50s film star
> 1950s = setting for the ad
> Elvis Presley = iconic 50s singer
> Marvin Gaye = singer of *I Heard It Through the
> Grapevine* – soundtrack of the ad
> 1968 = year the song was released
> Barbara Nokes = the advertising executive who
> created the ad
> Nick Kamen = actor in the ad
> Madonna = wrote a song for Nick Kamen

3

- Focus the students' attention on the highlighted
  words in the article. Ask them to discuss with a
  partner what they think they might mean.

- Ask the students to use the highlighted words to
  complete the glossary at the bottom of the article.

a) conjure up	f) haunting
b) couldn't care less about	g) heart-throb
c) epitomise	h) nostalgically
d) fiercely	i) rugged
e) fussy	j) strip off

4

- Groupwork. Put students into small groups. Tell them
  that they're going to create their own TV advert. Ask
  them to turn to page 129 and follow the instructions.

- Allow the students plenty of time to discuss the
  questions and make notes of their answers, before
  asking them to compare their ideas with other groups.

Grammar (SB page 102)

Relative clauses

1

- Focus the students' attention on the examples in the
  margin and point out that the expressions in bold
  are relative clauses. Then go through the instructions
  and ask the students to look at the sentences specified
  in the article and underline the relative clauses in
  them. Ask them to work in pairs and to choose the
  description that best defines the function of each of
  these relative clauses.

- Check answers with the class and make sure that
  everyone understands the concept of defining and
  non-defining relative clauses. Ask them to look at the
  punctuation and to say what punctuation mark is
  used to show that a relative clause in non-defining.

> It represented youthful rebellion, radical chic
> and sex appeal, <u>which was perfect for Levis'
> intended positioning of their brand in the
> market</u>. – TYPE 3
>
> Her eyes are directed at the jeans <u>that are
> hanging out of the machine.</u> – TYPE 2
>
> Unlike the majority of adverts, this ad was
> created by a woman, Barbara Nokes, <u>who was
> creative director of the London-based agency,
> Bartle Bogle Hegarty.</u> – TYPE 1
>
> a comma

Language note
Vocabulary: relative clauses
(See Student's Book page 140.)

2

Pairwork. Working in the same pairs, the students look
at the pairs of sentences and identify the most suitable
follow-up for each sentence.

> a) 1   b) 2   c) 2   d) 1   e) 2   f) 1   g) 1
> h) 2

3

- Focus the students' attention on the main sentences in Exercise 2 and the list of types of relative clause in Exercise 1. Get the class to identify the type of relative clause that each sentence contains.

- Discuss which of the relative pronouns cannot be used with non-defining relative clauses.

---
a)
a) TYPE 2 (defining)
b) TYPE 3 (non-defining)
c) TYPE 3 (non-defining)
d) TYPE 1 (non-defining)
e) TYPE 2 (defining)
f) TYPE 1 (non-defining)
g) TYPE 2 (defining)
h) TYPE 3 (non-defining)

b) that
c) which

---

4 Grammar *Extra* 10, Part 1

Ask the students to turn to *Grammar Extra* 10, Part 1 on page 140 of the Student's Book. Here they'll find an explanation of the grammar they've been studying and further exercises to practise it.

1
a) a job that you are interested in ~~it~~
b) a bank account that never runs out ~~it~~
c) a boss who you get on with ~~him~~
d) a car that never breaks down ~~it~~
e) a government that you voted for ~~them~~
f) a friend who never lets you down ~~she~~
g) a home that you are happy in ~~there~~
h) a partner who you are in love with ~~her~~

2
a) He bought me an expensive dress, which I didn't really like.
b) Adam, who is almost never late, turned up at 10.30 this morning.
c) That women, who looks like my sister, works in our shop.
d) Mike's father, who lives in France, is in advertising.
e) There's a lift in the building, which you can use to go to the top floor.
f) Ellen got me a really nice jacket, which was a complete surprise.

Listening & Speaking (SB page 104)

1

Go through the questions with the class, then ask the students to discuss them in pairs. Encourage them to report back to the class on their discussion.

2 🔊 **3.11**

- Ask the students if they believe everything they read in the newspapers. If they don't, ask them for examples of things they've read in a paper which they either didn't believe or which subsequently turned out not to be true. Ask the students if they think all newspapers are equally reliable. Make sure they understand the words *tabloid* and *broadsheet*.

- Go through the instructions with the class and put the students into pairs. Play the recording and ask them to explain to each other why the actress isn't happy with the tabloid editor.

- Check answers with the class and then ask the students to say who they sympathise with most and why they sympathise with a particular person. Then have a class vote to find out who gets the most sympathy.

The tabloid editor's newspaper said that Shelley and her co-star had taken a bath together in her hotel room. The co-star is married to a good friend of Shelley's. The newspaper said the bath was filled with $5,000 worth of champagne. Shelley's co-star's wife is filing for divorce.

🔊 **3.11** (P = Presenter; S = Shelley Russell; J = Jim Falmer)

P: *Good evening and welcome to Talkback. Recently, the tabloid press have been under fire yet again, this time for their apparent disregard for truth and accuracy.*

  In the studio tonight we would like to welcome Shelley Russell, Oscar-winning actress, and Jim Falmer, editor of The Daily Post.

  Shelley Russell, let's start with you. Do you think there should be greater restrictions placed on the press and the stories they print?

S: *Yes, absolutely. I can't open a newspaper or magazine without reading stories full of false information about myself or people I know. It's getting …*

J: *Sorry, but I can't believe that you're actually complaining about free publicity. I mean, I remember, Shelley, before you were famous, you were begging us to write features about you … anything …*

S: *If you would just let me finish – of course the press have been important. I'm an actress and I understand the power of the press. But the thing is, I rarely seem to read anything true about myself these days. Take last week – your paper wrote this story about me and my co-star, who incidentally happens to be married to a very good friend of mine – taking a bath together in my hotel room.*

J: *Oh that. That was …*

S: *Hang on, I haven't finished. You went on to say that the bath was filled with $5,000 worth of champagne. Now, …*

J: *Well, that was just a bit of fun. I don't think you should take that too seriously.*

S: Oh really! You don't think that it's at all serious that my co-star's children woke up to the headline: SHELLEY GETS BUBBLY WITH SHAUN IN CHAMPAGNE BATH or that his wife is now filing for a divorce …

J: Look, I don't know whether …

S: Anyway, to get back to what I was saying … The point I'm trying to make here is that famous people have families with feelings. I am sick of the gutter press making up stories just so that they can splash sensational headlines across the front page and sell more newspapers – it's irresponsible and it messes up people's lives.

J: Look love, you're just angry about that particular article because the photos we printed of you weren't very flattering. Anyway, we made a public apology and said that there'd been some inaccuracies in the article.

S: Yes, but what you didn't say was what the inaccuracies were, so …

P: If I could just come in here. I think we need to address the root of the problem. Jim Falmer, why do certain newspapers continue to print these stories when it's obvious that they are not true?

S: To increase circulation and make more money.

J: If you would let me answer the question – I think we have to look at the relationship between fame, the public and the press. The public are fascinated by fame and scandal, and they love to read about their favourite stars. The problem is, it's not always clear what's true and what isn't. I mean, if a newspaper prints something scandalous or embarrassing about a famous person, they're bound to deny it, but that doesn't mean it's not true.

S: Are you trying to say …?

J: No smoke without fire, if you ask me.

P: Well, I'm sorry to interrupt you, but we'll carry on after this short break for some travel news …

3

- Ask the students to read the sentences. Allow them to work with a partner to decide who said each one and note this down.

- Tell students to choose words from the box to replace the highlighted words in sentences a–f. Then play the recording again for students to check their answers.

a) P – under fire; disregard
b) TE – begging; features
c) C – incidently
d) C – gutter press; splash
e) P – root
f) TE – scandalous; 're bound to

4

Ask the students to complete the phrases with the words in the box. You could play the recording as they work to help them. Then play it for them to check their answers.

a) but   b) finish   c) is   d) on
e) saying   f) is   g) was   h) here
i) question   j) is   k) but

Language note

Vocabulary: spoken discourse markers
These discourse markers are very common in (heated) discussions. In a normal conversation, people wait for the speaker to signal he/she has finished speaking before the next one starts. In a discussion like this, all parties are constantly trying to interrupt the speaker to get their point across, and the speaker has to defend his/her territory by using some of the devices here (e.g. *If you would just let me finish …*) or by raising his/her voice just enough so that it shows he/she hasn't finished making his/her point.

5

Write the headings on the board and ask the students to say which column to write the phrases in. Don't clean the board before the next exercise.

Interrupting:
Sorry, but …
Hang on …
What you didn't say was …
If I could just come in here …
I'm sorry to interrupt you, but …

Responding to an interruption:
If you would just let me finish …
Anyway, to get back to what I was saying …
The point I'm trying to make here is …
If you would let me answer the question …

Introducing a point:
But the thing is …
The problem is …

6

Groupwork. Put the students into groups and ask them to discuss the statements. Tell them to look at the board and use the phrases in their discussions. Encourage the groups to report back to the class on their ideas.

Grammar (SB page 105)

Emphasis (cleft sentences)

1

Pairwork. Focus attention on the sentences in the margin. Then read out the two sentences in the exercise. Ask the students to discuss in pairs how the emphasis changes in sentence B. Check their answers, then ask them if they can remember which sentence Shelley Russell used in the listening.

The speaker uses *what … was* to emphasise the object of the sentence.

She used sentence B.

Language note

Pronunciation: emphasis (cleft sentences)
(See Student"s Book page 140.)

2

- Do the first one with the class as an example, then ask the students to work individually to change the emphasis of the remaining sentences by using the sentence beginnings provided. As they work, go round giving extra help where needed.

- Check answers with the class before asking the students to say whether or not the sentences are true for them.

> a) What I don't understand is why I never seem to have any money.
> b) The thing I like about weekends is (that) I can go shopping with my friends.
> c) What really annoys me is people who only talk about money.
> d) What I feel like doing tonight is going to the cinema.
> e) The thing I hate about winter is (that) it gets dark so early.
> f) What I'd really like to do in the future is live and work abroad.

3

- Ask the students to read and discuss the statements in pairs. Tell them to decide which one of them is true. Allow them to compare notes with another pair before checking with the class.

- Ask the students to stay in the same pairs and to correct the false statements using the information in the box and the sentence beginnings given.

> Statement c) is correct.
> a) It wasn't George Bush who was the Republican candidate, it was John McCain.
> b) It wasn't Jude Law who replaced Piers Brosnan as James Bond, it was Daniel Craig.
> c) –
> d) It wasn't John Grisham who wrote *The Da Vinci Code*, it was Dan Brown.
> e) It isn't Brad Pitt who plays Captain Jack Sparrow in *Pirates of the Caribbean*, it's Johnny Depp.
> f) It isn't Juliette Binoche who is married to Nicolas Sarkozy, it's Carla Bruni.

Cultural notes

George W. Bush /dʒɔːdʒ bʊʃ/ (born 1946)
George W Bush was the 43rd President of the United States. He first became president on 20th January 2001, and was re-elected on 2nd November 2004. He's the eldest son of the 41st U.S. President, George HW Bush.

John McCain /dʒɒn m(ə)keɪn/ (born 1936)
American politician. McCain was the Republican Presidential candidate for the 2007 election, eventually losing out to Barack Obama.

Jude Law /dʒuːd lɔː/ (born 1972)
(See notes about Jude Law on page 80.)

Pierce Brosnan /ˈpiːəs ˈbrɑznən/
Pierce Brosnan is an Irish actor, film producer and environmentalist. He was the fifth James Bond and acted in the role for four of the films. Other films he has starred in include *Dante's Peak*, *The Thomas Crown Affair* and the musical *Mamma Mia!*

James Bond /dʒeɪmz bɒnd/
(See notes about James Bond in Review A, page 33.)

Kate Moss /keɪt mɑs/ (born 1974)
Kate Moss is an English model. In recent years, she's established herself as a fashion designer and has released collections in the UK and in the US.

Johnny Depp /ˈdʒɒni dep/ (born 1963)
Johnny Depp's film debut was in *Nightmare On Elm Street* (1984). Six years later he starred in the film *Edward Scissorhands* (1990). His most popular films to date are probably the *Pirates of the Caribbean* film in which he plays the role of Captain Jack Sparrow. His other films include *Sleepy Hollow* (1998), *Chocolat* (2000) and *Sweeney Todd: The Demon Barber of Fleet Street* (2007).

John Grisham /ˈdʒɒn ˈɡrɪʃəm/ (born 1955)
American novelist best known for his legal drama books, many of which have been turned into films like *The Firm* (1993) and *The Client* (1994).

Dan Brown /dæn braʊn/ (born 1964)
American author famous for his controversial book *The Da Vinci Code* (2003), which quickly became an international best seller. Dan Brown is especially interested in cryptography (the study of hidden messages and codes), which is a recurring theme in his books.

Brad Pitt /bræd pɪt/ (born 1963)
American actor who shot to fame in 1991 in the film *Thelma and Louise*. Other films he's starred in include *Seven*, *Fight Club* and *Ocean's Eleven*. He was married to the actress Jennifer Aniston (2000–2005). He started a relationship with Angelina Jolie in 2005. They have three biological children and three adopted children.

Juliette Binoche /dʒuːliˈet ˈbɪnɒʃ/ (born 1964)
Juliette Binoche is an Academy award-winning French actress famous for her roles in the films *The English Patient* (1996) and *Chocolat* (2000).

4 Grammar *Extra* 10, Part 2

Ask the students to turn to *Grammar Extra* 10, Part 2
on page 140 of the Student's Book. Here they'll find an
explanation of the grammar they've been studying and
further exercises to practise it.

3
a) What I love about my country is the fantastic
   weather.
b) The thing I like most in a person is their sense of
   humour.
c) What I enjoy most is playing tennis.
d) The thing I hate most about studying English is
   the tests.
e) What we all need in life is a stress-free job.
f) What I don't understand is why I never have
   enough free time.

4
a) It was in Paris that he met his wife.
b) It was only when he phoned that I understood
   how serious it was.
c) It was you that broke that cup, not Ian.
d) It was Ben that stole the cake, not Amy.
e) It was money that he wanted, not love.
f) It is the computer that Sam spends all her time
   on, not the phone.

Pronunciation (SB page 105)

1 🎧 3.12

- Read the instructions with the class. Ask them to
  read the sentences and decide which words are most
  likely to be stressed. Point out the underlining and
  the pause marks in the example. Ask the students to
  do the same for the remaining sentences. Encourage
  them to say the sentences aloud as they do this, so
  that they get a feel for what sounds right.

- Play the recording for them to listen and check their
  answers. Then play it again for them to repeat the
  sentences. When they've done this chorally, ask for
  individual repetition.

---

a) What I <u>love</u> about <u>Peter</u> // is his <u>wicked</u>
   sense of <u>humour</u>.
b) The <u>thing</u> I can't <u>stand</u> about this <u>country</u> //
   is the <u>weather</u>.
c) What I <u>really hate</u> about my <u>job</u> // is having
   to <u>work</u> at <u>weekends</u>.

---

d) What I find <u>annoying</u> about <u>politicians</u> // is
   that they <u>never</u> give a <u>straight answer</u>.
e) The <u>thing</u> I find most <u>difficult</u> about <u>English</u>
   // is the <u>spelling</u>.
f) What I would <u>really like</u> to do // is to <u>take</u> a
   year <u>off</u>.

Language note

Pronunciation: emphatic stress
English is a stress-timed language, so you would
commonly stress the most important words in the
sentence – the words which carry the meaning.
In a typical sentence this would mean stressing
several nouns and a verb or two.

2

Pairwork. Ask the students to take turns to finish the
sentences and give their opinions.

Reading & Vocabulary (SB page 106)

1

- Ask the students which, if any, of the James Bond
  films they've seen. Put them in pairs and ask them to
  discuss the questions before they read the article and
  to note down their answers. Then ask them to report
  back to the class on how many of their ideas were
  mentioned.

- Ask the students for their reactions to the article. Are
  they aware of product placement in films? Do they
  find it annoying or distracting?

Mentioned in the article:
a) *Dr No, Die Another Day, Quantum of Solace,
   Casino Royale, Goldfinger*
b) Sean Connery (*Others:* Roger Moore, George
   Lazenby, Timothy Dalton, Pierce Brosnan and
   Daniel Craig)
c) Smirnoff, Avon, Omega, Aston Martin

Cultural notes

James Bond /dʒeɪmz bɒnd/
(See notes about James Bond in Review A, page 33.)

Gemma Arterton /ˈdʒemə ˈɑːtətən/ (born 1986)
British actress best known for her roles in *Quantum
of Solace* (2008) and *The Boat That Rocked* (2009).

2

FCE Exam Practice

Paper 1: Reading Part 2 Gapped Text

Go through the instructions with the class and ask them
to decide which sentences go in which gaps. Remind
them that one sentence doesn't fit anywhere. As they
work, go round giving help where needed and pointing
out features such as time references and pronouns,
which can help them decide.

1 G   2 B   3 E   4 F   5 A   6 H   7 C

3

Pairwork. Ask the students to work in pairs and to decide on the correct order for the summary. Check answers with the class.

Correct order: 4, 10, 1, 7, 3, 11, 5, 8, 2, 9, 6

4

Put the students into pairs and ask them to discuss their favourite movie characters.

Speaking: anecdote (SB page 107)

For more information about how to set up, monitor and repeat Anecdotes, see page xx in the Introduction.

- Go through the instructions and the questions with the class. Give the students a minute or two to decide which film they're going to talk about. Then ask them to look at the questions and think about their answers to them. Allow them to make notes of what they're going to say and how they're going to say it, but discourage them from writing a paragraph that they can simply read out. Go round, monitoring and giving help where necessary.

- Put the students in pairs and ask them to take turns to tell their partner about a film they've seen. Encourage them to ask each other follow-up questions to get further information. Then ask some pairs to report back to the class about what they found out.

Useful phrases (SB page 108)

1 🌐 **3.13**

- Focus the students' attention on the illustrations which show posters for a variety of different film genres. Ask them which type of film they'd choose to go and see.

- Explain that all the people they're going to hear are about to see one of these types of film. Ask them to listen to the recording and say which one it is.

> d) *The Slime*

> 🌐 **3.13** (I = Interviewer; G1 = Girl 1; B1 = Boy 1; B2 = Boy 2; G2 = Girl 2; G3 = Girl 3; B3 = Boy 3)
>
> **1**
> I: Excuse me. Do you mind if I ask you how do you feel about seeing this movie?
> G1: A bit nervous actually. I don't know quite what to expect, but I think I'm going to be scared.
>
> **2**
> I: Excuse me – are you feeling nervous about seeing this movie?

> B1   Yeah a little uneasy, I must admit ... but I've brought my girlfriend, so I can hold her hand if I get scared.
>
> **3**
> I: How do you feel about seeing this movie?
> B2: I'm looking forward to being frightened to death.
>
> **4**
> I: What are you expecting from this film?
> G2: To be scared stiff – hopefully.
>
> **5**
> I: Do you think you're going to enjoy seeing this film?
> G3: Er, no – I don't think enjoy is the right word. But I've heard so much about it that I can't wait to find out what it's all about. In fact, I feel quite apprehensive, but I love horror films, and this one sounds as if it's going to be really scary.
>
> **6**
> I: Any expectations?
> B3: Well, I've been visiting the website for a while now and I'm really looking forward to finding out what happens. I expect it to be absolutely terrifying!

2

- Ask the students to underline the words they think match what the speakers said.

- Play the recording again for the students to listen and check their answers.

- Go through the instructions and make sure that the students understand that of the two remaining options in each phrase, one doesn't form a common collocation. This is the one they should cross out. They should tick the other.

> 1 'A bit / Totally / Extremely ✓ nervous, actually.'
> 2 'Yeah, distinctly ✓ / utterly / a little uneasy, I must admit.'
> 3 'I'm looking forward to being scared ✓ / nervous / frightened to death.'
> 4 'To be scared / afraid / bored ✓ stiff – hopefully.'
> 5 'I feel completely / terribly ✓ / quite apprehensive.'
> 6 'I expect it to be absolutely / quite ✓ / very terrifying.'

3

Explain the difference between gradable adjectives and absolute adjectives (see Language notes). Ask the students to look at the sentence frames and decide which adjectives go with which and how the meaning of *quite* changes in the two frames.

> A: boring, disappointing, entertaining, funny, good, interesting
> B: amazing, brilliant, dreadful, extraordinary, ridiculous, spectacular
>
> In A 'quite' means *fairly* or *rather*
> In B 'quite' means *completely* or *absolutely*

4 🔘 3.14

Play the recording, asking the students to listen and say what the general reaction to the film was.

Negative

🔘 **3.14** (I = Interviewer; G1 = Girl 1; B1 = Boy 1; B2 = Boy 2; G2 = Girl 2; G3 = Girl 3; B3 = Boy 3)

1

I: *So, how was it for you?*

G1: *Extremely disappointing. I wasn't the least bit scared, and you know from the start that everybody dies, so there's no suspense. Anyway, the characters are so annoying that I felt like killing them myself. It does not live up to the hype.*

2

I: *What did you think of it then?*

B1: *Absolute rubbish. My girlfriend fell asleep, and I spent the last half of the movie with my eyes shut – not because it was scary – but because the camera angles made me feel sick. Don't see it if you suffer from motion sickness. In fact, just don't see it.*

3

I: *So were you frightened to death?*

B2: *No way. After all the hype, it was a massive letdown.*

4

I: *What did you think?*

G2: *Over-hyped nonsense. I spent most of the time waiting for something to happen. I feel completely disillusioned.*

5

I: *Did the film live up to your expectations?*

G3: *No, it didn't. I don't think I've ever been so bored in my entire life, and I still haven't got a clue what it's about. In fact, there's no story to speak of. This film is a perfect example of hype over substance.*

6

I: *Your verdict?*

B3: *A total waste of time. I was bored out of my mind. The website was much more entertaining than the film.*

5

- Go through the instructions with the class and ask the students to try to remember and note down the exact words that the speakers used. Allow them to work in pairs or small groups if they wish.

- Play the recording again for them to listen and check their answers.

1 extremely	2 the hype	3 Absolute
4 massive	5 completely	6 entire 7 total

6

- Pairwork. Put the students in pairs and ask them to discuss the worst films, TV programmes, concerts or sports events they've seen recently. Encourage them to use the useful phrases to describe their feelings.

- As they work, go round taking note of any particularly good opinions which could be repeated for the class.

Vocabulary Extra (SB page 109)

Collocations

1

- Pairwork. Ask the students to read the text and identify the collocations. Ask them to match them to the categories listed below the text.

- Ask the students to check their answers in the dictionary extracts and to find and add more collocations to the categories.

> a) extremely important
> b) important aspect, useful information, informed decisions, practical suggestions
> c) cause problems
> d) difficulties arise
> e) soon realize

2

Go through the instructions and the example with the class, then ask the students to work individually to rewrite the text.

> Recognising and using collocations is a particularly important part of learning a language. Learners quickly realize that particular words regularly and naturally combine with each other. However, deciding which words go with which can cause confusion. Occasionally, problems arise when the wrong word is used. Fortunately, good dictionaries provide valuable information to help learners make strategic decisions. This page offers some helpful suggestions.

3

- Ask the students to look at the collocation boxes for *information* and *decision* and to focus first on the verb collocates. Go through the examples with the class and ask them to divide the other verb collocates into the two meaning groups for each word.

- Ask the students to choose two verb collocates for each noun that are new to them and which they think would be useful to learn. Get them to write a definition and an example sentence for each one, using a dictionary if necessary.

> **information**
> *give*: convey, disclose, divulge, leak, provide
> *get*: access, acquire, collect, elicit, extract, find, gather, glean, obtain, receive, retrieve
> **decision**
> *make*: arrive at, come to, make, reach, take
> *reject*: overrule, overturn, quash, reconsider, rescind, reverse

4

Go through the instructions and the example with the class, and ask them to match the other adjective collocates with their meanings.

> **information**
> a) accurate information
> b) additional/further information
> c) classified/confidential/inside information
> d) up-to-date information
> e) relevant/valuable information
>
> **decision**
> a) tough decision
> b) a momentous decision
> c) an informed decision
> d) a unanimous decision
> e) strategic decision
> f) controversial

5

Pairwork. Ask the students to look at the collocation boxes for *issue* and *problem* and to discuss in pairs how they could arrange the verb and adjective collocates in different groups according to similarity of meaning.

> **Verbs used with *issue***
> address, confront, tackle *an issue*
> consider, examine, explore, raise *an issue*
> cloud, complicate, confuse, fudge *an issue*
> dodge, duck, evade *an issue*
>
> **Adjectives used with *issue***
> contentious, controversial, divisive *issue*
> important, key, major, pressing *issue*
> sensitive, thorny *issue*
> unresolved *issue*

> **Adjectives used with *problem***
> big, fundamental, important, major, pressing, real, serious *problem*
> insoluble, intractable *problem*
>
> **Verbs used with *problem***
> address, alleviate, overcome, resolve, solve, tackle *a problem*
> cause, create, pose *a problem*
> encounter, face *a problem*
> compound, exacebate *a problem*

6

Ask the students to look in their own dictionaries to find out how information about collocations is shown.

Further practice material

Need more writing practice?

→ Workbook page 63
- Writing a film review.

Need more classroom practice activities?

→ Photocopiable resource materials pages 181 to 183
  Grammar: *Relative clauses*
  Vocabulary: *Sorry to interrupt …*
  Communication: *Inspirational marketing*
→ Top 10 activities pages xv to xx

Need DVD material?

→ DVD – Programme 10: *Bright futures*

Need progress tests?

→ Test CD – *Test Unit 10*

Need more on important teaching concepts?

→ Key concepts in *New Inside Out* pages xxii to xxxv

Need student self-study practice?

→ CD-ROM – Unit 10: *Sell*

Need student CEF self-evaluation?

→ CEF Checklists pages xxxvii to xliv

Need more information and more ideas?

→ www.insideout.net

11 Student *Overview*

Section & Aims	What the students are doing
Vocabulary & Reading SB page 110 Education; *is likely to / is expected to* Reading for gist and detail	Talking about the qualities of good teachers and students. Matching beginnings and endings of questions about education. Reading an article about people who proved their teachers wrong. Studying the language of predictions.
Pronunciation SB page 111 Abbreviations	Practising the pronunciation of common abbreviations. Working out what abbreviations stand for.
Speaking: anecdote SB page 111 Fluency practice	Talking about a favourite or least favourite teacher at school.
Listening & Vocabulary **SB page 112** Listening for gist	Talking about appropriate ages for taking responsibility for your life. Listening to parents who are worried about their daughter's future plans. Choosing the appropriate word to complete extracts from the interview. Completing statements and saying whether they agree with them.
Reading & Grammar SB page 112 Reading for detail Future forms	Reading an interview and choosing the most appropriate future forms.
Grammar SB page 113 Future forms and future time clauses	Completing a table with future forms. Identifying main and subordinate clauses. Completing sentences about the future.
Reading & Vocabulary SB page 114 Reading for gist and detail Exaggerated language	Discussing backpacking. Reading an article about students who go backpacking. Matching words to definitions. Choosing a favourite backpacker's story.
Vocabulary SB page 115 Exaggerated language	Identifying exaggerated language. Rewriting a story to make it more dramatic. Matching exaggerated expressions with their meanings.
Speaking SB page 115 Fluency practice	Writing a dramatic story from prompts and telling the story to other students.
Useful phrases SB page 116 Diplomatic language (making negative characteristics sound positive)	Putting questions from an interview into a logical order. Reading advice about job interviews and suggesting ways in which a candidate could improve his skills. Matching model answers to questions. Writing and practising job interviews.
Writing *Extra* page 117 CV and letter of application	Categorising tips for writing a CV under the headings DO and DON'T. Reading a CV and identifying what is wrong with it. Making improvements to the CV. Identifying the inappropriate parts of a letter of application.
Writing WB page 67	Writing a letter of application.

11 Student *Teacher's notes*

Vocabulary & Reading (SB page 110)

1

- Pairwork. Ask the students to think about what makes a good teacher and to write a list of qualities. Allow them to compare their lists with other pairs and then try to produce a class list of the three most important qualities.

- Do the same to produce a list of the qualities that make a good student.

2

- Do the first one as an example with the class. Then ask the students to match up the remaining questions.

- Ask the students to compare their answers in pairs before checking with the class. Allow them time to think about their answers to the questions, then discuss them in pairs.

> a) 8   b) 1   c) 4   d) 6   e) 3   f) 7
> g) 2   h) 5

3

- Go through the questions with the class first so that they know what information to look out for. Give them plenty of time to read the text and find the answers.

- When you've checked the answers, ask the students to read the article again and underline the expressions from Exercise 2 that are used in it. Point out that one of the expressions isn't used. Ask them to identify which one.

> a) Ann   b) Henry   c) Adams
> 'get a grant' is not used

4

- Go through the underlined structures with the class first and make sure they understand that these are used to make predictions about the likelihood of something happening. Give them plenty of time to read the text and find matching expressions.

- Encourage the students to use the expressions in sentences of their own.

> Text A: She is bound to fail the exam.
> Text B: She is unlikely to go on to further education.
> Text C: Henry is not expected to gain a place at university.

5

- Ask the students to work individually to complete the predictions, then allow them to compare their answers in pairs before checking with the class.

- Discuss with the class the likelihood of these things happening in their own country or countries. Encourage them to use the expressions they've just learnt and to predict when these things might occur.

- Pairwork. Put the students into pairs. Ask them to discuss and write down three more predictions about the future of education in their country or countries. Then ask them to discuss their predictions with other pairs.

> a) are expected to   d) are likely to
> b) are likely to   e) are bound to
> c) is highly likely

Pronunciation (SB page 111)

1 🌐 3.15

- Explain the difference between abbreviations and acronyms. (See Language note below.)

- Focus attention on the list and ask the students to think about which ones are acronyms. Then play the recording for them to listen and repeat. Ask them to tick the ones which can be pronounced as words.

- Play the recording again for them to underline the stressed letters in those which aren't acronyms.

> 1 AIDS ✓   2 BS<u>c</u>   3 C<u>V</u>   4 DI<u>Y</u>
> 5 FA<u>Q</u>   6 MB<u>A</u>   7 NATO ✓   8 OPEC ✓
> 9 Ph<u>D</u>   10 PIN ✓   11 UNICEF ✓   12 VA<u>T</u>

Language notes

Pronunciation: abbreviations and acronyms

- Abbreviations and acronyms both use letters to represent words, but acronyms can be pronounced like words, e.g. AIDS, NATO, OPEC, PIN and UNICEF.

- *VAT* is usually pronounced as individual letters, but when combined with *man* to make *VAT man*, it's always pronounced as an acronym.

2 🌐 3.16

- Pairwork. Ask the students to work together to decide what the abbreviations stand for. Ask them to highlight those which are connected with education.

- Play the recording for them to check their answers. Then ask what the equivalent abbreviations are in their own language or languages.

> 1 Acquired Immune Deficiency Syndrome
> 2 Bachelor of Science
> 3 Curriculum Vitae
> 4 Do-it-yourself
> 5 Frequently Asked Questions
> 6 Master of Business Administration
> 7 North Atlantic Treaty Organisation
> 8 Organisation of Petroleum Exporting Countries
> 9 Doctor of Philosophy
> 10 Personal Identification Number
> 11 United Nations International Children's Emergency Fund
> 12 Value Added Tax
>
> Abbreviations to do with education are:
> BSc   MBA   PhD

Cultural notes

Exams: GCSE, BSc, MBA, PhD

GCSE (General Certificate of Secondary Education) is an examination in a range of subjects taken at 16 in England and Wales; BSc is an academic degree taken in maths and science subjects in the UK; MBA is a Master's degree in business administration and PhD is an advanced degree recognised in many countries.

Organisations: NATO /ˈneɪtəʊ/, UNICEF /ˈjuːnɪsef/, OPEC /ˈəʊpek/

NATO is an international military alliance formed in 1949; UNICEF is an organisation that provides emergency food and healthcare to children in war situations around the world; OPEC is a group of 12 oil-producing countries which have formed an economic alliance.

Speaking: anecdote (SB page 111)

For more information about how to set up, monitor and repeat Anecdotes, see page xx in the Introduction.

- Go through the instructions and the questions with the class. Give the students a minute or two to decide which teacher they're going to talk about. Then ask them to look at the questions and think about their answers to them. Allow them to make notes of what they're going to say and how they're going to say it, but discourage them from writing a paragraph that they can simply read out. Go round, monitoring and giving help where necessary.

- Put the students in pairs and ask them to take turns to tell their partner about their favourite or least favourite teacher at school. Encourage them to ask each other follow-up questions to get further information. Then ask some pairs to report back to the class about what they found out.

Listening & Vocabulary (SB page 112)

1

Groupwork. Go through the questions with the class, then ask them to discuss them in small groups. Get each group to report back to the class on what they decided.

2 🌐 3.17

- Go through the sentences with the class before playing the recording, so that they know what information to look out for.

- You may need to play the recording again to give the students a chance to decide which is the best summary.

> b)

🔘 **3.17** (I = Interviewer; Mrs B = Mrs Barrington;
Mr B = Mr Barrington)

I: *What is Saffron going to do when she leaves school?*

Mrs B: *Until a few months ago, she was going to go to university, but she's changed her mind. Now she reckons she's going to make it in the pop world.*

I: *And how do you feel about that?*

Mr B: *We think she's making an enormous mistake.*

I: *But surely she can go back to her studies if her music career fails.*

Mr B: *That's true, but once she gets a taste of freedom, she'll find it more difficult to go back to college. I just think it's such a waste – in three years' time, she'll have got her degree and she'll still be young enough to try out the music business. At least if it doesn't work out she'll have a qualification behind her.*

I: *Have you discussed this with her?*

Mrs B: *Of course, but she's made up her mind. We're just hoping that she'll get it out of her system and then come to her senses and go back to her studies. When I left school, I didn't go on to university, and I've regretted it ever since. I just don't want her to make the same mistake I did.*

I: *Will you support her while she's trying to be a pop singer?*

Mr B: *You mean financially? No. She won't be living at home, and we can't afford to pay for her to live in London, so it's up to her to make it work.*

3

Encourage the students to think back to what they heard and try to decide which is the correct alternative in each extract. When they've done as many as they can, play the recording for them to check their answers.

a) make	b) taste	c) behind	d) system
e) senses	f) up		

Language note

Vocabulary: colloquial expressions
Note that the only words that change within these fixed phrases are the object pronouns (*me, you, him/her*, etc.) and the possessive adjectives (*my, your, his/her*, etc.). For example: *She might as well get it out of **her** system; It's up to **them**; He needs to come to **his** senses.*

4

- Pairwork. Ask the students to work together to use the expressions from Exercise 3 to complete the statements appropriately. Remind them that they'll need to make some changes.

- Check answers with the class before giving the students time to think about whether or not they agree with the statements. Then discuss this as a class, encouraging the students to give reasons for their opinions and to say whether they think their parents would agree with them.

a) get it out of your system	d) make it
b) a taste of freedom	e) up to you
c) behind you	

Reading & Grammar (SB page 112)

1

Pairwork. Focus attention on the photo. Point out that this is Saffron, the girl in the listening. Ask students to work with a partner and use the context to choose and underline the most appropriate future forms in the conversation.

1	my A-levels start
2	I'm going to concentrate
3	I'm going to be
4	I'm going to find
5	I'm moving
6	you'll be able
7	we might have to
8	it's going to be
9	we'll have had
10	I'll be staying
11	I'll give
12	it'll be

Cultural note

A levels
The Advanced Level General Certificate of Education exams are usually taken in three or four specialised subjects at the age of 17 or 18 in the UK.

2 🔘 3.18

Play the recording for the students to check their answers to Exercise 1. Then put them in pairs. Ask them to think about the question and then discuss their answers with their partner. Encourage the pairs to report back to the class.

I: *You're leaving school soon, aren't you?*

S: *Yes, my A-levels start next week, but I'm not too bothered about the results, because when I leave school I'm going to concentrate on my music career. I'm the lead singer in a band and I don't need any qualifications to be a pop star. I see my future very clearly – it's obvious that I've got what it takes to be successful. I'm going to be incredibly famous and fabulously rich.*

I: *So you've already got a contract then?*

S: *Er, no, not as such. Actually, we haven't got a manager yet, but the minute I've taken my last exam, I'm going to find a really good one.*

I: *So, do you intend to continue living at home?*

S: *No way. I'm moving to London as soon as I've left school. London's where it all happens in the music industry.*

I: *Do you think you'll be able to live off your music right from the start?*

S: *Well, if we don't make it straightaway we might have to get part-time jobs for a few months or something. I know it's going to be hard at first, but I bet you, by this time next year, we'll have had a single in the charts.*

I: *And where do you see yourself in five years from now?*

S: *In five years' time I'll be staying in posh hotels and won't be able to walk down the street without being recognised. In fact, I'll give you my autograph now if you like – it'll be worth a fortune in a few years' time!*

Grammar (SB page 113)

Future forms and future time clauses

1

- Pairwork. Ask the students to complete the table with examples of different future forms from the interview with Saffron on page 112. As they work, go round giving extra help where needed.

- Check answers with the class, going through the table and pointing out the various uses of the different forms.

> a) Example 1: … it'll be worth a fortune in a few years' time!
> b) Example: … we might have to get part-time jobs …
> c) *be going to*; Example 1: I'm going to concentrate on my music career.
> d) Example: I'm moving to London …
> e) Present simple
> f) Example: I'll be staying in posh hotels …
> g) Future perfect

Language note

Grammar: future forms and future time clauses
(See Student's Book page 142.)

2

Focus attention on the sentences and ask a student or students to read them aloud. Go through the instructions and point out the underlining and circling in the example. Then ask the students to discuss and do the same for the three sentences.

> a) … ⟨the minute⟩ (I've taken my last exam), I'm going to find a really good one. (line 14)
> b) … I'm moving to London just ⟨as soon as⟩ (I've left school). (lines 16–17)
> c) … ⟨if⟩ (we don't make it straight away), we might have to get part-time jobs… (lines 21–22)
>
> 1 The main clause
> 2 Present simple and present perfect (present continuous also possible)
> 3 When the subordinate clause comes before the main clause.

3

Ask the students to work individually to complete the sentences. Do the first one with the class as an example if you wish. Allow the students to compare their sentences in pairs before checking answers with the class.

> a) fail; will kill
> b) 'm going to grow; leave
> c) 'm never going to read; 've taken
> d) 'll like; get
> e) isn't coming out; 's done
> f) finish; 'm going to set up

4

- Ask the students to work individually to complete the sentences. Remind them that these should be true.

- Put the students into pairs to compare and discuss their sentences. Ask them to report back to the class on any particularly interesting sentences.

5 Grammar *Extra* 11

Ask the students to turn to *Grammar Extra* 11 on page 142 of the Student's Book. Here they'll find an explanation of the grammar they've been studying and further exercises to practise it.

> 1
>
> ### FCE Exam Practice
>
> **Paper 3: Use of English Part 4 Transformations**
>
> 1 She might not pass the exam.
> 2 I've arranged to see the director at 3 pm.
> 3 As soon as I've finished this test, I'm leaving.
> 4 I'm going to concentrate on my acting career.
> 5 By this time next week, the builders will have finished.
> 6 If you can't come with us, we won't go.
> 7 He's not coming out until he's finished his homework.
> 8 I think the team is going to win today.

| 2
Students' own answers. |

Reading & Vocabulary (SB page 114)

1

Groupwork. Put the students into small groups and ask them to discuss the questions, then to report back to the class on their ideas.

2

• Ask the students to look at the photo and at the title of the article. Ask them what they think the article will be about and if they think they'd enjoy this kind of experience.

• Go through the instructions and explain the expression *to take something with a pinch of salt* (to be slightly wary about believing what someone says). Then ask them to read the first part of the article and answer the question.

| Because travellers tend to exaggerate and embellish their stories. |

Cultural notes

Queensland
Named after Queen Victoria, Queensland is the second largest state in Australia, and is situated in the north east of the country. The Great Barrier Reef runs parallel to the Pacific coast of Queensland. It's a popular tourist destination.

Victoria Falls
A waterfall in the Zambezi River on the border of Zambia and Zimbabwe.

3

• Give the students time to look back through the text and find matching words and expressions.

• Check answers with the class before asking the students to say whether they know anyone who tends to exaggerate and embellish the stories they tell.

| a) buzz
b) tales
c) exaggerate and embellish
d) dodging
e) rite of passage |

4

Go through the instructions with the class, making sure that everyone understands that these are two versions of the same backpacking story. Ask the students to read both versions and decide which they prefer and why.

Vocabulary (SB page 115)

1

• Ask the students to read version 2 of Tom's story on page 114 again. Point out that describing ants as being the size of lobsters is exaggeration. Ask them to find ten more examples of exaggerated language.

• Allow the students to compare notes in pairs before checking answers with the class.

| dirty / filthy
full of / swarming with
big ants / huge ants that looked like lobsters
which had swollen up / which had swollen up like a balloon
trying to kill them / going berserk trying to kill them
I spotted one on the ceiling / I spotted an enormous ant on the ceiling
I hit it / I bashed it
I fainted / I blacked out
had hit my head / had dented my skull
I was taken to hospital / I had to be rushed to hospital
I had five stitches / I had emergency surgery |

Language note

Vocabulary: exaggerated expressions
The expressions in this section range from simple exaggeration (*dirty – filthy*) to hyperbole (*I was feeling ill – I was at death's door*). This is very common when spicing up a spoken story and, in some cases, has entered the common vocabulary; instead of saying *He was angry (about something)*, it's as common to say *He freaked out*. Other examples include: *I'm hungry = I'm starving; I'm thirsty = I'm parched; She cried a lot = She cried her eyes out; He was overweight = He weighed a ton*, etc.

2 ● 3.19

• Pairwork. Ask the students to read both versions of the second story. Point out that there's exaggerated language in both versions and they need to find this and combine elements of the story to make it as dramatic as possible.

• Play the recording for the students to compare with their stories.

| (See audioscript on page 117.) |

⊙ 3.19

Tom's second story

While I was travelling, I got an incredibly painful tropical ear infection after I fell into a stinking latrine. Feeling like death, I lay in bed with a raging fever for what felt like a lifetime. Wracked with pain, I couldn't face eating anything and I lost so much weight that I looked like a skeleton. Eventually, I managed to get hold of some antibiotics which brought me back from death's door.

3

- Ask the students to work individually to match the expressions with their meanings.
- Read the example sentence to the class, then ask the students to choose three expressions from column A and use them in sentences of their own.
- Ask the students to compare their sentences in pairs or small groups. Then ask some of them to read their sentences to the class.

a) 3   b) 9   c) 4   d) 10   e) 1   f) 7
g) 2   h) 5   i) 8   j) 6

Speaking (SB page 115)

1

Pairwork. Read the instructions to the class and point out that they can use their own ideas as well as the notes given. Ask the students to work together to devise their stories and encourage them to make them as dramatic as possible.

Language note

Vocabulary: linkers
These discourse markers provide cohesion in a text. This selection concentrates on: sequencing events (*To begin with*, *Then*, *Later*. Others include: *After that*, *Next*); expressing attitude (*To my horror*, *Suddenly*. Others include: *To my surprise*, *Naturally*, *Obviously*), and ending the story (*In the end*, *It turned out that*. Others include: *Finally*, *At last*).

2

Put the pairs together to create small groups and ask them to tell their stories to each other.

Useful phrases (SB page 116)

1 ⊙ 3.20

- Focus the students' attention on the picture. Ask the students to identify the situation (a young man being interviewed for a job).
- Put the students into pairs and tell them that they're going to hear the young man, Sam, being interviewed for a job. Ask them first to put the interview questions into what they think is the most logical order.

- Play the recording for them to check their answers. Then have a class discussion on whether or not Sam will get the job.

Correct order: e), f), c), b), g), d), a)

⊙ 3.20 (I = Interviewer; S = Sam)

I: Ah, come in. Sam, isn't it?

S: Yes.

I: Well Sam, tell us a little about yourself.

S: Um, well, I'm 24, and I was born in Swindon. I like football. In the winter I go skiing and in the summer, I like sailing and windsurfing. Oh, and I'm a black belt in karate. Well, I say I'm a black belt. In fact, I'm a brown belt but I'm taking my black belt in a few days, so … um, anyway, I graduated last year, and now I'm looking forward to getting a job.

I: OK. And why do you think you'd be right for a position in this company?

S: Oh, well, er, I'm interested in what your company does. Um, I haven't really thought about it.

I: In your opinion, what are your greatest strengths?

S: I'm outgoing and friendly, so I get on well with people.

I: What would you say your weaknesses are?

S: My weaknesses? I can't think of any. Ha ha. Oh, I know – I tend to be at my best in the afternoon. Mornings are tricky.

I: Right. And what are your long-term objectives?

S: To be the best I can be – and to make lots of money.

I: What would you like to be doing in five years' time?

S: Lying on a beach in the Caribbean! Ha ha.

I: Do you have any questions you'd like to ask us?

S: Er, no. I'm fine.

I: Right, well, we'll be in touch.

2

- Ask the students to read the advice on how to do well in a job interview.
- Discuss with the class how Sam could have improved his interview skills. Play the recording again, if necessary.

He shouldn't have waffled about his sporting achievements.
He shouldn't have suggested that he didn't have any weaknesses.
He should have been more enthusiastic (not implying he didn't work well in the morning) and he should have found out about the company to give the impression of being interested in the work.
He should have prepared for the interview better.

3 ● 3.21

- Ask the students to match the model answers to the questions. Allow them to compare answers in pairs.
- Tell them that they're going to hear another interview and that they should listen and check their answers. When they've done this, ask them which of the highlighted phrases could be used in other interview contexts.

---

1 b   2 e   3 c   4 f   5 d   6 a   7 g

All of them could be used in other contexts.

● 3.21 (I = Interviewer; L = Layla)

I: Ah, come in. Layla isn't it?

L: Yes, that's right.

I: Well Layla, tell us a little about yourself.

L: OK. I graduated from university last year, and since then I've been travelling in Asia and Australia. That was a great experience, but now I'm ready to embark on my career and I'm very keen to work for a company like yours.

I: OK. And why do you think you'd be right for a position in this company?

L: Well, I've always been interested in working in the media. I think I'm well suited to this kind of work because I work well under pressure. I don't have much experience yet, but anything I don't know, I'm willing to learn.

I: In your opinion, what are your greatest strengths?

L: I'm highly motivated and conscientious. I'm a team player, but equally I can work on my own.

I: What would you say your weaknesses are?

L: I would say my greatest weakness has been my lack of proper planning in the past. However, since I've come to recognise that weakness, I've taken steps to correct it.

I: Right. And what are your long-term objectives?

L: I'd like to gain some experience in this field for a few years, and then decide which area I want to specialise in.

I: What would you like to be doing in five years' time?

L: Ideally, I'd like to be managing my own team.

I: Do you have any questions you'd like to ask us?

L: Yes, I'd like to know a bit about the training opportunities in this job.

I: Yes, that's a good question. We believe in on-going training here, and we provide regular opportunities for our staff to attend relevant courses.

L: Oh, that sounds great.

I: Right, well, thank you for coming in Layla. We'll be in touch.

4

- Pairwork. Go through the jobs with the class and make sure everyone understands them. Then put the students into pairs to write an interview for one of the jobs (remind them that they can use their own idea for the job if they wish). Try to make sure that several pairs choose each option. Go round helping with vocabulary where needed and making sure that the students use the highlighted useful phrases from Exercise 3 in their interviews.
- Ask the students to practise their interviews. Ask a few confident pairs to perform theirs for the class.

Writing *Extra* (SB page 117)

CV and letter of application

1

- Make sure that the students understand what a *CV* is (*curriculum vitae*: an account of a person's education, qualifications, job experiences, skills and interests, which is used when making a job application). Focus their attention on the list of tips and tell them to decide which are things you should do and which are things you should not do when writing your CV.
- Check answers with the class and see if anyone has any other tips.

DO:
a) be honest
d) use a clear layout
e) use bold and italic for headings
f) include dates
g) check for spelling and typing errors

DON'T:
b) mention your bad points and failures
c) try to be amusing
h) use family or friends as referees

2

- Ask the students to work individually to read Sam Arnoldson's CV and to use the tips in Exercise 1 to identify the places where Sam has gone wrong.
- When they've finished, ask them to compare their answers with a partner.

- The CV looks overly familiar and the layout is poor.
- There are number of spelling errors, e.g. *educasion*, *personnel*, and typing errors, e.g. *compUter*.
- No dates are included.
- Sam has tried to be amusing with the use of emoticons, the funny email address and the mention of blood donating as a 'personal interest'. This wouldn't go down well.
- He has included his own mother as a referee.
- The language is too informal.

3

- Pairwork. Go through the example with the class and point out that there are ways of making most things sound a lot better than they are without being dishonest.
- Put the students into pairs and ask them to look at the rest of the items under *Employment* and *Skills* in Sam's CV and to think of ways to make them sound more formal and positive. When they've finished, ask them to turn to page 130 and read the improved version of Sam's CV.

4

- Ask the students to read the letter and then go back and cross out the parts that they think are inappropriate.
- Allow them to compare their answers in pairs before checking with the class.

Sam's letter with the inappropriate sections crossed out:

To whom it may concern DO NOT PUT THIS LETTER IN THE BIN!!!!!

Dear Sir or Madam or Mademoiselle,

I am writing to apply for the post of holiday representative advertised in *The Times* this week. As you can see from my curriculum vitae enclosed, I do not have a great deal of work experience and no experience whatsoever as a holiday rep. However, what I lack in experience I am willing to make up for in enthusiasm and hard work.

Since I left college in June last year, I have been in continual employment. First of all I worked as a shop assistant where I learnt a lot about the retail industry. But it was my mother's shop and we argued all the time. After that I worked in a ski resort in France where I enjoyed working as part of a team and improved my spoken French. I left because the pay was rubbish and I never had time to go skiing.

Through the variety of posts I have held, I have learnt important interpersonal skills, improved my knowledge of European languages and have gained extensive computing skills. I feel the job you are offering will enable me to put these skills into practice.

As I'm unemployed at the moment, I can be available for interview at your convenience.

Yours faithfully,

Sam Arnoldson ☺
Sam Arnoldson

5

Ask the students to write their own CV and letter of application for a job as a holiday representative. Tell them to follow the tips on writing a CV and to check their work thoroughly for appropriate language before they hand it to you for checking.

Further practice material

Need more writing practice?
→ Workbook page 67
- Writing a letter of application.

Need more classroom practice activities?
→ Photocopiable resource materials pages 184 to 186
  Grammar: *Future forms*
  Vocabulary: *Exaggerated expressions*
  Communication: *A good bet*
→ Top 10 activities pages xv to xx

Need DVD material?
→ DVD – Programme 11: *A special place*

Need progress tests?
→ Test CD – *Test Unit 11*

Need more on important teaching concepts?
→ Key concepts in *New Inside Out* pages xxii to xxxv

Need student self-study practice?
→ CD-ROM – Unit 11: *Student*

Need student CEF self-evaluation?
→ CEF Checklists pages xxxvii to xliv

Need more information and more ideas?
→ www.insideout.net

12 Home *Overview*

Section & Aims	What the students are doing
Reading & Vocabulary SB page 118 Reading for specific information Houses	Discussing dream houses. Reading an article about two unusual houses and discussing which one they prefer. Completing collocations.
Grammar SB page 118 Participle clauses	Completing a table with sentences containing participle clauses. Rewriting sentences using participles.
Vocabulary SB page 120 Furnishings	Matching furnishings to rooms. Discussing furnishings.
🔊 **Speaking & Listening SB page 120** Fluency practice Listening for detail	Looking at photos of rooms and discussing them and the people who might own them. Listening to a psychologist talking about what our rooms say about us and matching interpretations to rooms.
Grammar SB page 121 Nouns and quantity expressions	Completing extracts from descriptions of rooms. Completing sentences with appropriate endings. Choosing the correct verb form in sentences about quantity.
Speaking: anecdote SB page 121 Fluency practice	Talking about their favourite room.
Reading & Speaking: SB page 122 Reading for specific information Fluency practice	Reading an extract from *Sons and Lovers* by D H Lawrence and answering questions. Putting a character's morning routine in the correct order. Talking about the relationship between the characters in the story.
🔊 **Listening & Vocabulary** **SB page 122** Listening for specific information Morning routines	Listening to people from different countries talking about what they have for breakfast. Matching food items to people. Talking about daily routines and breakfast habits.
🔊 **Useful phrases SB page 124** Saying hello and goodbye	Completing expressions for saying goodbye in a conversation. Matching phrases with appropriate responses. Writing a conversation.
Vocabulary *Extra* SB page 125 Get it right	Completing statements with *actual / actually* or *current / currently*. Choosing the verb or verb phrase which is the odd one out. Underlining the correct alternative. Catagorising nouns as countable or uncountable. Identifying the common error in sentences and identifying ones they commonly make. Finding examples of correct usage in their dictionaries.
Writing WB page 71	Writing a description of a holiday home.

12 Home *Teacher's notes*

Reading & Vocabulary (SB page 118)

1

• Pairwork. Explain the concept of a 'dream' or ideal house. Go through the list of possibilities with the class, then ask them to discuss in pairs how they imagine their dream house. Make it clear that they should use their own ideas and not confine themselves to those in the book. Then ask the pairs to report back to the class.

• Focus attention on the two photos on page 119. Ask the students not to read the article yet, but to think about which of the features listed they would expect each house to have.

• When they've finished predicting the features of each house, ask them to read the article and find out if they were right.

> The earth shelter is eco-friendly, is light and bright, is quiet.
> The lighthouse is in the middle of nowhere, has a terrace, has bedrooms with en suites, is on the coast, has amazing views.

Language note

Vocabulary: house

There are some differences between American and British English when describing types of house or accommodation. For example:

Br E *flat* = Am E *apartment*.

Br E *block of flats* = Am E *apartment building* or *condominium* (for a small group of flats, each owned by the occupier).

Br E *a terraced house* = Am E *a row house* or *town-house*.

Br E *bungalow* = a house on one level, Am E *bungalow* = a house that is small and compact, usually on one level.

2

Put the students into pairs and ask them to discuss which of the two houses they'd prefer to live in. Make sure they give their reasons and encourage them to report back to the class.

3

• Pairwork. Ask the students to try to complete the collocations without looking at the article.

• When they've done as many as they can, allow them to look at the article again and check their answers.

• Ask the students to discuss their answers to the questions and report back to the class on their ideas.

> a) fuels   b) heating   c) cred   d) display
> e) dark   f) door
> *Possible answers:*
> a) coal, oil, gas, etc.
> b) September, October, November
> c) the right clothes, a cool place to live, fashionable friends, etc.
> d) national celebrations, for example, Guy Fawkes, New Year, etc.
> e) close blinds, curtains and shutters and switch off all lights, etc.
> f) to say hello, to ask for a favour, to borrow some sugar, etc.

Grammar (SB page 118)

Participle clauses

1

• Go through the sentences in the table with the class. Ask the students to identify the relative clauses in the sentences in column 2. Then ask them to find two appropriate sentences from the article on page 119 to complete column 3.

• Check answers with the class and go through the information on participle clauses in the margin.

> 1) We're in a bungalow covered in earth.
> 2) You will see a ship coming in.

Language note

Grammar: participle clauses
(See Student's Book page 142.)

2

- Go through the example with the class and then ask the students to work individually to rewrite the remaining sentences. Allow them to compare answers in pairs before checking with the class.

- Ask the students to discuss with a partner whether any of the sentences are true for them.

> a) My apartment block, built in the 1990s, is quite modern.
> b) My own apartment, located on the top floor, is very light and airy.
> c) Every morning I am woken up by the sun streaming through my window.
> d) My bedroom is full of souvenirs collected on my travels.
> e) The neighbours living opposite us are very friendly.

3 Grammar *Extra* 12, Part 1

Ask the students to turn to *Grammar Extra* 12, Part 1 on page 142 of the Student's Book. Here they'll find an explanation of the grammar they've been studying and a further exercise to practise it.

> **1**
> a) That man speaking very loudly is my cousin.
> b) The people living in my street are very friendly.
> c) The glasses kept in that cabinet are very expensive.
> d) The rooms overlooking the back of the house are the best.
> e) The pizzas sold in that place are the best!

Vocabulary (SB page 120)

1

- Point out that the headings in the table are all rooms in a house. Ask the students to work in pairs and to decide which of the furnishings listed in the box they'd expect to find in each room. Point out that some may appear in more than one room.

- Allow them to compare their answers with other pairs before checking with the class. Find out if anyone has any of these items in an unusual place in their own house.

> *Possible answers:*
> In the kitchen: a dustpan and brush; an ironing board; a sink, tea towels; a tumble dryer
> In the bathroom: a shaving socket; a shower curtain; a towel rail; a washbasin
> In the living room: candlesticks; a fireplace; a mantelpiece; ornaments; patterned wallpaper
> In the hallway: coat hooks, a doormat

2

- Ask the students to read the lists of items and decide which part of a room they'd associate with each group. Then check with the class and make sure everyone understands all the items. (*Parquet* is a kind of wooden flooring made up of small blocks fitted together.)

- Ask the students to tick all the items in Exercises 1 and 2 that they have in their homes. Find out who has the most items.

> a) a floor   b) a window   c) a wall
> d) a front door

Speaking & Listening (SB page 120)

1

- Pairwork. Go through the instructions and the questions with the class. Ask them to discuss the questions in pairs, giving as much detail as possible. With weaker classes, you might like to begin by simply getting the students to describe what they can see in the photos.

- Ask the pairs to report back to the class on their opinions. Write on the board any adjectives they come up with to describe the sort of people they think the rooms belong to.

FCE Exam Practice

Paper 5: Speaking Part 2 Talking about photographs

Here is a more formal exam practice alternative to Exercise 1.

- Pairwork. Read the following instructions as if you were the examiner.

Student A. Look at these two photographs. They show two different sitting rooms. Compare the photographs and say what kind of person you think each room belongs to. (Allow about 1 minute.)

Student B. Which room do you like best and why? (Allow about 20 seconds.)

- You could then swap the students round and use the same photos to repeat the activity. Better still, find two more photos of contrasting rooms from a magazine or brochure, i.e. two different kitchens or two different bedrooms. Use the same instructions as above with the new photos.

2 🌐 3.22–3.23

- Go through the sentences with the class, then ask them to decide which room each interpretation matches. Allow them to compare their ideas in pairs or small groups before you play the recording.

- Play the recording for the students to check their ideas. Encourage them to say whether they agree or disagree with the psychologist's assessment. Then ask them to turn to page 130 and read what the people who own the rooms think.

2

a) Room 1	d) Room 2
b) Room 1	e) Room 1
c) Room 2	f) Room 2

🌐 **3.22**

Room 1

This is obviously a family room. The leather sofa and armchair are nice big, comfortable seats which suggests that the priority here is comfort rather than style. I imagine a family with young children sitting on the sofa to watch a DVD or listen to a story.

There are far too many cushions and I'd say a woman was responsible for those. Cushions may look attractive, but nine times out of ten, they don't make seats more comfortable. But that's typical of the different ways men and women approach homes – men tend to be more practical, whilst women are more concerned with aesthetics.

So with that in mind, I imagine a woman will have chosen the candlesticks and house plants, and she will probably have been responsible for the family photos on the wall.

There are loads of different colours in this room with the green wallpaper, blue curtains and pattered carpet, but the big window and the mirror above the fireplace prevent the room from being too dark.

The room is rather untidy and but I imagine both parents go out to work and so they don't have much time to tidy up.

I think the people who live here are laid back, sociable people who enjoy entertaining. I don't think they're the sort of people who would worry too much if someone spills a little wine on the carpet.

🌐 **3.23**

Room 2

This one's more difficult because there are very few clues here about the type of person who lives in it. I think it's a man because there are hardly any personal objects on display – for instance, there aren't any family photos around the place.

But there's plenty of evidence to suggest that this is a successful career person, someone who spends most of his time travelling. There isn't really enough furniture to make this look like a home. There are a couple of leather and chrome chairs which are probably Italian and worth a lot of money – he certainly has good taste and may work in advertising or the media.

I think this is somebody who doesn't actually spend much time at home, and when he does, he's obsessively tidy. You only have to look at how his CDs are organised on the shelves to see that he likes things to be in order. The lack of decoration suggests that he wants to be ready to pack his bags and leave at short notice.

He has little time to socialise, except in a working context, and probably never entertains at home. He's single, and may be the sort of person who has problems with commitment in personal relationships.

Grammar (SB page 121)

Nouns and quantity expressions

1

- Focus the students' attention on the information in the margin. Point out that some of the quantity expressions can be used with both countable and uncountable nouns, but there are some which can only be used with one type.

- Pairwork. Ask the students to work in pairs to complete the extracts. Check answers before asking them to put the quantifiers in a logical order.

---

a) There are	d) There are
b) There are	e) There is
c) There are	f) There is

Logical order: c), f), b) e), d), a)

> **Language note**
>
> **Grammar: nouns and quantity expressions**
> (See Student's Book page 142.)

2

Pairwork. Ask the students to complete the sentences with the appropriate endings. Check answers before asking them to identify the meaning of the quantifiers in bold. Draw their attention to the difference in meaning between *few* and *a few*.

---

a) 2   b) 1   c) 1   d) 2
a) a little, a few   b) little   c) few

3

Ask the students to work individually to complete the sentences so that they are true for them. Then tell the students to compare and discuss their sentences in pairs.

4

- Do the first one as an example with the class, then ask the students to choose the correct forms.

- Check answers before asking the students to change the statements to make them true of their own home town or city. Also point out that they should add two more statements of their own before comparing their answers with a partner.

> a) isn't   b) 's   c) are   d) 's   e) are
> f) 's

5 Grammar *Extra* 12, Part 2

Ask the students to turn to *Grammar Extra* 12, Part 2 on page 142 of the Student's Book. Here they'll find an explanation of the grammar they've been studying and further exercises to practise it.

> **2**
>
> | | |
> |---|---|
> | 1 are | 5 little |
> | 2 much | 6 some of |
> | 3 few | 7 hardly any |
> | 4 plenty of | 8 a lot of |
>
> **3**
> Students' own answers.

Speaking: anecdote (SB page 121)

For more information about how to set up, monitor and repeat Anecdotes, see page xx in the Introduction.

- Go through the instructions and the questions with the class. Give the students a minute or two to decide which room they're going to talk about. Then ask them to look at the questions and think about their answers to them. Allow them to make notes of what they're going to say and how they're going to say it, but discourage them from writing a paragraph that they can simply read out. Go round, monitoring and giving help where necessary.

- Pairwork. Put the students in pairs and ask them to take turns to tell their partner about their favourite room. Encourage them to ask each other follow-up questions to get further information. Then ask some pairs to report back to the class about what they found out.

Reading & Speaking (SB page 122)

1

Tell the students that they're going to read an extract from a famous novel by D H Lawrence called *Sons and Lovers*. Ask the students to look at the photo of the kitchen on page 123 and to work individually to write three adjectives describing the room and three adjectives describing the life of the people who might live there. Allow them to compare with a partner and then have a class discussion of their impressions.

> ### Cultural notes
>
> **DH Lawrence** /diː eɪtʃ ˈlɒrəns/ (1885–1930)
> British novelist, poet and painter. The son of a miner, Lawrence was encouraged by his mother to become a teacher. The semi-autobiographical *Sons and Lovers* (1913) was his third novel and

established his reputation as an author ready to explore issues relating to emotion and human intimacy, subjects which at the time were regarded as taboo.

> ### *Sons and Lovers*
> This novel was written in 1913 and tells the story of Paul Morel, a boy born in a mining community in northern England. His complex relationship with his mother and his troubled relationships with his father, and with other women, dominate the story.

2

Give the students plenty of time to read the extract to find out if their ideas were correct. Then ask them to find the answers to the questions.

> a) Morel gets up at 5 a.m. (sometimes earlier) and goes to work at 6 a.m.
> b) For breakfast, he has tea, toasted bacon and a thick slice of bread with drops of fat from the bacon. For lunch he has two thick slices of bread-and-butter and cold tea with no milk or sugar.
> c) He loves having breakfast alone (' … he sat down to an hour of joy')

3

Encourage the students to try to put the routine in order without looking back at the text. When they've finished, allow them to read the extract again to check their answers.

> *Correct order*: 1, 9, 3, 2, 5, 7, 8, 6, 4

> ### Extra activity
>
> Ask the students to write sentences describing their own morning routine. They could then jumble these and get a partner to try to put them back in the right order.

4

- Groupwork. Go through the questions with the class, then ask them to discuss them in small groups.

- When they've finished, encourage them to report back to the class on their ideas, then ask them to turn to page 131 and to read the summary to check their ideas. Find out if anything surprised them.

Listening & Vocabulary (SB page 122)

1

Make sure the students can form the questions they'll need to find out the information. Give them a few minutes to mingle and ask each other their questions. They should then report back to the class on what they found out.

2

Pairwork. The students look at the list of food and drink items and answer the questions with a partner. Encourage them to report back to the class on their discussion.

> **Cultural notes**
>
> *Miso soup* /miːsəʊ suːp/
> A flavoursome soup from Japan containing miso paste, tofu and konbu (seaweed). It usually accompanies a meal of rice, fish and Japanese pickles.

3 🌐 3.24–3.26

- Ask the students to say which items they think are typically eaten in each country.
- Play the recording for them to check their answers.

> USA: eggs, bacon, pancakes, toast, orange juice, coffee
> GERMANY: jam, cereal, cold meat, bacon, ham, cheese, bread rolls, coffee, eggs
> JAPAN: green tea, rice, miso soup, omelette, pickled vegetables, grilled fish, seaweed

> 🌐 **3.24** (I = Interviewer; L = Lizanne)
>
> I: *Lizanne, you're from America. What do you have for breakfast?*
> L: *Er, eggs, bacon, pancakes, and a bit of toast on the side.*
> I: *And what to drink?*
> L: *Usually we start with orange juice and have lots and lots of coffee.*
> I: *And your eggs – how do you like to have them done?*
> L: *Sunny side up.*
> I: *What does that mean?*
> L: *That means that the yolk is facing upward – it's not been turned over.*
> I: *Thank you.*
>
> 🌐 **3.25** (I = Interviewer; N = Nicola)
>
> I: *Nicola, you're from Germany. Tell me about breakfast. What do you have for breakfast?*
> N: *Well, in Germany it's different. Some people like jam or cereals, but the typical breakfast is, of course, with cold meat like salami, bacon or ham, and cheese. And we always have hot bread rolls and coffee. But I don't like coffee very much. And, of course, boiled eggs – they are very important in Germany and very typical, with salt or pepper.*
> I: *You don't drink coffee for breakfast. What do you like?*
> N: *I like to drink tea.*
>
> 🌐 **3.26** (I = Interviewer; M = Michiko)
>
> I: *Michiko. What do you have for breakfast? What do you have to drink for breakfast?*

> M: *We drink green tea for breakfast.*
> I: *OK, and what about, what do you eat?*
> M: *We eat rice, miso soup, pickled vegetables, er, grilled fish – like salmon, and Japanese omelette, and seaweed.*
> I: *What, what do you have in the Japanese omelette? What does that …*
> M: *Japanese omelette is sweet taste, and it's different from the Western omelette.*
> I: *And miso soup. What is in that?*
> M: *Miso soup is a salty soup, which often has seaweed, vegetables and tofu.*

4

Ask the students to discuss their perfect breakfast in pairs. Encourage them to report back to the class on their discussion.

Useful phrases (SB page 124)

1 🌐 3.27

- Ask the students to look at the picture and to say what time it is and what they think the two people might be saying (it's night and they're saying goodbye). Explain that there are many different ways of saying goodbye in English.
- Ask the students to read the conversation and complete it with the words in the box. Allow them to compare their answers in pairs or small groups.
- Play the recording for them to check their answers. Point out that Ann and Bob are probably in love so they don't really want to say goodbye at all; that is why they're taking such a long time over saying it!

> 1) better   2) good   3) inviting   4) for
> 5) be   6) regards   7) will   8) Give
> 9) must   10) Take   11) you   12) carefully
> 13) Love   14) too   15) yourself,
> 16) already

> 🌐 **3.27**
>
> Ann: *I'd better be going.*
> Bob: *It was good to see you.*
> Ann: *Thank you for inviting me.*
> Bob: *Thanks for coming.*
> Ann: *I'll be off then.*
> Bob: *Give my regards to your family.*
> Ann: *I will.*
> Bob: *Give me a ring.*
> Ann: *Okay. I really must be off now.*
> Bob: *Take care.*
> Ann: *See you.*
> Bob: *Drive carefully.*
> Ann: *Love you.*
> Bob: *Me too.*
> Ann: *Take care of yourself.*
> Bob: *(as the car drives off) Missing you already!*

2 🌐 3.28

- Pairwork. Put the students in pairs and ask them to match the phrases with appropriate responses.

- Check answers and then get the students to identify which phrases are ways of saying hello and which ways of saying goodbye.

- Play the recording for them to check and repeat the useful phrases. When they've done this chorally, ask for individual repetition of the phrases.

a) 3	b) 10	c) 7	d) 6	e) 4	f) 1
g) 9	h) 8	i) 5	j) 2		

🌐 3.28

a) Fancy seeing you here!
   Oh, I come here all the time.

b) We must get together again soon.
   Absolutely, that would be lovely.

c) Good to see you again! You haven't changed a bit.
   Nor have you. As gorgeous as ever.

d) Safe journey!
   Thanks.

e) Long time no see!
   Yes, it must be over a year.

f) What have you been up to?
   Not much. The usual.

g) Thank you for everything.
   You're most welcome.

h) Hi how are you doing?
   Fine thanks. How about you?

i) You must come and stay again soon.
   I'd love to.

j) Keep in touch.
   I will.

3

- Pairwork. Ask the students to choose two of the exchanges in Exercise 2 and to write a longer conversation between two people. Tell them to decide on a context and to use the questions as prompts for ideas.

- When they've finished, ask them to practise their conversations and then ask several pairs to perform them for the class.

Vocabulary *Extra* (SB page 125)

Get it right

1–5

The first five exercises of this section are based on some of the most common learner errors at this level. The exercises are intended for the students to test themselves and then check their answers in the dictionary extracts at the side. Go through the information at the top of the page with the class and then ask the students to work individually to do the first five exercises and then

to check their answers. When checking with the class, ask the students to respond to the personal response questions after some of the exercises.

1
a) current
b) currently
c) actual
d) current, actually
e) actually

2 afford

3
a) with my parents
b) of children
c) politics
d) competitions
e) for products

4
All of them are uncountable.

The noun *advice* is interchangeable with any of the other nouns.

5
a) decrease <u>in</u> crime
b) dependent <u>on</u> their husbands
c) difference <u>in</u> grammar
d) increase <u>in</u> violent crime
e) reason <u>for</u> poverty
f) a solution <u>to</u> this problem

6

Ask the students to look in their own dictionaries to find example sentences that show the correct usage of six words or structures that they often use incorrectly.

Further practice material

Need more writing practice?
→ Workbook page 71
- Writing a description of a holiday home.

Need more classroom practice activities?
→ Photocopiable resource materials pages 187 to 189
   Grammar: *Is there much?*
   Vocabulary: *It's like talking to a brick wall!*
   Communication: *Home Sweet Home*
→ Top 10 activities pages xv to xx

Need progress tests?
→ Test CD – *Test Unit 12*

Need more on important teaching concepts?
→ Key concepts in *New Inside Out* pages xxii to xxxv

Need student self-study practice?
→ CD-ROM – Unit 12: *Home*

Need student CEF self-evaluation?
→ CEF Checklists pages xxxvii to xliv

Need more information and more ideas?
→ www.insideout.net

Review D *Teacher's notes*

These exercises act as a check of the grammar and vocabulary that the students have learnt in Units 10–12. Use them to find any problems that students are having, or anything that they haven't understood and which will need further work.

Grammar (SB page 126)

Remind the students of the grammar explanations they read and the exercises they did in the *Grammar Extra* on pages 140 to 143.

1

This exercise reviews relative clauses from Unit 10. When checking answers, ask the students to identify whether the relative clauses are defining or non-defining.

> a) who   b) which   c) who   d) who
> e) which   f) which

2

This exercise reviews cleft sentences from Unit 10.

> a) What really annoys me is people who talk at the cinema. / What really annoys me at the cinema is people who talk.
> b) What I like about Connie is her sense of humour.
> c) What I feel like eating tonight is steak and chips.
> d) The thing I can't stand about summer is the mosquitoes.
> e) What I'd really like to do is watch TV.
> f) What I don't understand is why he married her.

3

This exercise reviews future forms from Unit 11.

> 1 'm having
> 2 isn't going to be
> 3 might not get
> 4 'm not going to tell
> 5 'll help
> 6 'll have to support
> 7 starts
> 8 'll have left
> 9 'll be starting

4

This exercise reviews future forms and future time clauses from Unit 11.

> 1 've finished
> 2 've done
> 3 've organised
> 4 do
> 5 've done/'d done
> 6 won't be
> 7 don't get
> 8 'll be
> 9 is
> 10 'm going to tell

5

This exercise reviews participle clauses from Unit 12.

> a) My house, situated in the middle of town, was built one hundred years ago.
> b) These ornaments, given to me by my grandmother, are very valuable.
> c) The cat sitting on the windowsill had kittens last year.
> d) Those children playing in the photos are my brothers and sisters.
> e) The people living around here are very kind.

6

This exercise reviews quantifiers from Unit 12. Check answers with the class before asking the students to tick the sentences that are true for them.

> a) None/Few
> b) enough
> c) plenty of
> d) little
> e) far too much
> f) few

Vocabulary (SB page 127)

1

This exercise reviews words for looking at and seeing from Unit 10.

> a) staring
> b) gazing
> c) caught sight
> d) spot
> e) make out
> f) notice

2

This exercise reviews educational expressions from Unit 11.

> 1 pay
> 2 got
> 3 going on
> 4 fail
> 5 applied for
> 6 take
> 7 got

3

This exercise reviews expressions from Unit 11. Make sure the students understand that they have to modify some of the pronouns.

> a) up to (you)
> b) make it
> c) come to her senses
> d) behind
> e) get it out of his system

4

This exercise reviews exaggerated language from Unit 11. Make sure the students understand that they have to modify some of the pronouns.

> a) took my breath away
> b) over the moon
> c) at the end of my tether
> d) on its last legs
> e) at death's door
> f) dying for a drink

5

This exercise reviews words for furnishings from Unit 12.

> a) coat hook
> b) shelf
> c) radiator
> d) doormat
> e) letterbox
> f) bell

Pronunciation (SB page 127)

1

Remind the students that the boxes show the syllables of a word and the large boxes indicate the stressed syllables. Here they're being asked to classify words according to how many syllables they have and where the main stress falls. Encourage them to say each word aloud to get a feeling for what sounds right.

2 🔘 3.29

Ask the students to underline the stressed syllable in each of the words in the table. Then play the recording for them to check their answers. Play it a second time for them to listen and repeat.

1 and 2		
A: ☐☐☐	**B:** ☐☐☐☐	**C:** ☐☐☐☐
<u>a</u>dvertise	abso<u>lu</u>tely	e<u>pi</u>tomize
<u>e</u>vidence	disap<u>poin</u>ting	ex<u>pe</u>rience
<u>or</u>nament	edu<u>ca</u>tion	ext<u>ra</u>ordinary
<u>tho</u>roughly	tele<u>vi</u>sion	nos<u>tal</u>gically

Further practice material

Need more classroom practice activities?

→ Photocopiable resource materials page 190
  🔘 **3.30 Song:** *Suddenly I See*
→ TOP 10 activities pages xv to xx

Need progress tests?

→ Test CD – *Test Review D*

Need more on important teaching concepts?

→ Key concepts in *New Inside Out* pages xxii to xxxv

Need student self-study practice?

→ CD-ROM – *Review D*

Need more information and more ideas?

→ www.insideout.net

Resource materials

Worksheet	Activity and focus	What the students are doing
Unit 1		
1 Grammar *Would you mind telling me ...?*	Pairwork/groupwork: interview and discussion Direct and indirect question forms General tense revision	Asking appropriate personal questions and reporting information.
1 Vocabulary *Common ground*	Whole class: mingling Agreeing and disagreeing: *So/neither*	Sharing information and finding out about things in common.
1 Communication *You do, don't you?*	Groupwork: question forming Question tags	Finding out and checking personal information.
Unit 2		
2 Grammar *Tell me something about yourself*	Pair or groupwork: completing questions Adjectives and prepositions	Forming questions and interviewing each other.
2 Vocabulary *Vince's bike*	Pairwork: reading and analysis Features of formal and informal writing	Reading and analysing informal and formal language in context.
2 Communication *Single vowel dominoes*	Groupwork: pronunciation game Phonemes and phonetic symbols	Playing a dominoes game and matching single words with phonetic symbols.
Unit 3		
3 Grammar *Reported speech*	Pairwork: writing speech bubbles Reporting	Transforming direct and reported speech in mini-dialogues.
3 Vocabulary *Money talks*	Pairwork: Pelmanism game Money expressions/idioms	Matching money expressions.
3 Communication *Life is a journey*	Group or pairwork: reading and speaking Metaphors	Identifying metaphors and discussing personal situations.
Review A *When a man loves a woman*	Pairwork: song Revision of grammar and vocabulary from Units 1–3	Listening to and reading a song and finding meanings of phrasal verbs.
Unit 4		
4 Grammar *A dangerous adventure*	Individual and groupwork: writing a story Review of narrative tenses	Writing group story sentence by sentence.
4 Vocabulary *Phrasal verbs crossword*	Pairwork: completing crossword Phrasal verbs	Completing phrasal verbs in context.
4 Communication *Storytellers*	Groupwork: telling a story Linking words and expressions	Creating a book title and developing a story using suitable linkers.

Worksheet	Activity and focus	What the students are doing
Unit 5		
5 Grammar *Keep talking*	Individual and groupwork: speaking game Verb + gerund Verb + *to* + infinitive	Speaking for 30 seconds from a prompt to complete a board game.
5 Vocabulary *Wedding message*	Pairwork: word puzzle and discussion Wedding vocabulary	Decoding words to complete puzzle.
5 Communication *Old habits die hard*	Pairwork: grammar practice *will, would* and *used to*	Transforming sentences to describe present and past habits and states.
Unit 6		
6 Grammar *What have I been doing?*	Whole class: team guessing game Present perfect continuous	Guessing what someone has been doing from a description.
6 Vocabulary *Food fight*	Pair/groupwork: team game Food	Brainstorming food vocabulary and expressions.
6 Communication *Make the question*	Pair/groupwork: writing and sequencing race Passive questions	Making questions by sequencing individual words.
Review B *Big Yellow Taxi*	Pairwork: song Revision of grammar and vocabulary from Units 4–6	Listening to and reading a song and talking about dangers to the environment.
Unit 7		
7 Grammar *Pleasure and pain*	Groupwork: running dictation Modals of obligation	Dictating an extended text as accurately as possible.
7 Vocabulary *Word formation*	Pair and groupwork: team game Prefixes and suffixes	Adding prefixes and suffixes to form new words.
7 Communication *Pronunciation review*	Groupwork: board game Single vowel sounds, question tags, numbers and intonation	Answering pronunciation questions to complete board game.
Unit 8		
8 Grammar *Have you no scruples?*	Groupwork: speaking Unreal conditionals	Saying how they would react in different situations and guessing true or false information.
8 Vocabulary *Character search*	Pairwork: wordsearch and discussion Review of character adjectives	Finding and completing compound adjectives in a wordsearch puzzle and discussing personal qualities.
8 Communication *Face to face*	Pairwork: drawing and description Vocabulary describing face, ears, hair	Drawing a face and describing it to a partner for them to draw.

Worksheet	Activity and focus	What the students are doing
Unit 9		
9 Grammar *Why would a person do this?*	Groupwork: reading and discussion Modals of deduction	Reading different situations and creating plausible explanations.
9 Vocabulary *Word families*	Individual/pair/groupwork: spelling and pronunciation Patterns in word stress	Forming different words from root words and grouping them according to stress patterns.
9 Communication *Compare pictures*	Pairwork: speaking skills Making comparisons *Look/seem/appear*	Describing photographs in detail and asking questions about them.
Review C *Mozambique*	Pairwork: song Revision of grammar and vocabulary from Units 7–9	Listening to and reading a song and discussing places they have visited.
Unit 10		
10 Grammar *Relative clauses*	Individual/pairwork: grammar analysis Defining/non-defining relative clauses	Joining clauses together to make sentences.
10 Vocabulary *Sorry to interrupt ...*	Pair/groupwork: discussion Interruption devices	Using appropriate techniques/expressions to interrupt during discussion.
10 Communication *Inspirational marketing*	Groupwork: reading, discussion and planning Marketing	Devising marketing plans.
Unit 11		
11 Grammar *Future forms*	Class mingle: speaking and writing	Making and asking questions about someone's future.
11 Vocabulary *Exaggerated expressions*	Pair/groupwork: Pelmanism game Informal exaggeration	Matching expressions with exaggerated forms.
11 Communication *A good bet*	Pairwork: grammar analysis Review of grammar	Deciding on correct and incorrect sentences.
Unit 12		
12 Grammar *Is there much?*	Individual/pairwork: matching and discussion Quantifiers	Matching pictures with descriptions of quantity.
12 Vocabulary *It's like talking to a brick wall!*	Pairwork: reading and speaking Home expressions/idioms	Completing expressions related to houses or the home and discussing personal situations.
12 Communication *Home Sweet Home*	Groupwork: speaking and presenting House/Home vocabulary	Designing a home and presenting it to the class.
Review D *Suddenly I see*	Pairwork: song Revision of grammar and vocabulary from Units 10–12	Listening to and reading a song Reading a biography.

Teacher's notes

1 Grammar Would you mind telling me ...?

Page 151

Activity

Pairwork or groupwork: speaking.

Focus

Direct and indirect question forms; general tense revision.

Preparation

Make one copy of the worksheet for each pair of students. Cut up the cards as indicated.

Procedure

- Divide the class into pairs. Explain that the students are going to have the chance to ask questions to find out more about each other.

- Give each pair a set of question cards face down in a pile. Explain that each card has the start of a direct or indirect question. Elicit from the students why we use indirect questions (when the question is of a personal nature and/or when we want to be polite). Give the students a few minutes to think about the questions.

- Ask the students to take turns to turn over a question card and complete the question with anything appropriate to ask their partner. Encourage follow-up questions and discussion. The students continue asking and answering questions until all the cards have been used. Circulate and monitor, helping as necessary.

- When they have finished, pairs report to the class what they found out about each other.

Follow up

Ask the students to write the questions for homework.

Variations

This activity also works with groups of three to four.

An alternative to cutting up the questions is to give each student the complete worksheet and have them ask questions, crossing off each question as they ask it.

Another alternative is as above, but have the students circulate around the class asking different students the questions.

1 Vocabulary Common ground

Page 152

Activity

Whole class: speaking.

Focus

Agreeing (*so* and *neither*) and disagreeing.

Preparation

Make enough copies of the worksheet so that each student can take three cards. Cut up the cards as indicated.

Procedure

- Place the cards face down on your desk and ask the students to each take three.

- Ask the students to complete the sentence on each card with information that is true for them.

- Ask the students to walk around, pause with a student they meet and take turns to read their sentence or react to their partner's sentence. For example:

Student A: *I like eating lamb.*
Student B: *So do I. / I don't.*
Student B: *I didn't watch TV yesterday.*
Student A: *Neither did I. / I did.*

Encourage students to write the names of the students they speak to and put a ✓ next to the names of people who have the same information and a ✗ next to those who don't. If this is a new class, this is a good way for students to learn each other's names.

The students then continue circulating, pausing to read (or react to) the other sentences. Circulate and monitor, helping as necessary.

- When they have finished, the students report to the class what they found out about each other. For example:

I used to wear glasses as a child, and so did Sara.
I'm currently learning to ride a motorbike, but Juan isn't.

Notes

This activity works well as an ice-breaker with students who do not know each other very well.

You may want to precede the activity with some controlled practice of auxiliary verbs in different tenses, including examples with *never*. For example:
Student A: *I've never visited France.*
Student B: *Neither have I. / I have.*

1 Communication You do, don't you?

Page 153

Activity
Groupwork: speaking.

Focus
Question forms and question tags.

Preparation
Make one copy of the worksheet for each group of three students. Cut up the worksheet as indicated.

Procedure
- Divide the class into groups of three and give one of the question prompt sheets (A, B and C) to each student.
- Tell the students they are going ask each other the questions on their sheets. Allow the students a few minutes to prepare the questions. Before starting the activity, elicit a few examples:

  Teacher: *favourite colour?*
  Student 1: *What's your favourite colour?*
  Teacher: *country / like to visit?*
  Student 2: *Which country would you like to visit?*

- Ask the students to take turns to ask and answer all the questions. Explain that the students must not write down any of the answers.
- Tell the students they are now going to check how much they can remember by using tag questions. For example:

  Student A (to Student B): *Your favourite colour is blue, isn't it?*
  Student B: *Yes, it is. / Yes, that's right. / No, it isn't. It's red, actually.*
  Student A (to Student C): *And your favourite colour is green, isn't it?*
  Student C: *Yes, it is. / Yes, that's right. / No, it isn't. It's pink, actually.*

  Remind the students that, when checking information, the question tag is said with a falling intonation. The rising intonation is only used when asking a real question.

  Student B then asks his/her first question, and so on. For each correctly remembered fact the student gets one point. The students record their own points by putting a tick (✔) or a cross (✗) next to each question prompt. When all the facts have been checked, the student with the most points is the winner.

Follow up
Ask the students to change groups and report to each other as much as they can remember about the students in their first group.

2 Grammar Tell me something about yourself

Page 154

Activity
Pair or groupwork: completing questions and speaking.

Focus
Adjectives and prepositions.

Preparation
Make one copy of the worksheet for each student in the class.

Procedure
- Give one copy of the worksheet to each student and ask them to complete each question with a preposition.
- Once students have finished, divide the class into pairs and ask each pair to check they have the same prepositions. (See Answers.)
- Ask the students to interview each other and make a note of the answers they hear.
- Conduct an open class feedback to find out if students discovered anything interesting about their partner.

1	at	8	with
2	of	9	of
3	about	10	for
4	in	11	about
5	of	12	with
6	with	13	on
7	in	14	about

2 Vocabulary Vince's bike

Page 155

Activity
Pairwork: reading and analysis.

Focus
Raising awareness of features of informal and formal writing.

Preparation
Make one copy of the worksheet for each student. Fold the worksheet in half as indicated.

Procedure
- Write the words *bike, stolen, work, police, insurance* and *bananas* on the board and ask the students to predict what happened.

- Divide the class into pairs and give each student a copy of the worksheet, folded in half. Ask the students to read the e-mail version of the story and check their predictions.
- Ask the students to look at the underlined words in the e-mail and try to guess their meaning from the context. Do the first one as an example with the whole class, i.e. *nicked = stolen*.
- Ask the students to unfold the worksheet, read the formal letter and compare the language in it to the language in the e-mail. This may help clarify some of the language in the e-mail.
- Check the answers with the whole class.
- Ask the students to note any features or conventions that differentiate the informal and formal versions of the story. Do an example with the whole class first, e.g. the informal e-mail uses contractions (*they'll pay up*) and the formal letter avoids contractions (*I am writing*).
- Check the answers with the whole class.

Comparison of language:

e-mail	formal letter
nicked	stolen
locked up	locked ('up' is used to emphasise)
7ish	approximately 7.00 pm
got back	returned
when the penny dropped	as soon as I realised
go bananas	(not in formal letter, but 'go bananas' = 'become very angry')
for ages	(not in formal letter, but 'for ages' = 'for a long time')
no way	extremely unlikely
pay up	(not in formal letter, but 'up' is used to emphasise)
'cos	as (meaning 'because')
need	require
get to	travel to

Comparison of features or conventions:

e-mail	formal letter
contractions	no contractions
note-form sentences	full-length sentences
idiomatic language	formal language and phrasal verbs
abbreviations	full words
no set phrases	use of standard phrases, e.g. *I would appreciate it if ...*

Follow up

Ask students to think of something that has happened to them recently that they might complain about and then develop informal and formal texts about it, e.g. an e-mail to a friend and a letter of complaint.

2 Communication Single vowel dominoes

Page 156

Activity

Groupwork: pronunciation game.

Focus

The twelve single vowel phonemes and phonetic symbols.

Preparation

Make one copy of the worksheet for each group of three to four students. Cut up the dominoes as indicated.

Procedure

- Explain that the students are going to play a game of dominoes where single vowel phonetic symbols are connected to words which contain that single vowel sound.
- Divide the class into groups of three to four students and give each group a set of dominoes. Ask the students to divide the dominoes so that each person in the group has the same number.
- Ask the student who has the domino with 'dog' to start by placing this domino on the table. Tell the students to take turns to try to place their dominoes. For example:

If students do not have a domino that works, they miss a turn. The first person to play all their dominoes wins.

- Circulate, checking that students have found the correct connections.

/iː/	tree, tea	/æ/	hat, bag
/ɒ/	dog, watch	/ɔː/	door, four
/ɪ/	pin, swim	/ɜː/	bird, word
/ɑː/	car, heart	/ə/	the, teacher
/ʌ/	cup, sun	/e/	leg, bed
/uː/	shoe, school	/ʊ/	book, good

Follow up

Divide the class into different groups and play again.

Ask the students to think of more words for each vowel sound.

Notes

You may want to precede the activity with some revision of the phonetic symbols on page 18 of *New Inside Out* Upper intermediate Student's Book.

To maximise oral practice, ask the students to say each sound and word as they play.

3 Grammar Reported speech

Page 157

Activity

Pairwork: writing.

Focus

Making reported speech sentences.

Preparation

Make one copy of the worksheet for every pair of students in the class, cut in half as indicated.

Procedure

- Divide the class into two groups, A and B. Then divide all the students in group A into pairs and all the students in group B into pairs.
- Give each student in group A a copy of worksheet A and each student in group B a copy of worksheet B. Tell them to look at pictures 1–9. In each picture there are two people having a conversation (in a bubble) and one person reporting what was said.
- Ask the students to work together (A + A, B + B) to fill in the empty speech bubbles. If they see a sentence in reported speech, they have to provide the equivalent in direct speech. For example, in 1, Student A needs to complete what the young man is saying (*How much is this shirt?*) because in A the sentence has been reported. Student B has to write in the reported sentence (*He asked her how much that shirt was*) as in B the sentence is in direct speech. It would be useful to write these examples on the board so that you can point out the changes of pronoun in particular.
- Emphasise to students that they should **only** use *ask* or *tell* to report the speech.
- When all the pairs in A and B have finished writing, ask them to find a partner from the opposite team (A + B). The new pairs then take it in turns to read what they have written to the other, while the other checks if it is correct.
- When everyone in the class has read out their sentences, the activity is finished.

3 Vocabulary Money talks

Page 158

Activity

Pairwork: *Pelmanism* game.

Focus

The meaning of money expressions.

Preparation

Make one copy of the worksheet for each pair of students. Cut up the cards as indicated.

Procedure

- Divide the class into pairs and give each pair a set of pelmanism cards. Ask the students to place the cards face down on the desk.
- Explain to the students that on the cards there are ten pairs of expressions about money which are similar in meaning and the aim is to match these pairs.
- Explain that they should take it in turns to turn over two cards, one at a time. If the expressions are similar, the student keeps the pair and gets another turn. If the expressions are not similar, he/she turns the cards face down again and ends his/her turn.
- The game continues until all the pairs of cards have been won. The student with the most pairs is the winner.
- Check the answers with the whole class.

> She's a spendthrift. / She burns money.
> I'm broke. / I haven't got a penny to my name.
> It's worth a fortune. / It's priceless.
> She's stinking rich. / She's rolling in it.
> He lives from hand to mouth. / He lives on the breadline.
> It costs next to nothing. / It's dirt cheap.
> It isn't worth a bean. / It's worthless.
> It cost an arm and a leg. / It cost a fortune.
> I paid through the nose. / I paid over the odds.
> He lives like a king. / He lives in the lap of luxury.

Follow up

Give the cards to one student in each pair. This student says one of the expressions and his/her partner tries to remember the matching expression. Then students change roles.

Notes

You may want to precede the game with a matching activity. Ask the students to place the cards face up on the desk and match the ten pairs of expressions about money which are similar in meaning, using dictionaries if necessary.

3 Communication Life is a journey

Page 159

Activity

Pair and groupwork: reading and speaking.

Focus

Revision and practice of metaphors.

Preparation

Make one copy of the worksheet for each student.

Procedure

- Give one copy of the worksheet to each student. Elicit/Teach the literal meaning of any unfamiliar vocabulary.

- Divide the class into pairs and ask the students to choose which they think is the correct alternative to make metaphors. Encourage them to think about similar metaphors in their own language.

- Check the answers with the whole class, establishing meaning as you do this. Ask students to tell you metaphors which are similar in their own language.

- Divide the class into small groups. Ask students to think about times when any of the sentences were true for them and discuss these situations. Circulate and monitor, helping with vocabulary as necessary.

1	peak	9	food
2	odds	10	on top of the world
3	drifting	11	warm
4	digest	12	enemy
5	half-baked	13	race
6	sank	14	sea
7	rocky road	15	waste
8	precious		

Review A When a man loves a woman

Page 160

Activity

Pairwork: song.

Focus

Revision of grammar and vocabulary from *New Inside Out* Upper intermediate Student's Book, Units 1–3.

Preparation

Make one copy of the worksheet for each student in the class. Get the recording ready.

Procedure

- Ask the class if anyone knows Percy Sledge or any of his songs.

- Ask students to work in pairs and discuss the question in Exercise 1 for a few minutes. Then ask them to read the list of ideas in 2 and decide which they think are realistic and which unrealistic. When they have finished ask the class if anyone has any other ideas to add to the list.

- Ask students to listen to and read the song, and match a–h in Exercise 2 with lines in the song. One idea is not mentioned.

- Ask students to do Exercises 4 and 5 and then check the answers open class. If you have dictionaries available ask students individually to check the six phrasal verbs in Exercise 5 and see if they can find other meanings.

3
a) He'll never notice her faults. *line 4 'If she's bad, he can't see it. She can do no wrong'*
b) He'll do anything she tells him to do. *line 10 'He'd give up all his comforts … .'*
c) He'll love and respect her family. NOT MENTIONED
d) He'll spend all his money on her. *line 8 'Spend his very last dime'*
e) He'll give up everything for her. *line 3 'He'll trade the world for …'*
f) He'll never allow other people to criticise her. *line 6 'Turn his back on his best friend …'*
g) He'll think about nothing else but her. *line 2 'Can't keep his mind on nothin' else'*
h) He'll never cheat on her. *line 25 'He'd never want some other girl'*

4
a) – 2)
b) – 3)
c) – 1)

5
a) give up	give up
b) put down	put down
c) give up	give himself up
d) hold on to	hold on to
e) put down	put down
f) hold on to	hold on to

4 Grammar A dangerous adventure

Page 161

Activity

Individual and groupwork: writing a story.

Focus

Review of narrative tenses.

Preparation

Make one copy of the worksheet for each student in the class.

Procedure

- Divide the class into groups of three or four students. Explain that they are going to write a story about going on a dangerous adventure.

- Give one copy of the worksheet to each student. Give the students a few moments to look at the different stages. Then ask them to complete the first sentence. Encourage the students to be imaginative and amusing.

- Ask the students to fold their worksheet back so that what they have written is hidden and the next unfinished sentence is visible. Then ask them to pass their worksheet to the student on their left.

- Give the students enough time to complete the sentence that is now at the top of the worksheet, fold their worksheet back and pass it to the student on their left as before. If you feel that any students will take much longer than others you may want to state a time limit for the sentence completion, e.g. 60 seconds, to avoid a jam. Repeat this until all the sentences have been completed.
- When the last sentence has been written, ask the students to open out the completed story and read it to the others in their group.
- Ask the student to choose the most interesting or amusing story in their group, which they then read out to the whole class. The class listens to the stories and votes on the best.

4 Vocabulary Phrasal verbs crossword

Page 162

Activity
Pairwork: crossword.

Focus
Phrasal verbs.

Preparation
Make one copy of the worksheet for each student.

Procedure
- Divide the class into pairs and give each student a copy of the worksheet.
- Ask the students to complete the crossword with the missing verb of the phrasal verbs in the dialogues. Tell the students that they will need to put the verbs into appropriate tenses or forms.
- When the pairs have finished, ask students to compare their crosswords with another pair.
- Check the answers with the whole class.

Across		Down	
2	let		
4	put	1	stop
5	Go	2	look
6	use	3	turn
8	get	4	put
10	pick	7	dawned
12	gave	9	ended
14	made	11	come
16	doing	13	count
17	takes	15	came
19	see	18	saw
20	went		

4 Communication Storytellers

Page 163

Activity
Groupwork: telling a story.

Focus
Using linkers.

Preparation
Make one copy of the worksheet for each group of four to five students. Cut up the cards as indicated.

Procedure
- Elicit different types of book (romance, thriller, science fiction, biography, autobiography, history book, detective story, etc.).
- Divide the class into groups of four to five students and give each group the top section of the worksheet with the word cards removed. Ask the groups to make three new book titles using some of the words, e.g. *Love Ship* (a romance), *Robot Killer* (a science fiction story), etc. Ask the groups to read their titles to the class.
- Ask each group to choose one of their titles. Explain that each group is going to develop this story. Then ask the groups to decide on the first line of their story.
- Place a set of linker cards face down in the middle of each group. Students take it in turns to pick a card and add the next sentence to their story. For example, the first sentence of the story *Love Ship* is: *John and Camilla were sunbathing on the ship*. Student A picks up the card *because* and continues the story: *John decided to get some cocktails because he was thirsty*. Student B picks up a card and adds the next sentence to the story. This continues until all the cards have been used. (Encourage students to make notes about the story as they add each sentence to help them when they retell the stories.) Circulate and monitor, helping with vocabulary as necessary.
- Regroup the students to tell each other their stories.

Follow up
Immediately after the activity, it may be useful to conduct an error correction session based on the students' accuracy in using narrative tenses and linkers.

For homework, ask students to write up their stories or even create a class book of short stories. Consider copying this book and distributing it to other classes or displaying the stories on a noticeboard.

Notes
This activity is designed to practise linkers and the stories the students produce may not sound natural as there will be an unusually high number of linkers. This should be pointed out to the students, especially if they go on to develop and write up their stories.

5 **Grammar** Keep talking

Page 164

Activity

Individual and groupwork: board game.

Focus

Verb + gerund and verb + *to* + infinitive structures.

Preparation

Make one copy of the worksheet for each group of two to four students. Each student will need a counter and each group will need a dice.

Procedure

- Divide the class into small groups of two to four students. (Larger groups are possible if you have a particularly large class.)
- Give each student a counter and each group a copy of the worksheet and a dice.
- Explain the game:
  1 The students take turns to roll the dice, move along the board with their counter according to the number on the dice and talk, for thirty seconds without stopping, about the topic on the square.
  2 The students should begin talking by using the prompt in the square, putting the verb in brackets into the correct form. For example: *Something I really hate doing is ironing shirts because ..., I started learning English because ..., A famous person I'd really like to meet is Prince William because ...*
  3 One student in the group acts as timekeeper and the rest decide if he/she successfully spoke for the full thirty seconds without stopping. If successful, the student can play next time round. If not, he/she misses a turn.
  4 The winner is the first person to reach the 'finish' square.
- When they have finished, ask the students to report to the class anything interesting they found out about each other.

1 learning	9 singing	17 doing
2 doing	10 doing	18 to do
3 to watch	11 to do	19 doing
4 doing	12 to see	20 to do
5 to do	13 to eat	21 doing
6 to visit	14 doing	22 studying
7 to do	15 to meet	
8 to do	16 visiting	

Follow up

Give a copy of the worksheet to each student and ask them to write in the correct form of the verb.

Ask the students to choose one or more of the prompts and write a few sentences either about themselves or, from memory, about another student with whom they played the game.

Notes

The students, as a group or individually, can decide the correct form of the verbs before the game is played.

5 **Vocabulary** Wedding message

Page 165

Activity

Pairwork: word puzzle and discussion.

Focus

Revision of vocabulary related to weddings.

Preparation

Make one copy of the worksheet for each pair of students in the class.

Procedure

- Divide the class into pairs and give each pair a copy of the worksheet.
- Explain to the students that each number in the boxes corresponds to a letter of the alphabet. Their task is to decode the twelve words in the word puzzle. Tell them that each word is related to weddings. (if you want to set a competitive edge, you can either set a time limit or say that the first pair to finish is the winner.)
- When the first pair has finished (or the time is up), check the answers with the whole class.
- Then, ask the students to use the grid to decode the secret message. The secret message is a traditional saying which relates to what the bride should wear on her wedding day.
- Hold a class discussion about the saying in the secret message. How many countries have the same wedding superstition? Which other wedding superstitions or traditions are there?

> Word puzzle: wedding, photographer, vow, honeymoon, bouquet of flowers, church, reception, bridesmaid, ring, priest, veil, best man.
> Secret message: Something old, something new, something borrowed, something blue.

5 Communication Old habits die hard

Page 166

Activity

Pairwork: grammar practice.

Focus

Use of *will*, *would* and *used to* to talk about past and present habits.

Preparation

Make one copy of the worksheet for each student in the class.

Procedure

* Give a copy of the worksheet to each student and divide the class into pairs. Ask the students to work together to rewrite the sentences in either the past or the present, depending on which is already done.

* Point out the first two sentences as examples and explain that the transformation is straightforward: *will* is used for habitual actions in the present and *would* for habitual actions in the past, and the present simple is used for states in the present whereas *used to* is used for states in the past.

* As the students are rewriting the sentences, monitor closely, making sure no-one uses *use to* to describe a present habit (~~I use to study English~~ or ~~I am use to study English~~).

* After everyone has finished transforming the sentences, ask them to read through and tick the sentences which are true for them. Then ask them to read out those sentences to their partner. Explain that if someone has ticked both a past and a present sentence, they should practise the phrase '*I used to…* *and I still do*' to make it clear that this particular past habit is ongoing, although you wouldn't say '~~I would do … and I still will~~'.

Sample answers

1 I'll spend hours reading. I love it.
   I'd spend hours reading. I used to love it.
2 I used to love art at school. I'd paint a different picture every day.
   I love art at school. I'll paint a different picture every day.
3 Before leaving for school, I'd always take the dog for a walk. I used to love that.
   Before leaving for school, I'll always take the dog for a walk. I love that.
4 I'm a creature of habit. First I'll check my emails and then I'll have a coffee.
   I used to be a creature of habit. First I'd check my emails and then I'd have a coffee.

---

5 Before going to bed, I used to read my book. I'd usually drop off after about 15 minutes.
   Before going to bed, I read my book. I'll usually drop off after about 15 minutes.
6 During the school holidays I'd work for about six weeks. I used to enjoy the discipline.
   During the school holidays I'll work for about six weeks. I enjoy the discipline.
7 I'll watch around two hours of TV in the evenings and then I'll do my homework.
   I'd watch around two hours of TV in the evenings and then I'd do my homework.
8 I didn't use to have a car, so I used to walk everywhere.
   I don't have a car, so I walk everywhere.
9 At weekends I'll get up quite late. I'll usually read the papers and take it easy.
   At weekends I'd get up quite late. I'd usually read the papers and take it easy.
10 I used to have blond hair. Actually, I'd change the colour every month.
   I have blond hair. Actually, I'll change the colour every month.
11 I hate my car. It won't start if it's been raining.
   I used to hate my car. It wouldn't start if it had been raining.
12 My dad loves his car. He'll spend hours cleaning it at the weekend.
   My dad used to love his car. He'd spend hours cleaning it at the weekend.

6 Grammar What have I been doing?

Page 167

Activity

Whole class: guessing game.

Focus

Description using the present perfect continuous.

Preparation

Make one copy of the worksheet. Cut up the cards as indicated.

Procedure

* Divide the class into two teams, A and B, and place the cards in a pile face down on your desk.

* Explain the rules of the game:

1 A student from team A comes and picks up a card. This student has three minutes to describe to team A what he/she has been doing. The student can give any kind of information but must not use any of the underlined words in any form. For example, if the underlined word is *work*, he/she cannot use *worked*, *working*, etc.

2 During these three minutes the other members of team A can ask the student questions about what they have been doing to which he/she can only answer with *yes* or *no*.

3 If team A guesses the sentence in the allotted time, this team scores 10 points. If team A does not guess the sentence, or time runs out, it is team B's turn to try. If team B guesses correctly, it scores 5 points.

4 If the student describing the card mentions any of the 'forbidden words', his/her team loses 5 points and the turn goes to the other team.

5 Then, a student from team B comes to the front of the classroom and the game continues in the same way.

• The winner is the team with the most points at the end of the game.

Notes

If you have a very large class, you can divide it into two groups and then assign teams A and B within each group.

6 **Vocabulary** Food fight

Page 168

Activity

Pair/groupwork: team game.

Focus

Review of food-related vocabulary from Unit 6 of *New Inside Out* Upper intermediate Student's Book.

Preparation

Make one copy of the worksheet for each pair of students in the class, cut up as indicated.

Procedure

• Divide the class into two teams, A and B. Give each student in Team A a copy of worksheet A and each student in Team B a copy of worksheet B.

• Ask students to work together in their teams to prepare five items in each category. Encourage them not to go for the most obvious selection because afterwards the other team are going to have the chance to guess what they have written. If it's too easy, the other team will have the advantage. Allow them to check their ideas in Unit 6 of *New Inside Out* Upper intermediate Student's Book. It's very important that each member of the team writes exactly the same thing.

• When the students have finished preparing their categories, ask them to face each other. Team A starts by reading out the first category: '5 ways to cook food'. Team B then have one minute to call out as many ways as they can. Make sure they don't all call at once otherwise the other team won't hear them clearly. They must not look in the Student's Book.

After one minute, Team A says how many words Team B called out and that is the number of points which Team B are awarded. Play then passes to Team B and the above stages are repeated.

• When both teams have read out their categories and the time limit is up, count the number of points for each team. The team with most points is the winner.

6 **Communication** Make the question

Page 169

Activity

Pair/groupwork: sequencing and writing.

Focus

Passive questions.

Preparation

Make one copy of the worksheet for the class. You could make a copy in a larger size and then cut each of the nine sentences up as indicated and put them into separate envelopes. Number the envelopes 1–9. If you want to keep the words it is useful to stick them onto card for re-use.

Procedure

• Depending on the size of the class, divide the class into pairs or small groups. Give each pair/group one envelope with the cut up questions. If there aren't enough students to give out all the envelopes, either just give out as many as you can or let the students work on their own (although this is harder).

• Tell your students that, when you give the word, they should open the envelope and re-arrange the words inside to make a question. They should write the question down on a separate piece of paper and write the number of the envelope next to the question.

• Give them a time limit of between 30 seconds and two minutes, depending on the level of the class. Then ask them to put the pieces of paper back into the envelope and pass it to the pair/group to their left.

• This continues until every pair/group has written their questions. Once everyone has finished, check the answers in open class. Some students may have the prepositions at the end of the question. Allow this but explain that when writing it's normally preferable not to end the sentence in a preposition.

• If your students are keen to find out the answers, you can finish up with a quick quiz, with each correct answer worth one point. The pair/group with the most points is the winner.

Alternative

If you don't have time to cut up all the sentences, you could dictate each sentence to the class with the words out of order for each student to write down. When you have dictated all 9 they can start putting them in order with a time limit of 8–10 minutes.

> 1 At publication the next Olympic Games was 2012 in London, U.K.
> 2 4 million tonnes
> 3 Edvard Munch
> 4 Brazil
> 5 Dallas
> 6 The USA (four times)
> 7 *Ben Hur* (1959) and *Titanic* (1997). Both won 11 Oscars.
> 8 1889 (although construction started in 1887)
> 9 China (India is next. The biggest exporter is Thailand)

Review B Big Yellow Taxi

Page 170

Activity

Pairwork: song.

Focus

Revision of grammar and vocabulary from *New Inside Out* Upper intermediate Student's Book, Units 4–6.

Preparation

Make one copy of the worksheet for each student in the class. Get the recording ready.

Procedure

- Ask the class if anyone knows Joni Mitchell or any of her songs.
- Ask students to listen to the song without looking at the worksheet and decide whether it is about personal, environmental, or parking problems.
- Ask students to work in pairs to read the extract and answer the questions in Exercise 2.
- Ask students to read the song lyrics and find four examples of things that people take for granted.
- Students work with a partner to discuss the three biggest dangers currently facing the environment that we live in.

> 1 b)
> 2 a) In Hawaii
>   b) Green mountains and then a parking lot
>   c) Because she thought the parking lot spoilt the beautiful countryside
> 3 1 – paradise i.e. beautiful countryside
>   2 – trees (nature)
>   3 – birds and bees (nature)
>   4 – her partner/father

Notes

EXTRACT FROM WIKIPEDIA

"**Big Yellow Taxi**" is a song originally written and performed by Joni Mitchell.

Mitchell got the idea for the song during a visit to Hawaii. She looked out of her hotel window at the spectacular Pacific mountain scenery, and then down to a parking lot.

Joni said this about writing the song to journalist Alan McDougall in the early 1970's:

I wrote 'Big Yellow Taxi' on my first trip to Hawaii. I took a taxi to the hotel and when I woke up the next morning, I threw back the curtains and saw these beautiful green mountains in the distance. Then, I looked down and there was a parking lot as far as the eye could see, and it broke my heart... this blight on paradise. That's when I sat down and wrote the song.

The song is known for its environmental statement (from the lyrics "Paved paradise to put up a parking lot", "Hey farmer, farmer, put away that DDT now") and sentimental sound. The line, "Took all the trees, put 'em in a tree museum / And charged the people a dollar and a half just to see 'em" refers to Foster Botanical Garden in downtown Honolulu, which is a living museum of tropical plants, some rare and endangered.

In the song's final verse, the political gives way to the personal. Mitchell recounts the departure of her "old man" in the titular "big yellow taxi", referring to the old Toronto Police Service patrol cars that until 1986 were painted yellow. In many covers the departed one may be interpreted as variously a boyfriend, a husband, or a father. The literal interpretation is that he is walking out on the singer by taking a taxi; otherwise it is assumed he is being taken away by the authorities.

7 Grammar Pleasure and pain

Page 171

Activity

Groupwork: running dictation.

Focus

Writing an extended text. Further practice of modals of obligation.

Preparation

Make one copy of the worksheet for every 5 students in the class. Stick one text at eye level at the far end of the classroom, or outside the classroom, for each group of five students. The 'writer' in each group needs a sheet of paper and a pen.

Procedure

- Divide the class into groups of five and explain how to play: Each group should select one writer and four runners. The runners take it in turns to dictate a story to the writer. One runner from each team runs to the text, remembers as much as they can, and then runs back to the writer and dictates that part of the text. The next runner then runs to the text, remembers the next piece of the text, returns and dictates to the writer. Make it clear that the runners who are not running should be helping the writer with spelling and punctuation.

- When everyone has understood what they have to do, tell them to start. When everyone has finished running and writing, award the winning team 100 points; the team that finished second 90 points; the team that finished third 80 points, and so on.

- Ask each team to pass their completed text to the team on their left, so that no team has their own version of the text. Give each team a copy of the original story and ask them to check the text for mistakes. For each mistake, ask the students to subtract one point from the total score.

- At the end, when all the scores have been re-calculated, the team with the most points is the winner.

7 Vocabulary Word formation

Page 172

Activity

Pair/groupwork: team game.

Focus

Prefixes and suffixes.

Preparation

Make one copy of the worksheet for every pair of students in the class, cut up as indicated (or ask students to cut up).

Procedure

- Divide the class into pairs. Give each pair a copy of the worksheet. Ask them to work together to complete the table by putting three words under each suffix/prefix. For example, the suffix -ful combines with delight, stress and wonder to become delightful, stressful and wonderful.

- After the pairs have finished putting them in order, check answers in open class. Then ask the students to collect the pieces of paper. Make sure you keep one set of words.

- Draw the table (with the suffixes and prefixes marked) on the white board. Divide the class into two teams, A and B. Ask a member of Team A to come to you, and give them a red marker. Show the student one of the words. The student has to run to the board and write it under the correct suffix/prefix as they did before in their pairs. Meanwhile ask a member of Team B to come forward and give them a blue marker. Show them a different word. The student has to run to the board and write the word up. Keep this moving until all the words have been written on the board. Don't check any answers at this stage.

- When all the words have been written, check how many each team got right. The winning team is the one with most correct answers.

-ful	-less	-ish
delight	end	devil
stress	home	fool
wonder	relent	hell
dis-	**il-**	**im-**
honest	legal	mature
loyal	literate	polite
obedient	logical	possible
in-	**ir-**	**un-**
adequate	relevant	divided
appropriate	resistible	responsive
decisive	responsible	willing

7 Communication Pronunciation review

Page 173

Activity

Groupwork: board game.

Focus

Review of single vowel sounds, question tags, numbers and intonation.

Preparation

Make one copy of the worksheet for each group of four students (three players and one referee) in the class. The referee will need a copy of the sentences and the answers from the Teacher's Notes.

Procedure

- Divide the class into groups of four. Tell the students they are going to play a pronunciation review game. Explain there will be three players per group and one referee. The referee's job is very important. It is essential if possible that the referee has an understanding of phonetic symbols, so that he/she can adjudicate confidently.

Referee's notes

Sound sympathetic
That must be awful!
Oh, dear. You poor thing!

Sound unsympathetic
It serves you right then, doesn't it?
Oh well, you've only got yourself to blame.

Sound annoyed
Oh, she's always losing her glasses!
Oh, she will go on about her weight!

Question tags (asking for agreement)
You're not listening, are you?
It's cold, isn't it?
You don't understand, do you?

1 /ʌ/ *cuddle* (or *hug*)
2 check appropriate intonation
3 /uː/ *groom*
4 one – nil
5 /ɔː/ *resort*
6 'The' should be pronounced /ðiː/
7 /ɒ/ *crop*
8 falling intonation
9 /ʊ/ *should*

10 check appropriate intonation
11 /ɜː/ *curse*
12 the *and* should sound like /ən/
13 check appropriate intonation
14 /ə/ *banana* (should sound like /bəˈnɑːnə/)
15 /ɪ/ *stick*
16 check appropriate intonation
17 falling intonation
18 /æ/ *chat*
19 two hundred and ninety-four million, six hundred and forty-two thousand, five hundred and ten
20 /əˈbaʊt/ (the first sound is schwa)
21 /iː/ *mean*
22 *The* should be pronounced /ðə/
23 check appropriate intonation
24 /ɑː/ *starving*
25 Forty seven million, one hundred and twenty-three thousand, seven hundred and one.
26 check appropriate intonation
27 /e/ *trend*
28 falling intonation

- Tell your students the object is for the players to move around the board, answering questions to try to reach the finish first.
- The rules are simple. Player 1 flips a coin. If it's heads, the player moves two spaces; if it's tails, the player moves one square. The player will then have to carry out a task, which the referee will oversee:
  1 **Phonetic symbol and clue**. The player must guess the word.
  2 **Sound sympathetic / unsympathetic / annoyed**. The referee will point to a sentence which the player must say with the appropriate intonation.
  3 **Question tag**. The referee will give the player a sentence with a tag and explain that the intonation should be asking for agreement. Remind students that these have a falling tone at the end. All the other players can help the referee to decide on the intonation squares, if required.
  4 The remaining squares contain an **instruction**. The referee has the answers and can check them.
- If a player can't complete the task successfully, they must return to their original square and try again later. The winner is the first student to the finish.

8 Grammar Have you no scruples?

Page 174

Activity
Groupwork: speaking

Focus
Unreal conditionals.

Preparation
Make one copy of the worksheet for every three students in the class, cut up as indicated. Also two small pieces of blank paper per student.

Procedure

- Divide the class into groups of three. Give each group a copy of the worksheet, cut up, and ask them to place it face down on the table. Also give each student two small blank pieces of paper. Ask them to write 'TRUE' on one piece and 'FALSE' on the other and keep them safe.
- Explain the rules of the game:
  1 Player 1 takes a card from the top of the pile and reads the situation. Then Player 1 says how s/he would react in that situation, either by telling the truth or by telling a lie. But Player 1 must put a TRUE/FALSE card face down on the table, depending on whether it's true or false.
  2 The other players have to say if they think it's true or false.
  3 Player 1 then reveals whether he/she told the truth or a lie.

4 The players that guessed correctly score a point. Player 1 only scores a point if the other players were both wrong.

5 Play passes to Player 2, who picks up the next card on the pile and repeats the activity.

6 The game is finished when all the cards have been used up. The winner is the player with most points.

8 Vocabulary Character search

Page 175

Activity

Pairwork: wordsearch and discussion.

Focus

To review compound adjectives of character.

Preparation

Make one copy of the worksheet for each student.

Procedure

• Give each student a copy of the worksheet.

• Explain that there are fourteen words hidden in the puzzle (one is given as an example) and that the students have to find them to complete the compound adjectives. Tell them that they will use two words twice (*minded* and *headed*). When the students have found a word, they circle it in the puzzle and then write it in the appropriate space.

• Ask the students to compare answers in pairs, then check the answers with the whole class.

• Ask the students to work in pairs to discuss the follow up questions. Circulate and monitor, helping as necessary.

• When they have finished, the students report to the class what they discussed.

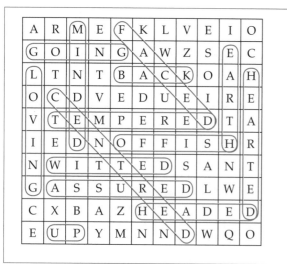

> (Answers to Ex 2a) and b) in brackets.)
>
> self-assured (+, confident)
> laid-back (+, relaxed)
> down-to-earth (+, unpretentious)
> absent-minded (–, forgetful)
> two-faced (–, hypocritical)
> stand-offish (–, unfriendly)
> warm-hearted (+, kind)
> bad-tempered (–, moody)
> self-centred (–, selfish)
> level-headed (+, sensible)
> easy-going (+, relaxed)
> big-headed (–, arrogant)
> open-minded (+, tolerant)
> stuck-up (–, snobbish)
> quick-witted (+, intelligent)
> fun-loving (+, sociable/outgoing)

8 Communication Face to face

Page 176

Activity

Pairwork: describe and draw.

Focus

Vocabulary relating to the face, ears and hair.

Preparation

Make one copy of the worksheet for each pair of students in the class, cut in half as indicated.

Procedure

• Give one half of the worksheet to each student.

• Explain that although they have two blank faces, they are only going to draw on one of them. They should be creative, even amusing, but most importantly have fun creating a face that they will be able to describe to their partner later.

• When all the students have finished drawing their faces, ask them to work with a partner, but not show their partner their picture.

• One student takes the role of describer, while the other takes the role of artist. The artist folds his or her piece of paper so that the face they drew is hidden, and the blank face is uppermost. The other student then describes in as much detail as possible the face they have drawn while the artist draws it. For example:

She's got high cheekbones, thin arched eybrows, full lips and a turned-up nose.

• Eventually, the artist will have drawn something resembling the other's picture.

• Students then change roles and repeat the process. At the end, students can compare their two pictures to see how accurately they described them.

9 Grammar Why would a person do this?

Page 177

Activity

Groupwork: reading and discussion.

Focus

Modals of deduction.

Preparation

Make one copy of the worksheet for each student.

Procedure

- Write the following sentence on the board: *A man cut off his own leg with a knife*. Brainstorm as a class what situation the man could have been in, and why he might have cut off his own leg, e.g. *He might have been trapped in a burning car after an accident so he must have cut off his leg to escape the flames.*
- Divide the class into small groups and give each student a copy of the worksheet.
- Ask the students to read the situations and make deductions in their groups about why the people involved might have acted in these ways. Circulate and monitor, helping with ideas and vocabulary as necessary.
- Conduct a class feedback session. Encourage discussion between groups to explain why their explanations are the most plausible.

Follow up

Ask the students to write down the ideas they discussed.

Ask the students to write situations of their own for other students to make deductions about.

9 Vocabulary Word families

Page 178

Activity

Individual/pair/groupwork: spelling and pronunciation.

Focus

Pronunciation patterns of selected word families.

Preparation

Make one copy of the worksheet for every student in the class.

Procedure

- Give a copy of the worksheet to each student and ask them to complete the first stage with the correct ending. In pairs, students check their answers.
- Ask the students to complete the table according to the pronunciation patterns of each word. Again, students check their answers in pairs.
- Divide the class into two teams, A and B. Ask a member of Team A to come to the front. Show them one of the root words (from your worksheet which is not completed) and ask them to write up the full word on the whiteboard and then pronounce it. For example, if you show the student '*mathema___*' under the 'adjective' heading, the student should write 'mathematical' and pronounce it according to this pattern: □□□□□□.

Note: The adjective formed from *economics* in this activity is *economic*. If anyone suggests the adjective *economical* you may want to point out that there is a difference in meaning: *economic* is connected with the money that a country or society or an individual has, e.g. *an economic disaster*; *economical* means spending money or using something in a careful way that avoids waste, e.g. *That car is very economical to run.*

- For writing the correct word, students score one point. For pronouncing it correctly, students score one point (even if they've written the wrong word). Extra points can be achieved when students write an adjective by calling out nouns which collocate with them (e.g. *mathematical equations* or *mathematical research*). The team with the most points at the end is the winner.

1 subject	person	Adjective (+ collocation)
scien*ce*	scien*tist*	scien*tific* (*advances/research*)
econom*ics*	econom*ist*	econom*ic* (*growth/research*)
gen*etics*	gen*eticist*	gen*etic* (*engineering*)
mathema*tics*	mathema*tician*	mathema*tical* (*equations/research*)
techno*logy*	techno*logist*	techno*logical* (*advances/research*)
chem*istry*	chem*ist*	chem*ical* (*reactions/weapons*)
bio*logy*	bio*logist*	bio*logical*

2 □□□□	□□□□	□□□□□	□□□
scientific mathematics economic economics	biology biologist economist geneticist technology technologist	biological mathematical technological	chemistry chemical scientist
□□	□□□	□□□□□	
chemist science	genetic genetics	mathematician	

9 Communication Compare pictures

Page 179

Activity

Pairwork: speaking.

Focus

Describing pictures using *look, look like, seem* and *appear*.

Preparation

Make one copy of the worksheet for each student in the class.

Procedure

* Divide the class into pairs and give each student a copy of the worksheet. Ask them to fold it in half along the dotted line. Tell them that they are going to take it in turns to speak about the pictures on their worksheet, without interruption, for one minute.

* While they are describing their picture, their partner should be listening and thinking of questions to ask them when they've finished speaking. There is a question at the top of their worksheet which they can be thinking about as they describe their picture. This exercise mimics Part 2 of the Cambridge FCE Speaking Test.

* The students can refer to *New Inside Out* Upper intermediate Student's Book page 92 (*look, seem, appear* etc.) and also contrasting linkers (*on the other hand, whereas* etc.). There are some on page 61.

* When the first student has finished speaking and has answered all questions, students change roles. The second student starts to talk about their picture while the first listens and thinks of questions to ask.

Review C Mozambique

Page 180

Activity

Pairwork: song.

Focus

Revision of grammar and vocabulary from *New Inside Out* Upper intermediate Student's Book, Units 7–9.

Preparation

Make one copy of the worksheet for each student in the class. Get the recording ready.

Procedure

* Ask students to group the words in the box according to the vowel sounds. (Note that *romance, glance* and *chance* have a short 'a' sound as used in US pronunciation.) Write them on the board to check. Ask students to turn their worksheets face down.

* Now play the song and ask students to number the words in the order they hear them.

* Ask the class if they know anything about Mozambique. Point it out if you have a globe or atlas in the classroom.

* Ask students to listen to the song without looking at the worksheet and decide whether it is about living, holidaying or going on a business trip to Mozambique.

* Ask students to turn over their worksheets and complete the expressions in Exercise 2. They can listen again to check their answers.

* Ask students to look at the expressions in 2 again and discuss the places they've visited with a partner .

1

8) be   9) free   7) sea

1) blue   2) two   4) you

5) chance   6) glance   3) romance

The song is about b)

2

a) aqua

b) cheek, cheek

c) two

d) speak

e) glance

f) ocean

g) peek

h) unique

---

10 Grammar Relative clauses

Page 181

Activity

Individual/pairwork: grammar analysis.

Focus

Defining and non-defining relative clauses.

Preparation

Make one copy of the worksheet for each student in the class.

Procedure

* Give each student a copy of the worksheet and ask them to work individually or in pairs to join the three parts of each sentence.

* Once they have done this ask students to work together to check they have the same sentences. Then check in open class.

* Ask the students to look at the sentences again and this time to change the relative pronoun to *that*, where possible. Sentences 2, 5, 6, 8 and 9 contain a defining relative clause and so the pronoun can change to *that*. The remaining sentences 1, 3, 4, 7 and 10 contain a non-defining relative clause (separated from the main clause by commas), and so cannot be changed.

1   Coca-Cola, which was first sold in 1885, was originally green.
2   The first novel that was written on a typewriter was *Tom Sawyer*.
3   Mel Blanc, who was the voice of cartoon rabbit Bugs Bunny, was allergic to carrots.
4   Barack Obama, who became the 44th U.S. President, was born in Hawaii.
5   Venus is the only planet which rotates clockwise.
6   The full name of the doll which most girls know as Barbie is Barbara Millicent Roberts.
7   The avocado, which comes from Latin America, has more calories than any other fruit.
8   Clocks which were made before 1670 had only one hand, the hour hand.
9   The animal that has fingerprints most similar to humans is the koala.
10 The World Wide Web, which links billions of internet users around the world, was devised in 1980 by an English physicist.

In sentences 5, 6, and 8 the relative pronoun *which* can be replaced by the relative pronoun *that*, because they are used in defining relative clauses. The relative pronouns in sentences 1, 3, 4, 7 and 10 are all used in non-defining relative clauses and can therefore not be changed to *that*.

10 Vocabulary Sorry to interrupt …

Page 182
Activity
Pair/groupwork: discussion.

Focus
Using interruption devices during discussion.

Preparation
Make one copy of the worksheet for each group of four students in the class, cut up as indicated. If you wish the students to cut up the phrases provide enough pairs of scissors for them to use.

Procedure
- Explain to your students that they are going to discuss some issues in small groups and that they should use some interruption phrases as they talk. Divide the class into groups of four and give each group a copy of the worksheet cut up as indicated. Each person in the group gets a set of interruption phrases and the group as a whole gets one set of statements.
- Tell the students that, as they talk, they should tick (with a pencil) the interruption phrases they use. The first person to use up all of their phrases is the winner. However, the phrases must be

used appropriately, otherwise it doesn't count. Alternatively, your students can cut out each phrase and put them down on the desk as they use them. This involves more fiddling around at the beginning but it is easier not to tick statements while they are talking.
- Student A reads out the first sentence and the whole group starts discussing the point. The student who reads out the statement should play devil's advocate (agree with the statement/take the opposite view from the rest of the group), just for the purpose of having a lively discussion.
- When all the statements have been discussed or when the students have had enough, stop the discussion and conduct a feedback session in open class about the topic they felt most strongly about.

10 Communication Inspirational marketing

Page 183
Activity
Groupwork: reading, discussion and planning.

Focus
Marketing plans.

Preparation
Make one copy of the worksheet for each student.

Procedure
- Write some famous brand names on the board, e.g. *Coca-Cola, Nike, Kodak*. Ask students to brainstorm globally famous brand names. Discuss what characteristics define a successful brand, e.g. name, logo, how global it is, cultural connotations, etc.
- Give a copy of the worksheet to each student. Ask the students to read the article.
- Ask the students to discuss the questions in pairs, then discuss with the whole class.
- Ask students to read the names of the inventions and discuss in pairs possible market opportunities for these products. Then conduct a class feedback session.
- Explain that the students are going to devise a marketing plan for one of the products. To make sure everyone understands, read the instructions and questions with the class.
- Divide the class into groups and ask the groups to prepare their marketing plans. Encourage students to think of a catchy brand name and a slogan for their product. Circulate and monitor, helping with ideas as necessary.
- Ask the groups to present their marketing plans to the class. The class can then vote for the best marketing plan.

Notes

If necessary, use the following skeleton marketing plan to help your students with the activity.

Sample marketing plan
1 Marketing objectives
2 Marketing strategy
3 Marketing budget
4 Marketing action plan

What are you offering?
Who are your customers?
Why should customers buy what you offer?
Where is your market?
What size is the market?
What is happening in the market?
Who/What is your competition?
How much should you charge?
How do you communicate with potential customers?
What after-sales service do you provide?

---

11 Grammar Future forms

Page 184

Activity

Class mingle: speaking and writing.

Focus

Using future forms.

Preparation

Make one copy of the worksheet for each student in the class.

Procedure

• Give one copy of the worksheet to each student in the class. Explain that they are going to ask one another some questions about their future.

• Explain that they should ask each other the questions and only write down the name of the person in the right-hand column who answers *'Yes'* to their questions*. Elicit the first question: *Are you going out for dinner tonight?* Ask them to find out more information, e.g. *Where are you going? What's your favourite kind of food?* etc.

• Ask them to stand up and mingle. Monitor carefully and only stop them when the first student has finished. Conduct a feedback session in open class.

Note

*For 'might be getting married soon' the ideal question is *Are you getting married soon?* (asking about something you consider already arranged). If the person answers 'Maybe', they write their name. For 'might start up their own business one day' the ideal question is *Do you think you'll start up your own business one day?* (asking for a prediction). Again, if the answer is 'Maybe' then write the name of the student.

11 Vocabulary Exaggerated expressions

Page 185

Activity

Pair/groupwork: *Pelmanism* game.

Focus

Informal exaggerated expressions.

Preparation

Make one copy of the worksheet for each pair/small group of students in the class.

Procedure

• Divide the class into pairs/small groups and give each pair/group a set of cards. Ask the students to place the cards face down on the desk.

• Explain to the students that on the cards there are twelve pairs of expressions which have the same meaning, but that one is an exaggerated way of saying the other. The students will have seen these expressions on page 115 of *New Inside Out* Upper intermediate Student's Book. The aim of the game is to match these pairs.

• Explain that they should take it in turns to turn over two cards, one at a time, and read aloud the expression on each card. If the expressions are similar, the student keeps the pair and gets another turn. If the expressions are not similar, the student turns the cards face down again and ends their turn. Encourage students when reading out the exaggerated expressions to put a bit more energy into reading them to make them sound exaggerated.

• The game continues until all the pairs of cards have been won. The student with the most pairs is the winner.

• Check the answers in open class.

I was happy / I was over the moon
There were a lot of people / The place was swarming with people
I was ill / I was at death's door
I started crying / I burst into tears
I was frightened / I was scared stiff
I was thirsty / I was dying for a drink
It was dirty / It was filthy
I was worried / I was going out of my mind
It was beautiful / It took my breath away
I was tired / I was on my last legs
It was very exciting / It was mind-blowing
I was desperate / I was at the end of my tether

Follow up

Cut some large photos out of a magazine/newspaper showing two people of any description who could be speaking to each other. Ask students in their pairs to choose one of the pictures and then to come up with a dialogue between the people, using as many of the exaggerated expressions as they can naturally fit in. Dialogues can be put up around the class or read out by each pair and then voted on by the class.

11 Communication A good bet

Page 186

Activity

Pairwork: grammar.

Focus

Review and consolidation of grammar from Units 1 to 11 of *New Inside Out* Upper intermediate Student's Book.

Preparation

Make one copy of the worksheet for each student in the class.

Procedure

- Divide the class into pairs and give each student a copy of the worksheet.

- Explain that the students are going to look at twenty sentences and decide if they are grammatically correct. Tell them they are also going to bet on how sure they are of their decision.

- Ask the students to work through the sentences putting a tick (✓) or a cross (✗) by each one. In the *BET* box the students write the number of points (from 1 to 5) they bet on their decision being correct. (5 points if they are certain, 1 point if they are really doubtful.)

- When most of the pairs have finished, check the answers with the whole class. Tell the students that if their answer was correct they win the number of points they bet. If it was incorrect, they lose the number of points they bet.

- Ask the students to add up the total number of gains and losses. The grand total will be the number of gains minus the number of losses. The winner is the pair with the most points.

1　The weather_'s been_ terrible ever since we arrived last Friday.
2　Do you mind telling me how old _you are_?
3　I'm very fond _of_ cats, but unfortunately I'm allergic _to_ them.
4　Correct
5　Lauren has long, straight, blonde hair.
6　Correct
7　As a child I _used to_ have a good memory but as I've got older it's got worse.
8　I'll never forget _seeing_ the eclipse of the sun last year.
9　Correct
10　I_'ve been watching_ television since _I came_ home from work this evening.
11　Correct

12　I was wondering why _he was_ always late for work.
13　Correct
14　All I want in life is ~~a~~ good health, ~~the~~ happiness and a little money.
15　If I were you, I_'d_ go to the doctor immediately – that cut looks very deep.
16　Correct
17　Centuries ago, people _used to_ think the world was flat.
18　Correct
19　Correct
20　He's _tried_ to break the world record four times but he has always failed.

Follow up

This exercise may well reveal some language areas that need reviewing. Be prepared to refer to the relevant units in the *New Inside Out* Upper intermediate Student's Book.

Ask the students, in pairs or small groups, to write some correct and incorrect sentences of their own for another pair/group to do.

12 Grammar Is there much?

Page 187

Activity

Individual/pairwork: matching and discussion.

Focus

Quantifiers.

Preparation

Make one copy of the worksheet for each student in the class.

Procedure

- Give a copy of the worksheet to each student in the class and ask them to work individually to complete the task. Explain that although some of the sentences have similar meanings, there is a picture that clearly illustrates the differences. There is one sentence to one picture, so students should ensure they have found a match for every one before they think they have finished.

- Once they have thought about each sentence and had time to think about the pictures, divide the class into pairs and ask each pair to compare their answers and justify their choices to each other.

- Check answers in open class, discussing each choice, its similarities and differences from other sentences.

1	L	5	G	9	D
2	J	6	C	10	F
3	A	7	E	11	H
4	I	8	B	12	K

---

12 Vocabulary It's like talking to a brick wall!

Page 188

Activity
Pairwork: reading and speaking.

Focus
Expressions/idioms related to the home and houses.

Preparation
Make one copy of the worksheet for each student. Cut the worksheet into two sections as indicated.

Procedure
- Divide the class into pairs and give each student a copy of the top section of the worksheet.
- Ask the students, in pairs, to complete the expressions/idioms by choosing the correct alternative. Encourage the students to think of any similar expressions in their own language and ask them to make calculated guesses if necessary. You may wish to allow the students to use a dictionary. You could introduce a competitive element where the pair with the highest score is the winner.
- Check the answers with the whole class.
- Give each student a copy of the discussion section of the worksheet. Ask the students to take turns to tell their partner about the people and situations. Encourage them to ask questions to find out more information.
- Ask the students to report to the class anything interesting from their discussions.

1 b	5 c	9 b
2 b	6 b	10 c
3 c	7 a	
4 a	8 c	

12 Communication Home Sweet Home

Page 189

Activity
Groupwork: speaking and presenting.

Focus
Review of vocabulary related to homes.

Preparation
Make one copy of the worksheet for each student.

Procedure
- Explain that students are going to design a home and then present it to the rest of the class.
- Divide the class into groups of three to four students and give each student a copy of the worksheet. Explain that the worksheet contains choices of possible locations, styles and features for their house. Allow enough time for each group to prepare their ideal home and draw a floor plan.
- Allow students some time to prepare their presentation. While students are preparing, circulate and monitor, helping as necessary.
- When all the groups are ready, ask each one to make its presentation. The class votes on the best presentation.

Review D Suddenly I see

Page 190

Activity
Pairwork: song.

Focus
Revision of grammar and vocabulary from *New Inside Out* Upper intermediate Student's Book, Units 10–12.

Preparation
Make one copy of the worksheet for each student in the class. Get the recording ready.

Procedure
- Ask the class what they know about KT Tunstall. Distribute the worksheets folded over so they can just see the photograph. Ask students to work in pairs to speculate about her age, nationality, etc.
- Tell students they are going to read a biography of the singer but first they need to choose from some alternatives. Ask them to unfold the worksheet. They should complete Exercise 1 individually.
- Now play the song and ask students to read the lyrics and listen and choose the best summary.

1 a) Scottish	d) flute and piano
b) Kate	e) Best Female Solo Artist
c) Chinese	f) *The Devil Wears Prada*
2 b)	

1 Grammar

Would you mind telling me ...?

Would you mind telling me ...?	What's the best thing about ...?
Would you say ...?	**Do you have any idea ...?**
Would you like to ...?	When did you last ...?
Do you consider yourself ...?	*Do you know ...?*
How long have you ...?	**I'd like to know ...**
Have you ever ...?	*What's the single most ...?*
How do you feel about ...?	What's your favourite ...?
Do you think you'll ever ...?	*Do you mind if I ask you ...?*
In an ideal world, ...?	**Could you tell me ...?**
When do you suppose ...?	**I was wondering ...**

1 Vocabulary

Common ground

I wouldn't like to _____
_____

I've never visited _____
_____

I usually wear _____
_____

I didn't _____
yesterday.

I've got a friend called
_____

My favourite film is _____
_____

I'm currently learning how
to _____

I don't want to _____
_____

I love listening to _____
_____

I can't _____
very well.

I had _____
for breakfast today.

I'll never _____
again.

I used to _____
_____ as a child.

I'm not keen on _____
_____

I've always wanted to _____
_____

Last Saturday I _____

1 Communication

You do, don't you?

A **F**IND OUT...

favourite colour?   country / like to visit?

where / born?   what / last film / see?

what / do last night at seven o'clock?

which languages / speak?   how long / learn English?

afraid of flying?   hobbies?

B **F**IND OUT...

favourite film?   what time / get up this morning?

married?   where / go on holiday last year?

lucky number?   mother's name?

what / do next weekend?

how long / have that hairstyle?   ride a horse?

C **F**IND OUT...

favourite food?   birthday?   who / look like / family?

nickname?   what / have for dinner last night?

how long / have these shoes?

where / go on holiday next year?

member of any clubs?   like classical music?

2 Grammar

Tell me something about yourself

1 Were you good ___ sports at school?

2 What animals or insects are you afraid ___ ?

3 Is there anything you are worried ___ at the moment?

4 Are you interested ___ politics?

5 What achievements in your life are you most proud ___ ?

6 Would you say you were satisfied ___ your level of English?

7 Do you believe ___ miracles?

8 Who or what have you got angry ___ lately?

9 Are you scared ___ flying?

10 What would you like to be famous ___ ?

11 Have you ever done something which you are now embarrassed ___ ?

12 What or who have you been fed up ___ in the last two weeks?

13 What type of music are you keen ___ ?

14 What are you excited ___ doing in the next 7 days?

2 Vocabulary

Vince's bike

From:	Vince	To:	Brenda

Subject:	Re: Bike Nicked!

Message:

Hi Bren!

Had a terrible day yesterday – someone <u>nicked</u> my bike! I <u>locked it up</u> outside work as usual. After work I went to the pub with Steve (my boss) and Roger (a colleague) for a few beers. I headed off at <u>7ish</u> because I didn't want to ride home too drunk. When I <u>got back</u> to where I'd left my bike, I found it had gone. At first I couldn't believe that someone had nicked it, but <u>when the penny dropped</u> I <u>went bananas</u>. I went straight to the local police station to let them know but I had to wait <u>for ages</u>. A policewoman eventually saw me after 45 mins and took down the details. She said there was <u>no way</u> they'd find whoever had nicked it, but they did offer to put me in touch with a victim support group! Anyway, I've written to the insurance company and I hope they'll <u>pay up</u> soon 'cos I <u>need</u> a bike to <u>get to</u> work. Anyway, such is life. Hope life with you is better – e-mail soon, Vince :(xxx

- **FOLD** -

Dear Sir/Madam,

I am writing to inform you that my bicycle (frame no. TTJ 58394751) has been stolen and to make a claim on my insurance policy (ref: VD/29684AA).
As requested, I have provided a report of what happened below.

The theft occurred on Thursday 5th June between 9.00 am and 7.00 pm.
My bike was securely locked outside my workplace (106 Piccadilly). I realised that the bicycle had gone when I returned from a social event with work colleagues at approximately 7.00 pm. As soon as I realised what had happened I went directly to the local police station and reported the incident. The police constable provided me with a crime reference number (CD346300), although she informed me that it was extremely unlikely that the thief would be caught.

I would appreciate it if you would process my claim as quickly as possible as I require a bicycle to travel to and from work.

Yours sincerely,

V. A. Desmond

Vincent A. Desmond

iː	dog	ɒ	pin	ɪ	car
ɑː	cup	ʌ	shoe	uː	hat
æ	door	ɔː	bird	ɜː	the
ə	leg	e	book	ʊ	tree
iː	watch	ɒ	swim	ɪ	heart
ɑː	sun	ʌ	school	uː	bag
æ	four	ɔː	word	ɜː	teac<u>h</u>er
ə	bed	e	good	ʊ	tea

3 Vocabulary

Money talks

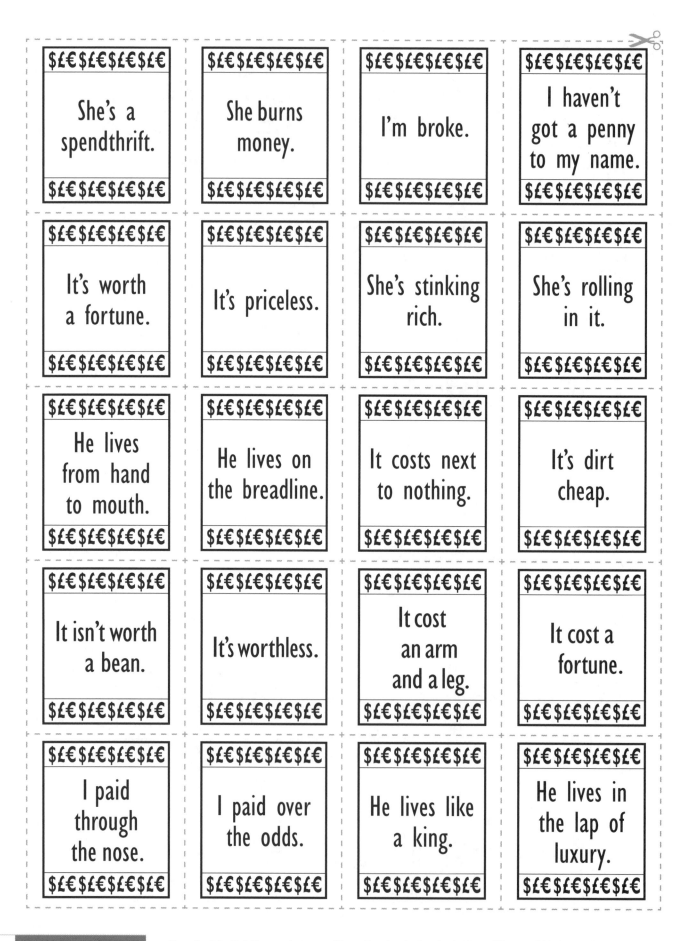

She's a spendthrift.	She burns money.	I'm broke.	I haven't got a penny to my name.
It's worth a fortune.	It's priceless.	She's stinking rich.	She's rolling in it.
He lives from hand to mouth.	He lives on the breadline.	It costs next to nothing.	It's dirt cheap.
It isn't worth a bean.	It's worthless.	It cost an arm and a leg.	It cost a fortune.
I paid through the nose.	I paid over the odds.	He lives like a king.	He lives in the lap of luxury.

New Inside Out Upper intermediate Teacher's Book © Macmillan Publishers Limited 2009

3 Communication

Life is a journey

I felt as if I was at a *crossroads* / ~~*roundabout*~~ in my life.

1 Choose the correct alternative to make metaphors.

1
I was at the *top /peak* of health.

2
I managed to do it even though the *odds / chances* were against me.

3
I spent years *drifting / floating* from one thing to another.

4
The news was difficult to *eat / digest* at first.

5
It was such a *half-fried / half-baked* idea I still can't believe it worked.

6
My heart *sank / slipped* when I heard the news.

7
It was a *rocky road / stony street*, but we're still friends.

8
It was one of the most *valuable / precious* moments in my life.

9
It gave me a lot of *drink / food* for thought.

10
I felt *on top of the world / over the earth*.

11
To my surprise they gave me a really *warm / hot* welcome.

12
I was my own worst *opponent / enemy*.

13
It turned into a *run / race* against time.

14
All I could see was a *sea / lake* of people.

15
It was a total *waste / loss* of time.

2 Think about times when these sentences have been true for you. Discuss in groups.

Review A

When a man loves a woman

When a man loves a woman was Percy Sledge's biggest success. It topped the US charts in 1966.

1 Work with a partner. Discuss in what ways men and women's behaviour changes when they fall in love.

2 Work with a partner. Read a list of ideas (*a–h*) about what a man will do when he is in love with a woman. Which ideas do you think are 1) realistic? 2) unrealistic?

a) He'll never notice her faults.
b) He'll do anything she tells him to do.
c) He'll love and respect her family.
d) He'll spend all his money on her.
e) He'll give up everything for her.
f) He'll never allow other people to criticise her.
g) He'll think about nothing else but her.
h) He'll never cheat on her.

3 🌐 1.34 Read and listen to the song. Match lines in the song to the ideas listed in Exercise 1.

a) *He'll never notice her faults. = line 4 'If she's bad, he can't see it.'*

Which idea is *not* mentioned?

4 Match the phrasal verbs with their meaning in the song.

a) put sb down
b) hold on to sth
c) give sth up

1) allow somebody to have something that was yours
2) criticize somebody publicly
3) hold something tightly or carefully

5 Each of these phrasal verbs in Exercise 4 has several different meanings. Complete these definitions and example sentences with the correct verb.

a) _____ to stop doing something that you do regularly = QUIT: *Have you ever tried to _____ smoking?*
b) _____ to kill an animal because it is old or ill: *In the end the dog had to be _____*
c) _____ to allow yourself to be arrested by the police = SURRENDER: *Police persuaded the man to _____ himself _____ before any more damage was caused*
d) _____ to not lose something = HANG ON TO: *_____ the receipt just in case they're the wrong size.*
e) _____ to pay part of the cost of something: *We've _____ a deposit on a new car!*
f) _____ to continue feeling or believing something: *They _____ the belief that she will come back one day.*

Look up the same phrasal verbs in your own dictionary. What other meanings can you find?

1 When a man loves a woman
 Can't keep his mind on nothin' else
 He'll trade the world for the good thing he's found
 If she's bad, he can't see it
5 She can do no wrong
 Turn his back on his best friend, if he puts her down

 When a man loves a woman
 Spend his very last dime *
 Tryin' to hold on to what he needs
10 He'd give up all of his comforts
 And sleep out in the rain
 If she said that's the way it ought to be

 Well, this man loves a woman
 I gave you everything I had
15 Tryin' to hold on to your high class love
 Baby, please don't treat me bad

 When a man loves a woman
 Deep down in his soul
 She can bring him such misery
20 If she plays him for a fool
 He's the last one to know
 Lovin' eyes can never see

 When a man loves a woman
 He can never do her wrong
25 He'd never want some other girl
 Yes when a man loves a woman
 I know how he feels
 'Cause baby, baby, baby, you're my world

 When a man loves a woman ...

* An American 10 cent coin

4 Grammar

A dangerous adventure

Complete one part of the story of a dangerous adventure.
Then fold the paper over and pass it to the person on your left.

Last year my friend and I were feeling adventurous and so we decided to go to ... (WHERE DID YOU DECIDE TO GO?)

— — — — — — — — — — — — — — — FOLD — — — — — — — — — — — — — — —

In preparation for our trip, I had ... (WHAT HAD YOU DONE?)

— — — — — — — — — — — — — — — FOLD — — — — — — — — — — — — — — —

As we set off on the first day of our adventure, we were wearing ... (WHAT WERE YOU WEARING?)

— — — — — — — — — — — — — — — FOLD — — — — — — — — — — — — — — —

A little while later, we heard a growl. We turned around and saw ... (WHAT DID YOU SEE AND WHAT WAS IT DOING?)

— — — — — — — — — — — — — — — FOLD — — — — — — — — — — — — — — —

We immediately ... (WHAT DID YOU DO?)

— — — — — — — — — — — — — — — FOLD — — — — — — — — — — — — — — —

Later that day, we met a group of people who had been ... (WHAT HAD THEY BEEN DOING?)

— — — — — — — — — — — — — — — FOLD — — — — — — — — — — — — — — —

We thought it would be fun to spend some time with them so we arranged to ... (WHAT DID YOU ARRANGE TO DO?)

— — — — — — — — — — — — — — — FOLD — — — — — — — — — — — — — — —

The best thing that happened to us was on the last day. (WHAT HAPPENED?)

It was the perfect ending to an unusual day.

4 Vocabulary

Phrasal verbs crossword

Complete the crossword with the missing verbs from the dialogues.

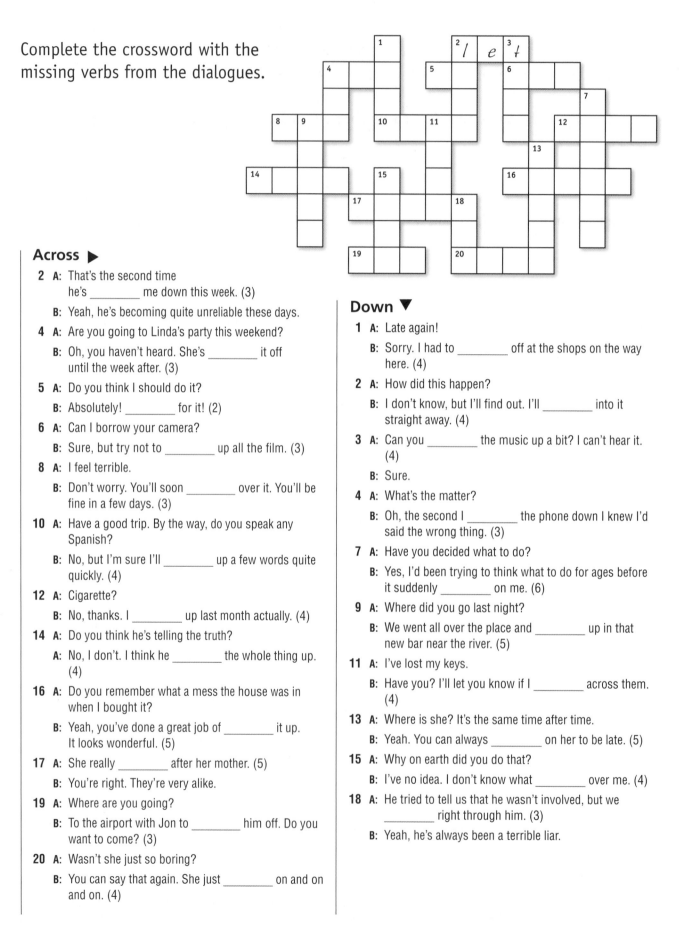

Across ▶

2 **A:** That's the second time he's _____ me down this week. (3)

    B: Yeah, he's becoming quite unreliable these days.

4 **A:** Are you going to Linda's party this weekend?

    B: Oh, you haven't heard. She's _____ it off until the week after. (3)

5 **A:** Do you think I should do it?

    B: Absolutely! _____ for it! (2)

6 **A:** Can I borrow your camera?

    B: Sure, but try not to _____ up all the film. (3)

8 **A:** I feel terrible.

    B: Don't worry. You'll soon _____ over it. You'll be fine in a few days. (3)

10 **A:** Have a good trip. By the way, do you speak any Spanish?

    B: No, but I'm sure I'll _____ up a few words quite quickly. (4)

12 **A:** Cigarette?

    B: No, thanks. I _____ up last month actually. (4)

14 **A:** Do you think he's telling the truth?

    A: No, I don't. I think he _____ the whole thing up. (4)

16 **A:** Do you remember what a mess the house was in when I bought it?

    B: Yeah, you've done a great job of _____ it up. It looks wonderful. (5)

17 **A:** She really _____ after her mother. (5)

    B: You're right. They're very alike.

19 **A:** Where are you going?

    B: To the airport with Jon to _____ him off. Do you want to come? (3)

20 **A:** Wasn't she just so boring?

    B: You can say that again. She just _____ on and on and on. (4)

Down ▼

1 **A:** Late again!

    B: Sorry. I had to _____ off at the shops on the way here. (4)

2 **A:** How did this happen?

    B: I don't know, but I'll find out. I'll _____ into it straight away. (4)

3 **A:** Can you _____ the music up a bit? I can't hear it. (4)

    B: Sure.

4 **A:** What's the matter?

    B: Oh, the second I _____ the phone down I knew I'd said the wrong thing. (3)

7 **A:** Have you decided what to do?

    B: Yes, I'd been trying to think what to do for ages before it suddenly _____ on me. (6)

9 **A:** Where did you go last night?

    B: We went all over the place and _____ up in that new bar near the river. (5)

11 **A:** I've lost my keys.

    B: Have you? I'll let you know if I _____ across them. (4)

13 **A:** Where is she? It's the same time after time.

    B: Yeah. You can always _____ on her to be late. (5)

15 **A:** Why on earth did you do that?

    B: I've no idea. I don't know what _____ over me. (4)

18 **A:** He tried to tell us that he wasn't involved, but we _____ right through him. (3)

    B: Yeah, he's always been a terrible liar.

4 Communication

Storytellers

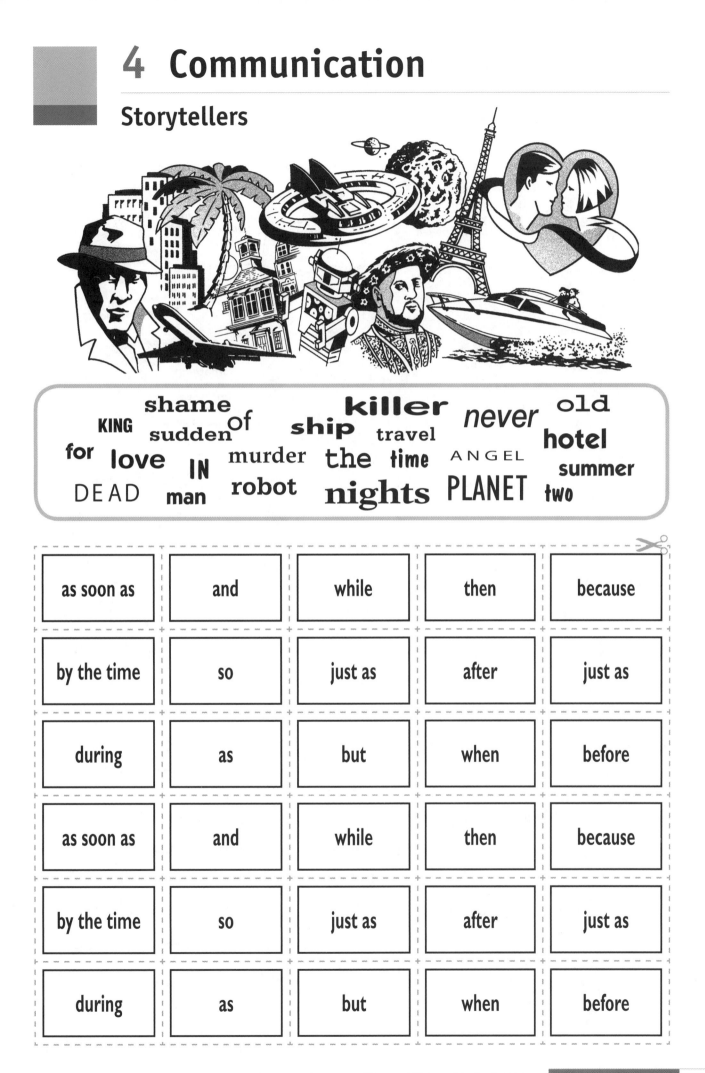

shame KING sudden of killer ship never old
for love IN murder the time ANGEL hotel
DEAD man robot nights PLANET summer two

as soon as	and	while	then	because
by the time	so	just as	after	just as
during	as	but	when	before
as soon as	and	while	then	because
by the time	so	just as	after	just as
during	as	but	when	before

Secret message

5 Communication

Old habits die hard

1 Rewrite each sentence in either the present or the past.

1 I'll spend hours reading. I love it.

I'd spend hours reading. I used to love it.

2 I used to love art at school. I'd paint a different picture every day.

I love art at school. I'll paint a different picture every day.

3 Before leaving for school, I'd always take the dog for a walk. I used to love that.

_____

4 I'm a creature of habit. First I'll check my emails and then I'll have a coffee.

_____

5 Before going to bed, I used to read my book. I'd usually drop off after about 15 minutes.

_____

6 During the school holidays I'd work for about six weeks. I used to enjoy the discipline.

_____

7 I'll watch around two hours of TV in the evenings and then I'll do my homework.

_____

8 I didn't use to have a car, so I used to walk everywhere.

_____

9 At weekends I'll get up quite late. I'll usually read the papers and take it easy.

_____

10 I used to have blond hair. Actually, I'd change the colour every month.

_____

11 I hate my car. It won't start if it's been raining.

_____

12 My dad loves his car. He'll spend hours cleaning it at the weekend.

_____

2 Tick the statements that are true for you.

6 Grammar

What have I been doing?

You've been <u>mowing</u> the <u>grass</u>.

You've been <u>working</u> at your <u>computer</u>.

You've been <u>walking</u> in the <u>rain</u>.

You've been <u>running</u> in the <u>forest</u>.

You've been <u>babysitting</u> for your <u>neighbour</u>.

You've been <u>dancing</u> with a <u>very attractive person</u>.

You've been <u>making</u> a <u>birthday cake</u>.

You've been <u>talking</u> to a <u>classmate</u> on the <u>phone</u>.

You've been <u>drinking</u> in the <u>pub</u> with your <u>classmates</u>.

You've been <u>studying mathematics</u> in the <u>library</u>.

You've been in town <u>shopping</u> for <u>new boots</u>.

You've been <u>travelling</u> by <u>train</u>.

You've been playing a <u>football match</u> with your <u>cousins</u>.

You've been <u>writing an email</u> to your <u>girlfriend/boyfriend</u>.

You've been <u>helping</u> your <u>little sister</u> with her <u>homework</u>.

Gabby's homework

You've been <u>doing</u> the <u>housework</u>.

You've been <u>lying</u> in <u>bed</u> because you've had <u>flu</u>.

You've been <u>doing</u> an <u>aerobics class</u> at the <u>gym</u>.

6 Vocabulary

Food fight

Write 5 ways to cook *food*	Write 5 adjectives which collocate with **dish**	Write 5 *vegetables*
Write 5 adjectives which collocate with **flavour**	Write 5 *food idioms*	Write 5 adjectives which collocate with **food**

- ✂

Write 5 *salad* items	Write 5 adjectives which collocate with **meal**	Write 5 different types of *restaurant*
Write 5 adjectives which collocate with **dish**	Write 5 types of *meat*	Write 5 adjectives which collocate with **plate**

6 Communication

Make the question

1

| IN | WHICH | COUNTRY | ARE | THE | NEXT | OLYMPICS | GOING | TO | BE | HELD | ? |

2

| HOW | MUCH | FOOD | IS | WASTED | EVERY | YEAR | IN | THE | U.K. | ? |

3

| WHO | WAS | *THE SCREAM* | PAINTED | BY | ? |

4

| WHERE | IS | MOST | OF | THE | WORLD'S | COFFEE | GROWN | ? |

5

| IN | WHICH | U.S. | CITY | WAS | J.F. KENNEDY | ASSASSINATED | ? |

6

| IN | WHICH | COUNTRY | HAVE | MOST | OLYMPIC GAMES | BEEN | HELD | ? |

7

| TO | WHICH | FILM | HAVE | MOST | ACADEMY AWARDS | BEEN | GIVEN | ? |

8

| IN | WHICH | YEAR | WAS | THE | EIFFEL TOWER | BUILT | ? |

9

| IN | WHICH | COUNTRY | IS | MOST | OF | THE | WORLD'S | RICE | PRODUCED | ? |

Review B

Big yellow taxi

Born in Alberta, Canada in 1943, Joni Mitchell is one of the great singer-songwriters of her generation. *Big Yellow Taxi* is one of her most famous songs.

1 🔘 2.20 **Listen to the song and decide whether it is mainly about:**

a) personal problems

b) environmental problems

c) parking problems

2 **Read an extract from an interview that Joni Mitchell gave in the early 1970s about the origin of the song.**

a) Where was she?

b) What could she see from her hotel room?

c) Why did she decide to write the song?

"I wrote 'Big Yellow Taxi' on my first trip to Hawaii. I took a taxi to the hotel and when I woke up the next morning, I threw back the curtains and saw these beautiful green mountains in the distance. Then, I looked down and there was a parking lot as far as the eye could see, and it broke my heart... this blight on paradise. That's when I sat down and wrote the song." [SOURCE WIKIPEDIA]

3 **The line 'You don't know what you've got till it's gone' is repeated four times in the song. Read the song lyrics. What are the four examples that Joni Mitchell gives to illustrate this idea? Do you agree with the idea? What other examples can you think of? Tell your partner.**

4 **Work with your partner. In your opinion, what are the three biggest dangers facing the environment?**

- **FOLD** -

Big Yellow Taxi

1 They paved* paradise
Put up a parking lot
With a pink hotel, a boutique
And a swinging hot spot
5 Don't it always seem to go
That you don't know what you've
got
'Til it's gone
They paved paradise
10 And put up a parking lot

They took all the trees
Put 'em in a tree museum
Then they charged the people
A dollar and a half just to see 'em

15 Don't it always seem to go,
That you don't know what you've
got
'Til it's gone
They paved paradise
20 And put up a parking lot
Hey farmer, farmer
Put away that DDT** now
Give me spots on my apples
But leave me the birds and the
25 bees
Please!
Don't it always seem to go
That you don't know what you've
got

30 'Til its gone
They paved paradise
And put up a parking lot

Late last night
I heard the screen door slam
35 And a big yellow taxi
Took away my old man***

Don't it always seem to go
That you don't know what you've
got
40 'Til it's gone
They paved paradise
And put up a parking lot

* paved = covered in concrete   ** DDT = poisonous chemical pesticide   *** old man = boyfriend, husband or maybe father

7 Grammar

Pleasure and pain

My wife and I wanted a honeymoon near enough to home that we didn't need to spend 12 hours on a plane, so we chose the Red Sea.

The hotel was clean and the staff polite. We didn't have to walk far to get to the beach. The sea was crystal blue and calm and the sand sparkled in the blazing sun. This is more like it, we thought.

I had never been snorkelling before. I hadn't really seen the point. However, we were in an exotic location and my wife was keen. The moment I put the mask into the water, I was hooked. It was full of tropical fish, in crisp, clear colour, right in front of my face!

We were entranced, so entranced that we stayed out for hours, oblivious to the sun beating down on our shirtless backs. It was only when we returned to our hotel that we realised there was a price to pay for our pleasure.

My back was on fire. It's easy to say now that I ought to have kept my t-shirt on. I know I should have told my wife to do the same. But I was too distracted.

We spent the rest of the day in our hotel room shower. The cold water cooling our lobster-red flesh. It was the only way we could get any relief. I have never known agony like it. We couldn't go out for several days.

So there we were in a holiday paradise, typical honeymooners in that we rarely left our room – though unfortunately not for the typical reasons!

7 Vocabulary

Word formation

-ful	-less	-ish
dis-	il-	im-
in-	ir-	un-

adequate	home	possible
appropriate	honest	relent
decisive	legal	relevant
delight	literate	resistible
devil	logical	responsible
divided	loyal	responsive
end	mature	stress
fool	obedient	willing
hell	polite	wonder

 New Inside Out Upper intermediate Teacher's Book © Macmillan Publishers Limited 2009

7 Communication

Pronunciation review

START

1 /ʌ/ Embrace someone affectionately

2 Sound sympathetic

3 /uː/ He marries the bride

4 Read the football score: 1–0

5 /ɔː/ A place that people go for a holiday

6 Pronounce this: The Eiffel Tower

7 /ɒ/ A plant grown for food e.g. corn

8 Question tag

9 /ʊ/ Use this word to give advice

10 Sound unsympathetic

11 /ɜː/ A bad, magical spell

12 Pronounce this: fish and chips

13 Sound annoyed

14 /ə/ Yellow fruit

15 /ɪ/ _____ out your tongue

16 Sound unsympathetic

17 Question tag

18 /æ/ A short, informal conversation

19 Say this number: 294,642,510

20 Pronounce this: about

21 /iː/ Cruel or unkind

22 Pronounce this: The Danube

23 Sound annoyed

24 /ɑː/ Very hungry

25 Say this number: 47,123,701

26 Sound sympathetic

27 /e/ A fashion

28 Question tag

FINISH

8 Grammar

Have you no scruples?

Imagine you saw someone shoplifting, would you report them?	If you gave your partner a present just before they split up with you, would you ask for it back?
Assuming someone on the street gave you some money they thought was yours, would you tell them you hadn't dropped any?	Supposing the person sitting next to you on the train fell asleep on your shoulder, would you move?
If your best friend had a haircut you hated, would you tell them the truth?	Imagine you were driving at night and you saw a woman standing by her car, would you stop and ask if she needed help?
Supposing you didn't like the service in an expensive restaurant, would you complain to the manager?	If you spilt some red wine on your boss's beige carpet, would you confess, even if no-one had seen you do it?
Assuming you're in a happy relationship, would you give your number to a good-looking stranger if they asked you for it?	Supposing your favourite band was coming to town for just one gig, would you skip work to go and see them?
If a friend had left their diary open and you just happened to be walking past, would you take a quick look?	Assuming you knew your daughter had lied on her CV to get the job at your friend's company, would you mention it to your friend?
Imagine a shop assistant gave you far too much change, would you tell them they had made a mistake?	If you and your friends all took, and passed, the same test, but you were the only one who didn't cheat, would you tell the teacher?
Suppose you were at a dinner party and you were served something you didn't like, would you eat it?	Imagine you accidentally scratched a car in a car park, would you leave a note with your name and number on it?
If you were with your friends and one of them told a joke you didn't get, would you laugh anyway?	Assuming money was no object, would you ever consider having cosmetic surgery?
Assuming you were sitting on the bus after a long, hard day, would you pretend you didn't see the little old lady without a seat?	If an old flame emailed you asking for a photo of yourself, would you send the most recent photo of yourself?

 New Inside Out Upper intermediate Teacher's Book © Macmillan Publishers Limited 2009

8 Vocabulary

Character search

1 Find words in the puzzle to complete the compound adjectives. The words go across, down and diagonally. (Two of the words in the puzzle need to be used twice.)

A	R	M	E	F	K	L	V	E	I	O
G	O	I	N	G	A	W	Z	S	E	C
L	T	N	T	B	A	C	K	O	A	H
O	C	D	V	E	D	U	E	I	R	E
V	T	E	M	P	E	R	E	D	T	A
I	E	D	N	O	F	F	I	S	H	R
N	W	I	T	T	E	D	S	A	N	T
G	A	S	S	U	R	E	D	L	W	E
C	X	B	A	Z	H	E	A	D	E	D
E	U	P	Y	M	N	N	D	W	Q	O

self-_____*assured*_____   laid-_____

down-to-_____   absent-_____

two-_____   stand-_____

warm-_____   bad-_____

self-_____   level-_____

easy-_____   big-_____

open-_____   stuck-_____

quick-_____   fun-_____

2 Answer the questions in pairs.

   a Which of these qualities are positive and which are negative?

   b Can you think of other words with similar meaning to the compound adjectives?
      e.g. *two-faced = hypocritical*

   c Which of these qualities are most important for you in a person? Which are the least desirable? Put them in order of most desirable to least desirable.

   d Which compound adjectives best describe you? Does your partner agree with you?

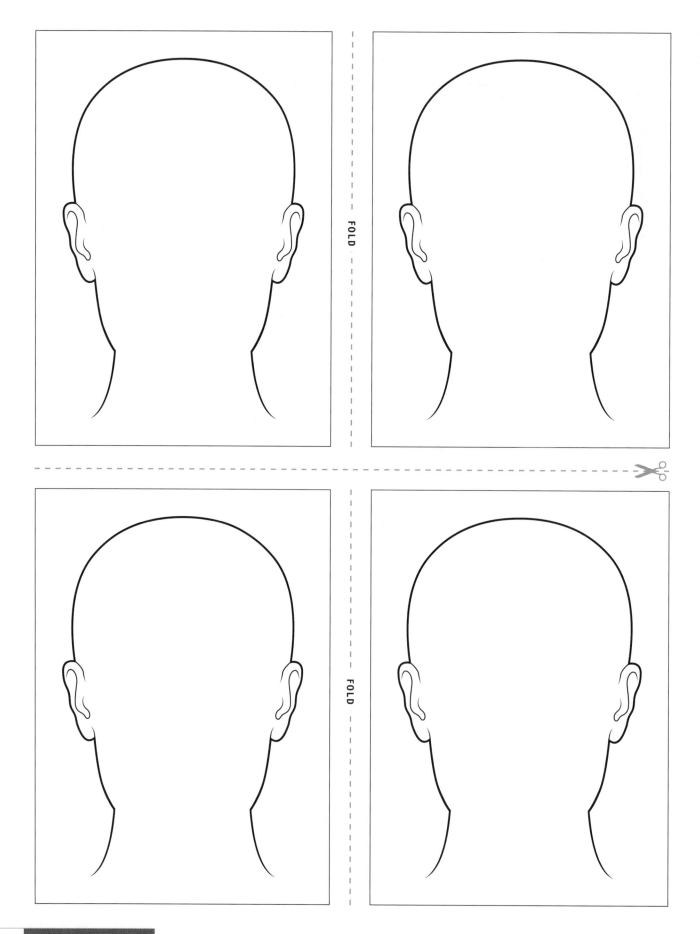

9 Grammar

Why would a person do this?

Sometimes it is difficult to understand why people do certain things. Read the following situations and discuss why the people involved might have done these things.

1 A sixty-year-old man risked his own life by jumping into a fast-flowing river to save a drowning child. The man had no biological or other link with the child, and just happened to be passing when he saw the child slip and fall into the river. The child's own father was by the side of the river when the incident occurred.

2 A woman gave birth to a baby girl and abandoned her within days. She left her wrapped up and warm in a basket outside a hospital at 4 am. Nobody saw her do this. There was a bottle of milk and a note in the basket. The note read: 'This is Rosie. Please look after her. Thank you.'

3 A forty-two-year-old woman inherited £10 million when her rich and famous parents suddenly died in a car crash. The woman immediately donated all her inheritance to various charities and lived in poverty for the rest of her life.

4 A 50-year-old man and his wife sat down to breakfast, as usual. After they had finished, and had washed the dishes, the man told his wife he was going to get a newspaper. He asked her if she needed anything and then left the house. His wife never saw or heard from him again.

5 A man was diagnosed with cancer. He continued to smoke twenty cigarettes a day, even though he had been told by his doctor that continuing to smoke greatly increased his chances of dying.

6 A woman wrote a best-selling novel. As soon as it was published she became a recluse, refusing all interviews or contact with the outside world. She never wrote another novel, nor did any other form of work for the rest of her life.

7 A woman spent five years applying for her dream job as a journalist with a national newspaper. Every time her application was rejected. When she was finally given the job, she wrote a letter to the newspaper saying that she had decided not to accept it.

8 A world-famous footballer on a salary of £65,000 a week accepted financial bribes from a bookmaker to fix the results of certain matches.

9 Vocabulary

Word families

1 Complete each word.

subject	person	adjective
scien_ce_	scien_tist_	scien_____
econom_____	econom_____	econom_____
gene_____	gene_____	gene_____
mathema_____	mathema_____	mathema_____
technolo_____	technolo_____	technolo_____
chem_____	chem_____	chem_____
biolo_____	biolo_____	biolo_____

2 Position each word in the table according to its pronunciation pattern so that, for each word, there is a word family consisting of noun (subject), noun (person) and adjective on the page.

> mathematics   genetic   chemistry   biologist   economics   mathematician   genetics
> chemical   technologist   economist   chemist   economic   economical   technology
> geneticist   biological   science   technological   scientific   mathematical   biology

9 Communication

Compare pictures

A

Student A: The following two photographs show different places to live. Compare these photographs and say what the advantages and disadvantages are of living in each place.

Student B: When Student A has finished, say in which of the places you would prefer to live.

Shoppers in Oxford Street, London, Britain – 19 Dec 2005

- **FOLD** -

B

Student B: The following two photographs show different types of holiday. Compare these photographs and say what the advantages and disadvantages are of each type of holiday.

Student A: When Student B has finished, say on which holiday you would prefer to go.

Review C

Mozambique

Singer, songwriter, author and poet Bob Dylan was born in Minnesota USA in 1941. His most famous works date from the 1960s and many have a political message. 'Mozambique' is one of his more light-hearted songs recorded in 1976 for the album 'Desire'.

1 Arrange the words in the box into three groups of three words with the same vowel sound.

| be   blue   chance   free   glance   romance   sea   two   you |

☐ _____   ☐ _____   ☐ _____

☐ _____   ☐ _____   ☐ _____

☐ _____   ☐ _____   ☐ _____

🌐 **3.08** Listen to the song and note the order in which you hear the words. Decide if the song is about

a) Living in Mozambique
b) A holiday in Mozambique
c) A business trip to Mozambique

2 Complete the expressions from the song:

a) the sunny sky is a_____ blue
b) all the couples dancing c_____ to c_____
c) a very nice place to stay a week or t_____
d) everybody likes to stop and s_____
e) say hello with just a g_____
f) lying next to her by the o_____
g) you turn around to take a final p_____
h) you see why it's so u_____

Listen again and check your answers.

3 Choose lines from the song in Ex 2 which remind you of places you've visited and tell your partner about these places.

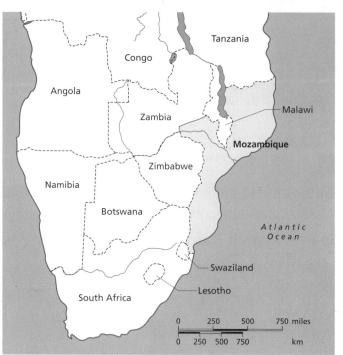

Mozambique

By writers Bob Dylan and Jacques Levy

1 I like to spend some time in Mozambique
The sunny sky is aqua blue
And all the couples dancing cheek to cheek
It's very nice to stay a week or two

5 There's lots of pretty girls in Mozambique
And plenty time for good romance
And everybody likes to stop and speak
To give the special one you seek a chance
Or maybe say hello with just a glance.

10 Lying next to her by the ocean
Reaching out and touching her hand
Whispering your secret emotion
Magic in a magical land.
And when it's time for leaving Mozambique

15 To say goodbye to sand and sea
You turn around to take a final peek
And you see why it's so unique to be
Among the lovely people living free
Upon the beach of sunny Mozambique

10 Grammar

Relative clauses

1 Coca-Cola,

2 The first novel

3 Mel Blanc,

4 Barack Obama,

5 Venus

6 The full name of the doll

7 The avocado,

8 Clocks

9 The animal

10 The World Wide Web,

is the only planet which

which comes from Latin America,

that has fingerprints most similar to humans

which was first sold in 1885,

who was the voice of cartoon rabbit Bugs Bunny,

that was written on a typewriter

which links billions of internet users around the world,

who became the 44th U.S. President,

which were made before 1670

which most girls know as Barbie

has more calories than any other fruit.

rotates clockwise.

was originally green.

had only one hand, the hour hand.

is the koala.

is Barbara Millicent Roberts.

was devised in 1980 by an English physicist.

was Tom Sawyer.

was born in Hawaii.

was allergic to carrots.

10 Vocabulary

Sorry to interrupt …

Discuss the statements.

1 These days there's very little point in getting married.

2 Sometimes it's necessary to hit children.

3 There's a direct relationship between the food you eat and the way you behave.

4 The world would be a happier place without bankers and politicians.

5 Graffiti is not art, it's vandalism.

6 The very poor should be prevented from having children.

7 There's nothing we can do individually about the environment – it's the responsibility of our governments.

8 Corporal punishment is an effective deterrent.

9 Footballers earn too much money and they don't have the good taste to spend it wisely.

10 The leopard can't change its spots. People born bad stay bad.

Introducing a point
But the thing is …
The problem is …

Interrupting
Sorry, but …
Hang on …
If I could just come in here …
I'm sorry to interrupt you but …

Responding to an interruption
If you would just let me finish,
Anyway, to get back to what I was saying,
The point I'm trying to make here is …
If you would just let me answer the question

Introducing a point
But the thing is …
The problem is …

Interrupting
Sorry, but …
Hang on …
If I could just come in here …
I'm sorry to interrupt you but …

Responding to an interruption
If you would just let me finish,
Anyway, to get back to what I was saying,
The point I'm trying to make here is …
If you would just let me answer the question

Introducing a point
But the thing is …
The problem is …

Interrupting
Sorry, but …
Hang on …
If I could just come in here …
I'm sorry to interrupt you but …

Responding to an interruption
If you would just let me finish,
Anyway, to get back to what I was saying,
The point I'm trying to make here is …
If you would just let me answer the question

Introducing a point
But the thing is …
The problem is …

Interrupting
Sorry, but …
Hang on …
If I could just come in here …
I'm sorry to interrupt you but …

Responding to an interruption
If you would just let me finish,
Anyway, to get back to what I was saying,
The point I'm trying to make here is …
If you would just let me answer the question

A new way to break the ice at the local pub

Traditionally, British pub-goers like their beer warm. But that could soon be a thing of the past with the first sub-zero draught lager, Arc, which comes topped with two centimetres of ice crystals. Brewers Bass have developed the revolutionary process. The beer is cooled to a temperature of −2°C and stored at high pressure to keep it from freezing solid. An empty beer glass is sprayed with chilled water and then, when the drink is poured from the pump the pressure is released and ice crystals form around the beer's gas bubbles.

"We knew we had something revolutionary when the lager scored exceptionally well in market research. Seventy-five per cent of participants said they would definitely buy the product," said David Griffiths, the new product development manager at Bass. But not all beer-lovers are convinced. Iain Lowe from the 'Campaign for Real Ale' believes drinkers will soon tire of what he calls a marketing gimmick. "At the temperatures at which they are talking of serving it you won't be able to taste anything," he says. "Beers should be served cool, but never iced."

Adapted with kind permission of *The Guardian* © from 'A new way to break the ice at the local' by Esther Addley, 5 September 2000

- What do you think of this revolutionary new product? Do you think that there would be a market for this product in your country? Why / Why not?

- What new products have recently entered the market in your country? Can you predict any revolutionary products of the future?

How much of a market do you think that there would be for the following inventions?

Talking computer · Self-driving car · Umbrella hat · Floating furniture · PET SHOWER · Robotic body massager · Motorised skate-board · Back massaging office chair · Motorised swimming costume · Spectacle de-mister

In groups, devise a marketing plan for the product in the newspaper article or one of those listed above. Remember the essential four Ps of marketing: *Product, Place, Price, Promotion*. Consider these questions when you write your marketing plan:

Product What identity does your product have? What does it do? Why will people want to buy it? Does it have a good brand name?

Place What geographical markets will you target and why? Will they be local, national, international? What social groups / types of customer is the product aimed at? How will the product be sold (Internet, high street, direct mail, etc)?

Price How much will the product cost? What type of profit margin do you expect? Will the product be priced differently for different markets? Will there be any special offers or discounts available?

Promotion How will you advertise the product (word of mouth campaign, magazines, broadcast media, posters)? What type of launch will the product have? What will the initial promotional budget be?

11 Grammar

Future forms

Find someone who ...	Name
1 is going out for dinner tonight	_____
2 will be sitting in the same seat in two hours' time	_____
3 thinks they will be rich and famous in the next five years	_____
4 will have finished some important exams by this time next year	_____
5 is going to celebrate their birthday in the next two months	_____
6 might be getting married soon	_____
7 will be studying English this time next year	_____
8 is meeting up with friends at the weekend	_____
9 is likely to start up their own business one day	_____
10 will be living in a different place in six months' time	_____
11 is going somewhere warm for their summer holidays	_____
12 is due to start a new course or job soon	_____

New Inside Out Upper intermediate Teacher's Book © Macmillan Publishers Limited 2009

11 Vocabulary

Exaggerated expressions

I was happy	I was over the moon	There were a lot of people
The place was swarming with people	I was ill	I was at death's door
I started crying	I burst into tears	I was frightened
I was scared stiff	I was thirsty	I was dying for a drink
It was dirty	It was filthy	I was worried
I was going out of my mind	It was beautiful	It took my breath away
I was tired	I was on my last legs	It was very exciting
It was mind-blowing	I was desperate	I was at the end of my tether

11 Communication

A good bet

SENTENCE		✓ or X?	BET
1	The weather was terrible ever since we arrived last Friday.		
2	Do you mind telling me how old are you?		
3	I'm very fond for cats, but unfortunately I'm allergic of them.		
4	Simon Brown, a specialist in contemporary music, was interviewed on the radio recently.		
5	Lauren has a long, straight, blonde hair.		
6	I've had a cold for three weeks now and I can't get rid of it.		
7	As a child I would have a good memory but as I've got older it's got worse.		
8	I'll never forget to see the eclipse of the sun last year.		
9	I don't have time to meet you today, but tomorrow is fine.		
10	I've watched television since I've come home from work this evening.		
11	Try to be more careful! That's the third time you've broken a cup.		
12	I was wondering why was he always late for work.		
13	If you aren't very good at running, why don't you concentrate on cycling instead?		
14	All I want in life is a good health, the happiness and a little money.		
15	If I were you, go to the doctor immediately – that cut looks very deep.		
16	If she hadn't slept in, she wouldn't have missed her flight.		
17	Centuries ago, people would think the world was flat.		
18	My parents wouldn't let me go to piano lessons so I taught myself.		
19	Why are you smelling the meat? Do you think it's off?		
20	He's been trying to break the world record four times but he has always failed.		

 New Inside Out Upper intermediate Teacher's Book © Macmillan Publishers Limited 2009

12 Grammar

Is there much?

Match the picture to the sentence.

1. There aren't any.
2. There are a few.
3. There are plenty.
4. There aren't enough.
5. There are too many.
6. There aren't many.
7. There isn't any.
8. There's a little.
9. There's plenty.
10. There isn't enough.
11. There's too much.
12. There isn't much.

12 Vocabulary

It's like talking to a brick wall!

1 Choose the correct alternative to complete the expressions.

1 He never listens to what I'm saying. It's like talking to a _____ *brick wall* _____ .

   a thick hedge   **ⓑ** brick wall   **c** wooden fence

2 The hotel we're staying in is OK, but nothing to _____ about.

   a send a letter home
   b write home
   c telephone home

3 He hit the _____ when I told him I'd scratched his car. He was so angry.

   a wall   **b** floor   **c** roof

4 I don't know the people who live _____ very well. They only moved in a month or so ago.

   a next door   **b** the next door   **c** at next door

5 I feel so relaxed here. It really is _____ .

   a a house from house   **b** a house from home   **c** a home from home

6 He smokes like a _____ . He really should give up.

   a fire   **b** chimney   **c** cooker

7 Aaarrrgh! If I hear that awful song one more time! It's driving me _____ .

   a up the wall   **b** through the door   **c** over the roof

8 We were hoping to go away for a few months, but I couldn't get time off work, so our plans went out of the _____ .

   a letterbox   **b** door   **c** window

9 We're really good friends. In fact, we got on like a _____ from the moment we first met.

   a burning house   **b** house on fire   **c** fire in the house

10 I feel terrible this morning. We had a night on the _____ last night.

   a bricks   **b** slates   **c** tiles

- ✂ - - -

2 Tell your partner about ...

1 a time when you felt like you were talking to a brick wall.

2 a place you've been which unfortunately was nothing to write home about.

3 a time when you, or someone you know, hit the roof about something.

4 the people who live next door to you.

5 somewhere which is a home from home.

6 someone who smokes like a chimney.

7 something which drives you up the wall.

8 a time when your plans went out of the window.

9 someone you get on with like a house on fire.

10 when you last had a night on the tiles.

12 Communication

Home Sweet Home

You're going to design a home and make a short presentation of it to the rest of the class. Money is no object, but you haven't got much time.

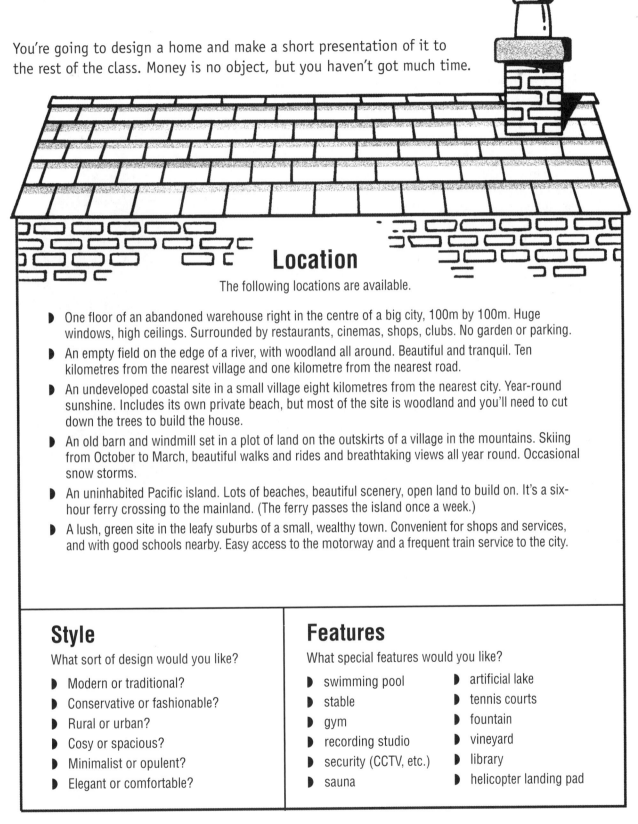

Location

The following locations are available.

- One floor of an abandoned warehouse right in the centre of a big city, 100m by 100m. Huge windows, high ceilings. Surrounded by restaurants, cinemas, shops, clubs. No garden or parking.
- An empty field on the edge of a river, with woodland all around. Beautiful and tranquil. Ten kilometres from the nearest village and one kilometre from the nearest road.
- An undeveloped coastal site in a small village eight kilometres from the nearest city. Year-round sunshine. Includes its own private beach, but most of the site is woodland and you'll need to cut down the trees to build the house.
- An old barn and windmill set in a plot of land on the outskirts of a village in the mountains. Skiing from October to March, beautiful walks and rides and breathtaking views all year round. Occasional snow storms.
- An uninhabited Pacific island. Lots of beaches, beautiful scenery, open land to build on. It's a six-hour ferry crossing to the mainland. (The ferry passes the island once a week.)
- A lush, green site in the leafy suburbs of a small, wealthy town. Convenient for shops and services, and with good schools nearby. Easy access to the motorway and a frequent train service to the city.

Style

What sort of design would you like?

- Modern or traditional?
- Conservative or fashionable?
- Rural or urban?
- Cosy or spacious?
- Minimalist or opulent?
- Elegant or comfortable?

Features

What special features would you like?

- swimming pool
- stable
- gym
- recording studio
- security (CCTV, etc.)
- sauna
- artificial lake
- tennis courts
- fountain
- vineyard
- library
- helicopter landing pad

Once you've chosen your site and discussed the style and features you want, you're ready to begin. Start by drawing a floor plan. Think about how many rooms you want. Do you want several floors or do you want everything on one floor? What furniture do you need? What kind of garden do you want? When you've finished, make your presentation to the class.

Review D

Suddenly I see

1 Look at the photo of singer-songwriter KT Tunstall and read the statements below. Choose the answers you think are most likely to be correct. Then read the Biography below to check your answers.

a) She is *Scottish / American / Australian*.

b) KT Tunstall's real name is *Karen / Kate / Keira*.

c) Her biological mother was half *Native American / Chinese / French*.

d) As a child she studied *flute and piano / violin / drums*.

e) At the 2006 Brit Awards, she won *Best Album / Best live act / Best Female Solo Artist*.

f) KT Tunstall's hit song 'Suddenly I See' was featured in the film *Mama Mia / Slumdog Millionaire / The Devil Wears Prada*.

> "Suddenly I See" is a song by Scottish singer-songwriter KT Tunstall. It is inspired by New York singer and poet Patti Smith.

KT Tunstall

KT Tunstall Biography

Scottish born singer-songwriter KT Tunstall, known to her family as Kate, was adopted by a couple of teachers. Her biological mother was half Chinese, and her biological father, whom she has never met, was an Irish folk singer. KT started playing piano and flute at a young age and she learned to sing by listening to Ella Fitzgerald. At 16, she taught herself the guitar.

KT Tunstall took the long road to success. She started singing and song-writing in her teens, and spent much of her 20s touring with a number of Scottish bands. She decided to go solo in 2002. She moved to London but a recording deal fell through and it was some time before she could secure a new deal. Many felt that at 27 she was too old! She got her breakthrough when a band pulled out of a TV show and she appeared instead. After that she became a commercial success, winner of the 2006 Brit Award for Best Female Solo Artist and nominated for a Grammy Award in 2007. Her biggest hit single, 'Suddenly I See' was played at the beginning of the film 'The Devil Wears Prada'.

2 🌐 3.30 Read the lyrics and listen to the song. Choose the best summary:

a) KT Tunstall wants to look like the woman in the song.

b) The woman in the song inspires KT to do well in her career.

c) The woman in the song makes KT want to give up what she's doing.

Patti Smith

- **FOLD** -

Suddenly I see

1 Her face is a map of the world, is a map of the world
You can see she's a beautiful girl, she's a beautiful girl
And everything around her is a silver pool of light
The people who surround her feel the benefit of it
5 It makes you calm
She holds you captivated in her palm

Chorus

Suddenly I see
This is what I wanna be
Suddenly I see
10 Why the hell it means so much to me

Suddenly I see
This is what I wanna be
Suddenly I see
Why the hell it means so much to me

15 I feel like walking the world, like walking the world
You can hear she's a beautiful girl, she's a beautiful girl
She fills up every corner like she's born in black and white
Makes you feel warmer when you're trying to remember
What you heard
20 She likes to leave you hanging on a word

Chorus x 2

And she's taller than most and she's looking at me
I can see her eyes looking from the page in a magazine
She makes me feel like I could be a tower, big strong tower, yeah
25 The power to be, the power to give, the power to see, yeah yeah

Suddenly I see
She got the power to be
The power to give
30 The power to see yeah yeah

Chorus

 New Inside Out **Upper intermediate Teacher's Book** © **Macmillan Publishers Limited 2009**

1. Reasons to be cheerful?
This week's lesson features contrasting feelings of optimism and pessimism in the face of current economic, political, social and environmental issues.

Level
Upper intermediate and above (equivalent to CEF level B2 and above)

How to use the lesson
1. Would your students generally describe themselves as optimistic, pessimistic or something in between? Ask them how optimistic/pessimistic they are with regard to national/global economic, political, social and environmental issues in their countries, and why.

2. Tell students they are going to read the opinions of three people about how optimistic/pessimistic they are. Give your students five to ten minutes to read through Worksheet A, encouraging them to look up new vocabulary. You could ask them to check if any of their ideas are mentioned. Tell them they are going to answer a series of questions on the text, but that they shouldn't write anything down at this stage.

3. Divide the students into pairs and hand out Worksheet B. Ask them to work together to complete the different types of comprehension questions in Exercises 1, 2 and 3.

4. Check answers in open class.

5. Ask the students if they particularly agree or disagree with any of the opinions expressed on Worksheet A, and if so, why.

6. Hand out Worksheet C and ask the students to work together to complete the crossword.

7. Check answers in open class.

Answers:

Exercise 1
1. Michael   2. Sam, Michael   3. Margaret   4. Sam, Margaret   5. Sam, Michael

Exercise 2
1. T   2. T   3. F   4. D   5. T   6. T   7. F   8. T

Exercise 3
1. He is referring to people complaining or grumbling about things.
2. He is less optimistic about future employment/unemployment, the chances of economic growth continuing, and his future standard of living.
3. Michael thinks people live longer these days because of better healthcare and better food.
4. The economic crisis.
5. Margaret refers to a declining sense of community, with people trusting and helping each other less than they used to, and to people being obsessed with earning as much money as possible.

Exercise 4
1. grumbling   2. growth   3. quality   4. privileged   5. higher   6. wealth
7. anxious   8. oil   9. democracy   10. easier

If the sentences have been completed correctly, *bright side* will read from top to bottom.

2. Related Websites
Send your students to these websites, or just take a look yourself.

http://optimistworld.com/Default.aspx
The website *The Optimist*, which specialises in 'daily good news headlines'. Accessible to upper-intermediate level.

http://news.bbc.co.uk/1/hi/health/635292.stm
A BBC article (2000) on medical research in the United States that suggested people with an optimistic outlook live longer. Accessible to upper-intermediate level.

http://www.france24.com/en/20090505-poll-shows-europeans-pessimistic-about-future
An article about a recent poll (May 2009) that suggests Europeans are pessimistic about the future. Accessible to upper-intermediate level.

Reasons to be cheerful?

WORKSHEET **A**

Sam

Whenever I watch the TV news I see things that make me anxious about the future. The current economic crisis is making me question various assumptions I had until recently – for example that I would probably never be unemployed, that economic growth would carry on indefinitely, and that when I got to my parents' age I would have a higher standard of living than they do now. And then there are the huge environmental problems around the corner. What will happen to food production as the planet continues getting hotter? What will happen to our way of life when we run out of vital natural resources such as oil?

Michael

Sometimes I look around me in Britain and I can't believe the number of people with long faces. It's partly the media's fault, though: on the front pages of most newspapers there's nothing but doom and gloom – crime, political scandals, global warming, etcetera. Every day the papers give the public something to complain about, and eventually it becomes a habit – I'm sure there are people who'd hate it if they didn't have anything to grumble about.

The truth is we live in a privileged part of the world at a privileged time in history. We have a standard of living beyond the wildest dreams of our great-grandparents. We live in a democracy and have freedom of speech. We have better healthcare and better food, which is why we live longer. Everyone has the opportunity to get an education, and to travel.

Sure, we've got a short-term economic crisis, but the long-term trend is for things to get better – so please can we cheer up a bit?

Margaret

I'm very grateful for a lot of things in my life but I see worrying changes in society and wonder how they will affect my grandchildren.

When I was growing up in the 1950s, life was harder in lots of ways – we were poorer, for a start – but there was more of a sense of community. We trusted and helped each other, whereas these days it seems a lot of people don't even know who their neighbours are.

Too many people these days seem obsessed with earning as much money as possible, then finding new ways to spend it. They have less time for each other. It's not wealth that makes you happy, though, is it? I'm not sure they have a better quality of life than we used to. In some ways it seems things are going in the wrong direction.

Reasons to be cheerful?

WORKSHEET **B**

Exercise 1

Decide for which of the three people (Sam, Michael, Margaret) the following statements are true.

1. They believe things will probably get better in the future.

2. They mention environmental problems.

3. They mention future generations.

4. They are not certain whether our current standard of living is better than in the past.

5. They mention the media.

Exercise 2

Decide whether the following statements are true (T) or false (F), or if the text doesn't say (D).

1. Margaret thinks it is a good thing to know who your neighbours are.

2. Michael thinks the media can affect people's attitudes.

3. Sam thinks he has less chance of becoming unemployed than he used to.

4. Sam does not have a good standard of living.

5. Margaret believes there is less of a sense of community these days.

6. Michael thinks life in Britain is better than in some other parts of the world.

7. Michael thinks British people's great-grandparents would not have been surprised by the rise in the standard of living that has taken place since they were alive.

8. Sam believes global warming is taking place.

Exercise 3

Answer the questions below.

1. What is Michael referring to when he says 'it becomes a habit'?

2. Sam mentions three ways in which he is less optimistic now than he used to be – what are they?

3. Why does Michael think people live longer these days?

4. Michael mentions something that he doesn't think will last a long time – what is it?

5. Which 'worrying changes' does Margaret refer to?

Inside Out

Reasons to be cheerful?

WORKSHEET C

Exercise 4

Complete the crossword below. If all the words are correct the two words that complete the expression 'look on the _____ _____', which means to focus on positive rather than negative aspects of a situation, will read from top to bottom.

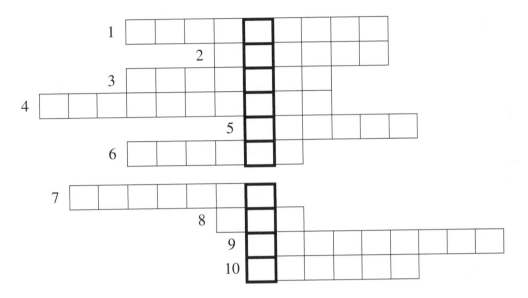

1. Michael thinks there are lots of people who should stop _____.

2. Sam used to assume economic _____ would never stop, but now he is not sure.

3. Margaret doubts whether young people's _____ of life has improved.

4. Michael believes people are _____ to be living in Britain today.

5. Michael believes the standard of living of people in Britain today is far _____ than that of their great-grandparents.

6. Margaret thinks many people believe _____ is more important than it really is.

7. Watching the TV news makes Sam _____.

8. Sam believes _____ is essential to our current way of life.

9. Michael refers to the fact that Britain is a _____.

10. Margaret believes that in lots of ways life today is _____ than it was in the 1950s.

Reasons to be cheerful? – Glossary

anxious adjective
worried because you think something bad might happen
His silence made me anxious.

assumption noun [count]
something that you consider likely to be true even though no one has told you directly or even though you have no proof
Your argument is based on a completely false assumption.

beyond (your) wildest dreams phrase
much better than you imagined or hoped

doom and gloom phrase
a feeling that a situation is very bad and without hope

environmental adjective
relating to the natural world and the effect that human activity has on it
The Minister discussed environmental issues.

freedom of speech noun [uncount]
the legal or natural right to say what you believe is true, without being prevented or punished

generation noun [count]
a group of people in society who are born and live around the same time
People retiring today are wealthier than the previous generation.

global warming noun [uncount]
the slow increase in the temperature of the Earth caused partly by the greenhouse effect increasing the amount of carbon dioxide in the atmosphere

grumble verb
to complain, especially continuously and about unimportant things
Children always grumble about school dinners.

indefinitely adverb
for a period of time that has no fixed end
It will keep indefinitely in a sealed container.

long face noun [count]
a sad, disappointed, or serious expression on someone's face
There were some long faces in the hall when the results were read out.

long-term adjective
continuing to exist, be relevant, or have an effect for a long time in the future
a good long-term investment

media noun [uncount]
radio, television, newspapers, the Internet, and magazines, considered as a group
Both political parties have accused the media of bias.

natural resources noun [plural]
valuable substances such as wood and oil that exist in a country's land and sea

obsessed adjective
considering someone or something as so important that you are always thinking about them, in a way that seems extreme to other people

privileged adjective
having advantages and opportunities that other people do not have, because you have a lot of money or high social status
Cynthia had a very privileged upbringing.

quality of life noun [uncount]
the enjoyment of life at a basic level, which includes being happy and healthy, rather than having lots of money

scandal noun [uncount]
talk or reports in the newspapers or on television about shocking events involving important people
He was tired of the endless stream of scandal offered by the tabloid press.

short-term adjective
lasting for a short period of time

trend noun [count]
a gradual change or development that produces a particular result

wealth noun [uncount]
a large amount of money and other valuable things
They used some of their wealth to build magnificent town halls.

worrying adjective
causing you to feel worried
The most worrying trend is the sharp decline in young readers.